French Tragic Drama

in the Sixteenth

and Seventeenth Centuries

French Tragic Drama in the Sixteenth and Seventeenth Centuries

GEOFFREY BRERETON

Methuen & Co Ltd
11 New Fetter Lane London EC4

First published in 1973
by Methuen & Co Ltd
11 New Fetter Lane, London EC4
© 1973 Geoffrey Brereton
Printed in Great Britain
by Richard Clay (The Chaucer Press) Ltd
Bungay, Suffolk

ISBN 0 416 07630 0 (hardback)
0 416 78920 X (paperback)

Distributed in the USA by
HARPER & ROW PUBLISHERS, INC.
BARNES & NOBLE IMPORT DIVISION

CONTENTS

FOREWORD

This book is designed as a single-volume survey of that important period of French drama which runs from the first native tragedies of the Renaissance to the culmination of 'classical' tragedy in the last decades of Louis XIV's reign. The field is vast, and to cover it within the limits that seem desirable if the book is to be of practical use and interest to the student and the general reader the treatment is necessarily selective. Comedy is omitted. Though many of its themes and situations occur in a different form in tragedy and, more particularly, in tragicomedy, the undeniable relationship (which still awaits a thorough investigation) is a matter of secondary importance in this period of drama as a whole. But even after respecting the traditional separation of the tragic and comic genres, one is still left with a wealth of material, most aspects of which have been the subject of numerous specialized studies. They include the contemporary movements of thought and sensibility, the political background, and the social and theatrical conditions which helped to shape the drama.

Account has been taken of all these wherever their relevance is apparent, but the main stress is on the plays themselves seen as types of drama, on the circumstances in which they were produced and their reception by contemporaries. The basic method is descriptive, since there is little value in critical interpretations if the works interpreted are hardly known. Unfortunately this must often be the case. One might assume a first-hand acquaintance with the plays of Corneille and Racine, though, even here, perhaps not with all of them. But one cannot do the same with Thomas Corneille, Quinault, Tristan, Du Ryer, Rotrou, Hardy, Montchrestien, or even Garnier. This is largely because of the inaccessibility of the works of these dramatists. In several cases they can be found only in the original editions or in later editions which have themselves become rare. This situation is slowly being remedied (see Bibliography), but there are still many interesting plays among the hundreds written which await a modern edition.

Academic and commercial considerations, in this case complementary, have focused excessive attention on Corneille and Racine, to the neglect of their contemporaries and predecessors. This is not to deny the pre-eminence of the two great tragic dramatists, but the impression is fostered that they were isolated talents, whereas they belonged to periods of intense dramatic and theatrical activity. The present book aims at giving at least some idea of this and, while I have virtually ignored the work of truly minor playwrights, I have devoted chapters to others whose plays are not only symptomatic of trends but are well worth reading in their own right. Most of these are now attracting the attention of scholars and in time no doubt will become more familiar ground. The most conspicuous exceptions at this date are Alexandre Hardy, important both as an influence and as a typically 'baroque' writer, and Philippe Quinault.

In view of this I have generally given priority to description over comment, providing summaries of their plays at the end of the chapters on Garnier, Hardy, Corneille and Racine, and outlining the plays of others in the chapters which concern them. A summary can never be a substitute for the actual reading of a text, but, where this is not readily available, it at least provides something concrete to which the reader can refer.

My debt to a great American scholar, H. C. Lancaster, will be apparent, as it must be for any writer who sets out to record and connect the successive phases of French drama in the seventeenth century. For an earlier period I owe a debt, lesser but still considerable, to the work of an eminent French scholar, Raymond Lebègue. The studies of many others, listed for the most part in the Bibliography, have influenced my own findings or helped me to arrive at new ones.

Among friends with whom I have discussed aspects of this book, I am particularly grateful to Professor R. C. Knight, whose careful reading of the finished manuscript saved me from a number of errors of fact or interpretation. For any that remain the responsibility is mine.

Finally, I would like to thank the Trustees of the Leverhulme Research Awards for the original grant of a fellowship which made it materially possible to start work on this book.

G.B.

February 1972

PROLOGUE

During the sixteenth century a fundamental change took place in West European drama. Italy, Spain, England, France were all affected by it. Although there were national variations in the dating of the change and in the nature of the new dramas which eventually grew up, certain radical distinctions between the old and the new became apparent in time in all these countries. The medieval drama had been the product of communities whose members participated actively in it, sometimes to the number of hundreds. The performances were usually out of doors in spaces not specially designed for the purpose and which could be adapted or extended in a variety of ways. The plays matched the material conditions in being episodic, of no uniform overall length, but easy to shorten or prolong and, considered as wholes, virtually formless. In contrast, post-medieval drama was performed by professionals before a public of non-participating spectators in buildings set aside for that particular use. The acting-space was relatively restricted, being confined to an indoor stage of fixed dimensions. The plays, considered as spectacles, were suited to the amount of physical action that could be shown on the new stages, while the number of characters was limited both by the size of the acting-space and by the supply of trained (and paid) actors available. The duration of the play was limited to the two or three hours during which a passive audience could be expected to remain receptive. In short, the drama was brought indoors, it was professionalized, and it was changed and tightened in form to satisfy the conditions of a performance that had to be completed in one session on one fixed spot.

Such is the general picture, though it may be qualified in the details. Medieval drama, including Mysteries, was sometimes performed indoors, a practice which became increasingly common in the fifteenth and early sixteenth centuries. There were examples of buildings used either exclusively or regularly for performances. There was an element of professionalism, though its extent and even the definition of the word in a pre-Renaissance context is debatable. Some of the plays were short and possessed, notably in the case of the French *moralité* and *farce*, a recognizable dramatic unity. On the other hand, the seventeenth century also had its lavish and episodic theatrical spectacles – though they were by then of a thoroughly professional and sophisticated kind and, except for the occasional court entertainment, always took place indoors.

Such qualifications have a certain force. They contain, among other things, the elements of the case which has been argued against a break in continuity at the Renaissance. Certainly there was no abrupt break over the field of drama as a whole and considered primarily as a matter of production techniques. Dramatists also persisted in their use of certain themes, particularly those drawn from the Bible and the martyrology, though they treated them differently. But when the period of transition was complete there can be no question that the final result was a new art-form in which the medieval tradition, though occasionally still discernible, was of no real importance.

So far as France is concerned, it is possible to illustrate the rift that eventually opened up between the two conceptions of drama by contrasting the spectacular productions of the late Mystery Plays with the performance of 'regular' tragedy and tragicomedy when these were establishing their ascendancy in the 1630s and 1640s. Though not the only kinds of drama practised in their respective periods, these can fairly be called the most representative.

In 1536 the town of Bourges mounted a production, of which several contemporary accounts survive, of the longest of all the Mystery Plays, the *Actes des Apôtres*. It was performed in the old Roman amphitheatre, covered for the occasion by an enormous canopy to shelter the spectators. Nearly 300 individuals were required to play its 500 different parts. The spectacle was presented as realistically as the scenic specialists of the time could devise. Ships could be seen sailing across the 'sea'. Angels, saints and magicians made vertical or lateral flights. Hell's mouth roared and spouted flame. Thunder answered from heaven. The tortures endured by martyrs and their atrociously varied forms of death were simulated at length with the help of dummies, trapdoors and other devices. The performance is said to have lasted forty days, during which the atmosphere of the town must have been one of continuous carnival. The time would not be too long to represent the separate lives of ten of the Apostles, together with other saints such as Stephen and Paul. Their stories, already expanded by medieval legend to embrace their miracles, their missionary journeys to foreign lands and their martyrdoms, were unfolded against a non-biblical background of Jewish and Roman history, but they also took in such New Testament scenes as the Ascension and Pentecost. There were comic episodes revolving, as usual, around the antics of devils.[1]

This vast religious adventure serial, containing crude humour, barbarous cruelty and an overriding element of the magical and the spectacular, was typical in its violence and colour of the late Mystery Plays. From its modest beginnings as an extension of the liturgy of the Church, religious drama had developed through the fifteenth century into an overblown entertainment catering for the broadest and even the lowest tastes. It was as splendidly vulgar as anything that has been attempted since by the twentieth-century cinema. One would not have thought in the first half of the sixteenth century that it was so near to extinction, for that was the period of some of the most lavish productions. The *Actes des Apôtres* was repeated in Paris in 1541 by the Confrères de la Passion at the Hôtel de Flandres, on a more restricted scale. The popular *Mystère de la Passion* was given an ambitious production at Valenciennes in 1547. The *Vieux Testament*, in its entirety the longest Mystery after the *Actes des Apôtres*, is recorded at Paris and several provincial towns in the thirties and forties and as late as 1557 at Draguignan. More markedly than the other French Mysteries, this was a compilation of a series of different plays, and the records of its performance may refer only to one or more of the separate episodes which could be extracted from it. (Among them were the stories, used by later dramatists, of Tobias, Judith, Esther and the sacrifice of Isaac by Abraham.)

Like the other great cycles, the *Vieux Testament* was full of spectacular effects, of noise, music, singing, dancing and even feats of horsemanship – this at Solomon's feast for the Queen of Sheba. Like them, it aroused astonishment, by predominantly material means, and played (though less blatantly than the *Actes des Apôtres*) on the two emotions of pity

[1] For a detailed study of this play, see R. Lebègue, *Le Mystère des Actes des Apôtres* (Paris, 1929).

and horror. Since these are constant aims of most non-comic drama, it might be asserted, on the highest theoretical level, that the medieval spectacle did not differ in essence from any other drama. But there are differences in the means employed which no history of drama can afford to ignore.

In the 1630s and 1640s 'regular' plays were beginning to establish themselves as the dramatic norm in the two theatres which Paris by then possessed. A landmark in those decades was the production of Corneille's *Le Cid* in the winter of 1636–7. Chiefly because of its happy ending, the play was at first called a tragicomedy and in other respects also it did not fully comply with the strict requirements of the tragic convention as this came to be understood a little later. Nevertheless, it can be taken as an outstanding and sufficiently representative example of the serious drama of its time.

Le Cid has twelve characters, if the Infanta's page is included. It has a playing-time of about two hours. The action is supposed to occupy twenty-four hours from beginning to end and to take place in various parts of the same town, represented conventionally rather than naturalistically. The elaborate theatrical machinery of the Mysteries has disappeared and there are no 'effects' of any kind. The only violent physical action on stage is a quarrel between two men in which one slaps the other's face and swords are drawn, but one quickly disarms the other and the fight is cut short.[1] The story of the play, however, includes two completed duels, of which one ends in a death, and a pitched battle in which a large force of raiders arriving in ships are attacked as they land and are bloodily defeated. These exciting events are not shown but reported. All the important action of the play is expressed through words in the mouths of actors, reinforced by gesture and facial expression but by nothing more spectacular. With the one exception of the abortive fight, the conflicts witnessed by the audience are verbal conflicts. The suffering seen is emotional, not physical. Yet the story of this play is obviously rich in opportunities for visual and aural effects. In most other periods and places a dramatist who neglected them would seem incompetent and a production which failed to exploit them apathetic and resourceless. For *Le Cid* this is not so. Not only has it proved a better and more lasting play than it could

[1] Even this degree of action was soon to be eliminated from tragic drama.

possibly have been if constructed in the spectacular convention, but audiences of the time showed that they liked it as it was.

So, almost exactly a hundred years after the Bourges production of the *Actes des Apôtres*, French drama produced this. The long process of transition had not been simple. What lay between will be described in the following chapters.

I

THE BEGINNINGS
OF FRENCH TRAGEDY

Early learned tragedies – influence of Muret and Buchanan on the *Pléiade*
group – Jodelle's *Cléopâtre* – his *Didon* – Grévin's *César* – tragedies of the
La Taille brothers – *De l'art de la tragédie* and the humanist conception –
popular 'tragedy' – the Protestant contribution: de Bèze's *Abraham sacrifiant*
– Des Masures's *Tragédies saintes*

The performance of Étienne Jodelle's *Cléopâtre captive* by a group of
students in Paris in the winter of 1552–3 has been held traditionally,
and on the whole rightly, to mark the beginning of native tragedy in
France. That play was the embryonic model of a dramatic form which,
with very considerable developments and modifications, was to persist
on the French stage for more than two and a half centuries. But it was
not only a starting-point. It was the product of a movement which had
been in progress for some time and of which it was seen by contemporaries as the successful culmination. The movement had originated
in Italy in the previous century when humanist scholars began the
rediscovery of the Greek tragic dramatists. It may be said to have
reached France in 1506 with the publication in Paris of Latin translations by Erasmus of two of the tragedies of Euripides, *Hecuba* and
Iphigenia. From then on, French practice followed that of Italy,
though with a considerable time-lag. Between 1506 and 1552 there was
a progression which, though not absolutely clear-cut, can be summed
up in general terms as follows: (1) translations from Greek into Latin,
a much more familiar language even in learned circles, (2) original
tragedies in Latin, (3) translations into French,[1] leading finally to
(4) original tragedies in French.

The first two categories of plays were composed for student

---

[1] e.g. from the Greek: Lazare de Baïf's *Électre* (1547, from Sophocles), Bocatel's
Hécube (1544, from Euripides), Sébillet's *Iphigénie à Aulis* (1549, from Euripides).

performance by teachers such as the great Scottish scholar George Buchanan, who made Latin versions of the *Alcestis* and the *Medea* of Euripides and wrote two original Latin plays on biblical subjects, *Baptistes* and *Jephtes*. All these were acted at the Collège de Guyenne at Bordeaux between 1539 and 1544. Montaigne, who was a pupil at the school, recalled with pride having taken part in them and also in plays by two of his other masters, Muret and Guérente.[1] Whatever Guérente wrote has disappeared – in common no doubt with much other pedagogic work which never reached publication – but Muret is remembered as the author of a *Julius Caesar*, performed at Bordeaux around 1545, which is the first definitely known original tragedy on a non-religious subject to be composed – though in Latin – in France.

By the early 1550s Muret had moved to Paris and was teaching at the Collège de Boncourt, where Buchanan also held a post for a time. Together with the Collège de Coqueret, Boncourt was the cradle of the main literary movement of the French Renaissance, centred on the group later known as the Pléiade. Nearly all the writers associated with the Pléiade were students and contemporaries at the two colleges: Ronsard, Du Bellay and Jean-Antoine de Baïf at Coqueret, and Belleau, La Péruse, Grévin, Jean de La Taille and Jodelle at Boncourt. The twenty-year-old Jodelle's tragedy can be seen as an experiment launched by this young group, very probably under the guiding influence of Muret and perhaps more distantly that of Buchanan. It may be described in retrospect as an awkward breakthrough into the field of dramatic literature of a genre which until then had been almost exclusively academic. The group's jubilation at their worldly success – quite apart from the gift of 500 crowns with which Henri II rewarded the author after the performance at court – goes to confirm this view.

The subject was the last hours of Cleopatra after the defeat and death of her lover Antony. This favourite story, which Jodelle was the first French writer to treat, was taken from Plutarch, as Muret's *Julius Caesar* had been. Jodelle's dramatic adaptation had features modelled on Greek tragedy and also on Seneca, whose more accessible and

---

[1] 'Shall I mention one youthful quality I possessed? I brought a bold and confident look and a flexibility of voice and gesture to the parts which I undertook to act. For I was scarcely twelve when I played the leading parts in the Latin tragedies of Buchanan, Guérente and Muret, which were performed in our Collège de Guyenne with some dignity.' (*Essais*, I, xxvi.)

rhetorical work had been available to French latinists throughout the century and whose influence, of undoubted importance, mingled with the influence of the original Greeks. In form, *Cléopâtre* came near to establishing the sixteenth-century pattern. It was divided into five acts separated by choruses and, although the acts were of disproportionate lengths (the material being inadequate to fill the last two), the principle of the five-act tragedy was at least affirmed. The play was written in a variety of verse-metres which included the alexandrine, at that date a novelty. Another embryonic feature of regular tragedy was the respect for the unities of time (sunrise to sunset) and, liberally interpreted, of place. It can be deduced from the text that the action takes place in various parts of the city of Alexandria, but since there was probably no scenery there was no need to locate the setting explicitly. Unity of action was observed without difficulty because there was so little of it.

This is the first criticism which a modern reader would make of what, from a later standpoint in history, can only be called an extremely thin play. Nothing happens which is not clearly laid down from the beginning, first by the ghost of Antony, which opens the first act with an exposition, and then by Cleopatra herself. Already the situation is seen as hopeless and the only way out is for Cleopatra to kill herself. By the last act she has done so, offstage. A messenger relates, not indeed her death, which he has not witnessed, but more remotely still the scene in the death-chamber after all is over. In the intermediate acts there has been no true variation of Cleopatra's intentions, nor has anything occurred to make a variation likely. A dramatic conflict and perhaps a change of direction appear superficially possible in Act III, in which Cleopatra confronts the victorious Caesar and his officers. The Queen appeals for clemency and the conqueror seems to grant it, but on both sides this is a feint and is known to be so by the audience. No new situation develops.

Jodelle's play is thus innocent of two features often considered essential to drama, conflict and suspense – unless for the suspense of waiting to see what Cleopatra will do one is prepared to substitute a secondary interest in the circumstances of her death. But this would demand more sensational treatment to provide an adequate climax. Shakespeare, using the same story from Plutarch, showed the death on stage. He also, besides introducing much other matter, began his play well before the defeat of Antony, when everything still hung in the balance. The whole material of Jodelle's tragedy provided Shake-speare with no more than his fifth act.

But such comparisons are beside the point. Had he been able to anticipate the methods of Shakespearian tragedy, it is inconceivable that Jodelle would have employed them. Negatively, he represented an extreme reaction against the popular Mysteries, though his delib-erate avoidance of the visually sensational was not compensated by an ability to create dramatic interest by other means. Positively, his aim was to arouse by verbal means, including poetic ornament, the Senecan *sentence* and the classical allusion, pity for the fate of an illustrious person. His conception of tragedy had resemblances with that of the public funeral ceremony, with comparable opportunities for lamentation, rhetoric and moralization. The theme can be summed up in one phrase: 'How are the mighty fallen!' In this last respect particularly *Cléopâtre captive* was typical of much French sixteenth-century tragedy.

It is obvious that the theme symbolized by the commonplace of Fortune's Wheel[1] is to be found in most tragedy. But often a complete turn of the wheel is shown, so that the destiny of the protagonist is seen to come full circle. If not that, the protagonist is first shown at the top of the wheel just before it begins to spin down. In Jodelle's type of Fortune Tragedy he is practically at the bottom when the play opens and the whole spectacle consists in the contemplation of his misery.

Jodelle's only other tragedy, *Didon se sacrifiant*, was a dramatization of the *Aeneid*, Book IV. Its subject was thus the desertion of Dido by Aeneas, her objections, reproaches, lamentations and, finally, her suicide. Alexandrines are used throughout, except in the choruses. There is a great predominance of feminine rhymes, which do not alter-nate with masculine rhymes on any discernible system, taking the play as a whole. Though the immensely long speeches of the protagonists make for torpidity, the tragedy is not without vigour. Aeneas's decision to obey the gods and leave Carthage is affirmed near the beginning and, although his conscience torments him, his determination never really wavers, so that there is little uncertainty on this count. But Dido's reactions, like those of her sister Anna, are varied, and she does

---

[1] Though medieval in origin, the symbol was still current in the sixteenth century, e.g. 'Ces tyrans, renversés au bas de la roue . . .' (Garnier, *Cornélie*, Act II). In England, it occurs at least as late as *c.* 1613, in Webster's *Duchess o ʃMalfi.*

not definitely resolve on suicide until the end of Act IV. Before this she has shown a capacity for violent recrimination and even irony which balances the self-pity of other passages. In her torments of passion she has a kinship with Phaedra, who is invoked by name. In her dealings with Aeneas there is a suggestion of other deserted heroines of tragedy, which makes it possible to see comparisons with Racine's Hermione and Bérénice. Most of all this was already in Virgil and Ovid, but Jodelle deserves credit for having expressed it in dramatic form and so having helped to introduce such themes to French tragedy. His *Didon* is more than an elegy.

The play's approximate date was probably 1560, but there is no record of its first performance, which was not attended by the publicity which *Cléopâtre* had enjoyed. More marked contributions to early tragedy were made by other members of the Boncourt–Coqueret group, Jacques Grévin and the brothers La Taille.

Grévin's *César*, a reworking in French of his master Muret's *Julius Caesar*, was acted by students in 1561. It cannot be said to lack dramatic movement, though the high point of Caesar's assassination is narrated, not shown. It ends with Mark Antony's successful attempt to turn the Romans, by his oratory, against Brutus and his fellow conspirators. In its versification the play marks a further step forward in the development of regular tragedy. Except for the choruses, it is written throughout in alexandrines with alternating masculine and feminine rhymes, in accordance with Ronsard's prescription.

Jean de La Taille's two tragedies both had biblical subjects, closely related to each other. In *Saül le furieux* he depicted the last hours of the Old Testament king, when he believed, with reason, that God was about to destroy him. The play has considerable interest as a study of a terrible and tormented character on the verge of madness. It contains the raising-up of the ghost of Samuel by the Witch of Endor and ends, after Saul's death, with a paraphrase of David's lament over Saul and Jonathan, the biblical *locus classicus* of the 'How are the mighty fallen' lament. Jean de La Taille succeeds in endowing the theme of the great man on his plunge to destruction with appreciable dramatic qualities. There is suspense and some movement, generated less by the story than by the psychology of the central character, which has suggestions of depth unusual for the period. Jean de La Taille's second tragedy, *La Famine ou les Gabéonites*, is, however, less interesting. It concerns the fate of the surviving members of Saul's family after their circumstances have become hopeless and aims at arousing horror and pity by means of rhetorical lamentation. The model is Seneca's *Troades*, which is followed closely, in spite of the difference of subject.

Jean de La Taille's younger brother, Jacques, composed six tragedies before dying of plague at the age of twenty in 1562. All six had classical subjects, but only two, *Daire* (Darius) and *Alexandre*, were preserved and printed. These cannot be rated much higher than school exercises.

In publishing his own two plays in 1572-3, the elder La Taille added a preface, *De l'art de la tragédie*, which was one of the more notable writings of its time on tragic theory and valuable as a representative statement of the ideas of his group. He invokes Aristotle's *Poetics* and Horace (the *Ars poetica*). He repeats the Aristotelian prescriptions that the story of a tragedy should be sufficiently lamentable in itself to move us to tears and that the heroes should be neither extremely wicked (and so deserving of punishment) nor entirely innocent. He recommends the peripeteia or unexpected reversal of fortune from happiness to misery – and also vice versa – to hold the interest of the spectator. Going, knowingly or not, beyond Aristotle, he insists on the unities of place and time ('a single day') and condemns violent physical action in the name of verisimilitude, since the audience, he argues, will always know that a killing on stage, and much more a crucifixion, is a faked effect. As for the disposition of a tragedy, it consists of five acts each complete in itself and followed by a chorus which 'discourses on what has just been said'. The action should begin near the middle or the end of the story – an echo, very probably, of Horace's precept to start *in medias res*, but which, too keenly applied, weakened suspense to vanishing-point, as had happened in the case of Jodelle.

Theoretical pronouncements such as this, taken with the plays we have just described – to which might be added the *Médée* of La Péruse (*c.* 1553), a vigorous imitation of Seneca – serve to define the aims and achievement of the Boncourt-Coqueret school of scholar-dramatists. They established a regular type of tragedy in five acts separated by moralizing choruses. They introduced the unities of time and place and, in practice, of action. They assumed an unhappy ending and opened near to the catastrophe. They replaced violence and spectacle by narrative, relying very largely on verbal effects to move the spectator. Their subjects were classical, i.e. taken from the Greek dramatists or

Seneca or from Greek and Roman history, and also biblical. Fairly early examples of both categories can be found outside the immediate Boncourt–Coqueret group. Such were the *Aman* of the Protestant André de Rivaudeau (composed *c.* 1558, published 1566), which uses the story of Esther, and the *Achille* (1563) and *Lucrèce* (1566) of Filleul. A curiosity at that date was Gabriel Bounin's *La Soltane* (1561), a partly regular tragedy based on a harem drama of recent occurrence and the distant forerunner of other Oriental tragedies.

Indeed early humanist tragedy placed no conscious restrictions on its subject-sources, though inevitably it drew heavily on its models in Greek and Roman tragedy. The insistence was on treatment rather than on subject. The treatment in this experimental drama had many weaknesses and nothing was produced comparable in quality to the contemporary achievements in non-dramatic poetry of Ronsard, Du Bellay and others. The highest expression of the movement's aims is found somewhat later in the plays of Garnier, whose work is considered in the next chapter.

II

Apart from the learned tragedy of self-consciously academic inspiration, a more popular type of drama continued, though little of it survives. The fashionable name of *tragédie* was sometimes given to plays which seem in fact to have been either Miracles or Moralities in the old tradition, or episodes taken from the long Mysteries. The latter had been banned in the capital in 1548 by edict of the Parlement de Paris, and other municipalities gradually followed suit, but in some of the provinces they persisted for many years on a modified scale. This popular activity, however, was disdained by the supporters of learned tragedy as fit only to amuse 'the servants and common people, but not serious persons' (Jean de La Taille). The only noteworthy attempts to link the old with the new were made by Protestant writers. The *Abraham sacrifiant* of Théodore de Bèze, first played by students at Lausanne in 1550, half qualifies as the first French tragedy, since it was earlier than Jodelle's *Cléopâtre*. Its author was a good humanist scholar who had studied in Paris before joining Calvin in Geneva. But the story (Abraham's preparations to sacrifice his son Isaac in obedience to Jehovah's command, and the last-minute reprieve, which gives a happy ending) had figured as an episode in the Mysteries, of which de

Bèze's language is sometimes reminiscent. Satan and an angel appear in the play, which is not formally divided into acts. The main metres are the decasyllabic and the old octosyllabic line; the alexandrine is not used. The unities of time and place are not observed, though the unity of action is. There is a strongly underlined moral: that it is imperative to obey God's will. Satan retires baffled, as in the Mysteries, and religious edification is the play's dominant feature.

The same may be said of the *Tragédies saintes* of Louis Des Masures, published at Geneva in 1563. This is a trilogy of plays on David and Saul. Although each works up to an apparent climax and could be performed separately, there is no inherent dramatic unity in their subjects or treatment. They are in fact a 'representation' of the events in certain chapters of the First Book of Samuel, interspersed with psalms, canticles, pious exhortations and *cantiques à danser* which clearly were danced to by the chorus. Because of its subject – the killing of Goliath by David and the triumph of the Israelites over their enemies – the first, *David combattant*, comes nearest to being a unified whole. The sequels, *David triomphant* and *David fugitif*, which deal with Saul's jealousy of David and David's flight into the desert, are further pieces of adaptation which the author, not surprisingly, fails to endow with dramatic necessity. The moral, illustrated by the action and stressed in the dialogue, is that the man who trusts in God need fear no evil. Satan, who constantly tries to intervene as a character in the course of events, is constantly frustrated. While appearing to envisage the multiple décor of the Mysteries for performance, Des Masures avoids opportunities for violent physical action with one notable exception. This is the combat between David and Goliath, which takes place before the audience and ends with the severing of the dead Goliath's head – a familiar trick in the medieval repertory of scenic illusions. As to the form, there is no division into acts. The verse is more varied than in the Mysteries, including the alexandrine among other metres. The *Tragédies saintes* are interesting as a hybrid type of play which had no ultimate development, and their weakness is underlined by the inevitable comparison with Jean de La Taille's 'classical' handling of similar material in *Saül le furieux*. By the 1670s Protestant writers had ceased their attempts to dramatize biblical stories. Catholic writers turned to them increasingly later in the century, but generally in the form established by the humanist scholars.

2

ROBERT GARNIER

Garnier's life and character – his contemporary reputation – form and nature of his tragedies – insistence on suffering – cultivation of mental torture – lack of dramatic suspense – lack of stoicism – the idea of retribution – moralization and application to the contemporary scene in *Les Juives* and other plays – a tragicomedy, *Bradamante* – Garnier's style – the oratorical tradition and the 'mighty line' – use of imagery – the lyric monologue – the chorus – summaries of Garnier's tragedies

Humanist regular tragedy is represented at its best by Garnier, who by the volume and quality of his work was easily the most important French dramatic writer of the century. Born, probably in 1544, at La Ferté-Bernard, a small town near Le Mans, Garnier was some twelve years younger than Jodelle and five to ten years younger than Jean de La Taille, whose birth date is uncertain. But, although he belonged to a slightly later generation than the Boncourt–Coqueret writers, his work was rooted in the same tradition of humanist scholarship and his relationship with the group was close and cordial.

Nothing is known of his early years and education before the time when he became a law student at Toulouse, where he showed his literary talent by winning prizes at the Floral Games of 1564 and 1565 and by writing laudatory verses to welcome the young Charles IX on his visit to the city in 1565. From Toulouse he moved to the capital to work as an advocate at the bar of the Parlement de Paris, and it was most probably then that he entered into contact with the Pléiade writers and formed at least literary friendships which remained with him for life. When his first tragedy, *Porcie*, was published in 1568 it was preceded by sonnets in its author's praise by Ronsard, Belleau and A. de Baïf. Similar tributes were exchanged throughout Garnier's literary career and culminated in his fine elegy of 1586 on the death of his 'cher Ronsard'.

After two or three years in Paris he was appointed to be a judge at

Le Mans and returned to his native district. Five years later (1574) he became *lieutenant criminel* of Le Maine, with responsibility for the criminal jurisdiction of the whole of his province. With his family he survived an attempt by their servants to poison them all during an outbreak of plague. The object was to make it appear they had died in the epidemic and plunder their possessions. He held his judicial post until 1586, in which year he was elected to the Grand Conseil of the realm, which sat in Paris. This considerable distinction seems, however, to have been honorary, involving Garnier in no active work.

The last few years of his life were obscure and apparently unhappy. Already in 1583, in dedicating his last tragedy to the King's favourite, the Duc de Joyeuse, he had expressed his disappointment in both literature and the law and complained, rather surprisingly, that for him they had proved equally barren. Two years after he had ceased to be *lieutenant criminel* his wife died, leaving him with two young daughters. He gave his temporary support to the Ligue, the ultra-Catholic subversive party whose efforts were directed against both the Protestant party of Henri de Navarre and the reigning monarch Henri III, assassinated in 1589. In political disgrace and confusion, Garnier died in 1590, aged about forty-six.

Garnier lived through troubled and dangerous times. The Wars of Religion, with their conspiracies, assassinations, massacres and barbarous local persecutions, were the background of his adult life. As an influential official, he could not have entirely avoided political involvement. As an administrator of justice, he was responsible for the application of particularly ruthless laws. It was his duty to order, and no doubt to witness, the kind of tortures deplored by his contemporary Montaigne, who had left the legal profession at the first opportunity. Garnier remained in it longer – there are no grounds for interpreting his retirement in 1586 as a repudiation – and his conscious attitude to the horrors of his age is difficult to assess, but it is legitimate to assume a certain ambivalence which carried over into his tragedies. On the one hand he deplores the suffering and unrest which torment his country, on the other he creates a drama whose basis is cruelty. No doubt this was a requirement of the tragic play as then understood, but, as will be seen, Garnier develops it to the psychological limit. Some reflection of his lived experience can be assumed here, subordinate though it may be to the tragic pattern as a whole.

As a type, Garnier was one of those lettered magistrates particularly common in sixteenth-century France. But for this member of the *noblesse de robe* literature was more than an occasional pastime or relaxation. He evidently considered his dramatic writing as something of a second career capable, among other things, of contributing to his material advancement. When he complained to Joyeuse of his fruitless labours, he was not of course thinking of direct monetary rewards, implying a kind of professionalism and a regular theatre inexistent at that date. He was no doubt regretting that too few official honours had come his way and that none of his plays had been performed at court.[1] On a less material plane, however, he was far from being a failure. Apart from enjoying the esteem of Ronsard's group, he saw his plays go through three collected editions between 1580 and 1583.[2] His achievement was recognized even in his lifetime, while soon after his death his reputation as a renewer of antique tragedy spread to England, where a translation of his *Marc-Antoine* by the Countess of Pembroke was published in 1592, and a translation of *Cornélie* by Thomas Kyd in 1594.[3] The hints of melancholy and frustration which Garnier's more personal utterances contain seem to have been less the effect of circumstance than of temperament.

II

Garnier published seven tragedies and one tragicomedy, all, except the first, in the ten-year period (1573–83) during which he was occupying his judicial posts at Le Mans.[4] He took his subjects from Roman

[1] There was, however, an adequate explanation of this in the fact that the Queen Mother, Catherine de Medici, had conceived a superstitious dislike of tragedies, believing they brought bad luck, and refused to include them among court entertainments. Cf. the anecdote, found in Diomedes and repeated by several sixteenth-century commentators, concerning Euripides' refusal to write a tragedy about King Archelaus when asked to do so. His reply was: 'May nothing ever happen to you which would be fit material for tragedy.'

[2] As for posthumous editions, over forty editions of various works of Garnier's, including poems, appeared between 1592 and 1619.

[3] See particularly A. M. Witherspoon, *The Influence of R. Garnier on Elizabethan Tragedy* (Yale and Oxford, 1924). Witherspoon saw the influence of Garnier, more or less direct, in ten other tragedies written by authors connected with the Countess of Pembroke's circle. He may have spread his net too wide. In any case the influence was limited, and marginal to the main development of English drama.

[4] For titles and dates, with summaries of the plays, see end of chapter, pp. 33–7.

history, largely as presented by Plutarch, though also by Appian and Cassius Dio; from Greek mythology, mainly derived through Seneca, but with some independent recourse to Sophocles and Euripides; from the Bible (*Les Juives*); and for his tragicomedy, *Bradamante*, from the then modern Italian poet Ariosto. In form, the tragedies confirmed and strengthened the example sketched out by Jodelle. All have five acts, separated by the chorus, which intervenes occasionally during an act to provide a lyric interval. The choruses are written in various metres, but outside them the alexandrine is used exclusively. Whatever the story derivation, the dramatic technique is predominantly Senecan. The unities are observed in a liberal fashion. The passage of time is not precisely marked, but in no case need it be more than a few hours. Place, as in Jodelle, is limited to one or more spots in or near the same city. There is, on the whole, unity of action, though in the more plotless of the plays this becomes unity of interest or of theme. Several different disasters may strike the same person or group of persons, whose anguish is the focal point of the tragedy. The most static of the tragedies, *Porcie* and *Cornélie*, simply offer the spectacle of a woman awaiting disastrous news, receiving it with lamentations, and either committing suicide or resolving to do so after an interval. In *La Troade*, the women and children of fallen Troy await the will of their conquerors and are carried off for rape or slaughter one by one. The general theme of *Les Juives* is similar: the fate of helpless captives at the hands of an implacable victor. The disasters accumulated in *Antigone* all befall a single family, through it striking directly or indirectly the heroine of the title. Even in *Hippolyte* and *Marc-Antoine* plot and peripeteia are subsidiary to the theme of misery, which is exploited to the full.

Basically this is the same as Jodelle's tragedy of lamentations, but it goes even further in its insistence on suffering, and it would hardly be an exaggeration to call the effect, if not the intention, sadistic. In nearly every case the characters who suffer on the stage are women. Their suffering is of course emotional, exteriorized in the wringing of hands, cries and sobs, ending sometimes in suicide before the audience (Cléopâtre, Phèdre, Jocaste). The physical sufferings – the killings and massacres which provoke the emotional suffering – occur offstage. They are narrated by messengers at length, touching off in the listening characters, already racked by apprehension or despair, new paroxysms of grief. Similar scenes occur in Greek tragedy and, more obtrusively, in Seneca, but in Garnier the use of them is so prominent as to appear obsessive. It parallels on the psychological plane the physical tortures and executions common in medieval drama, so that what the audience has before it is a transposition of the literal torments inflicted on female martyrs in the older plays. The parallel is drawn closer by the frequent use of words associated with physical suffering – not only *travail* (anguish), *tourmenter, gêner* (to torture), *bourreler* (to put to death), but even more concrete expressions such as *ardente tenaille* (red-hot pincers), *brasier* (brazier), *cuisante flamme* (searing flame). These are revealing metaphors, some bolder and nearer to the literal sense than others. When similar terms are found in seventeenth-century tragedy one tends to regard them as conventional, and indeed artificial. The word *flamme* in Corneille or Racine evokes no image of a martyr at the stake. Yet for their contemporaries there was no doubt rather more life in such metaphors, while for Garnier's there was probably enough for the association between physical and mental suffering to become explicit.

The language contributes to the dominant intention discernible in these plays: to present tragedy as a spectacle of suffering. Although it is mental suffering, its representation is near enough to the physical to be still crude. The characters writhe and scream in their despair. Funeral urns and dead bodies are brought on to the stage to increase the clamorous grief of the survivors. As a further turn of the screw, children are introduced in three plays. In *La Troade* the deaths of several young boys are described or reported.[1] In *Marc-Antoine* the children of Cléopâtre escape by being led to safety by their tutor Eufron, but only after their mother's heart has been 'rent', as she says, by the thought of what might happen to them:

EUFRON	Qui en aura pitié? Déjà me semble voir
	Cette petite enfance en servitude choir
	Et porter en triomphe.
CLÉOPÂTRE	Ah! chose misérable!
EUFRON	Leurs tendres bras liés d'une corde exécrable
	Contre leur dos foiblet.
CLÉOPÂTRE	O dieux! quelle pitié!
EUFRON	Leur pauvre col d'ahan vers la terre plié.

[1] It is sufficient to read the last act of this play to realize that 'drama of cruelty' is not an inappropriate term.

CLÉOPÂTRE   Ne permettez, bons dieux, que ce malheur advienne!

EUFRON   Et au doigt les montrer la tourbe citoyenne.

CLÉOPÂTRE   Hé! plutôt mille morts.

EUFRON   Puis l'infâme bourreau
Dans leur gorge enfantine enfoncer le couteau.

CLÉOPÂTRE   Hélas! le cœur me fend.

In *Les Juives*, the children of the Jewish queens are taken out to be butchered before the eyes of their father, who is then blinded. These cruel acts are not shown, but they are suffered by proxy by the mothers as they listen to the narration of them.

The messenger, or some character with an equivalent role, thus replaces the torturer of the crudely realistic type of play. His more obvious function is to recreate for the audience, by his demeanour and his words, the horror of a spectacle which can no longer be represented physically. His other function, subtler but no less important, is to harrow the feelings of the characters who listen to him and whose painful reactions are essential to tragedy of this kind.[1]

Garnier's plays constitute an early theatre of cruelty – conceived, it might be said, with the laudable object of moving the spectators to pity, but in which the means seem disproportionate to the end. The anguish experienced by the characters is so strongly stressed that ultimately it becomes deadening, so that pity is eliminated by either incredulity or revulsion. There are several ways in which this effect could be tempered and the sickening spectacle of the oppression of the weak by the strong made more tolerable. It is worth examining what use Garnier made of them.

III

A favourite method used by the dramatist, as by other story-tellers, to mitigate an impression of total despondency, is the cultivation of uncertainty, resulting in the suspense mentioned in the footnote below.

[1] Criticism of the messenger speeches in Garnier (and equally in Seneca and the Greeks) as unnecessarily long and tedious is beside the point. It is based on a different conception of drama (such as that expressed by Fénelon in his criticism of Racine's *Phèdre* in the *Lettre à M. Dacier sur les occupations de l'Académie* of 1714), in which mere news of an event is sufficient to resolve the suspense in which the audience has been held by uncertainty of the outcome. This type of suspense occurs in Garnier only occasionally and incidentally.

However black the outlook, there is a possibility of a change of fortune and an escape for the characters. These seem to have a chance, in the minds of either the audience or the characters, or both. It is true that when the story is traditional and the play is a tragedy, the audience can have little expectation of an ultimately happy outcome. But there may be moments of hope, fugitive chances of a reprieve, efforts on the part of the characters to react against their doom. Such things distract attention from the inevitability of disaster and introduce life and hope into the drama, even if sometimes ironically. It can be said at once, however, that the cultivation of suspense through uncertainty formed no part of Garnier's conception of tragedy, any more than of Jodelle's. If it occurs once or twice in minor instances, it is only accidental and any slender hope which may have been generated is quickly dispelled. In these tragedies the situation is usually seen and described as hopeless from the beginning. When debates occur which, in the mind of a modern reader, might well lead to a modification of a character's intentions and persuade him to adopt a different course of action, they remain, rather obviously, debates, initiated for their own sake and with no true dramatic function. The arguments on each side are marshalled, usually in the form of Senecan stichomythia, yielding what in effect is an academic or rhetorical exercise. The two chief subjects of debate are suicide (to be or not to be) and clemency (to pardon or to punish), but in neither case is there much doubt which way the verdict will go. If these exercises fulfil a dramatic function, it is not for any influence they might have on the plot, but for their psychological interest: they demonstrate the unshakeable resolve of some character to die, to exact vengeance and so on. But if it is just possible to detect this interest in Garnier, it remains, at most, quite secondary. There is very little in his tragedies (apart from a number of verbal parallels) comparable to the truly dialectical discussions found in Corneille, by means of which decisions are formed or modified and character is affirmed or revealed.

If there is no relief on this count, and none can reasonably be expected, the misery of the characters might still be transcended by fortitude. They could rise superior to their destiny by heroic disdain or stoic endurance and the tragic gloom would be lightened for the spectator because his pity would be tempered by admiration. But it was clearly no part of Garnier's purpose to illustrate stoicism in action, historically probable though this might have seemed. There are examples of what might perhaps be called stoic resignation – that of Porcie and Cornélie in the first two plays, of Polyxène and Astyanax in *La Troade*, of Antony and Cleopatra. But nearly all these deaths or decisions to die are accompanied by so much lamentation that the element of fortitude virtually disappears. In *Marc-Antoine* there would be an obvious opportunity, without changing the story in any way, for the two lovers to die not merely defiantly but triumphantly, exulting in each other's love and in the indestructibility of their own passion. This conception, however, is totally absent from Garnier. His lovers die, not in triumph but in despair, bewailing the misfortune which has brought them to that necessity.

Finally, the sufferings shown in tragedy may be justified as a retribution for wrongdoing. In the widest sense, this is a part of the conception of *hamartia*. More narrowly, it is the principle which allows satisfaction to be derived from the exemplary punishment of a criminal. Garnier invokes it on several occasions. Thus Antony is punished because he has allowed his warlike qualities to be dulled by luxurious living. Sédécie in *Les Juives* has rebelled against his overlord and the Jewish people have sinned collectively against their God. In *Antigone*, the two sons of Œdipe have pursued their rivalry without regard for the welfare of their city or their mother's supplications. At the end of the same play Créon's sufferings are declared to be the result of his unjust punishment of Antigone.

In all these instances, Garnier is aware of a need for justification and states it explicitly. But there are numerous other cases in which no justification is attempted, nor is one possible. On this score as on the others, one cannot deduce from Garnier's tragedies any consistent ethical or philosophical system, whether Stoic, humanist, Christian or even fatalistic.

Lacking a system, Garnier is nevertheless a moralist, of a conspicuous and persistent kind. His frequent moralizations take the form of *ad hoc* comments uttered either by the chorus which, as often in Greek drama, never hesitates before the obvious, or by individual characters. If the latter, they are expressed in *sentences* of the Senecan type. These short moral observations, arising out of the situation of the moment but capable of a more general application, are not integrated with the plot or the characterization. It hardly matters in whose mouth they are placed. They are not, in a modern sense, 'dramatic', and for a modern reader they are often intensely irritating. Yet they were certainly prized by Garnier's contemporaries and constituted for them one of the features of tragedy and not the least of its attractions.

In spite of the fragmentary nature of their moral content, Garnier's tragedies served a general moral purpose in his own view. He saw the miseries depicted in them as a reflection of his own times and pointed this out repeatedly in his dedications and elsewhere. *Porcie* is described on the title-page as a 'tragédie française, représentant la cruelle et sanglante saison des guerres civiles de Rome, propre et convenable pour y voir dépeinte la calamité de ce temps'. The dedication of *Marc-Antoine* draws a parallel between the civil wars of Rome and 'nos dissensions domestiques et les malheureux troubles de ce royaume'. That of *La Troade* claims that the spectacle of the disasters which befell 'our Trojan ancestors' should be of some consolation to Frenchmen in their present domestic troubles, since from the ruins of Troy there arose in due course, after the fall of the Roman Empire, 'cette très-florissante monarchie [de France]'.[1] The dedication of *Les Juives* contains the words 'Or vous ai-je représenté ici les soupirables calamités d'un peuple qui a comme nous abandonné son Dieu . . . Vous y voyez le châtiment d'un prince issu de l'ancienne race de David pour son infidélité et rebellion contre son supérieur.' The last sentence could be applied to Henri de Navarre, the leader of the Protestant party against his relative, the reigning king, Henri III.

The plays themselves also contain passages which it is easy to construe as allusions to the contemporary state of France. They help to link Garnier's drama to the political climate of his age and make it impossible to consider it as a product of purely academic humanism. But the idea of his *engagement* cannot be carried too far. The plays were certainly not conceived as polemical pieces. Most of the allusions in them are unparticularized. The stories of none of the tragedies as a whole could be applied to sixteenth-century conditions without the parallel breaking

---

[1] The allusion in this rather forced comparison would be clear to contemporary *literati*. According to the purely literary legend, the kingdom of France had been founded by an invented son of Hector, Francus, who escaped from Troy after its destruction, as Virgil's Aeneas escaped to found Rome. The legend was taken up again by Ronsard in *La Franciade*, published in the same decade as *La Troade*. It never struck roots.

down on vital points.[1] The most one can say is that Garnier was probably attracted to tragedy rather than to other genres because its preoccupation with 'choses funèbres et lamentables' suited his own reaction to his times; that he realized the topical potentialities in his themes and occasionally cultivated them, but was content to leave the moral on a general plane and was not dominated by it in writing his tragedies.

Nevertheless, he has a historic importance (after the Protestants, and particularly Des Masures) as the first French dramatist to admit openly the relevance of tragedy to contemporary conditions. Not less significant is the parallel which he allows to emerge, in three plays, between ancient Rome and France. Rome, rather than the national past, was to become the mirror in which Frenchmen regarded the idealized image of their own condition. It generated a stronger attraction than the biblical analogies, certainly more than the abortive identification with Troy, and more for a long time than Hellenic mythology in general – this in spite of the work of the humanist scholars and the fact that their ultimate dramatic source was Greek tragedy.

IV

Besides his seven 'lamentable' tragedies, Garnier wrote one tragicomedy, the curious and attractive *Bradamante*. The story of this was taken from Ariosto, to whom the somewhat fantastic characterization and motivation may be ascribed. We are now in the world of romance and of that special version of chivalry bred from romance, and therefore in a different order of the imagination from that of Garnier's other sources. Romance was a natural basis for tragicomedy, a word used with some uncertainty at first to describe what was felt to be an intermediate genre. It was applied especially to plays in which the love

[1] Thus, although *Les Juives* shows the punishment of a rebellious prince, sympathy is with him and his followers and certainly not with the tyrant Nebuchadnezzar who, if the parallel were complete, would have to be identified with Henri III, while the Old Testament Hebrews would be identified with the Protestants. This was necessarily very far from the mind of the Catholic Garnier who, in the same dedication in which he spoke of 'rebellion', sought to interest the King in his play. However, as Raymond Lebègue has argued, in his edition of *Les Juives* (Textes Français, 1949), p. 264, it was possible within the polemical framework of the sixteenth century for Garnier to condemn as illegitimate *any* rebellion against a ruling king without having to defend that king's personal character or actions. In this sense, *Les Juives* was a reply to the Protestant argument.

interest was dominant and which ended happily. Such plays might or might not contain 'comic' (in the sense of humorous) scenes and characters. *Bradamante* did.

Though neither the only nor the first sixteenth-century play styled a tragicomedy,[1] *Bradamante* was easily the most outstanding. It is set at the court of Charlemagne, who wishes to marry Bradamante, the daughter of one of his vassals, to the converted Saracen knight Roger. Bradamante's parents (portrayed as a homely couple, and who provide the main comic relief) are more attracted by the prospect of a match with Léon, the heir to the throne of Byzantium. Their daughter refuses to agree with them. She is in love with Roger who, however, has unaccountably disappeared. She has a further line of defence. She is a redoubtable swordswoman and Charlemagne has decreed that if Léon wishes to make her his wife he must first defeat her in single combat.

Léon now arrives at Charlemagne's court with a knight of unknown identity whom he has rescued from captivity and who in return has sworn to perform any service his rescuer may demand. Léon, a coward and a poor fighter, asks him to win Bradamante for him disguised under his own arms. The unknown knight, who is none other than the missing Roger, agrees in despair, incapable of breaking his word. He defeats Bradamante without bloodshed, by tiring her out, and slips away. Bradamante's marriage to Léon, the supposed victor, now seems inevitable, but Roger's sister Marphise, another warrior maiden, delays matters by declaring falsely that her brother and Bradamante have already taken secret marriage vows. Challenged, Bradamante merely hangs her head and remains silent. It is then suggested that Roger should be summoned from whatever part of the world he happens to be in to fight it out with Léon. The latter, intending once again to ask the unknown knight to take his place, readily and boastingly agrees. He then learns that his champion has disappeared and is utterly deflated.

In the last act he has learnt the truth. Roger has been found sitting miserably on his horse in the middle of a wood waiting for death by starvation, and has explained everything. After a brief combat of generosity Léon persuades him to take Bradamante and is himself

[1] H. C. Lancaster (*The French Tragi-Comedy*, Baltimore, 1907) counted some fifteen 'tragicomedies' between 1552 and 1600. But the majority of these were in fact Moralities, either religious or political, or barely disguised Miracle Plays.

compensated by a daughter of Charlemagne, suddenly thought of and mentioned for the first time fourteen lines from the end of the play.

This delightfully silly plot[1] allows a full measure of the dramatic movement, the incidental uncertainties and surprises so rigorously excluded from the tragedies. In its complications and the case of concealed identity on which it mainly turns it belongs to the comic order. Comically ironic use is made of this concealment, culminating in the scene in which Léon proposes to employ the unknown knight, who is Roger, to fight for him against Roger. The dilemma of Roger himself touches the ethic of chivalry, or what passed for that ethic in the sixteenth century, and would again in the seventeenth. There is a foretaste of Corneille's Rodrigue in the soliloquy (III. v) in which Roger debates whether his obligation to Léon involves giving up his mistress to him. Might he not solve his dilemma by letting her kill him in the duel they are about to fight? No, that would be a betrayal of Léon, and, he adds, on discovering the truth Bradamante might feel impelled to kill herself too. Some critics have also seen in Bradamante an ancestress of Corneille's heroines. She certainly shares their spirit and determination, though she is never in a situation in which she has to weigh such conceptions as duty and honour. Honour indeed gets an ambiguous handling in this play. Roger is sincerely ready to sacrifice everything for it, but the character in whose mouth the word is most prominent is Léon, precisely at the moment when he is about to behave most dishonourably. Having just arranged for Roger to take his place in the duel, he declares to Charlemagne:

> Bradamante est mon âme et ne crains de mourir,
> Si mourir me convient en voulant l'acquérir,
> Mais j'espère (et le ciel cette faveur me fasse)
> Qu'avecque de l'honneur je conquerrai sa grâce.

(III. iii)

---

[1] 'Silly' is not a criticism. The comic dramatist is licensed to be irrational, and the licence extends to many spectacles not primarily conceived as comic (e.g. operas), to heroic dramas and even, as will appear later in this book, to some plays styled tragedies. The line between tragedy and tragicomedy is often difficult to draw. There are also theatrical considerations. Conviction in the theatre may not coincide with the logic of the printed page.

On the other hand, he does not hesitate to surrender Bradamante to Roger when he discovers his identity, in obedience to the best tradition of brotherhood-in-arms. At the end of the play he is rewarded as an emperor's son and not as a villain.

It would be hazardous to take a modern view of this and conclude that Garnier was gently satirizing the code of chivalry, as Cervantes was to do some twenty years later. If he was concerned with anything more than the comic incongruity of the situation, he was putting forward a case for discussion: is an emperor's son obliged to behave as a perfect knight in every respect when love is at stake, particularly if he does not realize that anyone else's interests will be harmed?[1] The problem is not openly debated in this play, as were the questions of suicide and clemency in the tragedies, but the material for debate is implicit. Once again, drama was conceived as a catalyst for a society in search of new values – a search which entailed a re-examination of the old ones.

Bradamante seems to have been conceived as a play for the court although, as with his tragedies, Garnier failed to have it performed there.[2] It contains flattering references to Paris under Charlemagne (read, under Henri III), to the valour of the French knights and the beauty of the French ladies. There are allusions to the conflict between Christendom and the Saracens, who could be seen in the contemporary context as the Turks, defeated at Lepanto twelve years earlier but still powerfully established in Constantinople. In short, the analogies with the sixteenth century, including the background of crusading and chivalry, were more obvious than in the Greek and Roman tragedies and seemed well calculated to please an aristocratic audience. The setting of this 'most national of all the regular plays of the sixteenth

---

[1] Evidence that contemporaries saw no satire in the portrait of Léon is furnished by the summary of the story given in Vauquelin de la Fresnaye's *Art poétique*:

> . . . Léon, le voyant être Roger de Rise,
> De sa vaine poursuite abandonne la prise,
> Lui quitte Bradamante et, *courtois généreux*,
> Aide à conjoindre encor ce beau couple amoureux.

Extracts from this work can conveniently be read in H. W. Lawton, *Handbook of French Renaissance Dramatic Theory* (Manchester University Press, 1949).

[2] At least in his lifetime. Later, it became a favourite court play and was performed by members of the royal family in 1609, 1611 and probably 1613.

century'[1] was home ground, for though it derived from Italian romance, that in turn derived ultimately from the French *chansons de geste*. The characters had been kept alive, independently of Ariosto, in native romance, so that the court of Charlemagne and what it might be supposed to stand for was a conception familiar to Garnier's contemporaries.

V

Garnier's drama is poetic drama, making conscious – often over-conscious – use of the resources of poetry. The fact that much of his verse has little relevance to the dramatic structure is a weakness in modern eyes. On a different plane, the sight of a speech consisting of a page of close-packed alexandrines, followed by another page and another and quite probably more to come, is daunting to the eye of the student and demands considerable dedication even from the specialist. However, *tirades* which today require all the skill of a very exceptional actor to be even tolerable (this can be seen in the treatment of the much shorter *tirades* in Corneille and Racine by the company of the Théâtre Français) were usual form in the sixteenth century and entirely in line with the oratory of the law court and the pulpit. The spoken word could evidently be listened to by the hour without mental fatigue.[2] The loss of this faculty, bound up as it is with the whole theory of

[1] R. Lebègue, Notice in his edition of *Bradamante*.
[2] To quote one example only of the *développement oratoire* characteristic of Garnier. In *Porcie*, Act III, the philosopher Arée urges appeasement and an end to civil strife in Rome. Octave replies:

> Plutôt du jour flambant l'éternelle clarté
> Se joindra sociable avec l'obscurité;
> Plutôt l'alme soleil, rompant sa course égale,
> Donra ses premiers feux à la mer Atlantale,
> Et lassé de courir bornera son chemin
> Dans le flot indien qu'il redore au matin;
> Plutôt à flots courbés le Tybre porte-arène,
> Refusant de couler dedans la mer Tyrrhène,
> Raidira contre-mont ses refluantes eaux
> Et les fera ramper au sommet des coupeaux.

The entire sense of these ten lines can be conveyed in the one word: *Jamais*. However, it seems legitimate to argue that here, as in later tragedy, verbal pomp was offered in place of a deliberately excluded visual pomp, and hence to connect, in at least one significant way, baroque rhetoric with baroque spectacle.

communication, is merely recorded here as a self-evident historical fact. It has removed from our own reach a general response on which writers such as Garnier felt entitled to count, and which now can only be reconstructed academically. We are left with occasional responses to certain passages and qualities, well worth discovering and pointing out but not representing the whole of his art.

The rhetoric of the 'mighty line' appears in such famous passages as Nebuchadnezzar's boasting speech which opens Act II of *Les Juives*:

> Pareil aux Dieux je marche, et depuis le réveil
> Du soleil blondissant jusques à son sommeil
> Nul ne se parangonne à ma grandeur royale.
> En puissance et en biens Jupiter seul m'égale,
> Et encore n'était qu'il commande immortel,
> Qu'il tient un foudre en main dont le coup est mortel,
> Que son trône est plus haut et qu'on ne le peut joindre,
> Quelque grand dieu qu'il soit, je ne serais pas moindre.
> Il commande aux éclairs, aux tonnerres, aux vents,
> Aux grêles, aux frimas, et aux astres mouvants,
> Insensibles sujets. Moi, je commande aux hommes,
> . . . Tous les peuples du monde ou sont de moi sujets,
> Ou Nature les a delà les mers logés.
> L'Aquilon, le Midi, l'Orient je possède,
> Le Parthe m'obéit, le Persan et le Mède,
> Les Bactres, les Indois – et cet Hébreu cuidoit,
> Rebelle, s'affranchir du tribut qu'il me doit!

In such passages, influenced no doubt by Seneca but effective in their new language, an English reader can easily recognize the tone of Marlowe's *Tamburlaine*, a play belonging to the same decade. In a similar vein of uninhibited oratory Nebuchadnezzar's queen salutes the morning sun:

> O beau soleil luisant qui redores le monde
> Aussitôt que la nuit te voit sortir de l'onde,
> Rayonnante lumière, œil de tout l'univers,
> *Qui déchasses le somme et rends nos yeux ouverts,*
> Tu sois le bienvenu sur ces belles campagnes,
> Bienvenu le bonheur de qui tu t'accompagnes . . .

Garnier's imagery is as bold as his rhetoric. Nebuchadnezzar, exulting in the capture of the Royal Family of Judah, compares them to a family of wild boars which have fallen into the nets of his hunters:

> Je le tiens, je le tiens, je tiens la bête prise,
> Je jouis maintenant du plaisir de ma prise.
> J'ai chassé de tel heur[1] que rien n'est échappé.
> J'ai lesse et marcassins[2] ensemble enveloppé.
> Le cerne fut bien fait, les toiles bien tendues,
> Et bien avaient été les bauges reconnues.
> Les veneurs ont bien fait, je le vois. C'est raison
> Que chacun ait sa part de cette venaison.

In spite of Ronsard's opinion that the language of tragedy should be noble and elevated, Garnier is often ready to sacrifice dignity to the energetic metaphor, homely if necessary:

MARC-ANTOINE   Ains comme un porc ventru touillé dedans la
                fange,[3]
                A cœur saoul me vautrai en maints sales
                plaisirs.   (*Marc-Antoine*, III)

His Phèdre speaks of her passion in this way:

PHÈDRE   Le brasier [of love in my heart] étincelle et flamboie
          âprement,
          Comme il fait quand il rampe en un vieil bâtiment
          Couvert de chaume sec . . .   (*Hippolyte*, III)

In these realistic terms, going considerably beyond the parent passage in Seneca,[4] the Messenger describes to Andromaque the body of her son Astyanax after he has flung himself down from a high tower in Troy:

> Son corps est tout froissé, tout moulu, écaché,
> Rompu, brisé, gachi, démembré, déhaché,
> Sa tête par morceaux, la cervelle sortie,
> En bref vous ne verrez une seule partie
> Qui n'ait les os broyés plus menu que le grain
> Qu'on farine au moulin pour le tourner en pain.
>   (*La Troade*, IV)

---

[1] I have hunted so successfully.   [2] Sow and young boars.
[3] But like a fat-bellied pig rolling in the mire.   [4] Seneca, *Troades*, ll. 1111-19.

Besides heroic rhetoric and often direct and picturesque imagery (though it must be said that he makes more frequent use of the literary classical allusion) Garnier is capable of a grave simplicity which is effectively pathetic. Antigone refusing to leave her outcast father Œdipus sounds the equal, for a few lines at least, of Lear's Cordelia:

> Ne me commandez point que je vous abandonne.
> Je ne vous laisserai pour crainte de personne.
> Rien, rien ne nous pourra séparer que la mort.
> Je vous serai compagne en bon at mauvais sort.
> Que mes frères germains le royaume envahissent
> Et du bien paternel à leur aise jouissent,
> Moi mon père j'aurai, je ne veux autre bien,
> Je leur quitte le reste et n'y demande rien.　　　(*Antigone*, I)

The monologue is one of the strongest features of Garnier's plays and this is nowhere more evident than in *Bradamante*. There is the typically frenetic Senecan soliloquy (IV. ii) beginning:

> Gouffres des creux enfers, Ténariens rivages,
> Ombres, Larves, Fureurs, Monstres, Démons et Rages,
> Arrachez-moi d'ici pour me rouer là-bas.
> Tous, tous à moi venez et me tendez les bras ...

in which Roger expresses his violent despair in a manner foreshadowing so many later monologues in French drama.

The lover's lament, placed most naturally in the mouth of Bradamante, occurs several times in the play, notably in Act III, Scene ii:

> Et quoi, Roger, toujours languirai-je de peine?
> Sera toujours, Roger, mon espérance vaine?
> Où êtes-vous, mon cœur? Quelle terre vous tient,
> Quelle mer, quel rivage a ce qui m'appartient?
> Entendez mes soupirs, Roger, oyez mes plaintes,
> Voyez mes yeux lavés en tant de larmes saintes.
> O Roger, mon Roger, vous me cachez le jour,
> Quand votre œil, mon Soleil, ne luit en cette cour ...

This monologue, which contains a recurring couplet, not completely identical in each case but sufficiently similar to form a kind of refrain, is comparable to an aria without music. It is operatic in its effect, written to be recited to an audience sensitive to its repetitions, its well-developed comparisons and its verbal modulations. A break for applause would not be inappropriate at its end:

> Comme durant l'hiver, quand le soleil s'absente,
> Que nos jours sont plus courts, sa torche moins ardente,
> Viennent les Aquilons dans le ciel tempester,
> On voit sur les rochers les neiges s'afester,
> Les glaces et frimas rendre la terre dure,
> Le bois rester sans feuille et le pré sans verdure,
> Ainsi quand vous, Roger, vous absentez de moi,
> Je suis dans un hiver de tristesse et d'émoi.
> *Retournez donc, Roger, revenez, ma lumière,*
> *Las! et me ramenez la saison printanière.*
> Tout me déplaît sans vous, le jour m'est une nuit,
> Tout plaisir m'abandonne, et tout chagrin me suit.
> Je vis impatiente, et si guère demeure
> Votre œil à me revoir, il faudra que je meure,
> Que je meure d'angoisse, et qu'au lieu du flambeau
> De notre heureux hymen, vous trouvez mon tombeau.

This particular passage is fairly closely imitated from Ariosto, but Garnier can be said to have naturalized it in French drama. The principle of 'stopping to sing' is contrary only to a rather narrow conception of drama, that which demands that every speech should in some way advance the action. The aria type of monologue may of course do this also. It may serve to crystallize the character's intentions. But even when it serves only to confirm a state of mind which is already known, as in the above example,[1] it has a legitimate place in a play since it gives the audience an opportunity of savouring a situation and of identifying itself more closely with the emotions of the character.

A somewhat similar function is performed by the chorus whose utterances mark the ends of the acts in the tragedies (in *Bradamante*, a tragicomedy, there is no chorus) and provide a pause for reflection. It

---

[1] Which, however, is very opportunely placed. It immediately follows a monologue by Roger in which he expresses *his* despair and it precedes the scene in which the Emperor's son makes his formal challenge for Bradamante's hand.

must be admitted that too often they have nothing of interest to say, however melodiously they say it. Yet occasionally, as in *Les Juives*, they are sufficiently integrated into the play to provide an occasion for lyric poetry which is also dramatic. The interlude which they provide is again akin to music and could be replaced by it in a different theatrical idiom. Their eventual disappearance from French tragedy was not a total gain. A hundred years after Garnier, Racine welcomed the opportunity of introducing them into his tragedy *Esther*, which he described in the Preface as 'une espèce de poème où le chant fût mêlé avec le récit, le tout lié par une action qui rendît la chose plus vive et moins capable d'ennuyer'. Although Racine associated this with ancient Greek tragedy, his description could be applied with some aptness to sixteenth-century French tragedy – in which, however, the desirability of a 'linking through action' was less consciously felt.

GARNIER'S PLAYS

Porcie, tragedy, 1568
Story-sources: Plutarch, Appian, Cassius Dio.
   A sequel to the assassination of Julius Caesar. Act I: The Fury Mégère predicts new disasters for Rome, already torn by civil strife. II: Porcie, wife of Brute, awaits news of her husband's fate with black foreboding. In conversation with her Nurse, who attempts to comfort her, she contemplates suicide. III: The philosopher Arée deplores the warlike times he lives in. Octave enters, having defeated and killed Brute at Philippi, and swears vengeance on Caesar's remaining assassins in dialogue with Arée, who urges clemency. Marc-Antoine with his lieutenant and Lépide arrive, exulting also in the victory over Caesar's assassins. They envisage new conquests for themselves and Rome. IV–V: A messenger brings to Porcie the news of her husband's death in battle. He adds that he has also brought back his embalmed body. Porcie dies offstage by swallowing burning coals, all other means of suicide having been taken away from her. The Nurse stabs herself on stage with the dagger which she had removed from her mistress as a precaution. In his foreword Garnier remarks that this last death is his own invention 'pour envelopper [la tragédie] d'avantage en choses funèbres et lamentables, et en ensanglanter la catastrophe'.

Hippolyte, tragedy, 1573

The first French dramatization of the story of Hippolytus and Phaedra, closely modelled on Seneca's *Hippolytus*. Phèdre detests her absent husband, Thésée, and is tormented by desire for her stepson, Hippolyte, whom she is determined to win. She admits this freely (Act II) in a long dialogue with the Nurse, who strives to dissuade her from 'un crime exécrable', but finally, when Phèdre threatens suicide, resolves to help her. The Nurse attempts to persuade Hippolyte to respond to Phèdre's passion, but the misanthropic young hunter entirely fails to understand her. Finally Phèdre herself has to open his eyes by frankly declaring herself and imploring his pity. Hippolyte recoils in disgust and draws his sword to kill her. Phèdre begs him to do so, but he changes his mind and escapes, leaving her with the sword. Thésée now suddenly returns and a plot invented by the Nurse to shield Phèdre is put into practice. After veiled hints by the Nurse, Phèdre herself accuses Hippolyte of having raped her and produces the sword as evidence, saying he dropped it when he ran away. Blind with fury, Thésée calls down the vengeance of the god Neptune upon his son. In the last act the Messenger relates the death of Hippolyte, entangled in the reins and dragged over the ground by his bolting horses terrified by the appearance of a fabulous monster from the sea. Phèdre enters, stricken with remorse, confesses her crime and vindicates Hippolyte. She embraces Hippolyte's body which has been brought in, then stabs herself upon it with his sword. Thésée is left to lament his son and go on living miserably, as a greater punishment than suicide.

Cornélie, tragedy, 1574

Story-sources: Plutarch, Appian, Cassius Dio, Lucan.

The dramatic pattern is similar to that of *Porcie*, though the historic events referred to were anterior. Some were used again by Corneille in *La Mort de Pompée*.

Cornélie, twice a widow, is mourning the recent death of her second husband Pompée, murdered on landing in Egypt after his defeat by César. A messenger brings back Pompée's ashes to her in an urn – Cornélie is in Rome. Another messenger brings news of the death of her father Scipion after his defeat in battle. She decides to give honourable burial to them both before killing herself. (Act IV of the play, having little dramatic connection with the main action, introduces

Brute and Cassie, who resolve to oppose the tyranny of César. Then César enters, exulting in his recent victories, while Marc-Antoine warns him that he still has enemies at home.)

Marc-Antoine, tragedy, 1578

Story-sources: Plutarch, Cassius Dio.

The death of Antony and Cleopatra, after their defeat by Octavius Caesar at Actium. Although a note of doom is struck at the beginning, there is more vitality in this play than in Jodelle's version. (See above pp. 8–10.) Antoine is still alive during the first three acts, though determined to die and tormented by the belief that Cléopâtre has betrayed him by coming to terms with César. In Act II, however, Cléopâtre rejects this course and sends a reassuring message to Antoine (a sufficient illustration of Garnier's neglect of 'dramatic' opportunities is that the two lovers never meet on the stage). Cléopâtre is also resolved on suicide and overrides her confidantes' attempts to dissuade her. In Act III, Antoine again laments the loss of Cléopâtre's love (having not yet received her message), blames 'Volupté' for his downfall and reaffirms his decision to die. Act IV: César and his counsellor Agrippa discuss Antoine's fall and the pros and cons of showing clemency to him and his supporters. The discussion is proved academic by the entry of a messenger reporting that Antoine has stabbed himself, though he is not yet dead. He has been hauled up, desperately wounded, into the mausoleum where Cléopâtre has taken refuge. Agrippa suggests sending quickly to the mausoleum to seize Cléopâtre's treasures and – César adds – Cléopâtre herself, so that she can be led in triumph through Rome. Plutarch is followed faithfully in all this, but again there is no dramatic development. Act V shows Cléopâtre in the mausoleum with her attendants, her children, and the corpse of Antoine. The children are smuggled away. Lamentations. Cléopâtre dies on stage embracing Antoine's body, like Phèdre in Hippolyte.

La Troade, tragedy, 1579

Story-sources: Seneca's Troades, Euripides' Trojan Women and Hecuba.

A tale of the sufferings resulting from a collective disaster, the fall of Troy. While the surviving women wait outside the sacked city to learn their fate, the victors carry off the virgin priestess Cassandre to be Agamemnon's concubine, her sister Polyxène and the young Astyanax, Andromaque's son. The last two are slaughtered. All these atrocities are inflicted on members of the same family, that of Priam, King of Troy. The apprehension or narration of them make up the martyrdom of Priam's wife Hécube, who is continually present on the stage. A secondary martyr is Andromaque, tortured by the removal of Astyanax. The body of another child, Polydore, is found washed up by the sea. He has been murdered by a treacherous neighbouring king, Polymestor, to whom he had been sent for safety. In Act V the Trojan women wreak vengeance on Polymestor by killing his own two sons and blinding him. The combination of three source-plays enables Garnier to accumulate the narrated atrocities.

Antigone, tragedy, 1580

This play also shows an accumulation of disasters befalling a group – the family of Oedipus – but they are more varied than in *La Troade*. The main sources are the *Phoenissae* of Seneca, the *Antigone* of Sophocles, and the *Thebais* of the Latin epic poet Statius. There are also reminiscences of the *Oedipus Rex* and the *Oedipus at Colonus* of Sophocles.

In Act I the blinded Œdipe, wandering in the mountains with his daughter Antigone, recalls the events which led to his downfall and then disappears from the action. Acts II and III concern the struggle for the kingdom between his sons Étéocle and Polynice who kill each other in battle (reported). Their mother Jocaste, having failed to reconcile them, stabs herself on stage. The last two acts are more particularly the tragedy of Antigone, who has been present as an almost helpless witness at the earlier events, though suffering because of them. She sprinkles earth on the body of her brother Polynice, left unburied by order of her uncle Créon, and for this is condemned to a slow death by hunger immured in a cave. She hangs herself instead and her lover Hémon, Créon's son, kills himself on her body. Hémon's mother, Eurydice, kills herself also on receiving the news. Créon admits his responsibility for these deaths and prays for death as the tragedy ends.

Bradamante, tragicomedy, 1582
Story-source: Ariosto, *Orlando furioso*
    Summarized above, pp. 25–6.

Les Juives, tragedy, 1583

The story-source is biblical (2 Kings 24–5 and 2 Chronicles 36), but the general situation is similar to that of *La Troade*, and *Les Juives* carries reminiscences both of this earlier tragedy and of its sources.

Defeated by his overlord, Nabuchodonosor (Nebuchadnezzar), against whom he had rebelled, the Jewish king Sédécie (Zedekiah) is brought captive to Babylon, together with his wives, his children and his mother. Nabuchodonosor is determined to inflict exemplary punishment on him and this he finally does in spite of the pleadings of his own queen and of Sédécie's mother, Amital (Hamutal), who resembles Hecuba. The royal children, as well as various Jewish priests and elders, are slaughtered before the eyes of Sédécie, who is then blinded – all, of course, offstage. The mothers survive to lament, while a prophet predicts the ultimate restoration of Jerusalem and the coming of the Messiah.

The best-known and most successful of Garnier's tragedies.

3

FROM GARNIER TO HARDY

French tragedy between 1580 and 1610 – Montchrestien and his tragedies –
L'Écossaise – structure of this 'static' play and the humanist idea of tragedy
– Montchrestien's *Bergerie* – the contemporary theatre in England – in
Spain – relative poverty of French theatre – travelling companies in the
provinces – Paris and the Hôtel de Bourgogne – the flowering of the 1620s
– Bellerose and Montdory – foundation of the Théâtre du Marais – the
Parisian theatre in the 1630s and 1640s

Garnier's last tragedy, *Les Juives*, was published in 1582. For the period
1580–1610, more than seventy tragedies by other writers (excluding
Montchrestien, considered separately in this chapter) have survived
in print, while the titles of some thirty others, which were not printed,
are known. But this figure of a hundred-odd tragedies most probably
considerably under-represents the total production over the three
decades, and it is evident that 'tragedy' was a highly popular genre
during the whole period.

Disregarding for the moment the varied forms of these plays, it
is possible to establish a broad classification according to subject or
source, with a few examples of each category. The dates given are
those of first publication, sometimes later by several years than the
dates of known performances:

Biblical and Jewish: *Holoferne* (A. d'Amboise, 1580), *Tragédie du
meurtre commis par Caïn* (Lecoq, 1580), *Esther, Vasthi, Aman* (P.
Matthieu, 1585–9), *Sichem ravisseur* (Perrin, 1589), *Esaü* (Behourt,
1598), *La Machabée* (De Virey, 1599), *David persécuté* (Thierry, 1600),
Achab (de Marcé, 1601), *Dina, Josué, Debora* (Nancel, 1607), *Saül*
(Billard, 1610).

Classical Greek: *La Thébaïde* (Robelin, 1584), *Clytemnestre* (P.
Matthieu, 1589), *Pyrrhe* (Heudon, 1598), *Ulysse* (Champ-Repus, 1603),
Priam (Berthrand, 1605).

Roman, Plutarchan, etc.: *Didon* (La Grange, 1582), *Régulus* (Beaubreuil, 1582), *Sophonisbe* (Mermet, 1584), *Cléopâtre* (Montreux, 1595), *Horace*, *Dioclétien* (Laudun, 1596), *Octavie* (Regnault, 1599), *Coriolanus* (Thierry, 1600), *Monime* (Pageau, 1600), *Sophonisbe* (Montreux, 1601; Garel, 1607), *Panthée* (Guérin Daronnière, 1608; Billard, 1610).

French history, medieval or legendary: *Histoire tragique de la Pucelle* (Fr. du Duc, 1581), *La Franciade* (Godard, 1594), *Jeanne d'Arques* (?, 1603), *Merovée* (Billard, 1610).

French history, recent: *La Guisiade* (P. Matthieu, 1589), *Le Guysien* (Belyard, 1592), *Cléophon* (Fonteny, 1600), *Le Triomphe de la Ligue* (Nérée, 1607), *Gaston de Foix* (Billard, 1610).

Romance and exotic: *Isabelle* (Montreux, 1594), *Charite* (Poullet, 1595), *Radegonde* (Du Souhait, 1599), *Acoubar* (Du Hamel, 1603), *La Rodomontade*, *La Mort de Roger* (Bauter, 1605), *Adamantine* (Le Saulx, 1608).

A number of these tragedies were based on earlier plays rather than on their primary sources in the Bible, Plutarch and elsewhere. The influence of Jodelle, Garnier and Des Masures is often perceptible, pointing to the early growth of a self-perpetuating dramatic or theatrical tradition which was to be accentuated in the seventeenth century. The several *Sophonisbes* owed at least as much to Mellin de Saint-Gelais's adaptation of 1556 of the Italian *Sofonisba* of Trissino as to the original story in Livy. The two *Panthées* of 1608 and 1610 followed at least one earlier dramatization of the story, that of Guersens in 1571, and need not have been drawn directly from Xenophon. Others have no known dramatic precursors; this applies almost of necessity to those plays concerned with recent history, which tended to be drawn from life though at the same time deadened with propagandist features. In the Romance category, *Radegonde* derived from the medieval *Châtelaine de Vergy*; *La Rodomontade*, *La Mort de Roger* and *Isabelle* all from Ariosto independently of Garnier, though it is possible that his *Bradamante* had directed the attention of playwrights to the Italian poet; *Acoubar* derives from a French novel set in an imaginary 'Canada', while *Adamantine* is set among American Indians. Of some interest to English readers is the performance at Neufchâtel in 1581 of the *Roméo et Juliette* of Chateauvieux. No text survives, but, like Shakespeare's tragedy, it was no doubt ultimately derived from the *novella* by the sixteenth-century Italian, Bandello, in this case probably through Belleforest's translation.

As to the form of these plays, many still followed the pattern of humanist regular tragedy at its most declamatory and static. A few, such as the *Tragédie du meurtre commis par Caïn*, were simply Mysteries relabelled. Others were intermediary or unclassifiable. In these latter the number of acts might vary from two to seven, the choruses might disappear and the unities of time and place be disregarded. Some were evidently written for the medieval multiple décor. There was a return to medieval practice in showing spectacle and scenes of extreme physical brutality to the spectators; or it might be truer to say that in some of the provinces the medieval practice continued unchanged.

This prolific and varied production of tragedy was on a low literary level. It was the work of provincial schoolteachers and priests, local lawyers and officials, and in some cases possibly of small-time professional actors or the hack-poets who worked for them. There is no theoretical obstacle to such writers' producing good work, but in regular tragedy none even approached the level of Garnier. The only name that stands a little above the others in this category is that of Pierre Matthieu (1563–1621), at first a youthful headmaster in Franche-Comté, then a barrister, then historiographer to Henri IV. He wrote three tragedies on or around the perennial story of Esther, filled with didactic moralizations obliquely attacking the corrupt court of Henri III. His *Guisiade* was an attack on the Catholic Ligue after the author had rallied to Henri IV. His 'classical' *Clytemnestre* was a schoolboy work, written, it appears, at the age of fifteen. Almost negligible as drama, works such as these have a certain interest for the student of political literature and rather more, perhaps, for the student of baroque rhetoric. Native French critics, after picking out a few 'good' (i.e. vigorous but relatively sober) lines, speak of the whole as 'un étrange galimatias' (Lebègue), or conclude, as Faguet on Matthieu: 'D'ordinaire il a les défauts de son temps à un degré éminent: emphase, recherche, innovations puériles, mots composés.' One acquiesces, but had the total effect of these plays or of their unwritten successors been more forceful, it would not be difficult to change the emphasis and write approvingly of 'the exuberant fantasy of youth', of 'vigorous verbal invention', or even, without great exaggeration, of 'psychologically sophisticated linguistic structures'. It is not impossible that all this classically condemned *fatras* still awaits reinterpretation in that direction, resituating it, no longer disapprovingly, in its baroque context.

The same applies to some of the 'irregular' tragedies, in which untutored taste, pedantry and a kind of eccentric inspiration occasionally combine to produce remarkable linguistic effects – almost, it would seem, accidentally.

In such a mass of material produced in different places for differing purposes by writers with very uneven talents it is not easy to discern definite trends. It is customary to speak of the decline of regular humanist tragedy, constructed on the principles defined by various Renaissance theorists,[1] after Garnier. Viewed with hindsight in the light of the developments of the early seventeenth century (Hardy and others), this is clearly justified. But considering only the last two decades of the sixteenth century, for which the evidence is conflicting and far from complete, one would merely conclude that regular tragedy did not impose itself as the sole or even the dominant type. There was no strongly continuous development of the process initiated by Jodelle. But on the other hand, regular tragedies were still being written, while numerous others conformed to the regular pattern in part, so paying tribute to its influence on different levels of culture. The most noteworthy dramatist of his time, Montchrestien, wrote his wholly 'regular' tragedies around the turn of the century. He might be regarded as a latecomer, closing the first chapter of French classical tragedy, yet he was read and even acted.

Other conclusions are more certain and perhaps more significant. The first is that during 1580–1610 there was no slackening in the composition of tragic dramas in France. It was a nationwide activity and the fact that much of it was amateurish reinforces the point. Secondly, although the names and forms of medieval drama were concealed or obscured, the native habits of mind which underlay them were very far from dead. They persisted quite vigorously and were proving capable of either absorbing or combining with the Senecan and pseudo-Aristotelian influences of the academic tradition. What followed was not what an English reader, nourished on Elizabethan drama, might logically expect. In France things fell out differently.

II

Antoine de Montchrestien (c. 1575–1621) interrupts any theoretically consistent account of the development of French tragic drama. If

[1] Returned to below p. 111–12.

such an account is to be sustained, it is only possible to regard him as a latecomer, as has been suggested above. Writing some twenty years after Garnier, he composed six tragedies in the pure humanist classical convention with the usual five acts and choruses. The misery of his characters is less harrowing than in Garnier, their emotions are less stridently expressed. On stage there are no suggestions of physical violence, scarcely even a suicide.[1] His literary fastidiousness is in some contrast to his life, which was that of an impoverished middle-class son (his father had been a chemist in the Norman town of Falaise) determined to succeed by violent means if necessary, and sometimes by schemes which do not appear to have been over-scrupulous. He fought two duels, after the second of which he took refuge in the England of James I apparently for several years. Returning to France, he launched various business enterprises and published a justly famous (for its date) treatise on political economy. In politics and religion he seems to have sat on the fence, but towards the end of his life he took an active part in a Protestant insurrection and was surprised and killed at an inn while trying to recruit supporters for the Huguenot cause. His dead body was broken on the wheel and then burnt.

Like the non-dramatic verse which he also wrote, his six tragedies were the work of his earlier years. All were published in their final versions in the edition of 1604. The earliest, *Sophonisbe*, had first been printed in 1596. It was republished, very extensively revised and retitled *La Carthaginoise*, in 1601, together with four other tragedies: *L'Écossaise*, *Les Lacènes*, *David* and *Aman*. When these were reprinted, with some revisions, in 1604, a sixth tragedy, *Hector*, was added. Of the subjects, two were thus biblical (David's adulterous passion for Bathsheba and the familiar story of Esther and Ahasuerus), one Trojan (the death of Hector, with Andromache's fears and lamentations),[2] one from Plutarch (*Les Lacènes* or Lacedemonian Women concerns the fate of Cleomenes, King of Sparta), one, *Sophonisbe*, from Livy via the dramatization by Trissino, which it follows closely. There are no surprises here. Only *L'Écossaise*, dealing with the execution of Mary Stuart on Elizabeth's orders as recently as 1587, might seem to have a potentially exciting novelty. It interested contemporaries, is known to

[1] Except for the two which occur at the end of his first tragedy, *Sophonisbe*.
[2] Faguet considered this the worst of Montchrestien's tragedies, Petit de Julleville the best. Lebègue, so far as I can find, expresses no critical opinion.

have been acted at least three times between 1601 and 1604, and was the object of a protest by Elizabeth's ambassador in Paris.[1] Somewhat later, during his exile in England, Montchrestien presented the tragedy to James I, Mary Stuart's son, who was sufficiently impressed by it to intercede with the King of France in the author's favour. It contains numerous contemporary allusions of a general kind – to the gallantry and magnificence of the French kings, to conspiracies within England, to the threat from Spain then preparing to launch the Armada – and it relates in idealized terms the life of Mary Stuart from her early marriage to François II to her return to Scotland as a widow, her flight

[1] This was first brought to light by Dr Frances Yates in *Modern Language Review*, XXII (1927). The episode is a good illustration of the attitude of the authorities towards the theatre at that date. On 17 March 1602 Sir Ralph Winwood, English Ambassador in Paris, reports to Robert Cecil, Secretary of State, that 'since the beginning of Lent certaine base Comedians have publicklie plaied in this Towne the Tragedie of the late Queen of Scottes'. He has complained to the French Chancellor, who has charged the *lieutenant civil* 'to have a care, both that this Folly should be punished, and that the like hereafter should not be committed'.

While this tragedy cannot be identified with absolute certainty as Montchrestien's, it is highly probable that it was, particularly in the light of the next document quoted by Miss Yates. The tragedy here referred to bears Montchrestien's exact title. On 21 June 1603, Beauharnais, *lieutenant général* at Orléans, writes to the Chancellor that he has made inquiries about the comedians who performed at Orléans, some two months previously, 'une tragédie sur la mort de la feue royne d'Écosse'. They have now left for an unknown destination and he has only been able to learn that their leader was called La Vallée. However, 'j'ay recouvré ung livre de tragédies, la première desquelles, nommée "l'Écossoise" aultrement "le Désastre", est celle même qu'ils ont representée.' He sends this copy to the Chancellor for his inspection.

On 13 February 1604 NS, Sir Thomas Parry, the new English ambassador in Paris, writes to Cecil that the comedians, defying the prohibition, ventured 'this week' to perform 'ye tragedy of ye death of ye K. mother'. They have been arrested and are now in prison. 'Besides ye booke is suppressed and ye author and ye printer inquired after to tast of ye same cupp.'

In spite of this, it would seem that the French authorities took the matter less seriously than the embassy, since later in 1604 the new edition of Montchrestien's tragedies was published at Rouen, with a royal *privilège* dated 10 April. Further, Elizabeth had died in March 1603 and had been succeeded by James, who later approved of the play. One may plausibly assume, however, that the implications of the dynastic change escaped the new ambassador, who was merely continuing his predecessor's line of action. He may well have been shocked by the mere representation of 'ye K. mother' on a stage.

from there and imprisonment in England, and finally her execution, presented as an exemplary Catholic martyrdom. The first two acts are devoted entirely to Elizabeth, who is portrayed sympathetically. In Act I she conducts a long debate with a single counsellor on the question of clemency – the conventional theme – which she is determined to show towards Mary. In Act II she continues the debate more briefly with a *Chœur des Estats* (which can be interpreted either as a Council of Ministers or as a kind of parliamentary delegation), to whose arguments she finally gives her very reluctant consent. After their withdrawal, however, she decides to forbid the execution, or at least to postpone it. In Act III we learn, without transition or explanation, that the death sentence has been pronounced. The news is broken to Mary, who now occupies the centre of the stage (Elizabeth does not appear again) and resolves to die bravely (Act IV). In Act V her pathetic but edifying death is related.

As a dramatic exercise the story could hardly have been handled more ineptly, but this is perhaps as good a place as any to stop examining humanist regular tragedy for features which it neither possessed nor was intended to possess. Montchrestien, like Garnier, was clearly not interested in the dramatic qualities of movement, conflict, suspense and peripeteia. His method was to take a situation, often fully developed[1] and complete in itself, and to extract from it the maximum of emotional and poetic effect. Didactic effect also, so far as it is justified to consider the didactic content as a separate factor; but it is more satisfactory to count the commonplace reflections on the mutability of fortune and the inevitability of death as part of the emotional experience in Garnier and Montchrestien. While the modern mind draws a distinction between the emotion as experienced and the lesson drawn from it, it is not so certain that the sixteenth-century mind did the same. We doubt whether a 'philosophic' statement such as 'Alas,

[1] In the nature of things, the situation has to be defined for the audience, but this is done as early as possible with nothing withheld to leave an opening for surprise or suspense. The expositions in Corneille and Racine furnish the facts necessary to understand the drama that is about to follow. They do not prejudge the drama itself. In Garnier and Montchrestien there is not this clear distinction between a known past and an unknown future. When fresh events occur, as they must if there is to be any 'story' at all, their invariable tendency is to reinforce the situation under contemplation rather than to develop it.

she had to die', expressed at however great a length, was felt as less immediate than the plain lament in 'Alas, she is dead.' It was a prolongation or elaboration of it, and perhaps no more.

The exploitation of situations for their emotional or didactic yield resulted, as has been observed, in a static technique. When a play contains more than one situation, there is no effort to link them by dramatic necessity. The relation of one to another is that already laid down by history or the known 'story'. Since it happened that way, it is shown, but without regard for 'probability', whether overt or hidden. The structure of a play such as *L'Écossaise* is exactly that of a diptych. On one side is Elizabeth worrying over the insecurity of her throne as long as Mary is alive, but preoccupied much more with the sacredness of the royal blood in her rival (yet this is not developed to the point of an inner conflict); around her are the figures of counsellors expostulating. On the other side is Mary, an unhappy princess held in long captivity (her recalling of this is merely part of her portrayal) and now nobly preparing for martyrdom among her sorrowing attendants. The dramatically essential link between the two pictures – the decision to condemn Mary in spite of Elizabeth's reluctance – is practically omitted. It is, in pictorial terms, crowded into a corner of the second panel in the shape of a figure called Davison (or d'Avison in Montchrestien), the small political officer who has been detailed to announce the sentence to Mary. He deplores his mission at the beginning of Act III and later in the act discharges it quite briefly. Dramatically, this decision, with the debates and heart-searchings which led to it, would have been expected to fill the whole of Act III and perhaps Act IV. But in this kind of art it is unimportant. It does not even supply the centre panel of a triptych.

The analogy with pictorial techniques is a purely structural one. The same method of construction is used when a subject is represented on the stage in a number of tableaux, each one valued for its own sake at least as much as for its significance in a forward-moving series. Ballet, opera and pantomime all tend to conform to this conception, in which the story, reduced sometimes to no more than a theme, is of secondary importance. It is used perfunctorily as a framework for the different scenes, but need not be developed dramatically nor even, as Dr Johnson observed of eighteenth-century opera, rationally. However, in the types of entertainment which most readily dispense with it, the spectator is compensated by visual and aural effects: spectacle, dance, music. Renaissance regular tragedy offered none of these, but relied solely on the beauty, energy or flamboyance of the spoken word to fill their place. In itself it was hardly adequate to the purpose, but it would be mistaken to dismiss the work of Garnier and Montchrestien as abortive on those grounds. The so-called lyric elements so prominent in their tragedies are found in nearly all drama and certainly persisted strongly in the major French dramatists of the seventeenth century. The fact that they no longer occurred 'pure', but alternated or combined with other elements, does not obscure their survival, as will be seen later. Right up to Racine and beyond, the contemplative or analytic 'lyric' passage is found, though much more conspicuously in some of his predecessors. For writers whose talent lay predominantly in that direction, the logical course was to write for opera, once opera was established. But even spoken tragedy, and much more tragicomedy, had its operatic features, as they may now anachronistically be called. These formed an important part of the dramatic entertainment, which could hardly have dispensed with them without losing its contemporary appeal.

Meanwhile Montchrestien appears more interesting today as a poet than as a dramatist. He is hardly a great poet, but he is a competent one who repays study in the context of his time. His *lieux communs* are those of Chassignet and Sponde. His occasional *préciosité* suggests the influence of Desportes. Some of his verse also resembles that of Maynard and Racan, who were to follow him at a short distance in time. He therefore has a respectable place in the history of French poetry and deserves attention as a representative verse-writer of the turn of the century. But the implications of this lie mainly outside the history of drama and are not the subject of the present book.

It should be added that he wrote a *Bergerie* or pastoral, contained in the edition of 1601. Since it has been described somewhat differently by different authorities, it is worth devoting a few lines to it. It was clearly intended to be performed, though there is no record that it was. The preliminary list of *entreparleurs* includes Cupid, a naiad, a satyr and various named shepherds and shepherdesses. It consists of five acts divided into scenes. Each act ends with a chorus in verse of various metres. Unlike the usual dramatic pastoral, however, the main part of the text is in prose interspersed with verses. It would appear that the prose was intended to be spoken and some, if not all, of the verses to be sung,[1] including probably the choruses. Some of the longer verse passages in couplet-rhymed alexandrines may not have been sung.

III

To return to the general development of tragedy: it is of interest to recall the state of the drama at the end of the sixteenth and the beginning of the seventeenth century in the two neighbouring countries where it was most vigorous. First in England:

(a) *Authors.* Plays of the 'University Wits' (Lyly, Peele, Greene, etc.) in the 1580s and 1590s.

Kyd (1558–94): *The Spanish Tragedy* (?1587); translation of Garnier's *Cornélie* (pub. 1594).

Marlowe (1564–93): all plays 1587–93.

Shakespeare (1564–1616): all plays conjecturally dated 1591–1611.

Chapman (c. 1559–1643): tragedies based on French history, as *Bussy d'Ambois* (pub. 1607) and comedies, all c. 1598–1614.

Ben Jonson (1572?–1634): *Every Man in his Humour* (1598), *Sejanus* (1603), *Volpone* (1606), *The Alchemist* (1610), *Catiline* (1611), etc. Reprinted 1616, with 11 masques and 4 'entertainments'.

Beaumont (c. 1584–1616) and Fletcher (1579–1625): *The Woman Hater* (c. 1606), *The Knight of the Burning Pestle* (1607), *Philaster* (c. 1610), *The Maid's Tragedy* (c. 1611).

Webster (1580?–1625?): *The White Devil* (pub. 1612), *Duchess of Malfi* (1613?).

Also writing between 1600 and 1615: Dekker, Tourneur, Marston (*Tragedy of Sophonisba*, 1606) and others.

(b) *Companies.* Apart from the companies of boy actors (Windsor Chapel Children and Children of Paul's), who were already giving public performances in the 1570s and continued until after 1603, there were several adult companies created or sponsored by aristocratic patrons in the early 1590s and before. By 1594 three wholly professional companies (the Lord Chamberlain's Men, the Admiral's Men and

---

[1] e.g. II. iii:

LUCRINE	. . . Nous sommes découvertes aussi bien. Écoutez-les, ils chantent.
DEUX BERGERS	O doux astres d'amour qui gouvernez nos âmes Et versez en nos cœurs les désirs gracieux . . . etc.

Worcester's Men) had emerged and were recognized by the grant of royal licences. Their privileges were confirmed ten years later after the accession of James I, their names changing respectively to The King's Men, The Queen's Men and Prince Henry's Men. Though under royal patronage, these companies operated in effect as independent commercial ventures.

(c) *Theatres.* Inn-yards gave way to purpose-built buildings, of which the earliest was The Theatre, erected by Burbage in 1576. Several others followed. In 1600, London possessed four theatres in regular use: The Swan, The Globe, The Fortune and The Blackfriars. The last was a converted monastery building, the other three were new constructions. By 1615, three other theatres had been erected.

Developments in Spain can be summarized thus:

(a) *Authors.* Historians of Spanish drama encounter much the same difficulties in the dating and attribution of the very numerous plays of this period as do their English counterparts. Most of the following authors were already writing by 1615 – in some cases considerably before – but in one or two instances slightly later dates are all that can be taken as established, based on the certain evidence of publication.

Cervantes (1547–1616): early plays probably before 1585. Published 16 plays in 1615. Not very successful as a dramatist.

Lope de Vega (1564–1635): first play *c.* 1587. Continued writing for the stage until *c.* 1631. Claimed to have written over 1,800 plays in his life.

Tirso de Molina (1584?–1648): plays from before 1615 to 1625. Said to have written 300–400 in all. *El Burlador de Sevilla, El vergonzoso en Palacio, El condenado por desconfiado* (attrib.).

Vélez de Guevara (1569–1644): writing plays before 1614. Credited with composing 400.

Guillén de Castro (1569–1631): first volume of plays published 1618, including *Las mocedades del Cid.*

Ruiz de Alarcón (1581–1639): plays probably written 1615–25. Eight plays published 1628, twelve others 1634.

Mira de Amescua (1574?–1644): known to be writing in 1617.

A number of lesser dramatists were contemporary with these.

(b) *Companies and theatres.* A feature of Spanish drama, in addition to its popularity in Madrid, was the strength of its following in the provinces. Travelling companies of professionals are known to have been active in the mid-sixteenth century, giving somewhat crude performances. Their activities increased steadily, until in 1603 the number of licensed companies was officially limited to eight for the whole of Spain, increased to twelve in 1615. An unknown number of unlicensed companies also played in the villages and smaller towns. Constantly on the move, the companies rented *corrales* or courtyards generally owned by religious fraternities (*cofradías*) who used the proceeds to finance the hospitals that they maintained. While the performances were given in existing buildings as to the outer walls (sometimes they were the hospitals themselves), considerable construction work was done inside both to accommodate the spectators and to equip the stages; so that, as much as the purpose-built playhouses of London, many of the Spanish *corrales* could be regarded as regular theatres. Madrid possessed two from 1584, in succession to several earlier ones. Seville had at least three (though of perhaps less permanent construction) around 1580, and from then until 1600 there are records of similar theatres in all the big provincial cities. Legislation, bearing particularly on considerations of public order, morality and finance, testifies further to the vitality of the professional stage around the year 1600. In 1587, for example, the appearance of women on the stage was officially permitted, so regularizing a practice already current. The authorities disapproved, however, of the appearance of actresses in male attire. Conversely, the vexed question of boy actors in female roles was finally resolved in 1615 by their total prohibition from the stage. The Spanish theatre continued to flourish with few serious interruptions through most of the seventeenth century, while increasing interest in both amateur and professional productions was taken by the court.

If, therefore, one draws a broad outline of English and Spanish drama during the decades in question, one finds that both countries possessed what can reasonably be termed a flourishing professional theatre by the 1590s if not before. The companies of actors were there in some strength; buildings constructed or adapted for the purpose were set aside for their use. This process continued steadily between 1600 and 1620 – to look no further forward than the second of these dates. As for the dramatists, most of the English had finished writing by 1615 or had produced all their best work. The Spanish were a little later, but by the same date most of their greatest dramatists were also producing or beginning to produce prolifically to satisfy the needs of a large play-hungry public.

IV

France, in contrast, has a meagre record. Various reasons have been put forward for this: the anarchic state of the country during the last phase of the Wars of Religion, the indifference of the great nobles and, after the establishment of peace, the indifference of Henri IV to serious drama. To these political and material considerations is sometimes added the inhibiting influence of learned tragedy (we have already seen that this can be practically discounted) and, with rather more force, the fact that the best poets of the French Renaissance belonged to too early a generation to write for the theatre.

Most of these factors may have had a contributory effect, but it is difficult to see any of them as decisive. The last period of real anarchy lasted for only five years (1586–91), covering the assassinations of the Duc de Guise and of Henri III, and a grim siege of Paris by Henri IV. That this should have impeded the development of the theatre, at least in Paris, is understandable. So for several years after would be the neglect of dramatic performances by the aristocracy, preoccupied with other matters. But none of this need have caused more than a temporary halt, while the personal tastes of Henri IV can only have had a limited effect. Neither Philip II of Spain, who died in 1598, nor even Elizabeth of England (whatever may have been written to the contrary) gave much encouragement to the theatre. In both those countries the attitude of the court and the great nobles no doubt had a certain influence, but the early theatre was also and indeed mainly based on the support of the general public. This, as we have already partly seen, was true of France as well. One can see no theoretical bar to the growth of a flourishing professional drama after the Edict of Nantes of 1598 either in the capital, as happened in England, or both in the capital and in several of the big provincial towns, on the Spanish pattern. That it did not occur is still a matter of some surprise, and which has so far defied a satisfactory analysis. Meanwhile we can only describe the conditions as they existed.

The actual performance of plays by schoolboys, students and occasionally by amateur groups with an occupational bond (e.g. lawyers, nuns) continued to the end of the sixteenth century. During its last two decades also, if not earlier, there is plenty of evidence of the existence of travelling companies of professionals, as in Spain. Either these or the amateurs, and in some cases both, acted many of the plays listed above on pp. 38–9, in addition to the tragedies of Jodelle and Garnier and at least two by Montchrestien (*Sophonisbe* and *L'Écossaise*). The total picture of these activities has to be laboriously built up by research in municipal archives, a task magisterially begun by Gustave Lanson nearly seventy years ago and continued, in particular, by Raymond Lebègue. It is still incomplete and often inconclusive: the record of the passage of a troupe of actors may tell us little or nothing about its repertory and give no indication of the composition or quality of the troupe. But there is no room for doubt that the visits of travelling professionals were a familiar feature of life in the provincial towns. The evidence so far assembled points to special activity in the north and north-east with a vigorous extension into the Netherlands, though companies also visited such southern cities as Bordeaux and Toulouse. Finally, the names of two prominent leaders of companies emerge, that of Adrien Talmy, of whom not much is known, and of Valleran le Conte. Both were already active in the 1590s, separately and in association. Valleran, first heard of at Bordeaux in 1592, played the more important part in the history of the theatre.

Paris lagged behind the provinces. In 1600 and for some thirty years afterwards the capital possessed only one permanent theatre, the Hôtel de Bourgogne. It had been built in 1548 by the Confrères de la Passion, a fraternity of Parisian merchants and artisans who required a centre for their reunions and their own performances of religious and other plays. The profits went to the support of a hospital. From the beginning they held a monopoly, confirmed several times during the sixteenth century, of dramatic performances in Paris, which could only be given with their consent and on payment of most of the profits to them. Visiting companies who attempted to infringe their monopoly were constantly brought to heel by legal action. The Confrères themselves, whose acting seems to have begun on the level of Bottom and his cronies and to have improved little during the next half-century,[1]

[1] See S. W. Deierkauf-Holsboer, *Le Théâtre de l'Hôtel de Bourgogne*, I, pp. 22 and 35–6. Mme D.-Holsboer concludes that the Confrères clung to the old medieval repertory throughout the second half of the sixteenth century, continuing to

finally ceased their own performances and from 1597 became simply the landlords of a theatre available to any company ready to agree to their highly onerous terms. Their function was now identical to that of the *cofradías* in Spain. Their only interest in the theatre was a financial one.

The first attempts to hire the Hôtel de Bourgogne, in 1598, were all abortive. The French companies of Adrien Talmy and Valleran le Conte, an English company under one Jean Thays, of which it has proved impossible to discover more, and, at the end of the same year, two other French companies, all negotiated with the Confrères but finally failed to fulfil their contracts and played elsewhere in the capital, on payment of the dues which the Confrères were entitled to exact. All this points to the strong attraction for touring companies exerted by the capital in the year of the settlement of the Edict of Nantes.

In the following year, Valleran hired the Hôtel de Bourgogne and performed there, becoming the first *de facto* lessee together with a company of Italian actors, the two companies using the theatre on alternate days. This was one of the numerous Italian troupes which, beginning in the 1560s, constantly visited Paris, usually under royal patronage, and enjoyed invariable success. They occupy an important place in the history of the French theatre and, still more, in the development of French comedy.

During the next twelve years (1600–12) no company established any kind of permanency in Paris. Valleran was in financial difficulties by early 1600 and apparently left Paris that summer for a long tour of the provinces. He returned in 1606 and again in 1607, each time leasing the Hôtel for a few months. His most sustained efforts in the capital were made between 1609 and 1612, when he leased the Hôtel several times but always, it appears, unprofitably. In March 1612 his troupe broke up and he left Paris for good. The following year he was performing with a new company in the Netherlands and probably died a few years later.

Over the same period 1600–12 there are records of visits to Paris of one or two other short-lived French companies and of several Italian

---

present Moralities, *farces* and *soties* in satisfaction of the lowest tastes of the Parisian populace, which were theirs also. She also finds that, notwithstanding the interdiction of 1548, they sometimes performed Mysteries (*Le Vieux Testament* and two others in 1572).

troupes, but nothing else. The unavoidable conclusion is that, in what might have been a vital formative period in French serious drama, there was insufficient demand for this among the Parisian public. Valleran's repertory, mentioned in a document of 1598 and reaffirmed in 1611, consisted of 'tragedies, tragicomedies, and pastorals' which it is assumed were all or mainly composed by his *poète à gages*, Alexandre Hardy. They evidently went down well enough in the provincial towns, but were not appreciated in the capital. A further unfavourable factor was the grasping attitude of the Confrères who, not content with milking off all the profits of the Hôtel de Bourgogne, did their utmost to discourage performances elsewhere in Paris. When these did take place, it was in various buildings adapted temporarily, such as court-yards, *jeux de paume*, or on stages erected in the open, particularly at the fairs, while court performances were given in the Louvre. But until the early 1630s Paris had no second permanent theatre building to compete with the Hôtel.

It might therefore be argued that the obstructive tactics of the Confrères and their constant recourse to legal sanctions were a major obstacle to the development of the drama and should be added to the causes already mentioned. But had the demand been stronger it is inconceivable that their monopoly, or near-monopoly, would not have been broken earlier.

As it was, public taste seems if anything to have degenerated in the ten years following the final departure of Valleran le Conte. A new Italian troupe under Tristano Martinelli, known as Harlequin, played in Paris in 1613–14 and again in 1620–1. The only French company to lease the Hôtel de Bourgogne was that of the three *farceurs* Gros-Guillaume, Gaultier Garguille and Turlupin, who styled themselves the Comédiens du Roi (a title formerly used by Valleran) and drew large audiences to their very broad comedies for the best part of six years.

A change of direction became perceptible only in 1622. In that year two major companies arrived on the scene and laid the foundation of a great era of drama. The first styled themselves the Comédiens du Prince d'Orange, having performed at the Hague for Prince Maurice of Nassau. They were led by the actors Charles Le Noir and Montdory, who had once been members of Valleran's troupe in the provinces. The second company was led by Pierre Le Messier, known as Belle-rose, who was also a pupil of Valleran and was now considered as his successor. He had with him the same *poète à gages*, Alexandre Hardy. Soon after his arrival, Bellerose entered into association with the three *farceurs* mentioned above, who now, in addition to their comic stage names, assumed different stage names for their appearances in tragic parts.

The 1620s were a time of rapid expansion. Their theatrical history is characterized broadly by a steadily increasing rivalry between Bellerose and his associates, still styled the Comédiens du Roi, and the Comédiens du Prince d'Orange. These titles, assumed and retained for prestige reasons, did not imply continuous patronage and certainly no financial subsidy. They might be based on nothing more than a few command performances at court in the past, but they are convenient. The composition of the Comédiens du Prince d'Orange, in particular, changed several times and neither Le Noir nor Montdory was always among them. Nevertheless they preserved a certain identity. Their principal quarrel with the Comédiens du Roi was over the use of the Hôtel de Bourgogne which, as time went on, both wanted to lease at once. In 1625 and again in 1627, when the Prince of Orange's men had the theatre, Bellerose staged rival performances in the street outside and tried to prevent spectators from entering the building. He had come to look on it as his own theatre and he boldly pushed on with his claims in a successful legal action against the Confrères, which gave him the sole tenancy of the Hôtel on better terms than the landlords had exacted previously. He immediately took out a three-year lease on the theatre (1629).

The rival company, evidently accepting the situation, installed themselves in December 1629 in the first of several *jeux de paume*,[1] moving

---

[1] The *jeu de paume*, the ancestor of the modern court-tennis, reached the height of its popularity in the sixteenth century. The walled buildings in which it was played, also called *jeux de paume*, numbered, on the most conservative of the surviving estimates, 250 in the Paris of 1596. The game declined in the seventeenth century, leaving numerous buildings available for hire to actors. The average measurements of a *jeu de paume* were approximately 100 by 30 feet. It was usually roofed and a gallery for spectators ran along one or both of the longer sides and lent itself to conversion into *loges* for theatre audiences. The disposition of the *jeu de paume* – a narrow rectangle with the addition of a spacious stage at one end – was conserved when the Marais was rebuilt in 1644 after a fire. The Hôtel de Bourgogne, though originally built for theatrical performances and not adapted rom a *jeu de paume*, was of similar shape.

in 1634 to the Jeu de Paume du Marais. This became the capital's second permanent theatre, in its heyday outshining the Hôtel de Bourgogne.

These theatrical developments were paralleled by the appearance of talented dramatists. When Hardy returned from the provinces with Bellerose in 1622, he enjoyed considerable, if tardy, success. Twelve of his plays were performed at the Hôtel de Bourgogne between 1623 and 1626. He then broke with Bellerose, but performances of his plays probably continued for several years. Younger dramatists, such as Mairet and Du Ryer, began to make their mark. Rotrou, writing his first comedy, *L'Hypocondriaque*, probably in 1628, became Bellerose's *poète à gages* in succession to Hardy. Most important perhaps of all, Pierre Corneille gave his first play, *Mélite*, to Montdory, who performed it soon after his arrival in Paris in 1629 and went on to make of his association with Corneille one of the main factors in the success of the Théâtre du Marais.

Thus in the 1620s, though not before, the foundations of a flourishing drama were firmly laid in the French capital. There were the theatres, in existence or in active preparation, there were the competent professional actors, the authors to write for them and, evidently, a new public capable of appreciating and supporting entertainment above the level of the old knockabout farce. The plays produced by the authors mentioned above were for the most part pastorals, tragicomedies and relatively sophisticated comedies, such as those by Rotrou and Corneille. The cultural level of the theatre was rising and its social level was soon to be confirmed by the direct patronage, for better or worse, of Louis XIII, Richelieu and other influential figures.

V

It will be convenient here to anticipate the two following decades and continue the history of the Paris theatre in order to avoid the necessity of returning to it later.

In the 1630s and 1640s the rivalry between the Hôtel de Bourgogne and the Marais continued. The former was still directed by Bellerose, the second by Montdory until he was incapacitated by a stroke in 1637, and soon afterwards by Floridor, another great actor-manager. Although the company of the Hôtel, as the *troupe royale*, now enjoyed the concrete advantages of royal patronage and subsidies, it had difficulty in competing successfully with the Marais. The balance was only redressed by the forcible transfer of actors from one to the other on Louis XIII's command. On the last occasion when this seems to have occurred, Floridor himself was removed from the Marais to take over the management of the Hôtel de Bourgogne (1647). Corneille went with him. The supremacy of the Marais as a home of tragicomedy, tragedy and comedy was at an end, and the disorientated company only saved themselves by turning to the *pièce à machines*, a type of play with spectacular scenic effects comparable to those of the Mysteries, but now inspired by the contemporary Italian theatre.

These two companies sufficed for the theatregoing public. The failure of one or two other companies to establish themselves in the capital appears to prove it. The most notable venture was that of the Illustre Théâtre, constituted by the Béjart family and the young Molière, which managed to maintain itself for eighteen months in two different *jeux de paume* (1644–5) and then, deeply in debt, left for the provinces, not to return until thirteen years later (October 1658).

The existing theatre buildings may also be said to have sufficed without fundamental change. The Marais was burnt down in 1644 and quickly rebuilt on a slightly larger scale. This allowed for better seating for some of the spectators, dressing-rooms for the actors and probably an improved disposition of the acting-space, but the rectangular plan of the old *jeu de paume* was not altered. Three years later the interior of the Hôtel de Bourgogne, which was somewhat larger, underwent a long overdue reconstruction on similar lines to the rebuilt Marais. Estimates of the number of spectators these theatres could hold have varied enormously, but the most reasonable figure is about 1,500 for each. Since for much of the period under review they opened on alternate days, this would give an audience capacity for the two playhouses together of about 10,000 persons weekly, though the average would certainly be lower, since they would hardly be full for every performance.

There were no other permanent public theatres. As in the case of the Illustre Théâtre, and indeed of the original Marais, a *jeu de paume* could be adapted temporarily with the help of carpenters. There were large halls in the Louvre and in the palace of the Petit Bourbon near to it which were used for court entertainments, particularly ballet, and occasional command performances. Richelieu ordered the building of a theatre in his private palace which incorporated certain new features. He died a year after its inauguration in 1641 and it was used only rarely for court spectacles until, in the 1660s, it was occupied by Molière's company. As the Palais-Royal, it then became the third Parisian public theatre.

In the 1630s successful actors began to enjoy increased wealth and standing. Some became considerable property-owners. Their stage costumes, which they owned, were magnificent and costly. When Montdory was stricken with paralysis, Richelieu gave him a pension of 2,000 livres, which was increased considerably by gifts from other benefactors. The professional stage had attractions even for 'respectable' families. Montdory's successor Floridor was the son of a Protestant pastor who later turned Catholic. He himself entered the army, was a member of the Royal Bodyguard, and held the rank of ensign before embarking on his brilliant stage career. Though this was an outstanding example, it was not isolated. The image of the raggle-taggle players of the vagabond companies no longer fits such actors, though there were always obscure troupes in the provinces to which it could be applied.

The rewards of the Paris stage extended, though as always less lavishly, to the authors. There were better prospects of windfalls in the shape of gifts or other favours from influential patrons. There was also an improvement in the direct payments for plays, and successful dramatists were able to drive harder bargains. While Hardy in the 1620s is thought to have received 100 livres for each play, there are indications that in 1637 his successor Rotrou was able to obtain 600 livres a play from the Hôtel de Bourgogne. The circumstances here may have been a little exceptional, but there is no doubt that the theatre was now able to offer sufficient fame and money to attract talented writers. The outstanding success was Pierre Corneille, but it would be misleading to suggest that he stood alone in this first brilliant period of French drama.

Meanwhile, we must return to the earlier years of the century, when both theatre and drama occupied a less secure position.

4

ALEXANDRE HARDY

The problem of dating Hardy's plays – Hardy and Valleran le Conte – his split with Bellerose and his waning reputation – conclusion on probable dating – *Théagène et Cariclée*, a serial – classification of remaining plays – the *poèmes dramatiques* – pastoral in the French theatre and Hardy's pastorals – his tragedies and tragicomedies – groupings of these plays – structural peculiarities and superficial psychology – Hardy's style and language – his legacy to Corneille's generation – character-types and themes – love in Hardy – summaries of Hardy's plays

If any author could fill the gap in the development of French drama referred to in the last chapter, it could only be Alexandre Hardy. He was a writer of Spanish fecundity, throwing off plays at high speed for the entertainment of predominantly popular audiences. He had some learning, but not too much of it. His verse was often vigorous, if unpolished, his language sometimes comic or colloquial. He ignored the unities, his plays contained brutal incidents which violated the kind of proprieties observed by the academic dramatists, he worked professionally with a company of actors and at one time was probably an actor himself.

But if one bases high expectations on these qualities one is likely to be disappointed. Hardy was neither a skilful enough dramatist nor a great enough poet to equal even his good second-rank contemporaries in England and Spain. He fills uncomfortably the role one would so readily assign to him. Yet, with all his weaknesses, he is full of interest, both inherently as an idiosyncratic writer and as a representative of the kinds of drama then being produced in France. His influence, moreover, was certainly more persistent than is usually suspected. While he can hardly be claimed as an unrecognized genius, his work has suffered far more neglect than it deserves, largely owing to the absence of critical, or even readable, texts.[1]

[1] See below pp. 72–3.

It is first necessary to decide when his plays were written and performed, a question to which there is no one simple answer. One begins from the certainty that between 1623 and 1628 he published six volumes of plays which contain the whole of his surviving dramatic work – thirty-four plays in all. In addition, the titles of ten lost plays by Hardy, with notes or drawings for their representation on the stage, are given in the *Mémoire* of Mahelot, who was scene-designer at the Hôtel de Bourgogne probably from 1622 to 1635. All that Mahelot's *Mémoire* indicates, however, is that the lost plays, with three others which have been preserved and published, were in the repertory of that theatre in 1622 or later. A terminal date for their composition is 1632, when Hardy died, though in fact it is virtually certain that he ceased to be performed somewhat earlier. Mme Deierkauf-Holsboer's conclusion, based on solid though not incontrovertible reasoning, is that the Hardy plays listed by Mahelot were all performed for the first time between October 1622 and January 1627.[1]

These are fairly late dates, which cannot apply to all the plays surviving in print. In the Dedication of Volume II of his *Théâtre* (1625), Hardy describes the six plays it contains as 'un bouquet de six fleurs vieillies depuis le temps d'une jeunesse qui me les a produites: desquelles toutefois l'injure des ans n'a pu totalement effacer le teint et l'odeur'. That particular volume may have been made up of older plays than the rest, though on the other hand it was not unknown for authors of that period to plead youthful inexperience to appease their critics, and to exaggerate in that respect: still, it seems hardly possible in the context to date the six plays in the volume (*La Mort d'Achille, Coriolan, Cornélie, Arsacome, Marianne, Alcée*) much later than 1610–15, and for some of them one should perhaps go back to before that.[2] Further evidence of a more general kind is Hardy's statement in his foreword to *Théagène et Cariclée* (1623) that he had written the huge number of 500 plays, a claim which was increased in 1628 (*Théâtre*, Vol. V) to 'six hundred and more'. Even an author who could hack out

---

[1] D.-Holsboer, *Le Théâtre de l'Hôtel de Bourgogne*, I, pp. 155–67.

[2] One at least, however, *Cornélie*, based on the *Novelas ejemplares* of Cervantes, must have been written after 1613, the date of the Spanish original. Since it is also one of the plays in Mahelot's *Mémoire*, the earliest date of production would have been 1622, if one accepts Mme Deierkauf-Holsboer's arguments. In that case it is difficult to see why Hardy described it in 1625 as a *fleur vieillie*. See also p. 77, note 1.

a five-act verse-play in a few days would have required a considerable number of years before he could amass such a total. This leads to the question of how long Hardy had been writing and of when the *jeunesse* which he invoked should be dated.

It is supposed that he began to write for the stage towards 1595, an approximate date based again on his own statement in the foreword to *Théagène et Cariclée* that he had been doing so for thirty years, a figure which he repeats unchanged five years later in his foreword of 1628. On this and some other rather inconclusive evidence, he has been assigned the conjectural birth date of 1575, with the assumption that his dramatic career began when he was about twenty. It is further assumed, with every appearance of probability, that he became the *poète à gages* of Valleran le Conte during the latter's first recorded visit to Paris in 1598, and that he remained a member of Valleran's company from then on. He would thus have been the author, or prospective author, of some or all of the 'comédies, tragi-comédies, pastorales et autres passages' mentioned in the act of association of 16 March 1598 between Valleran and Talmy, and he would have continued to supply Valleran with the plays described in similar terms in later documents. In this way (and how else?) he would steadily have built up the formidable total of plays referred to in his published works.

All this is overwhelmingly probable, but his actual name does not appear on a document until 1611, when he puts his signature to a lease on the Hôtel de Bourgogne together with other members of Valleran's company. The fact that he does so, styling himself *comédien du roi*, is taken to signify that he was then working as an actor, in addition to his duties as 'paid poet' – for in the latter capacity his name was not required in legal contracts engaging the company's collective responsibility. In drawing this almost necessary conclusion, his biographer, Mme Deierkauf-Holsboer, supposes that he was resuming a profession which he had already exercised in the past, which is also highly probable, if not proved. She concludes further that his reason for returning to acting at this time was to help out his old friend and manager Valleran le Conte in one of his recurrent financial crises. If this was so, his effort was a gallant failure, since in March 1612, as has been seen in the previous chapter, Valleran abandoned Paris for good, presumably taking Hardy with him.

For the next ten years there is no trace of Hardy, but by 1622 he was apparently back in the capital writing plays for Bellerose, Valleran's successor at the Hôtel de Bourgogne, and enjoying enough success for his plays to be thought worth publishing. This and the fact that he was now attached to Bellerose as his *poète à gages* led in the autumn of 1626 to a split between them. Bellerose refused to release for publication more than a small proportion of the many Hardy plays which he had in his repertory. Owing to the nature of their contract these were indeed the property of the company, not of the author, and publication would make them available to other companies. Presumably they were to be numbered in hundreds, though it is impossible to say categorically that they included the plays written earlier for Valleran, the rights in which may or may not have been taken over by Bellerose on becoming, as is thought, his direct successor.

Exasperated by Bellerose's intransigence, Hardy left him and signed a contract with a newly formed company who styled themselves provocatively Les *Vrais* Comédiens du Roi. His plays, old or new, continued in demand for a short time, though by 1628 he was being overtaken by a younger generation of playwrights. His period of great popularity with Parisian audiences appears, then, to have been between 1622 and 1626, with a rapid fading-out subsequently. His position in the middle 1620s, to judge by the forewords of his published plays and the panegyrics printed with them, was that of France's leading dramatist. This position, however, was already subjected to attacks, against which he defended himself with vigorous invective, bluntly hammering both critics and the young upstarts who presumed to challenge him on the stage.

Of the thirty-four plays on which he must be judged, eight have been shown to have been new in 1626 or later, three were not earlier than 1620, and it is unlikely that any of the rest go back to much before 1610. In general terms, what survives may be said to be representative of Parisian drama through most of the 1620s, with an indefinite number of earlier plays included either to make up the volumes or on the fortuitous grounds that the author possessed copies of them. No sustained attempt has so far been made to establish a dating on the internal evidence of language or dramatic technique.

II

The first published, *Théagène et Cariclée*, appeared separately in 1623 with, it seems, a second edition dated 1628.[1] It has not been republished since and modern readers may have difficulty in finding it. It is a dramatization of the long Greek romance by Heliodorus and consists of eight *journées* each divided into five acts. Each *journée* is a separate play which, however, leaves the story incomplete, and is obviously designed as one of the instalments of a serial. The title-page runs in part: 'Les chastes et Loyales Amours de Théagène et Cariclée, Réduites du Grec de l'Histoire d'Héliodore en Huit Poëmes Dramatiques, ou Théâtres Consécutifs'. The work as a whole is usually classed as a *poème dramatique*, though the only original use of that term is in the title just quoted. Alternatively, its eight parts are 'tragicomedies'. The title of the first part is 'Cariclée, tragicomédie', and the running heads of each part are 'Tragicomédie I, II', etc.

Whatever the classification of this somewhat dreary work, its performance no doubt continued over a number of days, whether consecutive or not, and for that reason one would incline to assign an early date to it. The method of acting a long play in several parts over a period of time was that practised in presenting the old Mysteries. There are two other examples of its application to secular plays, both belonging to the turn of the sixteenth century.[2] The only indications that *Théagène et Cariclée* might be a later work are (1) its date of publication (1623), which would seem curious – though not unique – if it came long after the dramatic performances had been forgotten, and (2) the fact that two of the lost Hardy plays in the Mahelot *Mémoire* (*Pandoste* and *Parténie*) were in two *journées*. Inclusion in the *Mémoire*,

[1] I have not seen this edition. Rigal (*Alexandre Hardy*, p. 71) describes it as very rare and much more correct than the edition of 1623. Same publisher: Jacques Quesnel, Paris.

[2] In 1599 Valleran le Conte, on his second visit to Paris, agreed to share the Hôtel de Bourgogne with a company led by Benoist Petit. Their first production was to be a *roman*, of unknown title, of which each company was to present parts, performing in alternate weeks. The agreement broke down because of Benoist Petit's refusal to pass on the scripts to Valleran's actors. In the following year Robert Guérin contracted with the Confrères de la Passion to act various plays on their behalf, beginning with 'la continuation de tous et chacuns les jeux qui resteront à jouer de *Valentin et Ourson*'. (D.-Holsboer, *Le Théâtre de l'Hotel de Bourgogne*, I, pp. 47 and 54.)

it will be recalled, gives those plays a probable dating in the 1620s. Scherer notes four other plays in two *journées* whose dates range from 1618 to 1630–1.[1] All these, however, contained only two *journées*, and nothing approaching the eight *journées* of *Théagène* has been recorded for that period. On balance it seems that the most reasonable conjecture is to assign that work to the first decade of the century.

III

The five volumes of Hardy's *Théâtre* which followed *Théagène et Cariclée* contain two further works classed as *poèmes dramatiques*, five *pastorales*, so distributed that there is one in each volume, twelve *tragédies* and fourteen *tragicomédies*.

Each of these four categories merits consideration, both because of its significance in a formative stage of French drama and for its future potentialities. The only important absentee is the *comédie*, of which there is no example among Hardy's extant plays.[2] This was natural at a date when comedy was not a flourishing genre and the short *farce* satisfied the popular demand for broad humour. Comic elements and themes were frequent in the pastoral and the tragicomedy, but it was not until around 1630, with the early work of Rotrou and Corneille, that the full-length comedy began to come into general favour.

Poème dramatique was something of a blanket term, used, as has been said, to describe *Théagène et Cariclée*, but also applied to two other plays by Hardy of a different sort. These are *Le Ravissement de Proserpine par Pluton* and *La Gigantomachie*, both published in Volume III of the *Théâtre*. They are mythological plays in five acts, with gods and goddesses as characters, and have scenes set in such places as Olympus, Hades and Vulcan's forge on Etna, which easily lend themselves to spectacular stage effects. These are in fact necessitated by the subjects as Hardy treated them. Thus *La Gigantomachie* presents an assault by the Giants, sons of Earth, on Jupiter's citadel, which seems to be conducted with scaling-ladders and is repelled with the help of thunderbolts. The play ends with a banquet of the victorious gods at which Hercules is married to Hebe. These two *poèmes dramatiques* have an obvious kinship with the *pièces à machines* of a later period.

---

[1] See *Dramaturgie classique*, p. 111.
[2] Though he wrote at least one, *Le Jaloux*, which he sold to Bellerose in September 1625. See D.-Holsboer, *La Vie d'Alexandre Hardy*.

Though attached by Lancaster to the tragicomedies,[1] they are if anything rather closer to the pastorals.

The vogue of pastoral in France had been inspired by sixteenth-century Italian models (Tasso, Guarini, Groto and others) and by the *Diana* of the Spaniard Montemayor. The typical characters were idealized shepherds and shepherdesses engaged in the pursuit of virtuous love in Arcadian surroundings – often in Arcadia itself, which allowed for a Greek-derived mythology involving nymphs, dryads, satyrs and the more appropriate gods, such as Venus, Cupid and Diana. There was endless leisure. Nature smiled but also contained rocks from which despairing lovers could hurl themselves or threaten to do so. Frustration in love from various causes was the dominant theme and the hope of its removal maintained the interest in these lengthy works. In the end a patient wooing was rewarded, or there was a rearrangement of partners which proved equally satisfactory. Pastoral in general was a courtly mode of literature, lending itself to some analysis of erotic emotion but, more characteristically, to the respectful adoration of flawless Woman:

> Who is Silvia? What is she,
> That all our swains commend her?
> Holy, fair and wise is she;
> The heaven such grace did lend her
> That she might admirèd be.[2]

Its emergence in France at the turn of the sixteenth century may well presuppose a new and more civilized conception of sexual relationships, though the social reality of this traditional interpretation is not above question. At least it encouraged a new literary idiom, fostering polished and melodious poetry when written in verse and the growth of *préciosité* in various verbal forms. In prose, the most influential example was Honoré d'Urfé's novel, *L'Astrée* (1607–27). Though freely drawn on by other dramatists, d'Urfé's work was not, however, utilized by Hardy.

[1] Lancaster, *History*, I, p. 53.

La Gigantomachie is described as a 'poeme dramatic' [*sic*] on the title-page. I can find no such original description for *Proserpine*, but it is an entertainment of the same type.

[2] Shakespeare, *The Two Gentlemen of Verona*, IV.ii. Written *c*. 1594.

It would be a theoretical exercise to attempt to draw a precise boundary between pastoral and chivalrous romance, which often merged into each other. Broadly, pastoral embodied the ethic of the courtier, romance the ethic of the knight, but at this date at least the two were very likely to be the same person, bound by a single code of behaviour. If one accepts romance as the main basis of tragicomedy, as it was in Garnier's *Bradamante*,[1] there is thus a good underlying reason for the close relationship between tragicomedy and pastoral, since both incorporated similar attitudes and tended to express them in similar language. On a more superficial level, the introduction of chivalry into pure pastoral provided the characters with a wider field of action and allowed the story to include the kind of 'adventures' appropriate to the knight of fiction but impossible for the shepherd.

French dramatic pastoral had appeared in the 1590s with such works as the *Diane* and *Arimène* of Montreux. About twenty *pastorales* were published in the reign of Henri IV (1589–1610); from the period 1611–20 ten are extant; from 1621–30, twenty-six, including Hardy's five and Racan's notable *Bergeries*; for 1631–4 there were twenty-five; after this there was a fall-off so rapid that during 1635–9 only six are recorded and after 1640 almost none. These figures include sixteen plays described as *tragicomédies pastorales*, four *comédies pastorales* and even two *tragédies pastorales*.[2]

In the 1650s and 1660s there was a minor revival of the genre to which Tristan L'Hermite and Quinault contributed and, in time, Molière. The latter's unfinished *Mélicerte*, a *comédie pastorale héroïque*, and his short *Pastorale comique*, were both written hurriedly as parts of Benserade's *Ballet des muses* for the entertainment of the court (1666–7). The *Pastorale comique*, consisting entirely of singing and ballet, points to the ultimate destination of dramatic pastoral, which became opera. Already in 1659 an early opera was produced by Perrin and Cambert with the title of *La Pastorale d'Issy*. The main success of the same librettist and composer, *Pomone* (1671), was called a *pastorale*. In the following year the same description was given to the *Fêtes de l'Amour et de Bacchus* of Lully, who was then rising to supremacy in the operatic field. After this, however, there was a change; the term *tragédie lyrique* was applied to nearly all Lully's later operas, with some rare exceptions of minor importance.

While pastoral, whether spoken or sung, seems scarcely to belong to the history of tragedy, it cannot be left entirely aside. There is its relationship with tragicomedy. There is also the fact that the amorous situations and the melodious type of verse practised by writers of pastoral from the Racan of the *Bergeries* to Quinault, who became Lully's librettist, were not without influence on the tragic genre itself.

Hardy's pastorals lack the sophistication (beneath an appearance of simplicity) which the genre was to develop. Their verse also lacks musical qualities, although, since they are all written in decasyllables (whereas the rest of Hardy's plays are in alexandrines), it seems possible that a special diction was expected of the actors.[1] All have five acts, no regular choruses, a rustic scene and rustic characters, and stage effects requiring at least some machinery. The plots turn entirely on love, whose course is generally ruled by the conventions of comedy.

Alphée, described in the edition of 1626 as a 'pastorale nouvelle', exemplifies all these features. It contains a chain of lovers, headed by the chaste and beautiful Alphée, whose father, Isandre, keeps her secluded, having been warned by an oracle that her marriage will bring trouble to the house. She is, however, courted by the shepherd Daphnis. Daphnis is pursued by the middle-aged sorceress Corine, Corine by a satyr, the satyr by a dryad, the dryad by the shepherd Euriale, and Euriale by the shepherdess Mélanie. Alphée and Daphnis are betrayed by Corine, who tells Alphée's father that they are engaged in a culpable love affair. Daphnis threatens Corine with violence if she fails to withdraw the accusation, whereupon the sorceress changes him into a rock. After more angry words have been exchanged, she goes on to transform Alphée into a spring and Isandre into a tree. The shepherds of Arcady, led by Euriale, come together to compel Corine to undo the spell, whereupon she summons the satyrs to her help and conjures up a storm with thunder and lightning. At this point Cupid

---

[1] Hardy himself merely says that he is following the example of the great Italians, 'Tasse, Guarini et autres sublimes esprits, qui ont choisi les vers de dix à onze . . . pour mieux exprimer telles innocentes amours, et accommoder le langage à la chose.' (Preface to *Théâtre*, Vol. 3, 1626.)

appears as the *deus ex machina*, changes the metamorphosed characters back into their human shapes, and decrees three marriages: that of Alphée to Daphnis, of Mélanie to Euriale and of Corine to the grey-haired but 'encore vigoureux' Isandre. The principal satyr, a gross and comic creature, is ordered back into the woods to seek some suitable mistress there. In addition to the transformations, the storm and the appearance of Cupid, the stage effects include the voice of Echo, a usual feature of pastoral.

IV

Between Hardy's twelve printed tragedies and the fourteen tragicomedies it is not possible to draw a consistently clear dividing-line, since, whatever criteria are adopted, there are nearly always exceptions. What distinctions there are must be taken as general rather than absolute.

The clearest distinction is in the principle of the unhappy ending, which applies to all the tragedies except one (*Timoclée*) and to none of the tragicomedies except two, *Procris* and *Aristoclée*; these, however, are among the four plays alternatively described as tragedies in the *Argument* or the heading.

Another apparent distinction rests on the source. All the tragedies except one (*Lucrèce*) derive ultimately from Greek and Latin authors, and so also do the four tragicomedies alternatively titled tragedies (*Procris, Alceste, Ariadne, Aristoclée*). Only one other tragicomedy (*Arsacome*) is based on an ancient author; all the rest derive from modern works, predominantly Spanish. It is also significant that five, and perhaps six, of the tragedies have subjects previously treated by French dramatists,[1] whereas none of the tragicomedies, so far as is known, possessed predecessors on the French stage. While it would be rash to claim any exact insight into the workings of Hardy's mind, it seems possible that he regarded the ancient writers, even when they were in effect romancers, as in some way more classical, and so nearer to the tragic, than the moderns. It is also probable that he discovered his modern sources at a later date than his ancient ones, as part of a general trend away from

---

[1] These were *Didon* (Jodelle and others), *Mort de Daire* and *Mort d'Alexandre* (Jacques de La Taille), *Mort d'Achille* (Filleul), *Coriolan* (Thierry). There had been two plays entitled *Panthée* (G. Daronnière, 1608, and Billard, 1610) though it cannot be stated with certainty that they were earlier than Hardy's tragedy.

tragedy which began in the 1620s and which may have led him both to entitle his newer plays tragicomedies and to look for material appropriate to his conception of this genre.

The unities are royally disregarded in both categories. Hardy's plays were obviously written for a multiple décor, which in any case rules out the unity of place in its strict classical sense.[1] The unity of time is ignored as much in the tragedies as in the tragicomedies. Although it is possible to calculate that the action of one or two of the former could have been completed within twenty-four hours, it is clear that this would be accidental and that Hardy was never attempting to conform to any theory of dramatic time. Violent action on stage is equally common in both types. There are fights, murders, abductions, a double rape on stage (according to the dialogue),[2] while the most potentially spectacular scene – a battle and the firing of a city – occurs in a tragedy, *Timoclée*. The existing texts carry very few stage directions and it is clear that a good deal was left to the discretion and resources of those responsible for the production. Much of the physical action, however, was basic and must have been shown in some visible form.

One cannot base any generic distinction on the characterization. Royal and noble characters are more frequent in the tragedies because of the source-stories from which these were drawn, but they are also found in several tragicomedies. Commoners have important parts in the tragedies. Nurses and messengers appear in both kinds of play, while ghosts, dreams and forebodings are ubiquitous. Only the chorus might seem to represent an element peculiar to one genre and it is true that it appears in several tragedies but in only one tragicomedy, *Aristoclée*, an alternatively titled tragedy. But, as Lancaster has already pointed out, no definite conclusions can be drawn from the absence or otherwise of a chorus. Choruses may have figured in early performances of some plays which were not retained in the published texts. Hardy remarks, in the *Au lecteur* of his *Théâtre*, Vol. I, that 'les Chœurs y sont omis, comme superflus à la représentation, et de trop de fatigue à refondre'. The remark is evidently intended to apply to all the plays in that volume after *Didon*,[3] though even then Hardy is not

---

[1] See below pp. 122–3 for an account of the stage-setting in this period.
[2] *Scédase*, ll. 763–820.
[3] Three tragedies, three tragicomedies alternatively called tragedies, and one pastoral.

entirely consistent. The chief significance of this particular statement is that in 1624 choruses were not required in the performance of a play, but it throws no light on earlier practice or distinction of genres.

It seems, therefore, not unreasonable to consider all Hardy's tragedies and tragicomedies as a single body of tragic drama, without insisting on distinguishing features of which Hardy himself appears to have been uncertain. Within this body of plays as a whole, however, there are distinctions, of emphasis and treatment rather than of kind, which make it possible to outline certain broad groupings.

In the antique group may be placed *Didon*, *La Mort de Daire*, *La Mort d'Alexandre*, *La Mort d'Achille*, *Coriolan* and perhaps *Panthée*. All these, as has been seen, had certain or probable precedents in French tragedy. In the first four Hardy remains nearest to sixteenth-century learned tragedy, and one would be inclined to give them an early date for that reason. Two are opened by a ghost predicting woe. All four present in reasonably pure form the downfall of a great personage, accompanied by lamentations. The same might be said of *Coriolan*, but with a great deal more struggle and uncertainty before the hero finally meets his doom. None, indeed, is as short of movement and dramatic suspense as the typically 'regular' academic tragedy. The difference is perceptible if one compares Hardy's *Didon* with Jodelle's, in spite of the fact that the latter may well have provided Hardy with his general model. All these plays possess a well-developed 'political' interest, centred on the destiny of states or of great personages in their capacity as rulers or military leaders.[1] In several the love interest is absent or quite subsidiary.

To this group might also be attached *Timoclée*, partly because of its source (Plutarch) and because it has Alexander as its hero. But the play lacks unity and turns to spectacle and melodrama in the second half, with the exciting climax in which Timoclée lures her ravisher down a well (a similar stage property figures in *Scédase*) and strikes or prods him from above until he drowns in it. The only connecting theme in this tragedy is 'the generosity of Alexander', who finally pardons Timoclée and, from a classical point of view, it just bears definition in those terms. From a different and certainly more relevant angle, it is the stage representation of the fall of a city, preceded by the councils

[1] This is least conspicuous in *Panthée*. In *Didon* 'love' and 'politics' are in perfect balance. It is simultaneously the drama of Dido–Aeneas and Carthage–Rome.

and deliberations which led to the attack on it, and followed by the acts of brutality performed by the conquerors. If it were possible to establish on good grounds the order of composition of Hardy's plays, one might find that it was transitional between his approximation to regular learned tragedy and his more popular vein.

Meanwhile, there is a small group of mythological plays, broadly linked by the intervention or appearance of gods and goddesses and some open recourse to the supernatural. These are *Méléagre*, *Procris*, *Alceste* and *Ariadne ravie*. The importance of the supernatural varies. The goddess Aurora in *Procris* (a childish play as Hardy wrote it) might be just any free-sleeping female character. For dramatic purposes, the god Bacchus in *Ariadne* could as easily be a human prince, though his entry as a god provides scope for a spectacular stage effect. However, the supernatural occurs in none other of the tragedies and tragicomedies, with the exception of the quite minor episode of the spell and the enchantress in *Dorise*, where it is psychologically unnecessary.

Two tragedies stand a little apart from the others, though a view of them is inevitably coloured by later and better-known plays which derive from them. *Panthée*, if not attached to the antique group ('the generosity of Cyrus'), is the story of a noble and beautiful woman surrounded by other noble characters, with one partial exception, who nevertheless brings disaster through no intentional fault of her own. *Mariamne* embodies the story of a noble and beautiful woman surrounded by villainous characters who succeed in working her downfall. This play, presumably an early one, is opened by a ghost and ends with the lamentations of a repentant Herod. The main source is Josephus, whose *Antiquités judaïques* was first translated into French in 1578. No French dramatization of the story earlier than Hardy's is known. *Mariamne* is Hardy's only surviving play on a Jewish theme. He ignores biblical and Christian subjects. Equally he avoids Roman history, with the single exception of *Coriolan*.

All the remaining plays – three tragedies and eleven tragicomedies – are concerned unreservedly with private relationships: love, lust, friendship, jealousy, revenge – with no intrusion of a 'political' motif. It is true that kingdoms are at stake in *Arsacome* and *Phraate*, but that theme is entirely subsidiary to the love interest in both plays. The majority of the plays in this group are based on Renaissance story-writers (three are from Cervantes, one goes back to the ever popular

Decameron), who gave Hardy his potentially most interesting material. But he cannot be said to have made the best of it, dramatically or psychologically. Structurally, his plays are often chaotic. One can only explain this by postulating a salaried playwright who every now and then found a promising story or was handed one and given a few days in which to turn it into a full-length play ready for rehearsal. The necessary speed was attained by using a mechanical technique of verse-writing (though Hardy's verse has interesting features of its own and is not all mechanical, as will be seen later) and by following the story-line of the original with considerable docility, since there was no time to recast it. This usually resulted in badly proportioned plays, in which some acts were relatively empty, while others were incredibly con-gested.[1]

Psychologically, Hardy is somewhat disappointing. In several of his stories there are opportunities for black dramas of distorted passions which would be apparent not only to a modern, but to a Jacobean mind. Gésippe in the play of that name is so attached to his friend Tite that he not only gives him his bride but practically pushes him into her bed. The Count of Gleichen in *Elmire* takes a second wife without relinquishing the first and invites the two women to share him impartially in their 'nocturnes combats'. The empress's daughter in

---

[1] e.g. *Phraate*, Act IV: Philippe de Macédoine, having defeated his enemy Cotys of Thrace in the entr'acte, is joined in Scene i by his son Phraate who has escaped from Thrace after his affair with Philagnie, the daughter of Cotys. After a sketchy debate on clemency, Phraate is persuaded by his father to take over command of the Macedonian army. In Thrace, Philagnie discovers that she is pregnant and writes a letter to be sent to Phraate. The messenger is captured and brought to the defeated Cotys, who is conferring with his counsellors. Warned, Philagnie takes to flight to escape her father's wrath. The messenger also escapes and reaches Phraate with the news of what has happened. Philagnie, now on the point of giving birth, comes to a peasant's hut and persuades its owner to shelter her. The act ends.

There are other examples of acts overcrowded with incident and covering long stretches of time. In *La Force du sang*, Act III, Scene i, Léocadie begins to feel labour pains. Scene ii evidently takes place several years later, and leads to the accident in Scene iv in which Léocadie's seven-year-old son is knocked over in the street. The intermediate Scene iii shows Léocadie's ravisher, away in Italy, begin-ning to repent of his misdeed. If, however, these compressed acts were compre-hensible to popular audiences following the incidents of the play with excitement, it becomes pedantic and irrelevant to speak of faults in construction.

Félismène falls passionately in love with a girl disguised as a page. But Hardy accepts these situations at their face value, reproducing the external facts of his sources without change, inquiry or analysis. Over a whole potential field of darkly motivated jealousy, vengeance, lust and murder, he passes innocently, subscribing whenever possible, and sometimes incongruously, to the conventional doctrine of courtly or virtuous love, when a moment's reflection would have suggested to a more sophisticated writer that the sort of passion he was dealing with was neither. In this respect he was a simple dramatist writing for simple audiences. While writing plays intended to be tragic he used the ethical conventions of comedy. In several of his *Arguments* he speaks of the 'richness' of his subject. He merely means that it is rich in incident.

The bare summaries of Hardy's plays often suggest a more interesting work than the play turns out to be. The story, which is generally that of the original source, is the best part of it. For Hardy to have added or subtracted nothing in an adaptation for the stage would be impossible, but what he has added is less often an enrichment than a curiosity. For this, he certainly repays study. And first, on the grounds of his style and language.

V

It must first be repeated that Hardy's reputation has suffered unduly for lack of a modern critical edition, and indeed of any modern editions at all, with one honourable exception. Since the first publication of his plays in the 1620s, they have been republished only once, by the German editor Stengel in the nineteenth century. This edition is itself fairly rare today, but without it few would be able to read Hardy at all and to Stengel must go most of the credit for keeping his work alive. However, his critical apparatus is limited to some short lists of variants and corrections at the beginning of his Volume I, whereas Hardy stands at least as badly in need of detailed textual criticism as the other dramatists of his time. The available text must often be corrupt; in many places it seems incorrect or barely comprehensible. Part of the blame for this must rest with the printers, of whom Hardy himself complained.[1] Some, no doubt, remains with the author, but before characterizing him as 'turgid' it is well to take such factors as capricious

[1] In the *Au lecteur* of Vols I and IV.

punctuation into account. Hardy's plays are far from negligible, even considered as literature. On historical grounds (linguistic, prosodic, the technical development of drama) they are full of interest. It is extraordinary that so little has been done to present them in a more accessible form.

In the quotations that follow the spelling has been modernized and the punctuation sometimes altered. Various other minor corrections, not claimed as definitive, have been made where they seemed necessary.

An obvious feature of Hardy's plays and a powerful reason for their neglect as the more polished drama of the seventeenth century developed was the archaism of the language and the verse technique. The vocabulary contains words which had become discarded or obsolete by the 1620s: *los, soulas, couardie, géniteur, absconsé, cuider, oncques, cetui-ci* and others. The phrasing, imagery and versification had also become old-fashioned since the advent of Malherbe, whom Hardy mentions with some respect while saying that his precepts are not applicable to dramatic poetry. He invokes instead 'le grand Ronsard',[1] and elsewhere maintains that 'le style du bon Sénèque suivi de Garnier' is the right one for dramatic poetry.[2] His language and prosody were therefore already, or were fast becoming, out of date. Although in process of time the importance of this would become less apparent, the modern reader may also be disconcerted if he attempts to read Hardy without some knowledge of sixteenth-century French. The fact that he is transitional, or perhaps merely provincial, tells against him.

A second feature is his frequent use of the classical allusion, which too often becomes a cliché. His characters do not speak of dying, but say:

> Je tombe au gouffre Achérontide
>
> (*Méléagre*, 1006)

or:

> Crois que Cloton bientôt abrégera ma trame.
>
> (*Force du sang*, 1230)

While one may accept such language in Jodelle and Garnier, in whose work it has rather more life and is better sustained, it becomes

---

[1] See *Théâtre*, Vol. 3, the Dedication and the *Au lecteur*.
[2] In his pamphlet *La Berne de deux rimeurs de l'Hôtel de Bourgogne* (1628).

both tedious and incongruous in Hardy, many of whose situations are conceived and presented realistically, with considerable realism in the language. At the dénouement of *Cornélie*, based on the story by Cervantes, Hardy has to supply a speech for Lorenzo Bentivoglio in praise of the noble Duke of Ferrara, since Cervantes did not do so, but merely wrote: 'He staggered on his feet and cast himself at those of the Duke.' He does it in these terms:

> O prince de vertus divines ennobli,
> Onc un acte si beau ne coule dans l'oubli.
> Tant que Phoebus luira, compasseur des années,
> Que les cieux tourneront aux cadences données,
> Que Thétis en son sein nourrira ses poissons,
> Que l'alme Cérès produira nos moissons,
> Toujours ton los, célèbre en la troupe mortelle,
> Remplira l'univers . . .   (*Cornélie*, 1479 ff.)

In the original there is nothing like this, which belongs to a different order of literature.

Hyperbolic rhetoric, not necessarily based on the classical allusion, is often accompanied by a descent into utilitarianism:

> O Monarque des Cieux, architecte du monde,
> Comme ta providence occultement profonde
> Sait aux tiens le bonheur à temps restituer,
> Tes promesses à temps leur sait effectuer.
> Mais passons, cher ami, jusqu'en l'hôtellerie . . .
>   (*Elmire*, 1241–5)

Hardy's metaphors are sometimes badly assorted, introducing a note of inappropriateness which destroys the seriously meant effect:

> Le bouton dégouttant des larmes de l'aurore
> Plus avide n'attend le soleil à s'éclore,
> Les petits oisillons dans le nid affamés
> Un repas incertain de leurs parents aimés,
> La tourtre sa moitié par le bois écartée,
> Le pilote un bon vent à sa nef arrêtée,
> Que fiévreuse d'amour j'attends ce beau portrait,
> Cet aimable voleur qui mon âme soustrait . . .
>   (*Félismène*, 217 ff.)

In short, Hardy's taste was uncertain and rather rustic. His classical learning was undigested and reminiscent of the student who has failed to progress beyond pedantry to achieve a more confident handling of his material. His respect for the old modes of verse-writing stems from the same characteristic. He had learnt his craft, he believed, in the school of Ronsard, and could never see that anything better, or different, might come to be admired.

In one respect, however, he attempted to use an idiom which was of his own century as much as of the sixteenth. His subjects often necessitated the courtly love speech. Earlier poets such as Desportes as well as writers of pastoral gave him some models, but the language of *galanterie*, and indeed of *préciosité*, was alive and developing in his own day. Here again, Hardy's handling of the convention was somewhat rustic. He wavered between the metaphoric pseudo-Petrarchan and the naturalistic style of physical description as practised by the sixteenth-century *blasonneurs*. Thus Araspe soliloquizes upon his desperate passion for the captive Panthée:

> Fut-il onc un désastre, un malheur mémorable
> A la fière rigueur de mon sort comparable?
> Araspe, pauvre Araspe, hélas! que n'as-tu pris
> Plutôt à gouverner le terrestre pourpris
> Que, geôlier établi d'une beauté captive,
> Beauté, je le dirai, la plus belle qui vive,
> Tomber en ses liens, t'enferrer de ses fers?
> Quels extrêmes tourments n'ai-je depuis soufferts?
> Chagrin, triste, pensif, solitaire, malade
> Et de l'âme et du corps, par sa sorcière œillade,
> Œillade qui décoche un reste de chaleurs
> A travers les nuaux de ses humides pleurs,
> Œillade qui sans doute embraserait le monde
> Si son œil retenait cette larmeuse bonde,
> Œillade qui piteuse un rocher transirait,
> Que pour prendre les cœurs apostée on dirait,
> Œillade qu'un scadron d'autres beautés divines,
> Mises à nonchaloir, accompagnent voisines;
> Ce poil d'or crépelu, qui sans ordre flottant
> Va sur un col neigeux sans ordre voletant;

Ce front ainsi voûté qu'Iris le sien déploie
Quand la pluie annoncer sa mâitresse l'envoie;
Un vermillon de joue, emperlé de ses pleurs,
De telles que l'Aurore épanche sur les fleurs;
Une bouche de rose aux soupirs éternelle,
Qui, s'ouvrant, les baisers dessus ses bords appelle;
Et ce tertre jumeau d'un petit sein, mouvant
A l'accord des sanglots qu'elle soupire au vent.

(Panthée, 213–39)

In his enumeration of Panthée's charms Hardy goes one step further than the conventions of contemporary courtly poetry approved,[1] and he repeats this same minor error of taste on other occasions. He is uncertain of what can suitably be said and what not:

PAGE   Si la Princesse a pris médecine aujourd'hui.
DON FÉLIX   Purge, Amour, la rigueur qui cause mon ennui,
             Échauffant les glaçons de cette âme cruelle . . .

(Félismène, 615–17)

Elsewhere he is content with the usual well-worn comparisons: of the woman to a goddess or a huntress, of her beauty to a conquering force, of her glances to arrows, of her effects on her suitors to fetters or flames. Atalante, arriving for the boar-hunt in Méléagre with the sole intention of hunting the boar, is greeted admiringly by the men who have already gathered for the same purpose:

MÉLÉAGRE   Non, certes, ton secours amène dans ces lieux[2]
             Le vainqueur enchaîné du monarque des cieux,
             Amène de renfort les amours et les grâces;
             Avec leur moindre effort le monstre tu terrasses,
             Tu charmes sa manie, et ne faut autre dard,
             Autre chasse, autres rets qu'un amoureux regard.
ATALANTE   Ce bras décochera, non l'œil, chose solide,
             Capable d'arrêter sa fureur homicide . . .
PIRITHOÏS   Vaincre les cœurs humains suffit à ta beauté,
             Ailleurs à mon avis nouvelle en cruauté.

(Méléagre, 387–98)

---

[1] Though he was not alone in this in drama. See Scherer, Dramaturgie classique, p. 405.   [2] Stengel's text has yeux.

This same armoury of conventional metaphors furnishes a line of the same order as Théophile de Viau's much-derided line in *Pyrame et Thisbé*.[1] Hardy's Céphale has just shot an arrow by mistake at his wife Procris and sees her lying before him mortally wounded:

CÉPHALE   Mais montre-moi l'endroit où tu te sens blessée.
PROCRIS   Pour la seconde fois dans le cœur traversée,
           Une fois de tes yeux, et l'autre de ce dard,
           Dard, qui de nos moitiés va faire le départ.
CÉPHALE   Hé, Dieux! Ce traître dard m'accuse plus coupable,
           Il me rendra le ciel et la terre implacable.

                                        (*Procris*, 987 ff.)

VI

Such are the principal faults and eccentricities in Hardy's diction. They are almost enough in themselves (apart from the changes which took place in the dramatic *bienséances*) to explain the disfavour into which he soon fell, to be followed by a great blank of total neglect. But unacknowledged, or nearly so, were qualities which persisted in the next generation of dramatists who, one is obliged to conclude, had learnt at least something from Hardy. Other qualities, which did not persist, at least in tragedy, are praiseworthy and interesting in themselves and deserve a short consideration.

The realism of some of Hardy's language, necessitated by some of his situations, has already been touched on in its incongruous aspect. Because of the French conception of tragedy as an elevated genre, originated if not perfected in the sixteenth century, it will come to appear more and more incongruous until it is eliminated from tragedy altogether and assigned to the field of comedy. The tyranny of verse and, within that, the domination of one metre, the alexandrine, which became virtually absolute with the disappearance of the choruses,

[1]   Ha! voici le poignard qui du sang de son maître
            S'est souillé lâchement: il en rougit, le traître!
                                        (*Pyrame et Thisbé*, 1227–8)

Théophile admired Hardy and his language in this play is not much more sophisticated than Hardy's. *Pyrame* was probably first performed late in 1622 (printed 1623). What may be an allusion to it occurs in Hardy's *Cornélie*, 917–18:

            C'est là . . .
            Que se doit réunir à sa Thisbé un Pyrame.

made it hard to achieve variety of diction and vocabulary within the same play. Hardy himself lacked the expedient open to his English contemporaries of switching to plain prose when plain speaking was required. Instead, he was in the difficult position of having to satisfy in the same dramatic idiom the requirements of the elevated style and those of the realistic and even the comic. After him, the attempt to do this was progressively abandoned, but in his day it may not have seemed hopeless, and in any case the issue had not yet been clarified.

The well in *Timoclée* and *Scédase* is referred to by periphrasis: 'moite cercueil' and 'humide sépulture'; but it is also called by its common name: *le puits*. Often, however, there is no attempt at periphrasis and words and sentences inadmissable in later tragedy are used quite naturally. Some are gross. The wronged wife in *Procris* calls the goddess Aurora an 'orde putain'. For the jealous elder characters in *Méléagre*, the heroine is also a 'putain' and a 'paillarde'. In a scene which is admittedly comic (*Ariadne*, 1075 ff.) the insults exchanged between Silenus and Pan include 'bouc infect de luxure' and 'vieil mâtin hargneux'. The father in *Félismène*, fearing he will be late for an appointment, remarks:

Il faut ma montre consulter.   (35)

In *La Force du sang*, after the two lovers have swooned simultaneously, the mother exclaims:

Du vinaigre, de l'eau, vite, vite.   (1465)

From *La Force du sang* also can be quoted a perfectly concrete speech referring to a concrete action. Three young men are planning to snatch a girl away from her parents in the street and carry her off for rape:

ALPHONSE   L'ordre de l'entreprise
Veut que l'on fasse peur à cette barbe grise,
La pointe de l'épée au gosier lui portant;
L'autre n'a que la vieille à saisir s'ébattant;
A bras de corps tandis je chargerai ma belle
D'une course au logis fugitif avec elle.
Chacun s'écarte donc et ne me suive pas;
Même chemin tenu remarquerait nos pas.

(201 ff.)

In *Gésippe* the bride discovers that the man who has slept with her was not the bridegroom, but his friend who has been substituted for him by arrangement. The two men make what, from a realistic point of view, can only be considered rather lame excuses. The friend offers to kill himself if this will smooth things over. The bride replies:

> Ta mort, lâche abuseur, ne me rend impolue,
> Ne répare un effort de rage dissolue
> Qui met au désespoir mon esprit furieux,
> Qui me fait abhorrer le monstre injurieux,
> Abhorrer à l'égal un scélerat infâme
> Qui la première nuit maquerelle sa femme.

> (697–702)

It is not always possible to be certain whether Hardy was seeking a comic effect or not. He would seem to be doing so in *Lucrèce* (entitled unambiguously a 'tragedy') in the scene in which the lover descends from Lucrèce's window by a ladder which she undertakes to hold firmly at the top:

> Sus, descends; tu sais bien quelle heure doit promise
> Achever la partie amoureuse remise.
> Mes mains sans varier l'échelle assureront.

Two lines later his foot has slipped and his fall is about to arouse the household. The husband is soon up and out, suspecting robbers. He recounts, in what must surely be a brief parody of the conventional dream of tragic foreboding which Hardy introduces frequently in full seriousness, how he has dreamt that horns sprouted from his head:

> Il me semblait, vision chimérique,
> Au retour de la chasse, un ébat héroïque,
> Avoir las dans un bois sommeillé quelque temps,
> Deux fourchons au réveil hors du front me sortant,
> Ainsi qu'on les dépeint à un jeune satyr.
> Quel présage de là à votre avis se tire?

> (449–54)

In the same play there is an appropriate coarseness in the conversation of the prostitute Ériphile, which verges on the comic, although the final result of her insinuations is the death of all the protagonists.

Another prostitute, in the tragicomedy, *Cornélie*, provides an unreservedly comic episode. Brought into the house by a page, she is at first believed to be the heroine who has disappeared, and whose name she shares:

SANTISTEVAN	[*a servant*]. Fraîche, galante et belle,
	Vous la trouvez là-haut.
D. ANTOINE	Sais-tu bien que c'est elle?
SANTISTEVAN	Au nom de Cornélie on la connaît assez.
D. ANTOINE	Monte après moi, sans bruit.
COURTISANE	Hé! sus, sus, avancez!
	Notre humeur n'aime pas telle cérémonie.
D. ANTOINE	Certain Duc vous vient voir d'allégresse infinie.
COURTISANE	Un Duc, et de plus grands d'ordinaire j'ai vu.
D. ANTOINE	[*seeing her*]. O cieux! mon œil surpris d'un fantôme imprévu . . .
COURTISANE	Là, là, ne faites pas ainsi le difficile.
	Beaucoup des plus huppés des premiers de la ville . . .
D. ANTOINE	O louve misérable! O pendard effronté!
	Ce Prince se croira de nous deux affronté.
COURTISANE	Dieux! que le courroux lent a de sel et de grâce.
	Approchez, dédaigneux, et que l'on vous embrasse.

[*The others arrive.*]

COURTISANE	Que de gens pour me voir dans un lit découverte,
	La grande nouveauté!
BENTIVOLE	Que veut dire ceci?
ALPHONSE	Êtes-vous Cornélie?
COURTISANE	Oui, je la suis, et si.
	Ne faites pas le fin; un mien frère, à même âge
	Vous vaut bien, tout rempli d'esprit et de courage.
BENTIVOLE	O plaisante rencontre!
ALPHONSE	O misérable moi!
COURTISANE	Trouvée avec un page, est-ce là tant de quoi?

(*Cornélie*, 1138 ff.)

The elements which are certainly comic are provided, as is to be expected, by lower-caste characters: prostitutes, pages, the occasional procuress or intermediary, the satyr-like Pan in *Ariadne*. Nearly all revolve round sexual love.

A feature distinctive of Hardy, which makes him both harder to read and more interesting from the stylistic point of view, is his fondness for compression. This has been seen as a Latinate feature,[1] though the syntactical influence of Latin on a writer whose classical scholarship was as apparently superficial as Hardy's must remain doubtful. It may be due in part to his hurried and incorrect methods of composition, and even, in places, to printers' errors. It is none the less striking, is much too frequent to be invariably ascribed to carelessness or chance, and constitutes a special kind of dramatic shorthand which is peculiar to this author. Often it takes the form of an unusual word-order, or of a single adjective used either adverbially or elliptically:

> Menteur puissent les cieux
> Me bannir à jamais du soleil de tes yeux.
>
> (= 'Si je mens'. *Dorise*, 143–4)

Sometimes it is sustained over a passage of several lines:

> Ma coulpe ne saurait s'excuser infinie,
> Ma gloire n'être point de mes larmes ternie,
> Sans pouvoir néanmoins que dedans le tombeau
> Éteindre avec mes jours un amoureux flambeau.
>
> (*Dorise*, 207–10)

The third line of this is overconcentrated or overcharged, but the sense of the whole, as is apparent from the context, is:

> Ma coulpe [faute] qui est infinie, ne saurait s'excuser, ma gloire ne saurait n'être point ternie de mes larmes, tant que je ne pourrais éteindre en même temps que mes jours un amoureux flambeau, ce qui n'est possible que dans le tombeau.

[1] See particularly the long and valuable section (pp. 557–652) on Hardy's language, style and versification in E. Rigal's *Alexandre Hardy et le théâtre français* . . . (Paris, 1889). Though his account of Hardy's life and the theatrical background can now be seen to be quite unreliable, Rigal's discussions of the work are still valid.

The context also, which is made clear in the play, explains the general meaning of the following passage from *Cornélie*. The Duke, having contracted with Cornélie a first, entirely secret, marriage, is now proposing to contract a less secret one in the presence of her brother and a few friends, while still postponing the ceremonious public nuptials until his mother, who is lying ill, has either died or fully recovered:

> Allons mettre au chef-d'œuvre une dèrniere main,
> La pompe (malgré moi) nuptiale sursise,
> Faut qu'après la langueur maternelle on avise
> De la mort terminée, ou que par la santé,
> Notre désir augmente à demi contenté.
>
> (1512–16)

I have respected the punctuation of Stengel's edition, though it might be amended with advantage. Again, the last line as it stands may also require emendation, though the sense is not dubious.

Of course it is always possible to assume that when he wrote such passages Hardy was pressed for time and resorted to such language to express several ideas in too short a space. The same has been said of Shakespeare's later plays. In his case, virtue was born of necessity. This is frequently true of Hardy, who often gains in terseness more than he loses in strict grammatical correctness.

VII

It is now possible, and necessary in all justice, to point to Hardy's qualities as a dramatic poet which are free from personal peculiarities and contain a minimum of obscurities. It is easy to find many examples and a small selection will suffice as representative. He knows how to write the lyric speech, as this, in which Cyrus addresses the spirits of the dead Panthée and her husband:

> Allez vous réunir ensemble, belles ombres,
> Loin de soucis mortels, de misères, d'encombres.
> Sous les myrtes sacrés aux mânes bienheureux
> Récompensez vos maux de baisers amoureux.
> Que votre faim toujours s'apaise d'ambrosie,
> Et sans fin le nectar votre soif rassasie,

Que le peuple léger des esprits fortunés
Vous adore, de fleurs richement couronnés.
Moi, qui vous ai perdus en l'avril de vos âges,
Enveloppé parmi les martiaux orages,
Lairrai[1] de mon regret des monuments si grands
Que vous triompherez de l'injure des ans.
Un blanc marbre érigé portera vos figures,
Inscrits de leurs beaux noms avec vos aventures,
Et d'encens chaque année on les parfumera
Cependant que Phébus nos jours allumera . . .

(Panthée, 1175 ff.)

Or there is this, in which the classical allusions are, for once, utilized
to good effect. Alphonse is repenting of his rape of the innocent
Léocadie:

Oh, que la volupté, sorcière de nos sens,
Circé qui les transforme en lions rugissants,
Produit de peu de joie une longue tristesse.
Combien il fait mauvais la recevoir hôtesse,
Ceux qui l'auront logée assurés au partir
D'un salaire fatal et honteux repentir,
Assurés de nourrir dans l'âme béquetée
L'aigle perpetuel du hardi Prométhée.
Depuis que sa fureur brutale en cruauté
Au rapt m'émancipa d'une chaste beauté,
Ne sais quel aiguillon maniaque me reste,
Peu s'en faut compagnon du parricide Oreste,
Qui pense chaque jour cette vierge revoir
Les cieux à ma ruine et l'enfer émouvoir,
Horrible en cris piteux plomber son sein d'ivoire . . .

(Force du sang, 603 ff.)

As for rhetorical vigour in both soliloquy and dialogue, it is one of
Hardy's strongest points. He knows how to use stichomythia dramatically. In this extract from a longer dialogue, Coriolanus is refusing

---

[1] i.e. 'laisserai'. I am indebted to Professor R. C. Knight for this convincing
emendation. Stengel printed 'L'airain'.

to grant the Roman ambassadors milder peace terms than those already offered to them:

AMBASSADEURS	Console au moins nos maux d'une humaine réponse.
CORIOLAN	La première donnée emporte son destin.[1]
AMBASSADEURS	L'honneur de ton pays veux-tu mettre en butin?
CORIOLAN	Je n'ai point de pays qu'où ma fortune est bonne.
AMBASSADEURS	Rome est celle pourtant qui ton être te donne.
CORIOLAN	Rome est celle qui m'a voulu priver du jour.
AMBASSADEURS	A son ingratitude oppose ton amour.
CORIOLAN	Ne m'importunez plus d'une prière vaine.
AMBASSADEURS	A d'autres mieux venus nous résignons la peine.
CORIOLAN	A quiconque ce soit je défends revenir,
	Si à la paix offerte il veut contrevenir.

(*Coriolan*, 774 ff.)

In the following, Herod orders the torture of a eunuch who, he believes, knows the truth of a plot against him. This involves his wife Mariamne, who has been falsely accused both of having conspired to kill him and of having committed adultery with the eunuch's master:

HÉRODE	Prévôt, que de ce pas on le livre aux bourreaux.
	Qu'ils recherchent parmi le fer, le feu, les eaux,
	De quoi le tourmenter, le presser, le contraindre
	A nous notifier ce qu'il a voulu feindre,
	Et que son traître maître amené sur le champ
	J'examine d'un coup, l'affaire dépêchant.
PRÉVÔT	Sire, il ne tiendra pas à un devoir fidèle
	Que Votre Majesté le crime ne décèle.
	Nous y employerons l'artifice et l'effort.
MARIAMNE	Ha! chétif innocent, que je pleure ton sort.

[1] Probably meaning: 'La réponse déjà donnée contient le destin de Rome.'

HÉRODE   Pleure le tien plutôt, et folle ne présume
              Abuser de ma grâce ainsi que de coutume,
              Qu'on te traite avec plus[1] de respect, de faveur,
              Tes yeux n'ont plus d'attraits, tes baisers de saveur.
              L'exécration jointe à ce dol homicide
              D'amour et de pitié rend ma poitrine vide,
              Déracine ce peu qui restait là-dedans
              Par l'assiduité des forfaits précédents.
              Assure, assure-toi, qu'exemplaire punie,
              L'appareillé supplice attend ta félonie.
MARIAMNE   Quelle?
HÉRODE   Ma mort brassée et mon lit maculé.

                                        (*Mariamne*, 1089 ff.)

Hardy also uses repetition to good effect. Having just been told by
the Count that the Pope sanctions their marriage, Elmire is asked
whether she consents to it:

          Si mon ardente soif désire une fontaine?
          Si, courbant sous le faix, je veux reprendre haleine?
          Si je me veux tirer d'un dédale d'ennuis?
          Si je veux qu'un beau jour termine tant de nuits?
          Si, le pouvant, je veux de butte me soustraire
          Aux traits empoisonnés de fortune contraire?
          Oui certes, parvenue à ce contentement,
          Que l'esprit d'aise au ciel vole subitement.
          Mais l'excès d'un tel heur m'empêche de le croire,
          Crainte[2] avant le combat de chanter la victoire.

                                        (*Elmire*, 1773 ff.)

One might over-critically remark that this whole speech could be
reduced to a: 'Yes, darling, if it's really true.' But it differs from the
baroque emphasis pointed out in Garnier (see p. 28, note 2) and certainly found elsewhere in Hardy. It is dramatically important here
to make Elmire express her joy exuberantly.

Finally, there is indeed a touch of bombast in the following, given
the situation, which is merely that the speaker's beloved has refused to

---

[1] Conjectural emendation: *moins* for *plus*.   [2] *Crainte* = *de crainte*.

see him and has torn up his letter without reading it. But if abstracted from that situation and related to a stronger one it would not seem excessive and in any case it is good of its kind:

> Viens, tigresse, d'un coup me ravir la lumière,
> Soûle ta cruauté sur ce mourable corps,
> Tire son cœur empreint de ton portrait dehors,
> Bois le sang épuisé qui coule de mes veines,
> Et finis, t'appaisant, mes amoureuses peines,
> O pervers animal ennemi de raison!
> Tous maux à ton égard sont sans comparaison,
> Tu les surpasses tous chez quiconque t'adore.
>
> (Dorise, 516 ff.)

VIII

In spite of the pronounced swing in taste that was later to occur, it would be a mistake to suppose that nothing of Hardy survived in French drama. Even his verse-style was not entirely abandoned, but persisted with gradual modification in his successors. Looking back in 1660 on his own first, irregular comedy, Corneille remarked: 'Je n'avais pour guide qu'un peu de sens commun, avec les exemples de feu Hardy, dont la veine était plus féconde que polie, et de quelques modernes qui commençaient à se produire, et qui n'étaient pas plus réguliers que lui.'[1]

Somewhat disparaging though this is, it at least shows a recognition of influence, which extended in fact some way beyond *Mélite*.[2] The language of Corneille and his contemporaries quite often recalls Hardy, or at least the dramatic idiom which Hardy used, and it is justifiable to say that, but for him, they would not have written quite as they did. Clean breaks are rare in dramatic idiom, and 1630 was not 1550, nor, as some critics have sought to maintain, 1830. To limit this to one play, *Le Cid*, several echoes of Hardy can be heard in it:

> Ma mignonne, ôte-moi de scrupule . . .
>
> (Dorise, 347)

---

[1] *Examen* of *Mélite*.
[2] In the Dedication of *Don Sanche d'Aragon*, a *comédie héroïque* published in 1650, Corneille argues that the misfortunes of common people can make as worthy a subject of tragedy as those of kings and princes, and cites *Scédase* in support.

Several times Hardy uses the conventional *myrtes/cyprès* antithesis. Once at least the *myrtes* become *lauriers*:

> Tes stériles lauriers convertis en cyprès.
>
> (*Mort d'Alexandre*, 631)

These lines have a Cornelian ring in themselves, apart from the more precise reminiscence:

> ... un homme de mérite,
> Qui, la même prudence et la même valeur,
> Fut aux victorieux trahi par le malheur.
>
> (*Elmire*, 894–6)

With dawning recognition one comes upon:

> O désespoir horrible! ô rage insupportable!
>
> (*Procris*, 732)

then upon:

> O honte! ô désespoir! O paresse trop grande!
>
> (*Arsacome*, 1473)

until it finally crystallizes as:

> O rage! ô désespoir! O énorme infamie!
> Amis, vengez ma mort, une louve ennemie ...
>
> (*Félismène*, 1533–4)

Echoes are not strictly evidence,[1] but there are enough of them, here and elsewhere, to suggest that a detailed analysis of Hardy's

---

[1] The corresponding passages from *Le Cid* are:

> (1)   Ôte-moi d'un doute.
>   Connais-tu bien Don Diègue?
>   (397–8)
> (2) J'irai sous mes cyprès accabler ses lauriers.
>   (1196)
> (3) Sais-tu que ce vieillard fut la même vertu,
>   La vaillance et l'honneur de son temps?
>   (399–400)
> (4) O rage! ô désespoir! ô vieillesse ennemie!
>   N'ai-je donc vécu que pour cette infamie?
>   (237–8)

poetic language would substantiate the existing impression of continuity in Corneille and his contemporaries.

As for Hardy's moral universe, it is too chaotic for definite conclusions or comparisons to be drawn. All one can say is that some of the key-words of the Cornelian ethic occur frequently in Hardy, with what appear to be similar connotations: *honneur, vertu, gloire, renom, mérite.*

In more general terms, Hardy's drama represents a great progress beyond the academic drama of the sixteenth century towards the professional drama of the seventeenth. As will already have become apparent, it is full of action. Physical action shown on stage, together with the 'irregularities' which accompanied it, will be progressively discarded, but psychological action will remain and take on increasing importance. It already exists in Hardy to a degree unknown in the previous century, invested with the dramatic qualities of movement and suspense. Unless Hardy's plays were complete failures when performed (and evidently they were not) they must have been watched with excitement and curiosity: excitement aroused by the development and turns of the plot, curiosity to know what the final outcome would be. That is the chief point of the majority of them and, although Hardy was a somewhat clumsy playwright who often misused his opportunities as they can be seen with hindsight to have been, the intention and the lesson for future dramatists were quite clear. More than anyone else in France, Hardy established the conception of a play as the representation of a story which unfolds before one's eyes and whose end is not known before one reaches it.

In addition, the following features, common in the seventeenth century, but absent or rare in the sixteenth, are to be found in Hardy. They bear on themes, situation, or characterization:

Inner conflict and hesitation over a dilemma. Didon up to a point. Énée is truly tormented by the prospect of his betrayal of Didon, though it is difficult to read much hesitation into this. *Ariadne*: Thésée's discussion with Phalare on whether he shall abandon Ariadne and go with Phèdre. 'Mon honneur et ma foi' versus 'love'. *Elmire*: the heroine debates whether she should resist her passion or elope with the Comte de Gleichen: 'L'un prolonge ma gloire en m'abrégeant la vie / Et l'autre me contente encore qu'asservie, / L'un ramène l'honneur . . . L'autre . . . etc.' Definite hesitation here. *Force du sang*: Alphonse's speech quoted above, p. 83. An inner conflict in the sense of an attack of conscience, though no decision is envisaged or called for at this point of the play.

(2) *Argument leading to change of mind.* (In Corneille the arguments are developed with superior dialectical force and skill, but basically this is the same thing.) *Coriolan*: persuaded, though reluctantly, with foreboding. *Panthée*: Abradate, *idem*. *Mort d'Achille*: Priam persuaded to consent to the murder of Achille.[1]

(3) *The 'political' conspiracy.* Though varying in importance and nature, this is found in: *Mort d'Achille*, *Mort de Daire*, *Mort d'Alexandre* and *Mariamne*.

(4) *The magnanimous prince or hero. Panthée*: Cyrus. *Mort de Daire*: Alexander. *Mort d'Alexandre*: the tragedy is full of the praises of Alexander's virtues, though in fact he performs no 'generous' act in the play. *Timoclée*: the magnanimous Alexander pardons Timoclée in the last scene, though textually his praises go to her for her 'acte magnanime autant que glorieux' in murdering her ravisher, rather than hers to him for his magnanimity. An example of moral confusion or transference?

(5) *'Combat de générosité.' Phraate*: Phraate and Cotys offering each other the throne of Thrace. *Elmire*: between the two wives. *Gésippe*: between the two friends.

(6) *Evil or dangerous women. Méléagre*: the mother, evil in character and act. *Félismène*: the Princess Célie, the 'woman scorned', evil through circumstance and dies before she can work harm. *Mariamne*: Salome, though she has the excuse of acting for affection of her brother Herod; ruthless through mistaken loyalty. *Dorise*: Sidère, an *intrigante* who succeeds and is not condemned. The play is on a light register.

Needless to say, there are many more virtuous female characters, but none who is depicted as stoical, except perhaps Timoclée. Volomnie in *Coriolan* is not stoical, but full of misgivings and lamentations.

The love element is important in Hardy, particularly as a factor in the motivation and development of plot. As such, it is taken for granted as a strong natural force and resembles the love of the romance tradition. Passionate and predominantly sensual love leading to disaster

[1] It might be added that all these arguments have a conclusive outcome and are integrated in the plot. In this they are unlike the argument between Elizabeth and her counsellors in Montchrestien's *L'Écossaise* (see above, pp. 44–5).

occurs in *Mariamne, Alcméon* and *Procris* (if taken seriously). Virtuous love causing one or both of the lovers to perform noble acts occurs unequivocally only in *Frégonde* and, though in an unusual form, in *Elmire, ou l'heureuse bigamie*. The love of Panthée for her husband is virtuous and leads to a decision which brings disaster, but for her it is not a hard decision. No consistent ethic can be deduced from the surviving plays. They merely contain varying types of love which later dramatists would develop in their own ways.

One type which they did not develop, unlike the English dramatists of the Restoration, was that in which 'love' in the form of sexual appetite emerges as brutality. This is quite frequent in Hardy: in *Scédase, Timoclée, Aristoclée, La Force du sang*, while even *Mariamne* can be attached partly to the same category. But physical brutality in sex soon disappeared from the French stage together with brutality in other domains.

HARDY'S PLAYS

TRAGEDIES

Didon se sacrifiant
Source: Virgil. Probably also Jodelle, though no close verbal borrowings are apparent.

Énée, urged by Mercury (who appears on stage) to sail on from Carthage to Italy, deserts Didon after some hesitation and an inner conflict. Didon kills herself on stage. There is more suspense in this than in Jodelle's version, the dialogue is livelier and the speeches appreciably shorter, though still lengthy.

La Mort d'Achille
Sources: Dictys and Dares.

During the siege of Troy Achille falls in love with Polyxène, the daughter of the Trojan King Priam. On the pretext of a marriage he is lured to the temple of Apollo and killed by Polyxène's brothers, in spite of Priam's reluctance. The play has considerable dramatic movement.

La Mort de Daire
Source: Plutarch.

The defeated Daire (Darius) is conspired against by one of his own captains and left mortally wounded. The body is found by an officer of the victorious and magnanimous Alexandre and brought in to be buried by Daire's mother Sisigambe.

La Mort d'Alexandre

Sources: Plutarch and Quintus Curtius.

While Alexandre is in Babylon, Antipatre and his sons plot to poison him. Acts I–III are taken up by the plotting and by omens and predictions of disaster, leading to attempts to persuade Alexandre to leave Babylon. In Acts IV–V he is poisoned but still capable of much speech before dying. His followers praise him lavishly and take his instructions for the succession and provision for his wife Roxane. The plotters, though their identity is suspected in passing by Alexandre, are not discovered. The play has little dramatic point.

Timoclée, ou la juste vengeance

Source: Plutarch.

After long debate with his council, Alexandre decides to subdue the defiant city of Thebes. He also contemptuously turns away an embassy from the Athenians who tend to support the Thebans. Thebes is attacked and taken. In the conquered city the nobly born Theban lady Timoclée is raped by one of Alexandre's captains. This occurs near the end of Act IV, though it has been prepared in Act III by a dream in which the ghost of Timoclée's brother appears to her and predicts the course of events. In Act V Timoclée avenges herself by luring the captain down a well and drowning him in it. She is taken before Alexandre and pardoned by him.

Coriolan

Source: Plutarch.

The victorious general Coriolan is accused by the Roman people of arrogance and of ambitions to become a dictator and is banished from Rome. He joins their enemies, the Volscians, and returns as the leader of a besieging army which reduces Rome to desperate straits. After several missions sent to him by the Romans have failed, a group of ladies including his mother Volomnie persuade him to relent and raise the siege. As he has foreseen, he is killed by the indignant Volscians. Volomnie, the second hero, mourns him and predicts her own death.

This is a clear and logical dramatization of the story, unusually well constructed.

Scédase, ou l'hospitalité violée
Source: Plutarch.

Two Spartan gallants arrive at the house of the humble farmer Scédase during his absence. They rape his two daughters, kill them, and throw the bodies down a well. Having returned home and discovered the crime, Scédase goes to Sparta to obtain justice. When this is refused, he kills himself.

Panthée
Source: Xenophon and Philostratus.

Cyrus has conquered the Assyrians. Among his captives is the beautiful Panthée whose chastity Cyrus is determined to respect. He entrusts her to his lieutenant Araspe, who falls violently in love with her and declares his passion in pressing terms. She appeals through her nurse to Cyrus, who is enraged with Araspe but is induced by the nurse to forgive him. Panthée is freed to join her husband Abradate, hitherto an enemy of Cyrus. Abradate is at first jealous and suspicious of Cyrus, but after hearing Panthée's praises of the conqueror he is persuaded to abandon his own hopelessly defeated country and join him. He is killed in battle leading an army for Cyrus, whereupon Panthée, blaming herself for this misfortune, kills herself on his body.

Mariamne
Source: Josephus.

Hérode has forcibly married Mariamne, a princess of the Hasmonaean royal line, whose father and brother Hérode has killed to gain the throne. She refuses to sleep with him. Meanwhile Hérode's brother and sister, Phérore and Salome, plot against her, and falsely accuse her both of trying to poison him and of having committed adultery with a member of his court. In his rage after another refusal by Mariamne Hérode orders her to be beheaded. After this has been done he bitterly regrets his action and her death.

Méléagre
Source: Apollodorus.

A semi-mythological play. Diana has sent a monstrous boar to terrorize the country ruled by Méléagre. Unable to kill it himself, Méléagre sends for help and is joined by various supporters, including Thésée and the virgin huntress Atalante. A hunt is organized and the boar is killed. The trophy is awarded to Atalante, but Méléagre's uncles are jealous and take it from her. She complains to Méléagre, who has fallen in love with her and is about to marry her. He kills his uncles on the spot. Indignant at this, his mother Althée takes out a magic brand with which his destiny is linked and throws it on the fire. Méléagre dies in agony. Althée exults over this act of justice and predicts her own imminent death.

Lucrèce, ou l'adultère puni
Source: story by Lope de Vega, *El Peregrino en su patria*.
   Lucrèce, the wife of Télémaque, commits adultery with Myrhène. The pair are betrayed by a jealous courtesan who has been deserted by Myrhène and who is now consorting with Télémaque. Télémaque surprises his wife with her lover and kills them both. He is then killed himself by an indignant friend of Myrhène's.

Alcméon, ou la vengeance féminine
Source: Pausanias.
   The Theban prince Alcméon falls passionately in love with Callirhoé, who insists that he should divorce his present wife Alphésibée and should give her the precious collar which was his wedding-gift to Alphésibée. The latter surrenders the collar reluctantly, and smears it with a poison which drives Alcméon mad. In this insane state he kills his children whom she delivers to him deliberately. She then urges her two brothers to attack him. In the fight which follows all three are wounded fatally. Alphésibée resolves to die on her brothers' tomb.

TRAGICOMEDIES

The first four plays summarized below are also described as *tragédies* in the heading or in the text of the *Arguments*.

Procris, ou la jalousie infortunée.
Source: Ovid.
   The hunter Céphale is persuaded by Aurore, goddess of the dawn, to trick his loving wife Procris. Told by a shepherd that Céphale and Aurore sleep together in the woods, Procris follows her husband one night. Mistaking her for an animal, he shoots her unintentionally, regretting this bitterly afterwards. Hardy's uncertain treatment of this mythological theme inclines to the pastoral, but with the addition of lust and blood.

Alceste, ou la fidélité
Partial source: Euripides, *Alcestis*.

The basic story is that of Alceste dying voluntarily in place of her husband Admète, and then rescued from death by Hercule. But there are so many differences and additions in Hardy's version that this furnishes at most the bare theme, in spite of his claim in the *Argument* that his 'rich subject' is partly taken from Euripides. The recovery of Alceste is treated as one of the labours of Hercules, who is the real hero of the play. The goddess Junon appears, as well as the deities of the Underworld.

Ariadne ravie
Sources: Plutarch and Ovid.

Having slain the Minotaur with the help of Ariadne, Thésée promises marriage to her and escapes from Crete with her and her sister Phèdre. Realizing that he prefers Phèdre, he sails on with her, abandoning Ariadne on the Island of Naxos. Ariadne attempts suicide, but is rescued by the god Bacchus, returning from his conquest of the East. Her marriage to him is ample consolation for her sorrows.

The Phaedra–Hippolytus theme is present in this play in subsidiary form. Before deserting Ariadne, Thésée had promised to marry Phèdre to his son Hippolyte. Though she has not seen Hippolyte, Phèdre already longs for him and is persuaded with difficulty to accept Thésée instead and to betray her sister.

Aristoclée, ou le mariage infortuné
Source: Plutarch, *Amatoriae narrationes*.

Aristoclée has two suitors, the rich young nobleman Straton and a poorer neighbour, Calistène, whom she prefers. Both her father and an assembly of the citizens who are summoned refuse to decide between the rivals, for fear of starting trouble. Forced to make her own choice, Aristoclée timidly names Calistène. Straton appears to accept the situation and is invited to the wedding. He comes with a gang of bullies who ambush the wedding procession with the intention of carrying off Aristoclée. In the resulting struggle she is killed. Straton and his accomplices make off. Calistène, arriving too late, commits suicide.

Frégonde, ou le chaste amour
Source: Diego de Agreda, *Doce novelas morales y ejemplares.*

The Marquis de Cotron falls in love with Frégonde, the wife of Don Juan, a 'brave Spanish knight', but she resists him. Don Juan loses his fortune, then accepts the disinterested aid of the Marquis, in spite of Frégonde's misgivings. He receives an important command and is killed in battle. However, his ghost appears to Frégonde, says that he now knows of the Marquis's virtuous love, and urges her to take him as her second husband. This she does, after a scene in which the King of Castile persuades her that it would be an appropriate course. In the King's role here there is a certain foretaste of Corneille's *Le Cid.*

Gésippe, ou les deux amis
Source: Boccaccio, *Decameron.*

The young Athenian Gésippe has formed such a close friendship with Tite, a Roman youth living in Athens for his studies, that he does not wish his forthcoming marriage to come between them. He therefore offers his well-loved bride to Tite, whom he introduces into his bed on the wedding-night. Discovering the substitution the next morning, the bride, Sophronie, is ashamed and furious, but is eventually persuaded by Gésippe and her own family to accept Tite as her true husband, as the least scandalous solution. The happy pair leave for Rome.

Some time after Gésippe, struck by misfortunes, also goes to Rome where Tite and Sophronie are living in blissful prosperity (Tite is now a Senator). Gésippe, now destitute, stands outside Tite's door but is not recognized by him. Believing he has been ignored deliberately he goes to some waste land where he comes upon two thieves quarrelling over their booty. One kills the other and makes off. The Provost and his archers arrive, whereupon Gésippe accuses himself of the murder as a way of ending his life. Brought before the court of Senators, he is condemned to death as he had planned and then recognized by Tite who takes the killing upon himself. While Tite's improbable confession is being considered, the real murderer appears and is moved by conscience to confess. He is pardoned. Gésippe is taken home by Tite, who offers him his sister in marriage. The virtues of 'perfect friendship' are stressed throughout the play.

Phraate, ou le triomphe des vrais amants
Source: Cinthio.

Phraate, son of Philippe (Philip of Macedonia), arrives incognito at the court of his father's enemy, Cotys, King of Thrace. He begins his wooing of the reluctant Philagnie, daughter of Cotys. Meanwhile, two women agents of Cotys, sent to poison Philippe, have been caught in Macedonia and imprisoned. Returning home, Phraate frees them secretly and sends them back ahead of him to Philagnie, whom they help to persuade to sleep with him. Phraate gets away again and eventually joins his father after the latter has defeated Cotys in a first battle, but without capturing him. He is persuaded reluctantly to take over command of the Thracian army and the campaign. Philagnie meanwhile finds herself pregnant, leaves home to escape her father's anger, and takes refuge in a peasant's hut, where her child is born. Phraate defeats Cotys definitively and holds him prisoner. The missing Philagnie turns up, escorted by the peasant and carrying the baby. All is joy. Phraate generously restores Cotys to his throne.

Elmire, ou l'heureuse bigamie
Source: Hondorff.

After being captured by the Saracens in battle, the Count of Gleichen is befriended by Elmire, daughter of the Saracen King. She helps him to escape and goes with him, on promise of a Christian marriage, although he already has a wife in Germany. In Rome, the Pope gives him permission to have two lawful wives and he returns home, where the Countess, whose overriding wish is to have her husband back, accepts the situation and welcomes Elmire. The two women agree to share him in mutual admiration and harmony.

La Belle Égyptienne
Source: Cervantes, *Novelas ejemplares*.

A young nobleman, Jean de Carcame, falls in love with the gipsy girl Précieuse and joins the gipsies to win her, taking the name of Andrés. The gipsies get into trouble, being falsely accused of theft by a rich woman whom Andrés has rebuffed. In the resulting dispute Andrés kills a soldier. When the gipsies are taken before the Seneschal for judgement, Précieuse is recognized as the Seneschal's long-lost daughter, stolen by the gipsies as a baby, and Andrés's noble identity is also revealed. Pardon, rejoicing and marriage.

Cornélie

Source: Cervantes, *Novelas ejemplares.*

Alphonse, Duke of Ferrara, has contracted a secret marriage with Cornélie, a young woman of a less powerful family in the same city. She gives birth to a baby which she intends to send to the Duke, but it is handed by mistake to a young Spaniard, Don Juan, who is lodging in Ferrara with his compatriot, Don Antoine. He charitably takes the newborn child home and entrusts it to his landlady. Going out again, he goes to the help of a man who is being attacked by six others and helps to rout the assailants. Unknown to him, the man he has saved is the Duke of Ferrara and the attacking gang was led by Cornélie's brother Bentivole, attempting to avenge the honour of his sister, whom he believes to have been seduced. Meanwhile Cornélie herself has left home for fear of her furiously jealous brother. Meeting Don Antoine in the street, she begs for his protection and is taken back to the house which he shares with Don Juan. Here, to her astonishment and joy, she finds her own baby. By a further coincidence, Bentivole calls on Don Juan to enlist his help in obtaining satisfaction from the Duke: either he fights him or marries his sister. The rest of the play is devoted to clearing up the imbroglio. It ends in a total reconciliation, with the Duke preparing to marry Cornélie before witnesses, as had always been his intention. This happy ending is somewhat delayed by Cornélie's flight from the house of the two Spaniards. For greater safety she takes refuge with a hermit, who also accepts the baby. As a comic complication a page of Don Juan's has brought a prostitute into the house whose name is also Cornélie. This complication adds to the delay in tracking down the true Cornélie to the hermit's dwelling.

La Force du sang

Source: Cervantes, *Novelas ejemplares.*

The young Léocadie, out for an evening walk with her parents in the streets of Toledo, is carried off by a young nobleman, Alphonse, and raped in his house while unconscious. Turned out into the street, she finds her way home, with nothing to identify the house to which she had been taken except a statuette of Hercules which she had secretly picked up in the strange bedroom (in Cervantes the object is a crucifix). Alphonse leaves for Italy. Léocadie gives birth to a son, who is brought up in her parents' house as her nephew.

Some seven years later this son, Ludovic, is knocked over in the street by a horseman and picked up by Alphonse's father, who feels a strange tenderness for the boy (the 'voice of the blood'). Thanks to this accident, the boy's grandparents meet his mother and all is made clear. Alphonse is recalled from Italy to marry Léocadie in all honour and delight.

Félismène
Source: Montemayor, *Diana*.

Félix, a young Spanish gentleman, is in love with Félismène and intends to marry her, but is sent away by his father to the court of the German Emperor. There he falls in love with the Emperor's daughter, Célie. Félismène follows him in male disguise, is employed by him unrecognized as a page, and acts as his go-between with Célie. Célie falls in love with Félismène in her male guise, is put off by her, and dies in a sudden fit of fury. The rumour spreads that she has been poisoned by Félix, who flees from the court pursued by three young Germans. The last act has a pastoral setting, in which Félismène, who has also left the court and is now dressed as a shepherdess, is discoursing of love with other shepherds and shepherdesses. Into this scene burst Félix and his pursuers. Amazon-like, Félismène takes up her bow and arrows and between them they kill the three Germans. Recognition, forgiveness and marriage.

Dorise (entitled *Sidère* in the *privilège*)
Source: de Rosset, *Les Amants volages*.

The theme of the love-switch, treated fairly lightly. Salmacis loves Dorise, whom he wishes to marry, but he is desired by a second woman, Sidère. Licanor, a friend of Salmacis, secretly loves Dorise also and combines with Sidère in a plot to separate the pair. This they do by falsely telling Dorise that Salmacis has boasted of having slept with her. Dorise furiously drives away Salmacis and turns to Licanor, whom she eventually marries. Salmacis, in despair, disappears and takes refuge with a hermit. He is found by Sidère with the help of an enchantress, who removes a spell which has been cast over him. He awakes to love of Sidère and readily marries her.

Arsacome, ou l'amitié des Scythes
Source: Lucian, *Toxaris.*

Arsacome, a warlike but unwealthy Scythian, falls in love with the princess Masée, and she with him. Her father Leucanor, King of the Bosphorus, prefers a neighbouring prince, Adimache, who is a richer suitor. Proudly protesting that his only wealth consists in his two friends, Arsacome leaves for home. One of his friends then kills King Leucanor by treachery and brings back his severed head to Arsacome. The second abducts Masée, also by a trick, and takes her to Arsacome, to become his willing bride. The play ends with the three friends confidently preparing to defeat an attack by the outraged suitor, Adimache. *Arsacome* bears all the signs of an early play.

5

TOWARDS CLASSICAL TRAGEDY

Types of drama popular in 1620–35 – the rise of tragicomedy – Hardy and
his first critics: a new drama or not? – Racan's *Bergeries* and Théophile's
Pyrame et Thisbé – Jean Mairet and his early plays – theory of the unities in
the sixteenth century – the seventeenth-century debate – Schelandre's *Tyr
et Sidon* and Ogier's preface – Chapelain's *Lettre à Godeau* – Corneille's early
opinions – Mairet's progress towards regularity – his *Sophonisbe* – his subsequent career – stage settings and the unity of place

Between the early 1620s and the 1640s, the general trend of French
drama has been described, in broad terms, in this way: at first there was
a steep rise in the popularity of tragicomedy at the expense of tragedy,
followed by a conscious movement of restraint leading to the establishment of the new regular 'classical' tragedy as the dominant genre.
This is a simplification, no doubt useful to guide the student towards
the more enduring works in a mass of dramatic productions, but in-
exact in the detail and misleading in its implications if these are
interpreted rigorously. The initial decline of tragedy, though certain,
cannot be dated and documented with precision. The ensuing rise of
tragicomedy was a fact, but is not entirely clear in its origins. The eventual decline of tragicomedy, in its irregular and melodramatic form,
was a much slower process than is sometimes supposed, and in fact
was never completely definitive. Irregular drama persisted vigorously
in France, in coexistence with the new regular tragedy, to a much later
date than is commonly assumed. In the early part of the period the
influence of pastoral is also not to be discounted. These considerations
affect our evaluation not only of plays which are obviously irregular,
but also modify to a certain extent our judgement of plays which were
once claimed to be typically classical. It is therefore necessary to look
again at the evidence which survives from the period and so hope to
obtain a clearer view of the contemporary situation.

It will be recalled that publication of all Hardy's extant plays began in 1623 and ended in 1628. In considering this one author it does appear, on the grounds of dramatic method, that most of his tragedies represent an earlier phase and that from 1622 on (the probable date of his return to Paris) he was satisfying a general demand for melodramatic or romantic tragicomedy. This, however, rests on no proof and the only definite evidence, that of known publication, shows that in

TRAGEDY, TRAGICOMEDY AND PASTORAL, 1621–1648

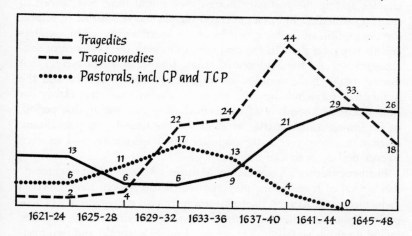

Totals of plays published in each four-yearly period from 1621 to 1648 with the exclusion of Hardy's plays

1621–7 inclusive, nineteen tragedies other than Hardy's were published as against three tragicomedies. Not until 1628 does the number of published tragicomedies begin to rise above that of tragedies – a position which is improved or maintained (with insignificant exceptions in two years) until the mid-1640s. A little earlier the number of published pastorals also begins to rise and from 1625 to 1634 is three times as high in aggregate as the number of published tragedies.

These statistics are not in themselves conclusive. A better indication of trends would be the records, with dates, of the actual performances of plays, but these are too incomplete or uncertain to serve as the basis of an analysis. A published play with a dated *privilège* is at least a reliable document, though one has to remember that numerous plays were never published and that the date of publication was almost invariably later than the first performance. As a working rule, with not too many exceptions, it can be taken to have occurred within a year of the performance.

A second uncertainty stems from classification. Not all 'tragedies', and still more not all 'tragicomedies', conformed to a type. There were also such hybrids as *tragicomédies pastorales* which are included in this chapter among the pastorals though they might have been added to the tragicomedies. But as a general principle it is reasonable to respect the description of a play given by the original author or his printers and to work on that. If, for example, following the evidence of self-classification and the evidence of publication dates, one observes that during 1628–31 the number of tragedies printed was two and the number of tragicomedies was nineteen (always excepting Hardy for both categories) one is justified in concluding that during that period, or beginning a little earlier to allow for the time-lag in publication, there was a steep rise in the popularity of tragicomedy and an even steeper decline in that of tragedy.

Further evidence is provided by Mahelot's *Mémoire*. This document[1] lists a total of seventy-one plays, of which forty-seven have survived to be identified. Among the forty-seven are two tragedies only (Théophile's *Pyrame* and Rotrou's *Hercule mourant*) and thirty tragicomedies, including three by Hardy. (There are also five *pastorales* and two *tragicomédies pastorales*. Eight comedies complete the total.) The value of this document as a means of dating the plays it lists is not, however, absolute. When editing it, H. C. Lancaster considered that it represented the repertory of the Hôtel de Bourgogne – that is, all the plays available to the company for performance, if required – in 1633–4.[2] The later specialist, Mme Deierkauf-Holsboer, disputes this, partly on the grounds that the *Mémoire* lists plays by Hardy which by 1633 would have disappeared from the repertory (though of this one cannot be sure). She concludes that Mahelot was listing plays performed at the Hôtel de Bourgogne between 1622 and 1635, but not *all* the plays and

---

[1] See p. 59 above.
[2] *Le Mémoire de Mahelot, Laurent, et autres décorateurs de l'Hôtel de Bourgogne et de la Comédie Française au XVIIe siècle* (Paris, 1920).

not in their chronological order.[1] Thus, the evidence of the *Mémoire* alone shows that tragicomedy had virtually replaced tragedy by 1634 or 1635 (though even these dates are approximate) but gives no definite indication of the date when the trend began. Was it from 1622, when Bellerose, with Hardy as his poet, was establishing his company in Paris; or was it near to 1628, when Hardy's star was apparently on the wane? On a long-term view, the difference of five or six years may seem to have slight importance, but it poses certain questions. Did the undoubted popularity of tragicomedy in the 1630s rise directly from and continue the example set by Hardy in the early 1620s? Did Hardy in his later years abandon tragedy, and indeed contribute to its decline? Or was there indeed a significant reaction against him and his type of play towards 1628 which led to the establishment of the regular and scenically restrained 'classical' tragedy which was to become the glory of the French stage and of the Comédie-Française technique in particular?

To these questions some answers must be attempted. Hardy's example seems to have been a more persistent force in the development of tragicomedy than is usually recognized. It is quite possible that he influenced the decline of tragedy in favour of the alternative genre, though the effect was not immediate, nor may it have been consciously intended. The reaction against him, which will be described below, was a partial one inspired by personal rivalries and bearing more on versification and language than on dramatic technique. It certainly did not change the course of French drama in the revolutionary way that has sometimes been suggested. This impression has been fostered by an excessive attention to critical pronouncements and other theoretical writings, but the practice of dramatists shows that much younger men than Hardy continued to write melodramatic and even violent tragicomedies for a long time to come.

II

The first sign of an embryonic new trend is to be found in the third volume of Hardy's *Théâtre*, published in 1626.[2] In the dedication (to Richelieu) he remarks that 'le style tragique un peu rude offense ordinairement ces délicats esprits de Cour, qui désirent voir une

---

[1] See *Le Théâtre de l'Hôtel de Bourgogne*, I, pp. 155 ff.
[2] The *privilège* is dated 28 May 1625, the *achevé d'imprimer*, 20 December 1625.

tragédie aussi polie qu'une ode, ou quelque élégie; mais aucune loi n'oblige à l'impossible . . .'[1]

The *Au lecteur* of the same volume shows that Hardy was beginning to come under fire on the grounds of purity of diction and correctness of versification, but his indignant defence is so turgidly expressed that it is difficult to be more specific than this. The most definite point is his grudgingly respectful mention of Malherbe, the influence behind the new prosody. But once again he protests that a style suitable for an ode or an elegy would be inapt for tragedy. When one remembers that he was writing lines to be spoken by actors to popular audiences, his reasoning is not without force.

Hardy's Volume IV, published later in the same year,[2] contains little polemical material beyond a general complaint in the Dedication that in the present age the best poets are the least sought after and 'il faut être aussi bon courtisan que mauvais poète pour faire fortune'. In the *Au lecteur* he points out that he has changed his printer, so eliminating a main source of the errors which disfigured his earlier plays and injured his reputation.[3] Two years later, however, he returns to the charge, in a tone which implies that he has been under new and heavier attack. In the Dedication to Volume V (*privilège* dated 24 July 1628) he calls on the Duc de Liancourt to pronounce between his own tragic muse – 'la plus grave des Muses vêtue à l'antique' – and 'le fantôme fabriqué par les rimeurs de ce siècle'. The *Au lecteur* contains his longest and most aggressive manifesto to that date. He begins with robust personal abuse against his detractors, some of whom he sees as affected court poets, 'qui sous ombre de quelques lieux communs pris et appris en Cour, se présument avoir la pierre philosophale de la poésie, et que quelques rimes plates entrelacées de pointes affinées dans

[1] It will be noticed that Hardy speaks of 'le style tragique' and of 'tragédie'. Elsewhere in the same dedication he offers Richelieu 'ce recueil de tragédies'. This particular volume, however, contains no 'tragedies', but is made up of tragi-comedies, mythological plays and a pastoral. This adds some support to our contention in the previous chapter that Hardy drew no rigorous distinction between the genres.
[2] The *privilège* is dated 26 June 1626.
[3] The change was from Jacques Quesnel of Paris, publisher of all the preceding volumes, to David Du Petit Val of Rouen. The subsequent and last volume, however, was published by François Targa of Paris.

l'alambic de leurs froides conceptions, feront autant de miracles que de vers en chaussant le coturne.'

This attack on *concettismo* is immediately followed by a gibe against certain 'excrements of the bar' who 's'imaginent de mauvais avocats devenir bons poètes en moins de temps que les champignons qui croissent.' Hardy then goes on, for the benefit of his inexperienced rivals, to define his conception of tragedy. The definition, though full of interest, is hardly what would be expected from this particular writer:

> ... je dirai que le sujet de tel poème [tragique], faisant comme l'âme de ce corps, doit fuir des extravagances fabuleuses, qui ne disent rien et détruisent plûtot qu'elles n'édifient les bonnes mœurs; que le vrai style tragique ne s'accorde nullent avec un langage trivial, avec ces délicatesses efféminées, qui pour châtouiller quelque oreille courtisane mécontenteront tous les experts du métier; que quiconque se soumet en tel ouvrage aux tyrannies de nos derniers censeurs déchet du privilège que la vénérable antiquité lui donne pour en venir à son honneur; que la disposition, ignorée de tous nos rimailleurs, règle l'ordre de ce superbe palais, qui n'est autrement qu'un labyrinthe de confusion, sans issue pour ces monstres d'auteurs; la grâce des interlocutions, l'insensible douceur des digressions, le naïf rapport des comparaisons, une égale bienséance observée et adaptée aux discours des personnages, un grave mélange de belles sentences qui tonnent en la bouche de l'acteur et résonnent jusqu'en l'âme du spectateur: voilà selon [*sic*] ce que mon faible jugement a reconnu depuis trente ans pour les secrets de l'art, interdits à ces petits avortons aveuglés de la trop bonne opinion de leur suffisance imaginaire.

At this point Hardy may have reflected that his own plays were not entirely free of 'extravagances fabuleuses', that they sometimes sinned against the austere nobility of 'le vrai style tragique', that their 'disposition' (organization or structure) was not invariably without confusion, that 'grâce' and 'douceur' did not invariably characterize his style, and that 'bienséance' was not always a feature of his characters and their dialogue.[1] He therefore abandons rational justification and employs the enormous weight of his experience and his relative success

---

[1] This early use of *bienséance* in a theatrical context has the sense of 'appropriateness' rather than 'propriety'.

to confound his critics: 'Et s'ils t'objectent que mes écrits franchissent souvent la borne de ces beaux préceptes, la vue, au pis aller, fera foi qu'entre six cents poèmes et plus de ce genre, aucun ne s'égare tant du bon chemin que le plus poli des leurs, pourvu qu'un arbitre capable et sans passion veuille prononcer là-dessus.'

III

Against whom or what was Hardy defending himself? Part of the answer is furnished by a pamphlet which he published late in the same year 1628, entitled *La Berne de deux rimeurs de l'Hôtel de Bourgogne*, in which he replies with crude and heavy invective to the young writers Auvray and Pierre du Ryer. These two had written letters to each other, unpublished but no doubt circulated in Paris, criticizing Hardy. Their date was probably October 1628, two or three months after the publication of Hardy's Volume V[1] and since both authors were lawyers it is a safe assumption that they were the 'excrements of the bar' referred to in that work. The controversy, already reflected there, was therefore not initiated by the critical letters. It could, in fact, be connected with Hardy's break with Bellerose and his switch from the company of the Hôtel de Bourgogne to a rival troupe, which had occurred in the autumn of 1626.[2] Bellerose's young authors would then be continuing an attack on Hardy which could well have begun as long as two years previously as part of a battle between rival theatrical companies, and in no fundamental sense on a point of dramatic doctrine. This accounts for all the facts we have so far reviewed except for the touchiness manifested by Hardy in the third and fourth volumes of his *Théâtre*, which were published *before* he parted from Bellerose. The assumption is that at that date (1625–6) he was already hearing criticisms of his old-fashioned language and verse-technique made by certain 'fastidious court wits' who followed Malherbe; in the subsequent years such criticisms were developed with a polemical intention by various theatre people who had a material interest in attacking his professional reputation. It would be hard, however, to maintain that his detractors were at that time aiming to establish a different type of play.

There were indeed few plays certainly or probably produced before

[1] The pamphlet and the letters were published by Émile Roy in the *Revue d'histoire littéraire*, XXII (1915). See also Lancaster, *History*, I, pp. 35–8.
[2] See above p. 61.

1629 which could be seen as serious challenges to Hardy. Of his two personal adversaries in the quarrel described above, Auvray made his début with a tragicomedy, *Madonte*, in 1628, and Du Ryer with *Arétaphile*, also a tragicomedy, in the same year. These had stories of violent love, blood and revenge, with a profusion of incident, and the main contrast with Hardy was that the style was more polished. That had also been true of two considerably earlier plays which came eventually to be seen as forerunners of a new cultured drama: Racan's *Bergeries*, a pastoral, and Théophile de Viau's *Amours tragiques de Pyrame et Thisbé*, a tragedy. (The probable dates of the first productions were respectively 1620 and 1622.) In its construction and its dramatic effects *Les Bergeries* did not differ radically from other pastorals of the period, including Hardy's own. But it avoided vulgarity and broad comedy and was visibly the work of a more cultivated man who was, moreover, an accomplished poet capable of writing harmonious verse within the limits of correctness laid down by Malherbe, his acknowledged master.[1]

As for Théophile, it is certain that he personally would never have attacked Hardy. He had died in September 1626, after the rigours of imprisonment and a long trial on the charge of atheism. Before that, he had contributed a eulogistic poem inserted in the first volume of Hardy's *Théâtre* – of which the *privilège* is dated 16 March 1624. In this poem he champions Hardy *against* Malherbe and his school, taking up what was precisely Hardy's own position as he defined it in his later volumes. There can be no comparison between the great tragic poet and these little men, Théophile asserts:

> . . . Jamais ta veine ne s'amuse
> A couler un sonnet mignard,
> Détestant la pointe, et le fard
> Qui rompt les forces à la Muse.
>
> Que c'est peu d'ouïr Cupidon
> En sonnet mollement s'ébattre,
> Aux prix de voir sur le théâtre
> Le désespoir de ta Didon.

[1] Racan, born in 1589, never wrote again for the theatre. From 1631 on he produced little except metrical versions of the Psalms, while leading the life of a country gentleman. Living until 1670, he could have seen several of Racine's earlier plays.

. . . Je marque entre les beaux esprits
Malherbe, Bertaut et Porchères,
Dont les louanges me sont chères,
Comme j'adore leurs écrits.

Mais à l'air de tes tragédies
On verrait failli leur poumon,
Et comme glaces du Strymon
Seraient leurs veines refroidies.

Tu parais sur ces arbrisseaux
Tel qu'un grand pin de Silésie,
Qu'un océan de poésie
Parmi ces murmurants ruisseaux . . .

Whatever qualities became discernible in Théophile's own tragedy
with the passage of time, it seems certain that *Pyrame et Thisbé* was not
deliberately composed to compete with Hardy, and, beyond that, it
was not immediately apparent that it followed a different dramatic
convention. It observes, no doubt deliberately, the unity of time, but
not strictly that of place. The dramatic construction is somewhat clumsy,
though there is a single main theme of dominant interest: the mutual
passion of the two young lovers and their determination to be united
in spite of all obstacles. Violent effects are limited to one sword-fight
on the stage in which Pyrame's would-be assassin is killed and to the
appearance of the lion which frightens Thisbé away.[1] This lion, incidentally, with the reminder of Shakespeare's burlesque of the story
in *A Midsummer Night's Dream*, makes it difficult for an English critic
to take the play as seriously as it really deserves. It has a similar theme
to *Romeo and Juliet* and ends in a similar double suicide. Pyrame believes
that his beloved has been devoured by the lion and kills himself.
Thisbé, returning, finds his dead body and stabs herself with his famous

[1] The text merely indicates that Thisbé thinks she hears and sees a lion, but there
can be no doubt that the beast appeared to the audience. Mahelot's *Mémoire* pre-
scribes 'a cave from which a lion comes out . . . and another cave at the other side
of the stage that he goes into'. In Mahelot's sketch of the scenery, the two caves
are shown on the right and left near the foreground. In Scarron's *Roman comique*
one finds: 'Each time I have seen *Pyrame et Thisbé* I have been less moved by the
death of Pyrame than terrified by the lion.'

blood-stained dagger.[1] Their two separate monologues fill the whole of the last act and open all the stops for the expression of pathetic emotion:

Mais que m'en sert ton dueil? Rameaux, prés verdissants,
Qu'à soulager mon mal vous êtes impuissants!
Quand bien vous en mourriez on voit la destinée
Ramener votre vie en ramenant l'année:
Une fois tous les ans nous vous voyons mourir,
Une fois tous les ans nous vous voyons fleurir.
Mais mon Pyrame est mort sans espoir qu'il retourne
De ces pâles manoirs où son esprit séjourne.

The tone is not very different from that of Garnier's *Bradamante*, and one can understand that it moved sentimental audiences to tears. What marred it on a longer view were the occasional conceits and the baroque excesses of some of the conceptions. Thus Pyrame, believing that the lion has devoured Thisbé, wishes that he could find some small uneaten piece of her:

Au moins si je trouvais d'un chef-d'œuvre si beau
Quelque sainte relique à mettre en un tombeau,
Je ferais dans mon sein une large ouverture,
Et sa chair dans la mienne aurait sa sépulture.
Toi, son vivant cercueil, reviens me dévorer,
Cruel lion, reviens, je te veux adorer.
S'il faut que ma déesse en ton sang se confonde,
Je te tiens pour l'autel le plus sacré du monde.

This is the very folly of love, if not something more psychologically peculiar, and in any case at least as extravagant as anything that Hardy wrote. Taking the play as a whole, however, it is true to say that most of the language is more chastened and more consistently harmonious than that of the old master. The versification is also more correct in the Malherbian sense, though not impeccable. Its affectations were more modern than those of Hardy, perhaps owing something to Marino. These qualities, added to the extreme pathos of the ending, endeared it to contemporaries and made it a lastingly popular and influential

[1] See above p. 77.

play. Nevertheless, it is hardly justified to see it in its immediately contemporary context as a definite break with Hardy.

This is attributed with stronger reason to Mairet, though here again there must be considerable reservations. Mairet was an aggressive young writer, attempting to push his way to the top in a manner not uncommon in the seventeenth-century theatre. For a long time, trusting to his own statement, historians of the drama believed him to be six years younger than his real age and to have composed his first play with brilliant precocity at the age of sixteen, and his second, which was a resounding success, at seventeen. In fact, his real birth date was 1604 and, coming to Paris from Besançon probably at the age of twenty-one, he wrote his first play then – an undistinguished tragicomedy, *Chryséide et Arimand*, and in the same year (1625) secured the patronage of the Duc de Montmorency. In the next year his *Sylvie*, a *tragicomédie pastorale*, was produced. It was acclaimed, and since it was, as the pastoral genre demanded, more polished and less violent than most of Hardy's work, and owed much to both Racan's *Bergeries* and Théophile's *Pyrame*, it became natural to consider it as the third notable production of a movement opposed to Hardy. This impression might be reinforced by the fact that Montmorency was also the protector of Théophile, who while in the Duke's household became a personal friend of Mairet. But the position is by no means so clear and simple. Any theory of rival cliques must meet the objection, not only of Théophile's admiration of Hardy which we have already mentioned, but of the fact that Montmorency was also a patron of Hardy, at least to the extent of allotting him a pension. A further objection rests on a question of dating. Hardy's Volume III, which contains his first vigorous defence of 'tragedy' against the 'mushroom rhymesters' of the day, and also a short, very ingenuous definition of the pastoral as he conceives it, appeared earlier than the earliest date that can be ascribed to Mairet's *Sylvie*. This play can hardly have been acted before 1626, and most probably in the autumn.[1] But the *achevé d'imprimer* of Hardy's Volume

[1] *Sylvie* was published in 1628. All modern authorities concur in dating its per-formance in 1626. Following Mme D.-Holsboer's interpretation of Mahelot's *Mémoire* (see *Le Théâtre de l'Hôtel de Bourgogne*, I, pp. 161-2) Bellerose's company performed sixteen plays in Paris during the years 1622-6. Thirteen were by Hardy and the others were *Pyrame*, *Chryséide* and *Sylvie*. The company were away from Paris during the last part of 1625 and much of 1626. They leased the Hôtel from 1 October 1626, and it must have been after that date that *Sylvie* was first per-

III is dated 20 December 1625, when Mairet was still almost unknown and hardly to be considered as a potential rival. Nor is it likely that at that stage in their relationship Mairet would be voicing criticisms of Hardy. One must therefore look elsewhere for the critics who had irritated Hardy, and one cannot name them. Their comments do not seem to have survived in print and perhaps they were only verbal. What can be said with certainty is that, before Auvray and Du Ryer did so in 1628, no French playwright is known to have criticized Hardy or challenged his position and his conception of drama.

How much do these personalities matter? They become important if they show a trend, or, in certain conditions, the absence of one, and it cannot be shown, in spite of a few isolated experiments and some pinpricks from literary purists, that there was any positive trend against Hardy before 1628. Even after that date, it was less a question of him directly than a controversy on new ground which arose. In this Mairet was certainly concerned.

IV

The unities of time, place and action had been prescribed or debated by theorists in the sixteenth century. Jean de La Taille, it will be recalled, had recommended all three.[1] André de Rivaudeau, in the preface to his play *Aman* (1566), came out strongly in favour of the unity of time – 'un jour ou un tour de soleil' – and even went on to suggest that the best tragedies were those in which the duration of the action represented was the same as the playing time. J.-C. Scaliger, a great classical scholar but, one can only assume, a man singularly lacking in imagination, also recommended the unity of time and appeared to associate it with the unity of place, both in the name of almost literal verisimilitude.[2]

---

formed. This was also the period of Hardy's split with Bellerose. This information reinforces the improbability of Mairet's having been among the early critics of Hardy. Before the autumn of 1626, he had one youthful play in a repertory which was almost the monopoly of Hardy, whose plays provided the company with their living. It is hard to imagine an aspiring author, however brash, disparaging an elder writer in such a position.

[1] See above p. 12.

[2] 'The matter itself is to be so conducted and disposed that it approximates as nearly as possible to truth . . . The battles and attacks before Thebes which are

Bound up with the unities, though of wider significance, was the general principle of *vraisemblance* which, together with *bienséance*, was to play so important a part in the theory and practice of seventeenth-century drama. In the sixteenth century neither had yet been named and discussion of them was at most implicit. The condemnation of violence on the stage formed part of the concept of *bienséance*. La Taille had really linked the two when he wrote: 'Aussi se garder de ne faire autre chose sur la scène qui ne s'y puisse *commodément et honnêtement* faire, comme de n'y faire exécuter des meurtres et autres morts, et non par feinte ou autrement, car chacun verra bien toujours [ce] que c'est.'

When this subject began to be debated again towards 1630, no open reference was made to the sixteenth-century critics, who were either forgotten or ignored. Instead, there was a direct appeal to the ancient Greeks and Latins, or to the modern Italians. There are four texts of particular interest at this stage.

In 1628 Jean de Schelandre published a new version of his play *Tyr et Sidon*. This had first appeared twenty years earlier as a 'tragédie' which attempted to conform to the old regular pattern, with choruses and long narrations of much of the action, though the plot was full of melodramatic incidents. In refurbishing it in 1628, Schelandre retitled it a 'tragicomédie', expanded it into two *journées* or parts for successive performances, showed on the stage most of the physical action which had previously been narrated, introduced comic and even indecent scenes, and gave the play a happy ending which it had lacked before. He made a slight concession to contemporary taste by reluctantly agreeing to polish his verse on the insistence of his friend, the young critic Colletet,[1] but the effect was minimal. All in all, the play in its new form was wilder and less organized than almost any of Hardy's and its appearance just then would certainly not suggest that the trend was against melodramatic tragicomedy. It is, however, the

completed in a couple of hours do not please me. Nor is it the sign of a careful poet so to manage things that one goes from Delphi to Athens or from Athens to Thebes in a moment of time . . . so that the actor has scarcely time to breathe . . .' From *Poetices libri septem* (1561), trans. H. W. Lawton, *Handbook of French Renaissance Dramatic Theory*, pp. 140–1.

[1] See also Lancaster, *History*, I, p. 314.

preface written for it by Schelandre's young friend François Ogier which defines the question with more precision.[1]

Ogier begins by attacking the unity of time, precisely on the grounds on which Scaliger and others had defended it: that of verisimilitude. Whereas the Scaliger school had found it unrealistic to suppose that the action of a play should last a much longer time – it might be months or years – than the time which the audience literally spent watching it, Ogier reasoned that it was unrealistic to crowd into a single day numerous happenings which must have taken longer. He instances and even criticizes certain Greek tragedies for this temporal overcrowding, adopting the general assumption that they literally obeyed the unity of time. It is clear, of course, that two different conceptions of what constitutes a play are opposed here. The play constructed upon a single theme, with faithful concentration on the emotional crisis to which it leads, easily obeys and may well require the unity of time. Much Greek drama falls into this category, as did the humanist tragedy of the sixteenth century, at least in intention. So, later, did the French 'classical' tragedy which the seventeenth century eventually evolved. Here, the unity of time has a merely mechanical importance as one of the factors in a general drive towards psychological concentration. The seventeenth-century theorists were no doubt mistaken in stressing a contributory element more strongly than the whole principle of dramatic construction which was really at issue, but it was on this ground that the debate became engaged. Also, the twenty-four hours rule provided critics with an easy practical test by which to fault plays which did not observe it for reasons which were more complex than appeared.

The kind of play which Ogier was defending was in no way concentrated or unified, but full of incidents which, as he remarked, could not have occurred in a single day. He considered this multiplicity of events a dramatic virtue, even of Greek and Roman drama. The ancient dramatists, he maintained,

prévoyant bien que la variété des événements est nécessaire pour rendre la représentation agréable, ils font échoir en un même jour quantité d'accidents et de rencontres qui, probablement, ne peuvent

[1] Ogier's Preface can be read in H. W. Lawton's *Handbook*.

être arrivés en si peu d'espace. Cela offense le judicieux spectateur, qui désire une distance, ou vraie ou imaginaire, entre ces actions-là . . .

Ogier's conviction that the 'variety of the events' was what constituted a play's attraction was allied in his mind with another conviction that the events should be represented and not simply narrated and led him to condemn the longwinded choruses and messenger speeches of Greek drama. He then went on to champion tragicomedy, which he saw as a mixture of the grave and the comic, on the grounds of realism. In real life there is a mingling of joy and sadness, high seriousness and triviality. Why should this not be so on the stage? It remains, he continues 'de faire parler chaque personnage selon le sujet et la bienséance' – by which last word he means neither decency nor consistency of character, but the fitting of language to the particular situation.

Ogier's plea for freedom and for external truth to life can be variously interpreted. Either he was advocating a 'new' theatre – though one which would in effect be a continuation of Hardy – or he was defending the 'old' theatre, again as represented by Hardy and by his own author, Schelandre. Was his manifesto conceived in an offensive or a defensive spirit?

In his final paragraph he protests against 'nos censeurs modernes' who are likely to skim over all the finest features of our tragicomedy, 'et laisseront en arrière tant d'excellents discours, de riches descriptions et autres rares inventions toutes nouvelles qui s'y rencontrent, pour s'arrêter à quelques vers un peu rudes et à trois ou quatre termes qui ne seront pas de leur goût.'

This is the familiar protest against the always unnamed critics of bold or colloquial language and irregular prosody of whom Hardy complained. Bearing upon the idiom suitable for poetic drama, it is separate, at least at this stage, from the larger question of dramatic construction and technique.

On the smaller point of idiom Ogier appears to write defensively, as he also wrote defensively about the unity of time, before passing vigorously to the attack. Both, however, are handled as points which are open to argument, and it is difficult to read the Preface as a whole as the vindication of a cause which Ogier felt to be in decline. The practice of most dramatists for some time after would also suggest that any such feeling would have been premature.

Two years after Ogier's Preface came the century's first known explicit defence of the unity of time by a French critic. In his *Lettre à Godeau sur la règle des vingt-quatre heures* (1630) Chapelain[1] recommended it in the name of *vraisemblance*. Taking as his authority the ancient Greeks, he assumed that the ruling principle of their poetry was *imitation*, which he interpreted as the art of persuading the spectator that the spectacle he was watching was a reality. In order to 'profit' from it by being 'purged of his disordered passions' (a misinterpretation of Aristotle), he must be led to be 'présent à l'action du théâtre comme à une véritable action' and the twenty-four hours rule, he considers, was observed as a means to this end. Otherwise the spectators would reflect that the action they were watching could not have taken place in the time that they spent in the theatre and the illusion of reality would be broken. This was basically the same argument that Scaliger had used, though presented more persuasively and with a greater show of reason. Recognizing that even twenty-four hours were too long for a literal coincidence between fictional time and playing time, Chapelain concluded that the missing hours should be supposed to have elapsed between the acts, 'où le théâtre se rend vide d'acteurs et où l'auditoire est entretenu de musique ou d'intermèdes'.[2]

Chapelain's letter, which was no doubt circulated but was not published until later, is symptomatic of a debate which had certainly been engaged by 1630. Further light is thrown on it by Corneille's preface to his tragicomedy *Clitandre*, published in 1632. In introducing

---

[1] Jean Chapelain (1595–1674) was a rationalist critic of considerable influence in the development of French seventeenth-century classicism. Historically, he provided a link between Malherbe and Boileau, although the latter derided him. An original member of the Académie Française, he was responsible for drawing up that body's *Sentiments* criticizing *Le Cid*. He was consulted in matters of patronage by both Richelieu and Colbert and recommended official rewards for Racine's early efforts. His own principal poetic work, the epic poem *La Pucelle*, was a disastrous failure.

[2] This concession, which came to be generally adopted, in fact destroys the whole case. If the audience can accept the passage of a few hours of fictional time during a short interval, it can equally well accept the passage of days, weeks or months.

this, his second play, probably first acted early in 1631, Corneille observed:

> Que si j'ai renfermé cette pièce dans la règle d'un jour, ce n'est pas que je me repente de n'y avoir point mis *Mélite* [his first play, a comedy], ou que je me sois résolu à m'y attacher dorénavant. Aujourd'hui quelques-uns adorent cette règle, beaucoup la méprisent: pour moi, j'ai voulu seulement montrer que si je m'en éloigne, ce n'est pas faute de la connaître.

In the same preface Corneille contrasts the Greeks and Latins with the 'moderns', and sides, though in moderate terms, with the latter: 'Je leur porte [aux anciens] du respect comme à des gens qui nous ont frayé le chemin et, qui après avoir défriché un pays fort rude, nous ont laissé à le cultiver.' He condemns the messenger speech and the 'long and boring' narration in favour of represented action, and calls the latter technique 'cette nouveauté'. Some of his arguments closely echo Ogier's, perhaps consciously, and he includes the familiar point which Ogier had made also, after Théophile and Hardy, that a play is not truly comparable to 'a sonnet or an ode'. His deduction, however, is different. Whereas his predecessors had argued that a short poem could well be more polished, in short more 'literary', than a play, Corneille maintained that a 'modern' play was a result of skill and planning, constructed according to its own rules – and not something tossed off in the heat of inspiration, as the short poem might be. This was a turning of the tables, and perhaps a deliberately perverse one, but like the rest of the Preface it shows an energy of conviction in the twenty-six-year-old dramatist and certainly does not suggest that the case for 'irregularity' advanced by Ogier was regarded as anything but a live issue at this date.

V

On the other side was Mairet. His successful *Sylvie* of 1626 was followed by another *tragicomédie pastorale*, *Silvanire*. The former play had observed none of the unities. The latter, derived from a formless dramatic pastoral in largely unrhymed verse by Honoré d'Urfé (*Sylvanire*, 1625), aimed at observing them all and was a relative failure. Publishing the play with a preface in 1631, Mairet recalled that some two years previously he had been encouraged by two aristocratic patrons (the Cardinal de La Valette and the Comte de Cramail) to compose a pastoral on the much-admired Italian model. Having examined the works of the great Italians, Tasso, Guarini and 'Guidobaldi' (Guidobaldo Bonarelli), he concluded that their secret was none other than that they had modelled themselves on the ancient Greeks and Latins, 'whose rules they observed more scrupulously than we have done so far'. He therefore recommends the observance of all the three unities, liberally conceived, and particularly of the rule of twenty-four hours. This part of Mairet's manifesto may be seen as a direct reply to Ogier, just as Corneille's preface to *Clitandre* appears to have been a reply to Mairet.

Mairet's observations (which included references to Aristotle and Aelius Donatus, but none to the sixteenth-century commentators) were symptomatic rather than original. They were, incidentally, evidence of an interest now being taken in the drama by certain cultivated aristocrats, but in themselves they were of no great importance. They have acquired this in the light of Mairet's subsequent activities. His next play, *Les Galanteries du Duc d'Ossone* (1632), was a comedy with a somewhat licentious love-plot. It violated *bienséance* in several particulars, notably in a bedroom scene. It respected none of the unities.[1] This was followed by a tragicomedy, *Virginie* (1633), in which Mairet endeavoured to observe the rules which he had so far recommended only for the pastoral. The plot, however, is that of a romantic melodrama which fits uneasily into the twenty-four-hour framework which Mairet provided. However, he persisted by substituting narration of the numerous incidents for physical action, although there is one represented episode in which two swordsmen run each other through. If Mairet may be regarded as a consistent experimenter rather than as a literary opportunist, *Virginie* can be seen as a logical step on the way to his principal achievement.

This was *Sophonisbe* (1634) which was both 'regular' and a tragedy – in which consisted its comparative novelty. The story, whose main original source was in Livy, had been dramatized in Italian by Trissino (1524) and later by several Frenchmen including Montchrestien (1596 and 1601) and Montreux (1601). Others, including Corneille and Voltaire, were to take it up after Mairet. While no doubt owing

[1] The unity of place at this date is discussed below on pp. 111–16. The scene of this play was a street above which were three rooms, two of them bedrooms.

something to his predecessors in drama, Mairet reconstructed the story with a view to both *bienséance* and regularity. His play opens with a confrontation between Sophonisbe, Queen of Numidia, and her elderly husband Syphax, the King. Their city of Cirta is threatened by Massinissa, another Numidian who is allied to the Romans, and at this critical moment Syphax has intercepted a letter from his wife declaring her love for Massinissa. There is a plausible motive for this in the fact that earlier in life Sophonisbe had been betrothed to Massinissa, but had been forced to marry Syphax instead.

In Act II Syphax has hurried off to repel an attack on the city. Sophonisbe, remaining in the palace (on stage), deplores the irresistible passion which causes her to burn with 'feux illégitimes' for her husband's enemy. Attendants report the progress of the battle to her and finally a messenger announces the fall of the city and the death of Syphax.

In Act III Massinissa appears outside the palace. He prepares to take it with the minimum of bloodshed, in order to secure the Queen before she can escape. Inside, Sophonisbe, having accepted the advice of her attendants to try to win over Massinissa by her beauty before adopting the ultimate recourse of suicide, awaits and meets her conqueror. He is indeed won over, in a scene of mutual compliments and flattery, and proposes immediate marriage, to which she consents. The pact is sealed with a kiss, the only theatrical 'impropriety' – according to later standards, but not those of the time – which the play contains.

Act IV opens the next morning, after the wedding-night. The two are blissfully happy and Sophonisbe reveals her youthful passion for Massinissa, of which he had been unaware. Immediately after, news is brought that the Roman military leaders have arrived, which bodes ill for the future of the pair. Scipio insists that Massinissa should deliver up Sophonisbe, the enemy of Rome. Massinissa refuses and begs Scipio's lieutenant Lelius to intercede for him with his chief.

Act V brings Scipio's definitive refusal. The only concession he can make, since the Senate's formal order to him is to have Sophonisbe sent to Rome, is to give the Queen an opportunity of killing herself and so escape the humiliation of being led in triumph. Faithful to a promise made earlier and prompted by a letter which is brought to him from Sophonisbe, Massinissa sends her his 'present' by the same bearer. It is a cup of poison, which Sophonisbe drinks. In the closing scene Massinissa stabs himself over her body, on stage.

All this action is represented in a framework of mechanical regularity. The scene is some rooms in the royal palace and an open space just outside in which Massinissa appears with some Roman soldiers at the beginning of Act III. Sophonisbe does not budge from the palace, but sends her attendants to watch the battle for her from the city walls offstage in Act II. The duration, which Mairet is careful to mark, begins at some hour on Day One and could end by the same hour on Day Two. During that time Syphax has discovered his wife's treachery, the fateful battle has been fought, Massinissa has married Sophonisbe, and the Romans have arrived and enforced their decision. But this does not appear incredible. In the matter of the wedding, Mairet promotes both *vraisemblance* and *bienséance* by causing Sophonisbe's first husband Syphax to be killed in the battle, whereas in the original story he was a prisoner and still alive. He also supplies a more civilized explanation of Massinissa's impetuousness than that of his hot Numidian blood mentioned by Livy: he knows that the Roman leaders are near and hopes that, by presenting Sophonisbe as his wife, he will be in a stronger position to protect her. Finally, the spirit of both tragedy and romance are satisfied by his suicide on her body. In all the previous versions Massinissa had gone on living, as he also did in Corneille's later *Sophonisbe*.

The interest of the play is faithfully concentrated around a beautiful and passionate heroine complemented by a lover of considerable moral stature. Massinissa understands that his political and military future lies in continued friendship with all-powerful Rome and he surrenders to the stronger force of love in full awareness of the consequences. His attitude and his decisions are as much stoic as romantic, corresponding to the unyielding severity of the Romans in the play. There is some stoicism too in Sophonisbe's decision to die rather than surrender. There is both pride and defiance in the speech she makes before taking the poison and, when this is compared with the self-pitying speeches of Cléopâtre in Garnier's *Marc-Antoine*, it is apparent that a new element has entered French tragedy thanks to a development in moral characterization.

Nevertheless, the stoic and resistant qualities of the two chief characters are still subservient to the theme of the tormented woman which, with its opportunities for pathos and sadism, was perhaps the main resource of French tragedy over so many decades. The victim may protest and struggle, but in the end she is destroyed. The general impact of the play may still be called romantic – an effect strongly reinforced by the melodious qualities of the verse and the long aria-type mono-logues which Mairet wrote with skill. His principal achievement, or at least that of which he boasted,[1] was to have moved his audiences to tears of sympathy with the lovers, and this with an economy of means which rightly caused his play to be considered a model in the future.

VI

While *Sophonisbe* was certainly a landmark, it was hardly, at its date, a turning-point. Though the number of tragedies grew markedly in the five years following after its performance, there was an even steeper rise in the number of tragicomedies, and in neither category was observance of the unities yet established as a general rule. In tragedy it was in the process of becoming accepted, though successful authors, such as Benserade and Scudéry, felt able to ignore it in some of their plays. In tragicomedy, it was very far from absolute. It was disregarded in at least half of the numerous tragicomedies produced between 1635 and 1640. Many of these showed violent or spectacular action on the stage and still based their appeal on the 'variety of events' recommended by Ogier.

Mairet himself wrote two more tragedies closely after the successful *Sophonisbe*. His *Marc-Antoine* or *Cléopâtre* (1635) dramatized a story which had evident resemblances with that of his first tragedy and observed the unities. His *Solyman*, probably not acted until late 1637 but composed earlier, was a romantic Turkish melodrama based on the Italian original of Prospero Bonarelli. The story was that of the sixteenth-century prince Mustapha, executed by his father together with the princess whom he loved as a result of the intrigues of his stepmother Roxane and the Grand Vizier. It could have pointed the way to Racine's *Bajazet*. In spite of the rich plot, the unities were technically respected in it.

After this Mairet abandoned tragedy altogether in favour of romantic

---

[1] '. . . cette tragédie, qui se peut vanter d'avoir tiré des soupirs des plus grands cœurs et des larmes des plus beaux yeux de France . . .' (*Sophonisbe*, Dedication to the Chancelier Séguier.)

and sometimes irregular tragicomedies, of which he wrote four: *L'Illustre Corsaire* (produced 1637), a story, probably taken from a novel, concerning the adventures of a prince turned pirate and his recovery of his long-lost love; *Roland furieux* (1637–8), taken from Ariosto and depicting the hero driven mad by love in a pastoral setting; *Athenaïs* (1638), the story, drawn from Caussin's *La Cour sainte*, of a beautiful pagan girl who is converted to Christianity and marries the Emperor Theodosius II of Byzantium at the instance of his sister Pulcheria; *Sidonie* (1640), a fantastic tale, based on a novel, of oracles, omens and dreams, set in a fictional Armenia.

The second and fourth of these plays violated the unity of time. The first two contained comic elements and popular language. The last two turned on melodramatic tricks or surprises. All were noticeably lacking in the 'classical' purity of structure and tone aimed at in *Sophonisbe*. When allowance is made for an updating of the language, they were, in fact, in the tradition of Hardy, little more respectful of either *vraisemblance* or *bienséance*, and based on the same kind of sources that he used.

Mairet's abandonment of 'pure' tragedy soon after his highly success-ful venture in it has been attributed to his envy of Corneille, with whom he realized he could not compete in 'classical' drama after the triumph of *Le Cid* (January 1637). This view is untenable. Though Mairet showed himself bitterly jealous of Corneille in the Quarrel of *Le Cid*, it was not because he felt that his own formula had been taken over by a better dramatist than himself. Such explanations may fit a broad theory of dramatic development but they hardly accord with the facts. *Le Cid* was presented when new as a tragicomedy and acclaimed as such by the public, who loved it for its romantic features. It observed the unities with considerable difficulty, as will be seen later. Corneille did not write classically regular tragedy until 1640, when his *Horace* was produced in the same year as Mairet's final play. Mairet's change of direction appears rather to provide further evidence of the continued vitality of melodramatic tragicomedy between 1637 and 1640. His constant ambition was to write a successful play, and he can be assumed to have been sufficiently responsive to current trends to believe that his best chance of doing this was in tragicomedy. Mairet, of all people, would have been capable of following up *Sophonisbe* with other 'pure' tragedies had he judged it opportune.

Sidonie was this careerist's farewell to the theatre. Thanks to highly placed patrons he now turned to a career of diplomacy on behalf of his native province of Franche-Comté, at that date a Spanish possession. He represented it in Paris for several years, then retired to Besançon, where he died as an honoured citizen in 1686, having survived Corneille and outlived the production of all Racine's plays with the exception of *Esther* and *Athalie*.

VII

The theoretical debate of the 1630s had turned largely on the unity of time. The unity of place was secondary and was mentioned, for example, in the remarks of the Académie on *Le Cid*.[1] The question calls for some description of theatrical practice.

Since the beginning of the century it can be assumed, and from 1622 it can be affirmed with certainty, on the evidence of Mahelot's *Mémoire*, that the stage of the Hôtel de Bourgogne showed a multiple décor which was a modification of that usual in the Mysteries, necessitated by the space restrictions of an indoor theatre and influenced also by Italian ideas of scenic design. A typical set comprised a backcloth representing some such scene as a sea, a city, a palace or a temple, with compartments on each side of the stage representing other places. The number of these compartments varied. Most commonly there were two on each side, giving, with the back-centre space which could also be utilized, five localities simultaneously visible to the audience. The minimum would be three. Each play had different scenery, always disposed on these principles, but, once set, it did not change basically in the course of the performance. Until some date in the 1640s[2] there was no front curtain to conceal scene-changing,

[1] 'Quant au théâtre [i.e. the stage-setting], il n'y a personne à qui il ne soit évident qu'il est mal entendu dans ce poème, et qu'une même scène y représente plusieurs lieux. Il est vrai que c'est un défaut que l'on trouve en la plupart de nos poèmes dramatiques et auquel il semble que la négligence des poètes ait accoutumé les spectateurs. Mais l'auteur de celui-ci, s'étant mis si à l'étroit pour y faire rencontrer l'unité du jour, devait bien aussi s'efforcer d'y faire rencontrer celle du lieu, qui est bien autant nécessaire que l'autre, et faute d'être observée avec soin, produit dans l'esprit des spectateurs autant ou plus de confusion et d'obscurité.' From *Les Sentiments de l'Académie Française sur la tragicomédie du Cid* (*Œuvres de Corneille*, ed. Marty-Laveaux, Vol. XII).

[2] The date is still debated. In any case the front curtain, when introduced, seems to have been used only at the beginning and the end of a play, and not to facilitate changes between acts.

though one or more of the side compartments were sometimes covered with a curtain or painted cloth, which could be removed to provide what in effect was a partial scene-change. In the last act of Mairet's *Sophonisbe* a curtain or 'tapestry' is raised to reveal the dead body of the heroine, over which Massinissa stabs himself after a speech of lamentations. This and much other evidence proves that the side compartments were often practicable (bearing a functional resemblance to the Elizabethan inner stage), so that actors could appear in them and play their parts in the place literally represented. Much more frequently, however, they simply used them (by entering from behind them or standing near them for a moment) as an indication of the fictional spot where they were supposed to be, and then conducted the action on the central part of the stage, which was open and spacious.

All Hardy's plays were evidently written for this type of setting, which continued in general use throughout the 1630s and in some cases considerably longer, particularly for tragicomedies. When, therefore, the theorists and, a little later, some of the dramatists, began to demand unity of place, they were moving against the practice of the theatre as it then existed. All but the most rigorous of them were at first satisfied if the stage represented several places in the same city or rooms in the same palace with an open space outside, but they did not accept wide distances between the localities shown. Gradually, however, even this came to appear too lax, and a literal unity of place was simulated in the 'classical' theatre of the second half of the century. The famous *palais à volonté*, the pillared hall in which all the proceedings of the drama took place, was created and served as the setting of the majority of Racine's tragedies. Prescribed originally in the name of *vraisemblance* in the same way as the unity of time, this scenic convention may be thought to violate plausibility as strongly as the temporal convention. Different characters who, realistically, would not have appeared and discussed their affairs on the same spot, nevertheless are made to do so. But there are signs that the single setting, once it had imposed itself, was regarded as notional rather than as realistic. Audiences accepted it as an acting-space without inquiring critically how or why the characters happened to have come there.

No definite date can be given for the substitution of a *décor unique* to the modified *décor simultané* of Mahelot's time. It was gradual and not consistent for all plays. The second seems always to have been available for comedies. It is even found as late as 1678 in a tragedy, Thomas Corneille's *Le Comte d'Essex*, which requires two places, a palace and a prison.[1] This, however, must have been exceptional, for it was in tragedy that the trend towards scenic concentration was strongest. The *lieu unique* in the strict sense is found for the first time in 1640 in d'Aubignac's *Zénobie* and Pierre Corneille's *Horace*,[2] but other writers did not immediately adopt the convention. Corneille himself required two different rooms for the action of his next tragedy, *Cinna* (1640–1).

When, therefore, in 1638, the Académie faulted *Le Cid*, a tragicomedy, for disregarding the unity of place, it was being hypercritical.[3] At that date no plays had yet been represented in a *lieu unique*, whatever the desideratum. Most probably, what had shocked the compiler of the Académie's *Sentiments*, though he put it in other terms, was the confusion produced in a spectator's mind by the multiplicity of places required by the action. The original *décor* had comprised four or five different compartments.[4] To a literal mind, expecting a realistic representation, it is not surprising that there was some doubt as to exactly where the characters were supposed to be in various scenes. The ensuing simplification of stage-settings may well have stemmed as much from the desire of dramatists and managers to make their performances more comprehensible and attractive to their audiences as from a doctrinaire compliance with critical theory.

The ultimate development can be seen in the notes of the scene-designer Michel Laurent, a successor of Mahelot's at the Hôtel de

---

[1] See Scherer, *Dramaturgie classique*, p. 186.

   Ibid., p. 189.

[3] See footnote on p. 122.

[4] See D.-Holsboer, *Histoire de la mise en scène*, p. 55: '. . . la scène représente à l'arrière-plan le palais royal, la salle du trône et le cabinet du roi; sur l'un des côtés de la scène la chambre de l'Infante, sur l'autre côté la maison du comte et de sa fille; devant le palais et entre ces deux derniers compartiments se trouve une rue.' It is not absolutely clear whether the first three places mentioned formed three separate compartments, or whether the 'palace' was a central backcloth visually linking the throne-room and the king's private cabinet. A contemporary wrote: 'Tantôt la scène est le Palais, tantôt la place publique, tantôt la chambre de Chimène, tantôt l'appartement de l'Infante, tantôt du roi, et tout cela si confus etc. . . .' *Jugement du Cid, par un bourgeois de Paris*, quoted Scherer, *Dramaturgie classique*, p. 187.

Bourgogne, outlining the requirements for a production of *Le Cid* in the late 1670s. The stage now simply represents a room, a virtually unlocalized acting-space, with four doors leading into it to indicate from where the actors have come.[1] The problem had by then been solved with 'classic' simplicity, at the expense of any visual attraction which scenery might provide.

To sum up: unity of place meant nothing to Hardy and there was no provision for its observance on the stage of his time. In the 1630s it was usually satisfied by the indication of several localities within easy walking-distance of each other. After 1640 it was interpreted more strictly as applying to a single fixed spot, and this interpretation gained in force until, in tragedy, it became virtually absolute. Concurrently, spectacle and machinery became divorced altogether from the 'regular' play and followed a separate development in the elaborate *pièces à machines* and eventually in opera.

It may be added that, while most of the evidence on which the last few pages are based is drawn from the stage practice of the Hôtel de Bourgogne, that of the Marais, where Corneille's plays (until *Héraclius*) were originally produced, seems to have been similar. After 1647, the Marais turned to the machine-play, as observed in an earlier chapter, and henceforth was of minor importance in the production of tragedy.

[1] See Lawrenson, *The French Stage*, p. 108.

6

PIERRE CORNEILLE:
THE FIRST PERIOD, 1629–1651

Corneille's background and character – his early comedies – *Clitandre* –
Médée – *L'Illusion comique* – *Le Cid* – ethos of *Le Cid* – Guillén de Castro's
Mocedades – the Quarrel of *Le Cid* – the first Roman tragedies from *Horace*
to *Pompée* – general characteristics and dating – plays from *Rodogune* to
Pertharite – general features – melodramatic tendencies – plot complication
– love and chivalry – the plays individually and their fortune: *Rodogune* –
Théodore – *Héraclius* – *Andromède* – *D. Sanche d'Aragon* – *Nicomède* –
Pertharite – Corneille's first retirement – summaries of plays to 1651

Pierre Corneille was born at Rouen on 6 June 1606 of a middle-
class Norman family. His father was *maître des eaux et forêts* for the
district, a supervisory post requiring legal knowledge and training.
After an education by the Jesuits, the son also studied law, qualified
as an advocate at the Rouen bar, but soon acquired two official posts
in the Rivers and Forests and the local Court of Admiralty, concerned
with the navigation of the Seine. He retained both posts for over twenty
years, conscientiously discharging his functions, which were principally
those of a magistrate, at the same time as his other activities. Throughout a long life as a writer, official and devoted family man, he remained
attached to the provincial bourgeoisie – shrewd, canny and prudently
conscious of money values – from which he sprang.

Contemporaries represented him as a socially clumsy figure, whose
conversation was incoherent and boring though he wrote divinely.
This cannot have been the whole truth, since he frequented literary
circles in Paris, joined fully in their polemics and intrigues, and
succeeded in cultivating the personal interest of various noble patrons.
Whatever the gaucheness of his personality, he knew how to use social
contacts in the furtherance of his literary career. Nevertheless he was a
solid rather than an exciting figure, whose character throws little light
on his work – or if it does, the connection has not yet been convincingly

established. That this member of the provincial *noblesse de robe* should have written plays filled with an idealistic ethos which have been interpreted as a typical expression of the aristocratic outlook is perhaps not as surprising as it appears, since a writer can project himself into attitudes quite foreign to his own lived experience. But it means that in this case the biography is of minor importance in a consideration of the work.

He began his dramatic career with a comedy, *Mélite*, written at Rouen and probably entrusted to Montdory when his troupe was performing in that town. Montdory took it to Paris and produced it there in December 1629, following it with four other comedies by Corneille in the next four years or so.

All these were comedies of love intrigue, full of misunderstandings, deceptions, threatened duels (but no actual duel on the stage) and switches of lovers. The endings were happy for most of the characters, though not for all. They stand near the beginning of French true comedy, as distinct from farce, and make of Corneille, together with Rotrou, one of its founding fathers. With their amorous complications and their analyses of sentiment they have a kinship with pastoral, without its spectacular and magic elements, and also with the kind of tragi-comedy exemplified by Hardy's *Dorise*. They are hardly comedies of manners (though Lancaster so classes them), beyond what is necessarily implied in their presentation of contemporary characters with the *mores* and reactions of the period. Realistic localization is developed in only one comedy, in the scenes in *La Galerie du palais* which show the merchants' booths and reproduce the backchat of the stall-keepers (I. iv–vii and IV. xii–xiv). It is true that the décor of *La Place Royale* also represented a well-known Parisian square, but as far as the dialogue and characterization are concerned any square with houses, on the conventional stage pattern, would have served just as well.

The comedies contain little physical realism or literally exact observation of contemporary life such as Molière was to excel in later, and on this ground they may be said to foreshadow the 'universality' of Corneille's tragedies. At least it is an indication. Certain characters, situations, dialogues and soliloquies also have their parallels in the tragedies. In Corneille's first play, *Mélite* faints on hearing a false report of the death of the man she loves, as did Rodrigue's Chimène (this is not in the Spanish original of *Le Cid*). In more than one comedy there are *stances* and stichomythia, again as in *Le Cid*. There is also, in *Mélite*, an interesting throwback to sixteenth-century tragedy, in which a character goes mad and imagines himself surrounded by the Furies and the deities of the classical underworld, though here this can be taken as burlesque.[1] The unities, disregarded or imperfectly observed in the first three comedies, are respected in the last two, *La Suivante* and *La Place Royale*.

In short, though these early comedies represent a different side of Corneille's talent and belong to a separate genre, it is at least possible to discern in them the hand of the same dramatist who wrote the later tragedies. The main general link is in the romantic interest and intrigue.

Of more immediate relevance in this account of tragic drama is *Clitandre*, produced immediately after *Mélite* (probably early in 1631) and Corneille's earliest experiment in non-comedy. At first styled a tragedy, it was described more appropriately in later editions as a tragicomedy. Except for one feature – respect for the unity of time, which is imposed incongruously upon the plot – it belongs typically to the class of violent romantic melodrama which Ogier had defended some three years before and which, at the date of production, still seemed to have a glittering future on the French stage. Looking back on it in his *Examen* from the viewpoint of 1660 with the humorous self-deprecation which is one of his most endearing qualities, Corneille observed that, after having been made aware of the irregularity of his first play, 'I undertook to write a regular play (that is, one observing the twenty-four-hour rule), full of incidents and in a loftier style, but quite worthless; in which I was completely successful.' He goes on to make all the points which need making against the feeble and chaotic structure of *Clitandre*. One does not know who the principal characters are or with whom to sympathize. The interest switches from one couple to another. The only quality which Corneille will concede to his early effort is that of the verse, powerful in places though mingled with *pointes*, although 'at the time this was not such a great defect'.

All this is justified. The verse-style does give promise of a great dramatic poet, indulging at times in the contemporary extravagance of the baroque conceit. The confusion of the plot is such that the prin-

---

[1] There is a somewhat similar throwback, seriously intended, in Corneille's first true tragedy, *Médée*. See Act I, Sc. iv, the passage beginning: 'Et vous, troupe avante en noires barbaries / Filles de l'Achéron, pestes, larves, furies . . .'

cipal impression is of various characters of both sexes, often in disguise, roving about a forest (nominally in Scotland) with murderous or lecherous intent. Misunderstandings predominate. There are killings and dead bodies on stage, and a notable example of horror is the scene in which a female character in male dress stabs out the eye of her pursuer with a pin so that he staggers about, still on stage, with blood gushing from the eye-socket.

The greatest potential interest is in the nominal hero, Clitandre, the favourite (this may be taken in a homosexual sense) of the Prince of Scotland and also in love with a female character. He is a self-pitying and introspective person who spends part of the play in prison labouring under a false accusation. The contrast with the typical Cornelian hero of later years need hardly be underlined. But before claiming that Corneille was capable of creating at least some elements of a character of the Hamlet or the Segismundo type, one must observe that Clitandre's role is almost entirely passive and that the play is not constructed to revolve round his fate or his character in any significant sense. He can hardly be called more than an accidental creation too faintly realized to leave a mark in the Cornelian psychology.

Some four years later, after writing four more comedies, Corneille produced a very different example of tragic drama. *Médée* (1635) was based on one of the grimmest stories of the ancient world, the subject of tragedies by Euripides and Seneca, and taken up again by the sixteenth-century humanists. There were several academic examples either in the original languages or in translation,[1] culminating in La Péruse's French adaptation of *c*. 1553, already mentioned in this book. The actor Talmy listed an unidentified *Médée* in his repertory in 1594 and this is easily the latest reference before Corneille to any play of that name, which is not known to have interested any French dramatist of the early seventeenth century. There is no good reason to doubt Corneille's own statement that he took his subject direct from Euripides and Seneca – and predominantly from the latter. Why he chose it is uncertain and one can do no better than accept the external explanation put forward by L. Riddle[2] and H. C. Lancaster: that it was to provide Montdory's troupe with a riposte to Rotrou's Senecan *Hercule mourant* produced shortly before by the rival company of the Hôtel de

[1] See Lebègue, *La Tragédie française de la Renaissance*, pp. 16–18.
[2] *The Genesis and Sources of P. Corneille's Tragedies . . .* (Baltimore, 1926).

Bourgogne. Both plays contain long scenes of suffering, in which the victims are shown in agony after putting on or handling a poisoned garment which eats into their flesh,[1] and this alone, together with the Senecan source and influence, exceptional at that date, seems to indicate more than a coincidence.

Médée obeys the unities of time and place (with the modified multiple décor) and has a strong if imperfect unity of interest. But it is far from observing the conventions of the infant regular tragedy. *Médée* is an enchantress. Apart from the on-stage scenes of suffering which her spells can cause, she wields a magic wand to free her friends from prison and immobilize her adversaries. She possesses a magic ring which makes its bearer invisible, and she makes her final escape, after killing her own children, 'en l'air dans un char tiré par deux dragons'. These are the effects of the machine-play developing the tradition of pastoral. Psychologically, the character of Médée herself can of course be interpreted as a foreshadowing of the heroic egoists who incorporate the Cornelian *moi* in the mature tragedies. She defies Fortune, the capricious tyrant-goddess of sixteenth-century tragedy. She feels the necessity of performing a willed act in order to realize her true nature (it is an act of vengeance):

> C'est demain que mon art fait triompher ma haine;
> *Demain je suis Médée*, et je tire raison
> De mon bannissement et de votre prison.   (IV. v)

In reply to her confidante she utters an almost too famous line, which, however, it is important to read in context:

> NÉRINE   Forcez l'aveuglement dont vous êtes séduite
> Pour voir en quel état le sort vous a réduite.
> Votre pays vous hait, votre époux est sans foi:
> Dans un si grand revers que vous reste-t-il?
> MÉDÉE   Moi:
> *Moi, dis-je, et c'est assez.*
> NÉRINE   Quoi! vous seule, Madame?
> MÉDÉE   Oui, tu vois en moi seule et le fer et la flamme,
> Et la terre, et la mer, et l'enfer, et les cieux,
> Et le sceptre des rois, et la foudre des dieux.   (I. v)

---

[1] There are possible reminiscences of Hardy's *Méléagre* and *Alcméon*. See the summaries of these two tragedies above, pp. 92–3.

One may read in this the superb defiance of a *moi* which feels that it is entirely self-sufficient, that it contains the whole universe within its own microcosm. When, however, one remembers that Médée the magician possesses supernatural powers which give her command over the elements of heaven, earth and hell, a different interpretation becomes possible. Elsewhere she says:

> Bornes-tu mon pouvoir à celui des humains?
> . . . La flamme m'obéit et je commande aux eaux.   (III. iii)

Before relating the blind integrity of her *moi* to that of Horace, Émilie or Polyeucte, one must make allowance for those supernatural powers and reflect that she can escape – and knows she can – from the consequences of her earthly acts in the dragon-drawn chariot.[1]

Conversely, if one insists on her psychological relationship with Corneille's later heroes, one must concede that these also rise in some way above nature, though not on the same secure basis of magic. On the whole, however, the relationship is incomplete and it is easier to see Médée as a forerunner of Corneille's evil queens (as Corneille did himself; see below p. 149) than of his stoical heroes and heroines. The play itself is of a totally different type from any of the tragedies he was to write in the future.

The magical features of *Médée* recur in the play which Corneille wrote immediately after it, *L'Illusion comique*. This also contains an enchanter, but a benevolent one, who invites a distressed father into his magic grotto and conjures up for him a vision of the adventures of the long-lost son whom he is seeking. These take the form of a love intrigue similar to those of the earlier comedies, but the last act appears to turn to tragedy with the death of the son and his newly acquired

---

[1] Médée reappears in Corneille's mythological machine-play, *La Toison d'Or* (1660–1). In a dialogue with her rival Hypsipyle (III. iv), she makes it clear that her overweening self-confidence is based on her supernatural powers:

HYPSIPYLE	Je suis reine, Madame, et les fronts couronnés . . .
MÉDÉE	Et moi je suis Médée, et vous m'importunez.
HYPSIPYLE	Cet indigne mépris que de mon rang vous faites . . .
MÉDÉE	Connaissez-moi, Madame, et voyez où vous êtes . . .

> [*With a wave of her wand she converts the scene into a horrible place filled with wild beasts and monsters who surround Hypsipyle.*]

And later (V. iv):

> C'est Médée elle-même, et tout l'art de Circé . . .

wife. The scene then changes to show a group of actors counting their takings. The grisly ending was merely a play they were performing and the missing son and his wife have in reality become prosperous actors in Paris. Corneille's entertainment ends with a panegyric upon the theatre spoken by the magician. It is now an honourable and lucrative profession and the father can feel proud that his son has adopted it.

The play belongs to the order of comedy, but it cannot be entirely passed over in an account of French tragedy in general or of Cornelian tragedy in particular. It has been studied as an example of baroque multiple illusionism (it contains a play within a play within a play) and compared on that score to an authentic tragedy, Rotrou's *Saint Genest* (1646) and even, however tentatively, to Calderón's *La vida es sueño*.[1] There is no question here of any direct influence by Calderón on Corneille, but some traces of Spanishness, perhaps suggested by Rotrou, are detectable in *L'Illusion*,[2] apparently for the first time in Corneille's work.

The verse is more consistently accomplished than in any of the previous plays, both in the comic and in some of the 'sublime' passages. It is, however, ironical that the most grandiloquently noble utterances are put in the mouth of the captain Matamore (a stage Spaniard for the French), a fantastically boastful and cowardly soldier of farce whom Corneille succeeds in endowing with poetic qualities going well beyond the conventional, as Shakespeare had done to a greater degree with Falstaff. This anti-hero can be appreciated as a curious burlesque before the letter of Corneille's real heroes, adopting similar attitudes and sometimes using similar language, only to end in ignominious deflation.

L'Illusion comique thus possesses a considerable interest in Corneille's experimental development, but it is experimental only. The author was hardly too severe on his own early work when he described it in the *Examen* of 1660 as a put-together play,[3] whose main justification was the success it had enjoyed on the stage.

---

[1] See Imbrie Buffum, *Studies in the Baroque from Montaigne to Rotrou* (Yale U.P., 1957).

[2] Particularly an explicit reference to several Spanish picaresque novels (I. iii).

[3] '*Tout cela cousu ensemble* fait une comédie dont l'action n'a pour durée que celle de sa représentation, mais sur quoi il ne ferait pas sûr de prendre exemple. Les caprices de cette nature ne se hasardent qu'une fois . . .'

II

Le Cid followed *L'Illusion comique* after an interval of about a year, since it was first produced at the Marais in January 1637. The play, belonging to the category of romantic tragicomedy,[1] was a new departure for Corneille, but one which – it seems inevitable to conclude – he had carefully planned on the basis of his now considerable experience of the theatre.

The dominant theme is love; the second theme, important though subsidiary, is revenge. The conflict between the two, each presented in their most honourable and imperative forms, engenders a psychological anguish in the two principal characters, a pair of perfectly high-minded young lovers for whom mutual admiration – or, in slightly different terms, socially conditioned moral approval – is an essential ingredient of love. The familiar lines by a contemporary seventeenth-century English poet, 'I could not love thee, dear, so much, loved I not honour more', sum up the ethos of the play, though to be accurate one should perhaps change the word 'more' to 'equally'. A deeper motivation has been read into Chimène's prevarications: whatever her feelings previously, she instinctively recoils from Rodrigue after he has killed her father. Corneille came near to making this point in his *Examen* of 1660, as also in his rewriting of the last scene of the play and the delay, of a year if necessary, conceded by the King of Castile before the wedding need take place. But all this, which suggests an attempt to convert a romantic play into a truly tragic one, is expressed textually in terms of *honte*, *reproche*, *médisance*, *vertu*, *bienséance* and *point d'honneur*, which evoke the social force of public opinion rather than a personal repulsion in the heroine. Sophocles' Antigone, one might say, was impelled to give her brother burial because she found it both socially right and humanly necessary. If it is possible to find traces of the second consideration in Chimène's reactions, they are very faint in the play as it stands.

There can be little doubt that contemporary audiences, like later ones, assumed an unequivocally happy ending – the union of the lovers

---

[1] When first acted and published (this in 1637), *Le Cid* was referred to as a tragicomedy. It went through several editions before being described as a tragedy for the first time in 1648.

– and interpreted the delayed wedding as a mere matter of propriety.[1] Delayed it must be, since Corneille was observing the twenty-four-hour rule, and when the play finished the body of Chimène's father must still have lain in the house awaiting burial. A marriage at that point in time would be equivalent to a rape beside the coffin, unthinkable in this order of drama. In *Le Cid* the young lovers are united after triumphing over great difficulties, internally experienced and particularly painful in the case of Chimène, who undergoes the torments of hope, indecision and despair before winning her happy reprieve from martyrdom. The result was in the romantic rather than in the tragic vein.

There is plenty of evidence that *Le Cid* was an immediate and resounding success. It updated, better than the numerous seventeenth-century plays and novels which had attempted the same thing, the knightly code of conduct in a society largely dominated by urban and feminine values. The conflict between the knight's martial qualities, his 'manliness' encapsulated in 'honour', and his qualities as a lover acceptable to discriminating women had been a familiar theme even in medieval literature. Nearer to Corneille's time, pastoral and its derivatives had dealt adequately with the second aspect, but it is hard, if not impossible, to find any presentation of the warrior who fits into the same idealized picture. Garnier's Italian-derived *Bradamante* dealt or played with the ethics of chivalry in their two main aspects, as we have seen. But this was fifty years before *Le Cid*,[2] and, even if taken as a serious statement, it only made the woman a match for the man by endowing her with similar martial qualities. If she was to command respect, as the courtly convention required, it must be by more feminine means than wielding a sword.[3]

---

[1] The Académie conceded this while regretting it. *Nature*, of course, in the following quotation, means the emotions based on blood-relationship, as always in seventeenth-century usage. Passionate love was not 'natural' in this terminology: 'Le poète, voulant que ce poème finît heureusement, pour suivre les règles de la tragicomédie, fait encore en cet endroit que Chimène foule aux pieds celles que la nature a établies . . .' (*Sentiments de l'Académie sur le Cid*).

Scudéry in his *Observations* assumed the same happy ending.

[2] A new dramatization of *Bradamante*, owing much to Garnier, had, however, been written by La Calprenède and produced in 1636, a year at most earlier than *Le Cid*.

[3] It is worth mentioning that, after *Clitandre*, none of Corneille's heroines or young princesses uses, or is reported to have used, physical violence, even including the

Le Cid, in its contemporary context, provided a skilful reconciliation of these contradictory elements. The hero Rodrigue was unfalteringly brave, a magnificent fighter in spite of his youthful inexperience, spirited yet modest when appropriate, and totally respectful of the heroine's feelings. Chimène was his moral equal, never swerving in her love for him, yet employing all the weapons at her command – tears, supplications, demands for justice – to secure his punishment for killing her father. Her motivation, like his, is 'duty', to use Corneille's own word, and this she obeys to the limit of her strength. She was, in fact, a variety of heroine new to the French stage, tenderly passionate, cruelly persecuted by circumstance, stoically determined, and finally discreetly triumphant in her inmost desires. It must be added that both she and Rodrigue expressed enough misgivings over the agonizing decisions which they had to make to appear sufficiently human to win the sympathies of any averagely sentimental audience.

Though earlier heroines of French tragedy and tragicomedy may have displayed love, endurance, defiance or self-sacrifice to a greater or more interesting degree than Chimène, none had combined them in the same appealing proportions, with the further prospect of a justifiably happy ending. Coupled with the mettlesome yet courtly Rodrigue, she was irresistible.

Corneille's source, Guillén de Castro's *Mocedades del Cid*, had presented him with these two characters and with all the essentials of the plot. The emphasis had been somewhat different, since the Spanish Rodrigo was a national hero whose legendary exploits gave him an almost superhuman status.[1] Nevertheless, his language in some of the scenes with Jimena is fuller of hyperbole and conceits than any of Corneille's courtly dialogues. Jimena, though never varying in her love for him, is even more tenacious than Chimène (the action and her

---

administration of poison. However aggressive their feelings, they act through the men. The strong-arm Amazon type is out of favour. Only two evil queens, Cléopâtre in *Rodogune* and Marcelle in *Théodore*, actually kill with their own hands.

[1] He kills in single combat the gigantic champion of the rival kingdom of Aragon, with which Castile is at war (Corneille reduces this to the duel for Chimène's hand between Rodrigue and Don Sanche in Act V). He goes on a pilgrimage and befriends a leper who is miraculously transformed into a saint and promises the hero immortal fame in reward for his good deed.

resistance last for three years), until even the King grows tired of her importunities. But the two principal characters could be adapted without great difficulty to the French stage, and the standards of honour which guided them were recognizably similar in both countries, even if more imperative in Spain. Adaptation of the plot was more difficult, since Castro's drama was in part a chronicle play and included certain events for the simple reason that they had occurred, or were believed to have occurred, historically. There was, in addition to the events mentioned in the last footnote, an important sub-interest concerning the succession to the throne of Castile, in which the young prince plays a vigorous part and develops a hatred of his sister, the Infanta. The feudal turbulence of the King's barons is also more prominent than in Corneille.

Corneille omitted most of this, concentrating his play round the love situation and eliminating as far as possible the epic and political elements. Several of Castro's characters were dropped, including the young prince, Don Sancho, whose name, however, was retained for another character. The plot necessitates a quarrel between the two fathers and also a battle in which Rodrigue proves his value to the kingdom as a leader. Shown in the Spanish version, with Moorish and Castilian soldiers scurrying across the stage, this battle is narrated in the French version. Altogether, Corneille's adaptation was a notable move towards concentration of interest and *bienséance*.

But it was by no means perfect. It observed the unity of place according to the scenic conventions of the period.[1] It deliberately observed the unity of time, but somewhat implausibly. Too much had to happen within the space of twenty-four hours, and the whole problem of the impropriety of Chimène's consent to marriage with Rodrigue was caused, or at least aggravated, by the exiguous time-limit. The unity of action was marred by the introduction of the Infanta, in her own mind a rival of Chimène for the love of Rodrigue, but this character loomed so large in the Spanish play that it may well have never occurred to Corneille to leave her out.[2]

In short, though *Le Cid* was consciously constructed to obey the new rules, it did so with difficulty, and was the work of a dramatist who at that date at least was still naturally drawn to the presentation

[1] See above p. 122 and pp. 124–5.
[2] Though her function in the action is minimal, she has character interest in her

of a subject through the 'variety of events' recommended by François Ogier. Technically this play was less purely unified than Mairet's *Sophonisbe*, although the principal tension inherent in the dilemma of the two lovers was better prepared and sustained.

The Quarrel of *Le Cid* followed, sparked off apparently by a boastful poem of Corneille's published within a few weeks of the first production. Corneille's role throughout was far from that of an innocent victim, as traditional piety has sometimes represented him, and he was to hit back later at some of his critics in no very delicate terms. But having, as it seems, started the affair, he had provided his literary rivals with an opportunity to attack his play, which at first had won nothing but praise. Mairet opened fire with a poem, *L'Auteur du vrai Cid à son traducteur français*, which accused Corneille of taking credit for a work which was little more than a translation. Scudéry, also a successful dramatist, published a long and reasoned criticism, the *Observations sur le Cid*, which was eventually submitted for an opinion to the newly founded Académie Française, together with the text of the debated play, after Corneille's consent had been obtained. Some six months later (December 1637), the Académie published its findings under the title of *Les Sentiments de l'Académie Française sur la tragicomédie du Cid*. This report was almost entirely the work of Chapelain, who made the first draft, amended it at the instance of Richelieu's intermediary, Boisrobert, and consulted his other colleagues principally on questions of wording.

Amid a large number of pamphlets and lampoons, which testify to the contemporary interest in the play and the acerbity of literary

---

relationship with the princesses of some of Corneille's later plays. Thus, her royal blood seems to preclude her marriage to a non-royal lover:

> Rodrigue, ta valeur te rend digne de moi,
> Mais, pour être vaillant, tu n'es pas fils de roi.

In this case, however, merit might overcome that obstacle (but for the existence of Chimène):

> Bien qu'aux monarques seuls ma naissance me donne,
> Rodrigue, avec honneur je vivrai sous tes lois.
>   Après avoir vaincu deux rois,
>   Pourrais-tu manquer de couronne?
>   (*Le Cid*, V. ii)

polemics at that date, the only two commentaries of value were Scudéry's and the Académie's. The second, it should be remembered, was
almost as much an evaluation of the first as a direct assessment of *Le
Cid*. Both made the kind of points we have already mentioned: the
overcrowding of incident, the functionless part of the Infanta, the
concettismo of parts of the dialogue. Both invoked the authority of
Aristotle, usually on mistaken readings, and of Heinsius, one of Aristotle's recent commentators. Both distinguished themselves from
modern criticism by underlining the importance of the moral effect
of a work of art, which they placed above its artistic excellence.

The phrase 'les bonnes mœurs' recurs in Scudéry's text in his arguments that literature should be conducive to them. Chapelain, taking
the same line even more conspicuously, seems to draw no distinction
between *bienséance* and *vraisemblance* in their basic senses. For him, the
moral and psychological implications are the same. Some of the
characters should/could not have behaved as they did. The alternative
motivations are not recognized by him. He therefore carefully scruti-
nizes, like Scudéry, the social behaviour of the characters of the play,
and sometimes condemns it as equally improper and improbable.
Many other points, which have no moral content, are considered on
the grounds of literal truth-to-life. Scudéry had argued that the Moorish
raiders could not have entered the port of Seville because it would have
been closed at night with a chain. The Académie solemnly takes up
this objection and observes in defence of Corneille that the river leading
to Seville is too wide to be barred by such means. This is hardly an
extreme example of the argumentation of much of the *Sentiments*.

Chapelain in particular examines the language of the play at length
and although, as in other matters, he often disagrees with Scudéry on
points of detail, this scrutiny illustrates the importance attached by the
doctes to questions of prosody, grammar, vocabulary and metaphor,
and continues the movement towards correctness so bitterly resented
by Hardy some ten years earlier. Dramatic theory in a deeper sense is
scarcely touched on. Chapelain briefly asserts the superiority of
pièces régulières over *pièces irrégulières*, accepts that *Le Cid* was intended
to be regular, but faults it because of the multiplicity of events and
Chimène's over-rapid consent to marriage with her father's murderer.

The *Sentiments de l'Académie* was designed as a tactful document.
Without abandoning criticism, it seemed aimed to offend neither

Scudéry nor – deeply – Corneille. The latter was defended here and there and a few verbal flowers were thrown at him. Since, however, he had been hoping for a clear refutation of Scudéry's strictures, he was far from satisfied.

This was predominantly a literary and critical quarrel. The extraneous factors were unimportant. The old theory that Cardinal Richelieu was hostile to Le Cid from the beginning through jealousy has long been discarded. He had the play performed twice in his own household, allowed the first edition to be dedicated to his niece, and permitted the honour of ennoblement to be granted to Corneille's father. A little later he supervised the examination of the play by the Académie, an infant body to which he had decided to give his protection, but the move was probably judicial rather than hostile. Richelieu the statesman wished to restore order to the dissension-torn world of letters by a wise and authoritative judgement, and when this came it was not an outright condemnation.[1]

It is always possible that Corneille was frightened by some other influential patron of one of his literary enemies, but the supposition rests on no known evidence. All that can be said is that, having produced one play a year on average before Le Cid, he waited for three years before producing his next (which he dedicated to Richelieu), and the gap is a long one. The flurry of the Quarrel, discouragement (though the 'persecuted' Cid remained highly popular), and a long period of reflection leading to a change in his dramatic methods appear to fill it. Though hypothetical, no other reasonable explanation has been advanced.

III

Horace, produced early in 1640, opens the sequence of four Roman tragedies which definitely established Corneille as the leading dramatist of his age and have been regarded ever since as his greatest and most typical contribution to drama. All were regular, with one slight reservation on the unity of place in *Cinna*. All had subjects taken from Roman history, which Corneille had not drawn on previously.

The Roman material, with the implications which stemmed from it

[1] M. A. Stegmann, in *L'Héroïsme cornélien*, I (1968), revives the hypothesis of Richelieu's hostility to Corneille in the Quarrel of *Le Cid*, but neither his arguments nor his evidence seem conclusive.

in the exaltation of the 'Roman' virtues, had been relatively neglected since Garnier. Hardy based one or two plays on it, but in using Plutarch showed a preference for his Greek subjects. Younger writers, both in tragedy and tragicomedy, also turned mainly to Greek or romanesque sources. But from 1635 Roman themes began to enjoy a noticeable popularity, possibly owing to the success of Mairet's *Sophonisbe* in the previous year. In a short period over a dozen plays of the kind appeared (if one includes the Dido and the Cleopatra stories), written by Scudéry, Rotrou, Du Ryer, La Calprenède and lesser men. There were two plays on Coriolanus, a subject already treated by Hardy. In 1637 an obscure Norman writer, Chaulmer, produced a play entitled *La Mort de Pompée*.

By 1638 the trend had died out, at least temporarily, so that, although Corneille was no doubt following fashion, he was belated. When his plays were written they revived the trend and confirmed it as the most appropriate expression of the French nation's image of itself in that period of history.

The 'Roman' ethos, as presented predominantly though not exclusively by Corneille, resulted in the theatre in characters of heroic proportions, not always presented as virtuous or exemplary, but motivated by the pursuit of various ideals which for them were absolute. Even when the motivation was shown to be morally or psychologically mistaken, it was never petty, and this aura of greatness was sustained by the firm eloquence of the dialogue written for actors trained in the rhetorical tradition. In this sense all Corneille's principal characters are cast in the heroic mould, tinged often with his age's conception of the severe Roman virtue, and the stories in which they figure are on the same elevated plane. 'La tragédie', he was to write in his *Discours du poème dramatique* (1660), 'veut pour son sujet une action illustre, extraordinaire, sérieuse.' Here he was paraphrasing Aristotle, with approval. Of his three adjectives, *extraordinaire* could be used equally well to justify melodrama of the anti-classical type, though Corneille's meaning here is probably no more than 'outstanding'. *Illustre* and *sérieuse*, however, can only typify heroic tragedy, of the kind in which he came to excel.

In his first four Roman plays the 'political' interest is conspicuous and important. Councils, conspiracies, decisions affecting the future of States or the fate or policy of rulers, are integral to the stories. Merely in themselves they have dramatic significance and excitement and they also lend themselves to endless interpretation and reinterpretation as allusions to contemporary political situations in a France mirrored in ancient Rome. But the love element is present in equal strength, making it impossible to maintain that Corneille had abruptly turned his back on romanesque drama, though he may have given it a new face.

Horace, the least romanesque of the first three tragedies, retains certain features of *Le Cid*, with interesting variations. The hero has all the martial virtues and proves his value to the State in a notable feat of arms. In this he resembles Rodrigue, but he lacks entirely Rodrigue's other quality – his worth as a lover. Horace is virile to the point of barbarity and in him there is no conflict with romance, so no dilemma. He is backed in this by his inflexibly patriotic father, reminiscent of Don Diègue,[1] who pleads his cause before the King and obtains his pardon. The other side of the case is presented in their various ways by the other four principal characters, who include Horace's own wife, Sabine, and his sister, Camille. All urge the claims of love which, however, are somewhat metamorphosed here since they are frequently and convincingly identified with the claims of common humanity. Camille's protest is the strongest and leads to her death at the hand of her outraged brother, whom she dares to reproach with killing her lover at a moment when he is drunk with triumph. Love, whether considered as a courtly accomplishment or as a plain human passion, must knuckle under in this play, though it is there and is expressed with eloquence. Horace never regrets his act and is finally disculpated in the interests of Rome. There would be irony if Corneille had set out to paint the portrait of a ruthlessly patriotic brute. But this is not so; the author's attitude is at the most ambivalent. His view of the character is summed up in his *Examen*, in which he writes of Horace's 'vertu farouche'.

The female characters in *Horace* are victimized, but not passively so. They speak their minds and are ready to die, displaying what might be called a Roman virtue, but they do not compete with the men in acts

---

[1] For Old Horace, however, the interests and honour of the family are secondary to those of the State, or rather derive entirely from its services to the State. In *Le Cid*, family honour was increased by services to the State, but subsisted independently. This change of emphasis can be seen with some plausibility as a rallying by Corneille to Richelieu's policy of centralization.

or influence the action (except fortuitously, in Camille's case). Their role in this play is thus not typically Cornelian, but given this particular story, it could hardly have been so.

In Corneille's next play, *Cinna*, a woman plays a decisive part in the action. Émilie, the daughter of a Roman nobleman, incites her lover Cinna to assassinate the Emperor Auguste in order to avenge her own father's death. The risks are great and she is doubtful about exposing Cinna to them, but *devoir*, *vertu* and *gloire* compel her, and also she has already obtained Cinna's promise to attempt to kill the Emperor as a condition of her marriage to him:

> Cinna me l'a promis en recevant ma foi,
> Et ce coup seul aussi le rend digne de moi.

Love of a romantic kind is thus associated with political action, and the basic situation is that of the knight who is expected to perform some outstanding deed in order to win his mistress. So imbued is Cinna with this ethic that when Auguste, ignorant of the plot against him, offers to abdicate voluntarily, Cinna persuades him not to. He must strike down the Emperor at the height of his power as an act of vengeance for Émilie, even though the political necessity of the act has disappeared.[1] He is tempted by another unwittingly double-edged offer of the Emperor's: to give him Émilie, the Emperor's protégée, in marriage. But Émilie's heart, he discovers, can only be won the hard way and, after some bitter heart-searching occurring at almost the exact centre of the play (III. iii and iv), he braces himself to keep his oath to her and proceed with the assassination of the man who trusts him.

Though after this events take a new turn, leading to a reconciliation of conflicting interests and a happy ending, it is clear that love of a particularly exacting kind, going a certain distance beyond the courtly convention, is the mainspring of this tragedy. The heroine's *vertu farouche* (which would be bloody-mindedness in quite a different ethos),

---

[1] Cinna has organized the conspiracy without mentioning Émilie to his fellow conspirators. Their aim is to rid Rome of a tyrant in the name of liberty. This motivation, which would be sufficient in itself in a French eighteenth-century tragedy, as it was in Shakespeare's *Julius Caesar*, is subordinate in Corneille to the romantic motivation.

dominating even her deeply felt love for Cinna, is finally overcome by the still higher *vertu* of Auguste, who in his generosity pardons and wins over his would-be assassins. Statesmanship possibly, but surrounded by what an aura of personal magnanimity!

In *Polyeucte*, which deals with a Christian martyrdom, it would appear more difficult to place a love interest. It is, however, present, expressed in a most courtly form. The love of the Roman Sévère for Pauline, the wife of the eventual martyr, forms an essential part of the play as Corneille wrote it. But the main story can exist perfectly well without it, and it is a complication or enrichment invented by Corneille, who did not find it in his primary source. Certainly the drama was intended to mingle the sacred and the profane, with the ultimate triumph of the former, and was an unusual conception for its date,[1] but whether this Christian tragedy was a work of true religion is an open question. The Roman ethos persists. The scene is the Roman province of Armenia. Three of the leading characters are Roman-born. In addition, the stoic resolution of the two Armenian martyrs is simply super-Roman and triumphs by a superior handling of the same moral weapons. Christianity for Polyeucte is what the State was for Horace, and for a moment at least it inspires him with the same 'inhuman' harshness towards his wife Pauline that Horace showed towards his sister and his wife (V. iii). Pauline is at once a victim, desperately tortured by her emotions, and a victor both in her conquest of them and in her ultimate defiant conversion to Christianity. In religious terms this might be called the Higher Love rising superior to the human love which she felt for Sévère, but it is in fact provoked by the pity and admiration which fill her after witnessing her husband's martyrdom. It can therefore be interpreted equally well as 'virtuous' love conceived by a supreme human effort, on the same level as that of other Cornelian heroines.

[1] Saint plays belonged to an old tradition, but were naturally rare in the professional theatre at this date. Baro's *Saint Eustache* (*c.* 1639), a spectacularly irregular play, was *Polyeucte*'s only close predecessor. A second *Saint Eustache* by Desfontaines and three other martyr tragedies, La Calprenède's *Herménigilde* and La Serre's *Thomas Morus* and *Sainte Catherine*, all appeared on undetermined dates at about the same time as *Polyeucte*. They are unlikely to have suggested Corneille's subject to him and some at least may have followed his tragedy. Later, Desfontaines wrote a *Martyre de Saint Genest* (1644), followed closely by Rotrou's more famous *Véritable Saint Genest* (1645).

The 'political' interest of *Polyeucte* should not be overlooked. There is a strong theme in the question of the central government's policy towards the subversive Christians of the provinces, and this is worked out principally through the character of Félix, whose problems as Governor of Armenia are as much administrative as emotional.

La Mort de Pompée is primarily a political drama. Here again there is a weak ruler, more treacherous and more interesting than Félix, manœuvring to retain his power which ultimately depends on Rome. (The theme of Roman intervention, with unpleasant consequences for the local rulers, had been used notably by Mairet in *Sophonisbe*. Adopted several times by Corneille, it persisted at least as far as Racine's *Mithridate*.) Ptolemy of Egypt, with his hesitations, his ruses and his acts, furnishes the plot of the play, which otherwise would fall to pieces. Round him are noble Romans, the magnanimous Caesar, Cornelia, the grief-stricken but implacable widow of Pompey who, like Garnier's heroine, carries round the ashes of her husband in a little urn. They recognize and salute the Roman virtue in each other and prove it in their acts,[1] but it is the despicable Ptolemy and his counsellors who set and keep the machinery in motion.

Cleopatra is there too, in love at this point with Caesar (Antony is still only a gleam on the horizon), and this gives rise to a scene of somewhat incongruous *galanterie* (IV. iii). But the romantic element is not developed in this play. It serves to motivate Caesar's support of Cleopatra's claim to the throne of Egypt, while Cleopatra herself uses it principally to further her political ambitions.

In *Pompée* Corneille wrote a play which, though the story is perfectly clear, lacks unity of interest. From this point of view it is the weakest of his four Roman tragedies and already announces the more diffuse and tumultuous tragedies which he was to produce after it.

IV

These four plays on which, after *Le Cid*, Corneille's main reputation has always rested, are regular in all outward respects. They observe the unities and the *bienséances*. Violence is narrated and never repre-

---

[1] The easy way for Cornelia to avenge herself on Caesar would be to allow Ptolemy to proceed with his plot to assassinate him. She disdains this as ignoble – and besides, a Roman ought not to be murdered by mere Egyptians – and persists in the hard way, much as Cinna did in the earlier tragedy.

sented, with the one doubtful exception of the scene in which Horace kills his sister.[1] Structurally, the linking of the scenes, though not always impeccable, was done well enough to silence criticism. Unity of interest was usually attained by a skilful combination of elements which, as has been seen in the last few pages, were not always obviously compatible. Profuseness of incidents was subordinated to the single plot-line, no doubt with difficulty on Corneille's part, but with apparent smoothness in the finished product, with the partial exception of *Pompée*. In short, these plays were, for their date, exemplary illustrations of the emergent classical doctrine, and as such exerted a powerful influence on the development of French tragedy.

As 'tragedies' they ended, not in disaster, but in triumph, exaltation, reconciliation or compromise. They contained dire events for certain characters, but the principal characters emerged victorious, either materially or morally, or both. In a wider context than that of the French theatre, one would prefer to class them as heroic dramas. The psychological motivation, as expressed in the dialogue, sometimes appears extraordinary to the modern mind. But it is consistent within itself and rests on a view of the human condition which possesses at least historical importance and underlay a system of personal relationships which evidently proved workable.

But Corneille would still not be a great dramatist without his mastery of language, which had been steadily growing until it reached its peak in *Cinna*. He had now forged a verse idiom which compensated, so far as that was ever possible, for the lack of physical action and spectacle in the theatre. The stateliness of his great speeches, the vigour and subtlety of his verbal duels, the ornamentation of his amorous dialogues – cliché-ridden though they may now appear – created verbally (and, in their peculiar way, psychologically) an entertainment which could grip his audience. All this was used dramatically, in the sense that it belonged to the action and advanced it. The resounding moral commonplaces had a bearing on character and situation. The debates were truly dialectical. Though on conventional themes such as suicide and clemency, their outcome mattered and was not foreseen from the

---

[1] In some of the early productions the killing seems to have occurred on stage, though Corneille's intention, indicated by his stage directions, was always that Camille should be pursued offstage and that her dying cry should reach the audience from the wings.

beginning. They could change the attitude of a character and the development of the plot in a manner not attempted in the sixteenth century, and rarely in previous tragic plays in the seventeenth.

The four tragedies which set this standard were performed within a period of about three years. The dates have been confused in the past and still cannot be established with complete accuracy, but they fall most probably within these limits: *Horace*, February–March 1640; *Cinna*, winter of 1640–1; *Polyeucte*, winter of 1641–2; *Pompée*, 1642–3.[1]

In the same winter in which he composed *La Mort de Pompée*, says Corneille, he was also writing *Le Menteur*, a comedy based on a Spanish model. He followed this successful play with *La Suite du Menteur*, and at about the same date as this (October 1644 or later) his new tragedy of *Rodogune* was performed.

V

The seven plays which Corneille wrote between 1644 and 1651 are too varied to be called a group, though several of them have common features. Their variety was a sign, not of an exhausted talent driven to search for novelty, but of the fertility of a dramatist at the height of his invention. In some respects these were Corneille's most interesting productions and, although only *Rodogune* and *Nicomède* have been generally ranked among his best plays, none of the others is negligible.

After *La Mort de Pompée*, Corneille ceased to draw predominantly on Roman history. There was Roman political influence or intervention in only two of his new plays, *Théodore* and *Nicomède*, and even these point to a growing interest in more barbaric or less 'classical' civilizations and manners, such as had already begun to manifest itself in *Pompée*. *Rodogune* is set in Syria, *Héraclius* in Byzantium, *Pertharite* in the Italy of the Lombards, while *Don Sanche* marked a return to Spain for the first time since *Le Cid* and the comedy of *Le Menteur*. One cannot, of course, say that there was any real attempt at local colour, and full allowance must be made for the influence of the contemporary French novel, whose romanesque ethos is recognizable in all these tragedies. But nevertheless there is a perceptible tendency to desert the well-trodden path of classical Rome in favour of less conventional subjects and ethics, not dissimilar to those which had

[1] See D.-Holsboer, *Le Théâtre du Marais*, Vol. I. Also Lancaster, *History*, II, Vols. I and 2.

appealed to Hardy.[1] The 'Roman' ethos of *vertu* and *gloire* persists, though sometimes in such distorted and peculiar forms that it throws some doubt on the whole concept as apparently established in the earlier tragedies. Meanwhile, the comparison with Hardy allows one to say that the predominant tone of these plays was melodramatic. Certainly it was melodrama according to the new conventions. The unities of time and place were not violated. The unity of action was preserved by most careful and skilful plotting. The *bienséances*, so far as they required the removal of shocking sights from the actual stage, were observed, although some of Corneille's plays of this period cry aloud for the representation of physical action in front of the spectator. Corneille narrates it, as excitingly as can be done in the circumstances, but his observance of the 'rules' in this sense is less a dramatic virtue than an enforced limitation.

All this shows that the basic concept of 'irregular' tragedy was still very much alive in the 1640s, though stage convention and a powerful section of public taste were combining against it. Corneille was ready to align himself with both (his most constant preoccupation, reasonably enough, was to write successful plays), but his natural inclination was towards the multiplicity of incidents and the surprising peripeteia, and only his great skill as a playwright enabled him to compose plays within the contemporary convention which would belong more appropriately outside it.[2]

In these plays taken as a whole, what is convenient to call the political interest is still strong. Except in *Théodore*, it bears on questions of the succession to a throne or of usurpation and is rarely distinguishable from the personal psychology of ambitious individuals, conditioned however by the obligations of rank and royal blood, to which a certain mystique is attained. This strong if conventional motivation is used

[1] As in *Méléagre*, *Alcméon*, *Frégonde*, *Gésippe*, *Phraate*, *Arsacome*.
[2] A traditional argument in favour of 'classical' tragedy requires the 'psychological' impact of events upon characters who are on stage to be more interesting than the spectacle of the events themselves. Such was the principle established by Garnier and brought to final perfection by Racine. (Nothing would be gained in *Bérénice* by bringing a Roman mob on stage at the end of Act IV. In *Bajazet* the potentially thrilling sight of Bajazet struggling with the mutes ordered to strangle him (Act V) would be of only secondary interest.) But in several of the Cornelian plays considered here this is not the case. The dramatic importance of the events is sometimes greater than the reaction of the characters to them.

(as already in *Pompée*), not so much ideologically as to provide the machinery of the plot, in which Corneille's interest is increasingly apparent.

In 'love' the virtuous variety persists, and persists strongly in many characters and situations. For perfect love, he or she must be 'worthy' of her or him. In some of these plays, this is beginning to look a little unnatural, but it is clear that Corneille's ethical assumptions could provide him with nothing else to put in its place. The only example of a 'natural' love-passion, unaffected by reason or *vertu*, in all these plays (and indeed in the whole of Corneille's dramatic production from *Le Cid* onwards) occurs in the person of Flavie in *Théodore*. Flavie never appears on the stage, is reported to have died for love of a man who remains totally unmoved, and has the sole function of motivating her mother's implacable hatred of the heroine. So much for *amour-passion* in Corneille.

Almost inseparable from virtuous love is the concept of chivalry. This is more prominent than in the earlier plays in the form of chivalry between men. A lover and even a husband (Pertharite) are ready to give up their beloved to a rival if they are persuaded that he has a stronger moral claim. This throws back to Garnier's *Bradamante* and applies to Placide and Didyme in *Théodore*, ultimately to Attale and Nicomède in *Nicomède*, and more conspicuously to the pairs of brothers or almost-brothers in *Rodogune* and *Héraclius*. The latter two pairs were a new departure in Corneille's scheme of characterization and are reminiscent of the two close friends in Hardy's *Gésippe*. But whereas personal friendship was the sole motivation in Hardy, Corneille finds additional and higher motivations: the claim to the throne and the interests of the woman herself. As a Cornelian princess, it was unthinkable that she should be handed over without her conscious and willed consent.

The strong-minded and virtuous young woman remains strongly in evidence – more so, in fact, than in the earlier plays, in which only the Émilie of *Cinna* can bear comparison with Rodogune, the Pulchérie of *Héraclius*, the Laodice of *Nicomède* and the Edwige of *Pertharite*. Rodelinde in this last play is persecuted certainly, in a way which a different dramatist might represent as the extreme of cruelty, but she fights back with such ferocity and scorn that pity is not the reaction she provokes. The only female victim to excite that emotion is the virgin martyr Théodore, but here, as will be seen later, Corneille went rather too far in devising a torture for her, and his public was revolted. Never, indeed, after *Le Cid* did he endow a character with that perfectly measured proportion of feminine strength and pathos which had made such an appealing heroine of Chimène.

As a foil to the resolutely virtuous heroines, and usually in opposition to them, Corneille introduced a new type of character, ultimately descended from the archetypal wicked stepmother of the fairy-tale. These ruthless elder women, inspired by ambition or desire for revenge, begin with the Cléopâtre of *Rodogune* (who was no connection with the Egyptian Cleopatra) and continue with the Marcelle of *Théodore* and the Arsinoé of *Nicomède* (though she receives forgiveness in the end). The Léontine of *Héraclius* is a character of similar conception, but she uses her powers of intrigue for good and therefore cannot be ranked literally with the others. In his *Avertissement* to *Rodogune*, Corneille calls the evil Cléopâtre 'cette seconde Médée', so pinpointing the immediate ancestry of these characters so far as he was conscious of it. But while looking back to his own early tragic heroine, he had developed the character in a contemporary direction and given it qualities which, while not over-subtle, made it psychologically plausible on a human plane.

These evil characters show passion, a hate-passion which absorbs them and cannot be justified rationally. The germ again is in Médée, in whom frustrated love for Jason had bred a blind obsession with revenge. This particular motivation, however, is not found in her successors.

It is important to remember that the tragedies of this period followed immediately after the comedy of *Le Menteur*, a play with a complicated plot revolving round mistaken identities. The same dramatic device reappears in several of the so-called tragedies, which in their construction belonged to the comic convention, according to the standards of the time. This fact may be obscured by the royal or noble standing of the characters and the bloodshed which sometimes resulted, but the ingenious imbroglios, the concealed identities, the revelations by means of letters, the surprising *coups de théâtre* (*Héraclius* and *Pertharite* are the outstanding examples) attach them far more closely to the comic order than to the tragic as exemplified in *Horace*, *Polyeucte* and even *Le Cid*. Today they can be justifiably classed as melodramas, but with characters belonging to the heroic tradition.

VI

The 'stories' of these plays are important and revealing. The reader is referred to the summaries on pp. 160–5, which, together with what has been written above, will indicate the main general features of Corneille's production in this period. The following short consideration of the plays in their chronological order will help to place them in their contemporary context and to illustrate their varied characteristics.

Rodogune, a 'strong' drama of love, ambition and revenge, with its spirited heroine and its evil queen-mother, was a contemporary success. It was dedicated to Condé, in gratitude for the 'protection' which the influential soldier-prince had given to the play. Reconsidering it in his *Examen* of 1660, Corneille declared his preference for *Rodogune* over all his other works, in these terms:

> On m'a souvent fait une question à la cour: quel était celui de mes poèmes que j'estimais le plus; et j'ai trouvé tous ceux qui me l'ont faite si prévenus en faveur de *Cinna* ou du *Cid* que je n'ai jamais osé déclarer toute la tendresse que j'ai toujours eue pour celui-ci, à qui j'aurais volontiers donné mon suffrage si je n'avais craint de manquer en quelque sorte à ceux que je voyais pencher d'un autre côté . . . [Dans cette préférence il entre peut-être] un peu d'amour-propre en ce que cette tragédie me semble être un peu plus à moi que celles qui l'ont précédée, *à cause des incidents surprenants qui sont purement de mon invention, et n'avaient jamais été vus au théâtre* . . . [our italics].

Surprising incidents of his own invention which were (excitingly) novel on the stage . . .[1] It would be difficult to suggest more adequately Corneille's conception of drama, not only in 1660 but throughout most of his career.

Corneille's diffident defence of *Rodogune* should not be taken to imply that the play was a failure. It seems to have ranked from the beginning among his most popular works. Later (1680–1700) it came fifth among his plays acted by the Comédie-Française, on a count of performances,

---

[1] At about the same date a *Rhodogune*, with a similar plot, by the minor dramatist Gilbert, was performed. Apart from Corneille's apparent, and sometimes transparent honesty, the balance of what evidence there is gives precedence to Corneille, with Gilbert deriving from him. See Lancaster, *History*, II, p. 506.

while throughout the eighteenth century until the Revolution it occupied the third place, immediately after *Le Cid* and *Le Menteur*.[1]

His next play, *Théodore*, was an instant failure and has remained neglected ever since. It was Corneille's second and last tragedy based on a Christian martyrdom, but it was much more than an attempt to repeat *Polyeucte*, similar though part of the situation is. It was an interesting, though over-bold, variation on the earlier play, with a female martyr in place of a male one. Though Théodore displays the same heroic constancy as Polyeucte, she is more vulnerable by the mere fact of her sex, and the response of an audience is necessarily different. It cannot be limited to simple admiration of a super-Roman *vertu*. The love interest, requiring such delicate handling that it ceases to be interesting, is also exploited differently. Used in *Polyeucte* to increase the importance of Pauline, who would otherwise have been a secondary character, and to integrate in the main action what could easily have been a sub-plot, in *Théodore* it is essential. Not at all to the psychology of the characters which, as Corneille himself recognized, is frigid and lifeless, but to supply the motivation from which the exciting action stems.

Vigorous in conception but defective in construction, the play might well have failed in any case. But there was a sufficient reason already in the subject. The whole plot hinged on the public prostitution of a virgin princess, and however hard Corneille tried to attenuate the impact of this theme by substituting narration for direct representation, it was naïve of him to believe that he had transformed it. What could not possibly be shown on the stage of that period, or of many others, was reported, but the still vivid description of the licentious soldiery fighting to get into the brothel to rape the heroine (who of course escaped at least this fate) inevitably still gave offence. It failed to gain in propriety while losing dramatic effectiveness. The general holocaust with which the play ends is also lost by being reported. This was really a subject for Hardy's period and one which Hardy, however clumsily, might have treated more effectively than Corneille.[2] Its choice by the latter was a mistaken though revealing decision.

[1] See ibid., II, p. 512.
[2] The somewhat similar story of St Agnes (on which Corneille probably drew) had indeed been dramatized, with a brothel scene, by Hardy's contemporary Pierre Troterel (*Tragédie de Sainte Agnès*, 1615).

After *Théodore*, Corneille changed direction again and wrote in *Héraclius* a fast-moving political drama with a happy ending. It had the most complicated plot of all his tragedies to date, and one which he clearly took pleasure in devising. His manipulation of 'history' was still freer than in *Rodogune*, and the whole imbroglio is really an invention pegged on the names of certain Byzantine emperors, as he points out himself in the *Au lecteur*. The complicated identities which make the basically logical story so hard to follow evidently did not prevent the play from being a contemporary success, though, as Corneille remarked in his *Examen*: 'I think that it ought to be seen more than once to obtain a full understanding of it.' This success in 1647 of what is in essence an involved tragicomedy is significant in the general history of French drama. The play remained popular throughout the seventeenth and eighteenth centuries. Between 1680 and 1793 it ranked seventh among Corneille's plays performed at the Comédie-Française, outdoing *Pompée* and *Nicomède* over this long period as a whole.[1]

Héraclius contains a near-violation of the scenic *bienséances*. In Act V, Sc. iii, the tyrant Phocas is about to order the immediate execution of one of the two princes (in fact, his own son) if the other will not admit his identity. Soldiers are on stage and one of them, as the scene is written, must be standing over the intended victim with drawn sword or some other weapon, ready to kill him at the word of command. This is averted, but only just, and one is bound to reflect that Corneille had come as near as he could to the actual representation of one of the barbaric execution scenes found in earlier drama.[2]

Part of the scene must be quoted, not only to illustrate this point, but to show the melodramatic suspense with which Corneille invests it. Martian is the threatened victim. Héraclius, wrongly believed by Phocas to be his son, is trying to save Martian's life. Octavian, a walking-on part named only in this scene, is a soldier or executioner:

PHOCAS   . . . Soldats, sans plus tarder, qu'on l'immole à ses
                yeux [aux yeux d'Héraclius];
                Et sois après sa mort mon fils, si tu veux.

[1] See Lancaster, *History*, II, p. 529.
[2] See for example Mahelot's lists of stage properties for two of Hardy's lost plays: *Parténie*: 'Il faut . . . une tête feinte' (though this was not certainly for an execution scene); *La Cintie*: 'Il faut pour un bourreau des cordes et une barbe.'

HÉRACLIUS	Perfides, arrêtez!
MARTIAN	Ah! que voulez-vous faire, Prince?
HÉRACLIUS	Sauver le fils de la fureur du père.
MARTIAN	Conservez-lui ce fils qu'il ne cherche qu'en vous; Ne troublez point un sort qui lui semble si doux . . .
PHOCAS	C'est trop perdre de temps à souffrir ces discours. Dépêche, Octavian.
HÉRACLIUS	N'attente rien, barbare! Je suis . . .
PHOCAS	Avoue enfin.
HÉRACLIUS	Je tremble, je m'égare, Et mon cœur . . .
PHOCAS (*à Héraclius*)	Tu pourras à loisir y penser.
(*à Octavian*) Frappe.	
HÉRACLIUS	Arrête; je suis . . . Puis-je le prononcer?
PHOCAS	Achève, ou . . .
HÉRACLIUS	Je suis donc, s'il faut que je le die, Ce qu'il faut que je sois pour lui sauver la vie.

Corneille's next production was to have been *Andromède*, an Italian-type mythological play based on the *Metamorphoses* of Ovid and intended to be performed with the elaborate décors and machinery of Giacomo Torelli. Besides the gods and the allegorical characters who descended or floated on the *machines* there were human characters and a story of human interest based on the relationship of Andromeda with her parents and her two suitors, Phineas and her rescuer, Perseus. Composed most probably in the second half of 1647, this production was postponed for extraneous reasons until early in 1650, when it was performed before the court in the Palais Bourbon (a slightly earlier performance at the Marais is possible but uncertain). While waiting, Corneille wrote *Don Sanche d'Aragon*, which was probably produced, before *Andromède*, in the last months of 1649. He styled this play a *comédie héroïque*, using the term almost for the first time to denote what was in fact a romantic tragicomedy with a happy ending. It contains some of his most lively and attractive verse-dialogue, particularly in Act I. It suggests the manner (as well as a theme) of Victor Hugo's verse dramas written nearly two centuries later, though executed with a lighter hand. The fact that parts of this play are imitated from Lope de Vega does not seriously diminish Corneille's skill in adaptation and fresh invention.

The initial success of this play, says Corneille in his *Examen*, was cut short by 'le refus d'un illustre suffrage' which caused it to disappear from the Paris stage and be relegated to the provinces. The identity of the eminent personage whose disapproval led to this virtual ban has not been established. The hypothesis that it was Condé is less probable than that it was Anne of Austria, the Queen Mother, or possibly Mazarin. Seen from a certain angle, there was a suggestive parallel between the relationship of these last two and the widowed queen of Corneille's play, surrounded as she was by aristocratic admirers but preferring a man of apparently obscure birth.[1] Whether Corneille had merely blundered into this parallel or whether he had consciously hazarded an allusion to the contemporary situation must remain a subject for speculation.

In any case he withdrew in his next play (after the court performance of *Andromède*) to the safer ground of ancient history, though even here keen-nosed critics thought they could detect references to contemporary personalities. *Nicomède* was a Roman play with a difference. The plot is rich and exciting, though not complicated. The principal characters, though not Roman themselves, have adopted the Roman virtues and stand by them defiantly. Their defiance is often exteriorized in irony, which was the most conspicuously novel feature of this tragedy. Until then, irony and double-take had been usual comic characteristics, and they have remained so since. Yet Corneille's experiment in incorporating these qualities in the character of Nicomède and so creating a new type of tragic hero came very near to success (there are certain scenes in which he goes too far). In modern terms, Nicomède combines the stiff upper lip with a capacity for bitter sarcasm.

The play, which was the first that Corneille gave to the Hôtel de Bourgogne, having left the Théâtre du Marais with the actor-manager Floridor after *Héraclius*, seems to have been well received. (All that Corneille has to say on this score is: 'La représentation n'a point déplu.')

---

[1] Though in title she was the Queen Mother, Anne of Austria was still virtually Queen of France, since her son, Louis XIV, was only eleven. Her personal relationship with Cardinal Mazarin, her Disraeli and rather more, was the subject of numerous innuendos and lampoons, especially provocative in 1649, at the time of the Fronde.

Its popularity was soon confirmed and grew during the remainder of the century. Between 1680 and 1700 the Comédie-Française acted it more frequently than any of Corneille's other plays except *Cinna* and *Le Cid*.[1]

About a year later, Corneille again indulged his fondness for the complicated plot and the melodramatic surprise in *Pertharite*, a play which embroidered on 'history' as freely as *Héraclius*. The conception is romanesque; the ethical assumptions seem almost a parody of those put forward seriously in a tragedy such as *Cinna*. Before, however, accusing Corneille of self-parody, one must recognize an alternative possibility: that, using a conventionally established ethos, in which neither he nor his audiences believed strongly at that date, he was playing an elaborate game of the emotions in a theatrical medium. From that point of view, this can be an instructive and fascinating play for the modern student. Contemporaries, however, did not appreciate it. It was evidently a complete failure, with no extenuating circumstances.

The effect on Corneille was to halt his career as a dramatist. 'Il vaut mieux que je prenne congé de moi-même que d'attendre qu'on me le donne tout à fait; et il est juste qu'après vingt années de travail je commence à m'apercevoir que je deviens trop vieux pour être encore à la mode,' he wrote with good enough grace in the *Au lecteur*. He retired to his native Rouen and occupied himself with an adaptation in French verse of the *Imitation of Christ*.

He had, however, left an escape-clause open. He had not, he said, made so definite a decision to leave the theatre that it could not be reversed, though it seemed highly probable that he would not write for it again.

CORNEILLE'S PLAYS
FROM *MÉLITE* TO *PERTHARITE*

(Only the tragedies and tragicomedies are summarized. The dates are those of first productions.)

Mélite, comedy, December 1629

Clitandre, tragedy, later styled tragicomedy, 1631
Possible partial source: Audiguier, *Histoire des amours de Lysandre et de Caliste* (novel, 1615).

[1] See Lancaster, *History*, II, p. 694.

The plot, too complicated to be adequately summarized here, is set forth in some 1,500 words in the *Argument* which Corneille published with the play.

A key character is the woman Caliste, who is loved by Rosidor who is loved by Dorise who is loved by Pymante. Clitandre, a relatively unimportant character in the action, is also in love with Caliste. Disregarding the numerous complications and misunderstandings, Pymante fails in an attempt to kill Rosidor, and the innocent Clitandre is put into prison in his place. When truth and justice finally prevail, Clitandre is released and married to Dorise, while Pymante, savagely maimed by Dorise in his pursuit of her, is sent for trial by the royal council. Rosidor is united to Caliste.

La Veuve, comedy, 1632

La Galerie du palais, comedy, 1633

La Suivante, comedy, 1634

La Place Royale, comedy, 1634

Médée, tragedy, 1635
Sources: Seneca, *Medea*, and Euripides, *Medea*.

The evil enchantress Médée has come to Corinth in pursuit of her errant husband Jason, who has deserted her with the intention of marrying Créuse, the daughter of Créon, King of Corinth. Créon orders her out of his kingdom, but allows her a day's grace and offers refuge to the children she has had with Jason, and whom she has brought with her.[1] In return for this supposed favour, Jason asks Médée to give her glittering dress to Créuse, who covets it. She does so, after having weaved a magic spell over it. When Créuse puts it on it burns into her flesh and has the same effect upon her father when he touches it. In their agony (on stage), Créon stabs himself, while Créuse expires after some time. Thirsting to punish Médée, Jason finds that she has already killed their young children, while she herself escapes in a magic chariot.

There is a secondary interest in the character of Égée, King of Athens, who is also in love with Créuse (Corneille: 'Pour donner à ce monarque

[1] Anouilh, in a new modernization of the subject (*Médée*, 1949), made the family travel in a caravan.

un peu plus d'intérêt dans l'action') and who attempts to abduct her. Imprisoned by Créon, Égée is delivered by Médée, to whom he promises refuge in his own kingdom.

L'Illusion comique, comedy, 1635–6 (see pp. 131–2)

Le Cid, tragicomedy, later styled tragedy, 1637
Source: Guillén de Castro: *Las mocedades del Cid.*

King Fernand of Castile appoints a new tutor (whose duties include instruction in arms) for the Crown Prince, and in so doing prefers the aged soldier Don Diègue to the vigorous Comte de Gormas. The Count's daughter, Chimène, is already betrothed to Don Diègue's son Rodrigue. Offended by the King's preference, the Count insults Don Diègue, who is too feeble physically to take up the challenge and calls on his son to avenge him. The hitherto unblooded Rodrigue does so, killing the father of his beloved Chimène. The rest of the play is taken up by Chimène's repeated pleas for the punishment of her father's killer, in spite of the dictates of her heart. Concurrently, Rodrigue repels a Moorish invasion, so confirming his bravery and his value to the State and earning the title of *Cid* (Lord). He also defeats in a duel a champion put up by Chimène. The King's final judgement is that Rodrigue and Chimène shall marry as originally intended, but only after a decent interval, of a year if necessary.

The emotional complications which make the play stem from the situation described. It should be added that the King's daughter, the Infanta, is also in love with Rodrigue, but is eventually brushed aside.

Horace, tragedy, 1640
Sources: in Dionysius of Halicarnassus and Livy.

The neighbouring cities of Rome and Alba are at war and to avoid a general battle it is agreed that each side shall name three champions to decide the issue between them. Rome's choice falls on Horace and his two brothers, that of Alba on Curiace and his two brothers. Horace is married to Sabine, an Alban woman and the sister of Curiace. Curiace is betrothed to Horace's sister Camille. Despite the pleas of the women, the warriors go out to fight. The combat is at first misreported, but it transpires that, after his two brothers have been killed, Horace has feigned flight, then turned and dispatched the three Curiaces one by one by his own hand, giving the victory to Rome. Bitterly reproached by Camille for killing her lover, Horace kills his sister for her un-Roman sentiments. His wife Sabine, even more indignant after Camille's murder, demands in vain the same fate. The last act is one of judgement, with the inflexibly patriotic father of Horace (and of Camille) pleading in his favour, Valère, a secondary suitor of Camille's, pleading against him, and Sabine urging a middle course (rejected): that she should be offered as a victim in her husband's place. The King, while condemning Horace's 'crime énorme', decides that his services to the State place him above punishment.

Cinna, ou la clémence d'Auguste, tragedy, 1640–1
Sources: Various, including Appian, Cassius Dio, Seneca, *De clementia*.

Émilie, whose father has been killed by César Auguste, has been brought up by the latter almost as a daughter. She plots, however, to avenge her father in a conspiracy which involves her lover Cinna and another Roman, Maxime, who later proves to be also in love with her. Preparations for the assassination are ripe when Auguste summons Cinna and Maxime – his trusted friends – and discusses with them his project of abdicating and retiring into private life. To Maxime's amazement, Cinna dissuades him. His secret motive is his promise to Émilie, which requires him to strike down Auguste at the height of his power. Later, the realization of Auguste's greatness of heart makes him begin to waver, but the implacable Émilie restores his determination.

The plot is now betrayed to Auguste by a servant of Maxime's, acting on his master's orders. Auguste is at once indignant, distressed and confused. Whom can he trust now? Shall he kill Cinna – and then, perhaps, himself? (Maxime is reported to be already dead.) Cinna is brought before him and, after an imperial harangue, is finally pardoned, as are Émilie, whose complicity is at last revealed, and Maxime, who proves to be alive after all. All praise his magnanimity and renounce their hatred, including even Émilie.

Polyeucte, tragedy, 1641–2
Source: Metaphrastes, adapted by Surius in *Vitae sanctorum*; probably also the Italian tragedy of *Polietto* by Girolamo Bartolommei.

Christianity is spreading in the Roman province of Armenia, governed by the Roman Senator Félix, who has recently married his daughter Pauline to the Armenian nobleman Polyeucte. The latter is converted to the new faith by his friend Néarque and baptized secretly, concealing the fact from his wife. Pauline has been troubled by a confused dream, in which her husband's life was threatened by an 'impious crowd' of Christians, by her own father Félix and, not least important, by a former lover of hers, Sévère, who has come to demand vengeance on Polyeucte. She and Sévère had been deeply in love in Rome formerly, but her father had forbidden the marriage because of Sévère's poverty. Later, Sévère rose to great influence and he now arrives in reality as the Emperor's emissary. He is thunderstruck by the news of Pauline's marriage, but is firmly told by her that, whatever her feelings, she intends to remain loyal to her husband.

In a religious ceremony in honour of Rome's victories, Polyeucte and Néarque mock the pagan gods and profane the altar. The fact that they are Christians is now public. Félix, already regretting his political blunder in marrying his daughter to the less influential man, is further alarmed at the prospect of Christian subversion in the province for which he is responsible. He has Néarque executed immediately, but spares Polyeucte whom he tries to persuade by every means to recant. Polyeucte remains irreducible against both Félix and Pauline and is finally led out to execution in his wife's presence. Pauline now declares herself a Christian. The wavering Félix also experiences a sincere conversion. Sévère, greatly moved, promises to plead with the Emperor in the hope of making him change his anti-Christian policy.

La Mort de Pompée, tragedy, 1642–3
Principal source: Lucan, *Pharsalia*.

Pompey, after his defeat by Julius Caesar at Pharsala, has sailed to Egypt for refuge. The Pharaoh Ptolemy is persuaded by his council to have him killed as he steps ashore. Ptolemy's sister Cleopatra, who should have shared the throne with him under the terms of their father's will, has opposed the killing, and then reveals that she is backed by Caesar, who is in love with her. When Caesar arrives with a huge fleet, Ptolemy tries to conciliate him, but finds that the murder of Pompey has not helped: Caesar admired Pompey. Pompey's widow Cornelia, who has been captured, is now brought in. She defies Caesar who, however, treats her with all honour. Ptolemy, aware of his own dangerous position, agrees to a plot by his council to fill

Alexandria with Egyptian troops and kill Caesar at a State banquet that evening. After a *galant* scene between Caesar and Cleopatra, in which Cleopatra raises the question of her reception in Rome if she should go there as a queen and begins pleading for clemency for Ptolemy's counsellors (she is unaware of their new treachery), Cornelia enters to reveal the plot against Caesar, which she has discovered. She desires his death, but not in such an ignoble fashion.

A battle takes place in the town (reported) in which Caesar is victorious and Ptolemy is killed. Caesar has Cleopatra proclaimed Queen of Egypt. Cornelia, completely uncompromising and now in possession of her cremated husband's ashes which she carries with her in an urn, warns Caesar against marrying a queen, declares her intention of rallying support against him, and leaves. The play ends with Cleopatra firmly established on the throne, though mourning her brother. Caesar's relations with her are left inconclusive.

Le Menteur, comedy, 1643

La Suite du Menteur, comedy, 1644

Rodogune, Princesse des Parthes, tragedy, 1644
Principal source: Appian, *Roman History* (*The Syrian Wars*), much altered.

Cléopâtre, Queen of Syria, has twin sons, Séleucus and Antiochus, by her first husband, King Nicanor. In the past Nicanor was believed to have died as a war-prisoner of the Parthians and Cléopâtre then married his brother Antiochus, of the same name as one of her sons. This older Antiochus was killed in battle. Nicanor proved to be still alive and marched back towards Syria with the intention of punishing his wife for her innocent infidelity and regaining the throne. He brought with him Rodogune, a Parthian princess whom he meant to marry to seal his alliance with Parthia. He also meant to disinherit his sons Séleucus and Antiochus in favour of his future children with Rodogune. Cléopâtre ambushed him on the way, killed him, it was said, with her own hand, and took Rodogune prisoner.

When the action begins, Rodogune is living in semi-captivity at the Syrian court. Cléopâtre is about to reveal the long-kept secret of which of her twin sons is the first-born; he will be crowned and married to Rodogune as an act of appeasement towards the Parthians. But in reality Cléopâtre wishes to keep the power for herself and destroy Rodogune. She offers her sons a bargain: she will name as king whichever of them kills the princess. The brothers are dismayed by their mother's ruthlessness and reject the proposal. Both are in love with Rodogune, but are bound together by so loyal a friendship that neither wishes to take advantage of the other. Rodogune, pressed to say which she prefers, eventually admits that it is Antiochus, but insists that her own royal blood obliges her to marry whichever of them is declared king. No less determined than Cléopâtre, she demands in her turn that one of them shall 'punish' his mother and so avenge the death of the old King Nicanor. While the brothers, horrified and defenceless, hesitate, Cléopâtre conspires. She names Antiochus as the elder, has Séleucus secretly killed, and prepares to poison Antiochus and Rodogune at their wedding-feast. The plan misfires. Cléopâtre herself drinks the poison and dies.

Théodore, vierge et martyre, tragedy, 1645
Sources: St Ambrose, *De virginibus,* and Surius, *Vitae sanctorum.* There are also evident parallels with *Polyeucte,* with suggestions similarly from a tragedy by Girolamo Bartolommei, *Teodora.*

Théodore, Princess of Antioch, has become Christian, secretly at first. She is loved by Didyme and would respond but for her new faith. She is also loved, without responding, by Placide, the son of Valens, the Roman Governor of Antioch. The Governor's evil second wife, Marcelle, wishes Placide to marry her own daughter by a previous marriage, who is languishing for love of him (this character does not appear, and dies later).

Marcelle persuades the weak Valens to condemn Théodore. He sentences her, not to martyrdom, for which she is quite ready, but to public prostitution if she will not recant. She is handed over to the soldiery but saved by Didyme – also a Christian now. On the pretext of going in to her first he changes clothes with her and she escapes so disguised. Didyme is arrested and brought before his rival Placide, who deals with him generously and offers to help the Christian lovers to escape to Egypt. Marcelle, however, intervenes. In a reported scene of great violence she fatally stabs Didyme, Théodore, who has returned to give herself up, and finally herself. Placide, arriving just too late to rescue the pair, stabs himself, whether fatally or not is left in doubt.

Héraclius, Empereur d'Orient, tragedy, 1647
Source: Germ in Baronius, *Annales ecclesiastici*, but the plot is Corneille's own invention.

Principal Characters:

Phocas, Emperor of Byzantium.

Héraclius, son of the Emperor Maurice (predecessor of Phocas, and murdered by him), believed to be Martian, son of Phocas; in love with Eudoxe.

Martian, son of Phocas, believed to be Léonce, son of Léontine; in love with Pulchérie.

Pulchérie, daughter of the ex-Emperor Maurice (and so, in fact, sister of Héraclius); in love with Martian.

Léontine, a noble lady, formerly *gouvernante* of Héraclius and Martian.

Eudoxe, daughter of Léontine; in love with Héraclius.

Exupère, a Byzantine nobleman.

The plot is too complicated to be adequately summarized. It rests on the supposed identities and relationships of the characters listed above. Léontine, after secretly substituting her own son Léonce to be slaughtered in place of the infant prince Héraclius, had then changed over the latter with the infant Martian, entrusted by Phocas to her care. Her object was that Héraclius should succeed to the throne, on the supposition that he was Phocas's natural heir. Only Léontine knows the whole truth, though Héraclius is informed of his own true identity when he grows up. The point comes at which Phocas, though determined to kill one of the two young men, does not know which is his son. Martian has been led to believe that he is Héraclius, and even the real Héraclius begins to doubt his own identity. There is a further complication in the danger of incest with Pulchérie.

Finally, Phocas is killed in a conspiracy promoted by Exupère, who had pretended to be his supporter while working against him. Héraclius becomes Emperor and marries Eudoxe, while Martian, alias Héraclius, alias Léonce, is fully contented with marriage to Pulchérie.

Don Sanche d'Aragon, comédie héroïque, 1649
Sources: *Don Pélage*, French novel by P. de Juvenal (1645), and *El Palacio confuso*, play by Lope de Vega and/or Mira de Amescua.

Isabelle, the widowed Queen of Castile, is urged by her subjects to choose a new husband, preferably from among the three noblemen whose names are put forward, the Counts Lope, Manrique and Alvar. Don Alvar, while unable to decline this honour, is really in love with Elvire, Princess of Aragon, who, together with her mother, Queen Léonor, has been living in exile at the court of Castile. These two are on the point of returning to Aragon to regain the throne. Also at the court of Castile is Carlos, a warrior of great prowess but of unknown origin. The Counts rebuke Carlos for presuming to take a seat in the Queen's presence when he is only a plebeian, whereupon Isabelle, who is secretly in love with him, ennobles him on the spot, hands him her ring and charges him to decide which of the three Counts shall marry her. His solution is to challenge them to fight him and then, if they beat him, each other; the winner to take the Queen. (The duel is postponed on Isabelle's orders and does not in fact take place.)

After much emotional skirmishing, particularly between Carlos and Isabelle and Alvar and Elvire, who cannot understand that her lover should be ready to fight for the hand of Isabelle ('To make myself worthy of *you*', is his sincerely meant reply), a report arrives that Carlos is really Don Sanche, the lost heir to the throne of Aragon. Certain that he is only the son of a humble fisherman, a fact which he has carefully concealed, Carlos strenuously denies the rumour. But the fisherman turns up in person. Carlos, though finally disgraced in his own mind, does not disown his 'father'. Further revelations follow. A letter proves that Carlos is indeed the Prince of Aragon, entrusted as an infant to the fisherman's wife, who has kept the secret even from her husband. Carlos/Don Sanche, now rightful King of Aragon, will unite his kingdom with Castile by marrying Isabelle. He gives his sister Elvire in marriage to her lover Alvar. The fisherman is to be honourably rewarded.

Andromède, a mythological machine-play, though styled a 'tragedy', 1650

Nicomède, tragedy, 1650–1

Principal source: Justin, *Historiae Philippicae*, Bks. 34 and 38, with probable borrowings from Rotrou's *Cosroès*.

Prusias, King of Bithynia, has married as his second wife Arsinoé, a dangerous and intriguing woman, determined to secure the throne for her son Attale and get rid of Nicomède, the son of Prusias by a first marriage. She tricks Nicomède into leaving an army which he has been leading successfully in the field to return to court, where she hopes he will fall foul of his father and of the Roman emissary Flaminius. The latter has come to ensure the succession to the throne of Attale, a Roman protégé, and to exclude the anti-Roman Nicomède. He also appears to favour the marriage of Attale to Laodice, the young Queen of Armenia, in captivity at Prusias's court. She and Nicomède, however, are firmly in love with one another.

The play continues with Nicomède defiant, Laodice determined, Attale wooing her fruitlessly, Arsinoé intriguing, Flaminius threatening, and the weak Prusias wavering continually. Finally, there is a popular revolt, provoked by the energetic Laodice, in favour of Nicomède. The latter has been imprisoned by his father but is freed by Attale, unexpectedly siding with him after his realization that he himself is only being used as the tool of Rome. Nicomède, now in command, forgives everyone, including Arsinoé. There are no deaths, except of minor characters, and the only slight cloud left at the end is uncertainty as to what Rome's reaction will be when Flaminius, who has grown to admire Nicomède, has returned to report to the Senate.

Pertharite, Roi des Lombards, tragedy, December (?) 1651
Sources: Paulus Diaconus; *History of the Langobards*, translated from the Latin by A. Du Verdier in *Diverses leçons* . . . (1577), and Erycius Puteanus, *Historiae barbaricae*, Bk. II. The historical events on which Corneille's play is distantly based occurred in the seventh century A.D. during the domination of Northern Italy by the barbarian Lombards.

Grimoald, formerly Duke of Benevento, has become King of the Lombards by conquest, after defeating the previous king, Pertharite, now missing and believed dead. Grimoald achieved this in fulfilment of his oath to Pertharite's brother Gundebert, who died in battle against Pertharite after exacting Grimoald's promise to avenge him as a condition of marrying his sister Edwige. But when the play opens Grimoald has transferred his love to Rodelinde, Pertharite's presumed widow. She refuses him scornfully, remaining faithful to her husband's memory. The situation is envenomed by the bitterness of the neglected Edwige, the rivalry of the two women, and the machinations of the

villain of the play, the Duke Garibalde. The latter has a secret interest
in his ambition to marry Edwige himself, as a step to usurping the
throne. He persuades Grimoald to threaten to kill Rodelinde's son, who
is in his power, if she persists in her refusal of him.[1] After hesitation
she takes up the challenge. She consents to the proposed murder and
even offers to join in it and then marry Grimoald as he demands.
They will have become partners in crime and both will lose their
gloire. After marriage, she will make his life a misery: 'On those conditions take my hand if you dare.'

At this point a *coup de théâtre* brings back the missing Pertharite,
but both Garibalde and Grimoald refuse to recognize him, and he is
imprisoned as an imposter. After strenuous efforts by Grimoald to
make him confess the supposed deceit (this involves putting pressure
on both Edwige and Rodelinde and a change in Grimoald's relationship
with them), Pertharite is allowed to escape, with an escort to see him
out of the kingdom. Grimoald now admits that he had recognized
Pertharite from the beginning, but concealed the fact for reasons of
state. A second *coup de théâtre* brings Pertharite back once more. His
party has been ambushed by the villainous Garibalde, whom, however,
he has killed before being recaptured. Grimoald: 'Oh God, all over
again!' ('Quel combat pour la seconde fois!')

But it is a *combat de générosité*. Grimoald, the moral hero of the play,
yields the crown to Pertharite. Edwige, having already released
Grimoald from his oath of vengeance given to her dead brother
Gundebert, is ready to marry him without a crown. Pertharite,
however, offers him the throne of Pavia, retaining Milan for himself
and Rodelinde. Rodelinde begs Grimoald's pardon for having mis-
judged him.

[1] The parallel between this situation and the theme of Racine's *Andromaque* was
pointed out by Voltaire. However, Rodelinde's reaction is quite different to
Andromaque's, as is the subsequent development of the plot.

7

CORNEILLE'S PRINCIPAL CONTEMPORARIES

Rotrou – his *Hercule mourant* and other secondary plays – *Saint Genest* – *Venceslas* – *Cosroès* – ethos and general qualities – Du Ryer – *Alcionée* – his biblical tragedies, *Saül* and *Esther* – *Scévole* – compared to *Cinna* – his romanesque tragicomedies – dramatic technique and verse-style – Tristan L'Hermite – two subjects from Hardy: *La Mariane* and *Panthée* – *La Folie du sage* – *La Mort de Chrispe* – contrast with Racine's *Phèdre* – *La Mort du Grand Osman* – other contemporary Turkish plays – Tristan's peculiarities as a dramatist – lyric qualities and use of imagery – political interest and love interest

The expansion of the theatre in the 1630s was matched by the appearance of a number of new dramatists attempting, with varying success, to meet its requirements. In addition to Mairet and Corneille, they included Scudéry, Benserade, Boisrobert, Desmarets, La Calprenède and Guérin de Bouscal. These last six produced some forty plays of the three main kinds in the decade 1630–40, Scudéry with thirteen plays being appreciably the most prolific. Greater talent, however, was shown by three other dramatists: Rotrou, Du Ryer and Tristan L'Hermite. If none of these was able to maintain his work consistently on the same level as Corneille's, none can be qualified as minor. All wrote a certain number of important plays which deservedly survived them.

II

Jean Rotrou, born at Dreux in 1609 of a family of lawyers, had become the *poète à gages* of Bellerose in succession to Hardy at the early age of nineteen after the performance of his first play, *L'Hypocondriaque*. From then on he provided the Hôtel de Bourgogne with a series of plays paralleling Corneille's contributions to the Marais, though at first on a more prolific scale. Between 1629 and 1637 he wrote twenty

	MAIRET	ROTROU	P. CORNEILLE	DU RYER	TRISTAN L'HERMITE
1634	*Sophonisbe*	*Hercule mourant*			
1635	*Marc-Antoine*	*Crisante*	*Médée*		
1636					
1637	*Solyman*	*Antigone / Laure persécutée* TC	*Le Cid* TC	*Lucrèce*	*La Mariane*
1638	*Roland furieux* TC			*Alcionée*	*Panthée*
1639	*Athenaïs* TC			*Clarigène* TC	
1640	*Sidonie* TC	*Iphigénie*	*Horace*	*Saül*	
1641			*Cinna*		
1642			*Polyeucte*	*Esther*	
1643		*Bélisaire* TC	*Mort de Pompée*		*La Folie du sage*
1644			*Rodogune*	*Scévole / Bérénice* TC	*Mort de Sénèque*
1645		*Saint Genest*	*Théodore*		*Mort de Chrispe*
1646		*D. Bernard de Cabrère* TC			
1647		*Venceslas*	*Héraclius*	*Thémistocle*	*Mort du Grand Osman*
1648		*Cosroès*		*Nitocris* TC	
1649		*D. Lope de Cardone* TC	*D. Sanche d'Aragon* CH		
1650			*Nicomède*	*Dynamis* TC	
1651			*Pertharite*		
1652					
1653					
1654				*Anaxandre* TC	

Dates are of first productions and accurate as far as is known.
The plays listed are tragedies except where otherwise indicated.

TC . . . tragicomedy
CH . . . comédie héroïque

surviving comedies and tragicomedies, in addition to a number of others which have been lost.[1] The tragicomedies were of the romantic and sometimes melodramatic kind which then dominated the stage. His first experiment in pure but not regular tragedy was his *Hercule mourant*, an imitation of Seneca's *Hercules oetaeus*, but with additions and developments of his own. This play, written for an elaborate multiple décor and ending with a machine-ascent of Hercules to heaven, was certainly produced at the Hôtel de Bourgogne in 1634 and, as has been suggested in the previous chapter, may have prompted Corneille to write his *Médée* to compete with it. A significantly earlier first production in 1631 has, however, been argued for *Hercule mourant*,[2] in which case it would be the first play openly described as a tragedy to appear on the Parisian stage since the publication of Hardy's works and even more notable as a pioneering experiment.

A return to Senecan subjects is a perceptible if secondary feature in the French theatre of the 1630s[3] which revived the tradition established by Garnier. Rotrou himself borrowed little more from Seneca, but looked back, as again Garnier had done, to the Greeks in two later tragedies. His *Antigone* (1637) was a marriage of two subjects (whereas Garnier had attempted to combine three): the struggle between the two sons of Oedipus, Eteocles and Polyneices (from the *Thebais* of Statius), and the personal tragedy of Antigone, determined to give her brother burial in defiance of her uncle Creon. But the subjects are not disparate and, in adapting them to the five-act form of his time, Rotrou was reasonably successful in preserving the unity of interest. His *Iphigénie en Aulide* (1640) derived from the tragedy of Euripides, with a few alterations which were Rotrou's own. At its date it was a lone experiment which is chiefly remembered for having exerted a certain influence on Racine, as, more importantly, did *Antigone*.

Concurrently with these derivations from Seneca and the Greeks, Rotrou was continuing to write both violent and romantic plays of a different order. His *Crisante* (1635) was an irregular tragedy, whose

[1] See Lancaster, *History*, I, pp. 310–11, footnote. Of Rotrou's entire production 35 plays have survived.

[2] See D.-Holsboer, *Le Théâtre de l'Hôtel de Bourgogne*, I, p. 163.

[3] The chief examples, besides *Hercule mourant*, were: La Pinelière, *Hippolyte* (1634–5?), Corneille, *Médée* (1635), L'Héritier Nouvelon, *Hercule furieux* (1637), Monléon, *Thyeste* (1637).

story, reminiscent of Hardy's dramas, was taken from Plutarch and other historians. It concerned the rape of a captured Queen of Corinth by a Roman centurion, her justification before her husband, and her eventual revenge and suicide. The centurion's severed head was brought on to the stage.

His *Laure persécutée*, probably produced in 1637, has a love intrigue, a happy ending and a fairy-tale atmosphere. Though styled a tragi-comedy, no doubt because of the royal standing of the characters and a peril of death which does not materialize, it comes in fact nearer to romantic comedy.

Another tragicomedy, *Bélisaire*, which in fact would qualify as a tragedy by the sombreness of its story, appeared in 1643 and resembled the tragedies which Corneille was to write in the same decade. Set in sixth-century Byzantium, it concerns the efforts of the Empress Theodora to kill the general Belisarius in order to avenge herself for having being refused in love by him. After having vainly employed several intermediary killers she attempts to stab him herself, but is prevented and taken before her husband the Emperor. She falsely accuses Belisarius of having made love to her, as a result of which the Emperor has his eyes put out and he dies. Theodora then confesses the deceit.

Bélisaire contained several features which have come to be looked on as Cornelian, and one which might be called Racinian. Belisarius is a *généreux*, winning over his would-be killers by his magnanimity. The Emperor Justinian also, in his early dealings with him, obeys the same magnanimous code. Theodora is a vindictive and ruthless woman (until her final confession) of the type of Corneille's female villains, all of whom, except Médée, she preceded. Her motivation is frustrated passion, as with Médée and as later, with greater sophistication, in Racine.

III

Up to this point in his career Rotrou had been a successful author of comedies – the most important part of his work – of tragicomedies of mixed kinds, and tragedies which it is possible to describe as experimental. He went on to produce the three important tragedies for which he is best remembered: *Saint Genest*, *Venceslas* and *Cosroès*.

The first, fully entitled *Le Véritable Saint Genest*, probably to distinguish it from *Le Martyre de Saint Genest*, a play by the minor writer

Desfontaines which is likely to have suggested the subject to Rotrou, was first produced in 1645. It was a saint play of a peculiar kind, modernized to fulfil the requirements of a theatre later characterized as baroque. Within the 'real' framework of a Roman court is acted the play-within-a-play of the conversion of St Adrian, martyred historically under Diocletian, who is represented as watching the play. The famous actor Genest, who plays the principal part, is converted to Christianity in the course of the performance and ends by proclaiming the fact from the stage in his own person, so defying the Emperor and inviting real martyrdom in his turn. The indefinite border-line between the real and the theatrical is maintained by the frequent references to stage practice. Genest and an actress are shown rehearsing their parts. There is a conversation about the scenery with the *décorateur*. Hangers-on of the court pester the actresses backstage and are called to order. When Genest departs from his role to make his personal profession of faith, the rest of the cast become confused and call on the prompter.

There are two parallel scenes of great interest (III. iv and V. ii). In the first Genest, playing the part of Adrian, is visited in prison by Adrian's wife Natalie, played by the actress Marcelle. Natalie reveals that she herself is secretly a Christian and promises her husband her full support in the terrible death which awaits him. In the second scene, in the 'real' prison, Marcelle blames Genest bitterly for joining a cause founded by 'un imposteur, un fourbe, un crucifié' and supported by the dregs of the population. She begs him to recant for the sake of the company, who without their leader will be lost and unable to gain a livelihood.

Such features, with the constant interplay between illusion and reality, have made it possible to regard the theme of this tragedy as a typical example of baroque metamorphosis. Genest begins by consciously acting the part of the martyr (the rehearsal scenes make this point clearly), then in performance he identifies more and more closely with the character, and finally he *is* the martyr and the part he is playing is indistinguishable from his real self. If that progression, as here baldly stated, were convincingly embodied in Rotrou's tragedy, this would be one of the most remarkable dramas of its time and indeed of French literature. But it falls somewhat short of that.

Imitated from a play by Lope de Vega[1] with probable borrowings

[1] *Lo fingido verdadero.*

from a Jesuit Latin play, Cellot's *Sanctus Adrianus* (1630), *Saint Genest* still bears the marks of the works of piety which inspired it. The unsophisticated psychology and the mechanical miraculous interventions carry over into Rotrou's tragedy and obscure the potentially more interesting development of character. Genest's incertitude begins to appear at an early stage (II. ii):

> D'effet comme de nom je me trouve être un autre;
> Je feins moins Adrien que je ne le deviens,
> Et prends avec son nom des sentiments chrétiens.

A little later in the same scene the heavens open (a familiar stage effect) and a voice speaks encouraging Genest to persevere towards his conversion. Almost convinced, Genest then wonders whether the voice was really supernatural or whether someone was playing a trick on him and expresses his doubts. He has however already shown himself to be ripe for conversion. He then acts the play before the Emperor's court, speaking with a realistic fervour which his audience greatly admires,[1] but without departing from his script. Finally in Act IV, Sc. iv he openly realizes his conversion. Heaven speaks again (flames are sent down from it supposed, no doubt, to be seen by Genest alone) and he leaves the stage to experience a miraculous baptism. From then on he is no longer the actor but the defiant Christian convert.

The significance of what was ostensibly a saint play on the professional Parisian stage at that date is not easy to determine, though there had been several undistinguished precedents.[2] Little is explained by referring back to the success some three years previously of Corneille's *Polyeucte*, with its quite different political and love interests – both absent from Rotrou's play. A more plausible assumption is that Rotrou wrote his tragedy to give the Hôtel de Bourgogne a martyr play to compete with Corneille's *Théodore*, which the Marais produced in the same year 1645. At least it was the only example of its kind in Rotrou's drama and was followed at an interval of two years by a totally different work.

[1] The interior play consistently glorifies the martyr, which is unrealistic in the circumstances in which it is supposed to be performed. Genest the actor had acquired a reputation for ridiculing the Christians on the stage.

[2] See above p. 143, footnote 1. If Du Ryer's two biblical tragedies of 1639–40 and 1642 are added, though they are quite different in character, it becomes possible to discern a minor revival of sacred plays in the early 1640s.

Venceslas, produced late in 1647, was again based on a Spanish original, *No hay padre siendo rey* by Francisco de Rojas Zorilla. First styled a tragicomedy, then a tragedy, it is, in broader terms, a drama with violent episodes and an ultimately happy ending. The real protagonist is not Venceslas, the ageing King of Poland, but his unruly son and heir Ladislas. This wild and impulsive prince, who had attempted to seduce the woman he loved until she made him understand she could be had only in marriage, who defies his father and suggests his abdication, who murders his own brother out of jealousy (though under the impression that he is a different man), is a character rare in the French drama of the time. In the end he is tamed, pardoned, and rewarded far more highly than his moral behaviour deserves,[1] and he is thus an incompletely tragic figure. But he can justifiably be seen as a *révolté*, impelled by passions (love and the urge to dominate) which take no account of any ethical code.

Venceslas has a political framework if attention is focused on the problems and actions of the old King. His reliance on his favourite, the Duke Féderic, and his elder son's resentment of the Duke's influence, could also fall into the political field. But, except for the King, love of various kinds supplies the overwhelmingly strongest motivation of all the characters: passionate love in Ladislas, conventional romantic love between his brother Alexandre and the Duchess Cassandre (who is the object of Ladislas's desires), and chivalrous love (exceptionally) in the Duke who hopes for the hand of Ladislas's sister and finally obtains it.

In *Cosroès* (1648) the motivation is reversed. There is a minor love interest which occupies little space in the play. The main action stems entirely from the political question of the succession to the throne of Persia. Sira, the second wife of the elderly King Cosroès, is determined that her own son Mardesane shall succeed him, to the exclusion of his half-brother Siroès. The latter, as the King's eldest son by a first marriage, has a prior right and is supported by the people, the army and the barons. Plots and counter-plots eventually result in the triumph of Siroès and his party.

---

[1] His father who, as King, is bound to uphold the death-sentence passed on Ladislas for the murder of his brother, abdicates in his favour as the only way out of the dilemma.

In this, the most immediately effective of Rotrou's tragedies, the vicissitudes are exciting and well organized, the characters well contrasted and clearly drawn. Most prominent is the ruthlessly ambitious Queen, akin to the Théodore of *Bélisaire* and to certain Cornelian characters.[1] The old King, weaker than his counterpart in *Venceslas*, is completely under her influence; a psychological explanation of his lack of self-confidence is contained in the fact that he killed his own father to gain the throne, a memory which haunts him and gives rise to a scene of remorseful madness (II. i) similar to scenes in sixteenth-century tragedy and in Corneille's *Mélite*.[2] The effective hero, Siroès, though not temperamentally irresolute, proves a weak leader of revolt because of the family ties which link him to his adversaries, and in the last act he is ready to give up all he has so far gained by submitting to his father's authority, to the horror of his supporters. However, he is too late. His opponents, including his father, commit suicide, and he is left in reluctant possession of the throne.

The moral values of this play are even less definable than in *Venceslas*. They consist purely in the glorification of royal power, with the assumption that the pursuit of a rightful claim to it justifies any acts. In balancing against this the claims of family affection, Siroès is not, it is true, explicitly blamed (though he is overridden by the events of the play and this could be interpreted as the dramatist's condemnation of his weakness). On the other hand, he is not commended either for his moments of compassion and one cannot relate them to any moral imperative of a general kind.

Rotrou's other plays of this period were two tragicomedies of lower quality, *Don Bernard de Cabrère* (1647) and *Don Lope de Cardone* (1649). Both had romanesque plots, enriched in the first of them by an element of ironical comedy, but neither adds anything to Rotrou's reputation. Shortly after this Rotrou died, at the age of forty-one. He held the post of *lieutenant civil* of his native town of Dreux and he returned there from Paris to fulfil his functions during an outbreak of plague which had already killed his cousin the mayor. He also fell victim to the epidemic.

[1] See above p. 149.   [2] Ibid., p. 128.

IV

The thirty-five known plays which Rotrou wrote in a little over twenty years were the work of a professional supplying a theatre-company with some of the regular material they needed. To a considerable extent, therefore, he followed or tried to anticipate public taste in the hope of a successful production, and some of what appear to have been his experiments, including *Saint Genest*, may require no profounder explanation. More than any of his contemporaries, except Scarron in comedy, he drew heavily on Spanish sources. But he was far from being a hack. He had too much talent as a writer and too much originality, even if limited in scope, ever to be dismissed in such terms. Yet he was hardly a great enough dramatist to create a world of consistent values, however artificial, and to search for this in his varied productions, partially rewarding as that process is with Corneille, would be a futile task with Rotrou. One can find recurrent features and even a development of them from play to play, but little on which to construct an ethical or social background of the kind which can be deduced from the work of the truly major writer.

His three important tragedies which we have considered came late in his career and almost, it would seem, as an accident. They cannot be seen in any sense as a fruition of his earlier work and there is the further consideration that they alternated with the two mediocre tragicomedies mentioned above. They possessed, as has been said, no definable moral background. There are some absolutes which are taken for granted: in *Saint Genest*, that Christianity is the right thing; in *Cosroès*, a legitimate claim to the throne; *Venceslas*, however, is an amoral play. In none of these are the claims of virtue, honour or chivalry of any great importance, while *gloire* (rarely mentioned) is a matter of reaching the highest eminence, the martyr's crown or the throne. The 'Roman' ethos, characteristic of Corneille's plays of 1640–3, is entirely absent from Rotrou's plays of only a few years later. Their interest lies in their characters, evil or good, and in the exciting development of the plots. The significance of this in the 1640s, so soon after the apparent triumph of regular 'classical' tragedy on the French stage, cannot be overlooked. These plays, like all Rotrou's later works, are technically regular in that they observe the unities of time and place and, in most cases, of action. But they are far from the models set up by *Sophonisbe*, *Cinna* or even *Horace*, and they illustrate the persistent attraction of melodramatic tragedy and tragicomedy.

Rotrou's dramatic verse, while not reaching the heights of gravity and *pompe* so admired in some of Corneille's plays, is a more than adequate instrument. It is supple and expressive, excellently suited to lively dialogue. When appropriate, his characters can speak with great vigour and even sarcasm. Occasionally his love-speeches are marked by preciosity but apart from that feature, inevitable at the date, his verse-style is neither affected nor laboured and lends itself admirably to the speaking voice.

V

Pierre Du Ryer (1600–58) was the son of Isaac Du Ryer, who held a court appointment as a King's Secretary and wrote two early dramatic pastorals and a collection of poems. At the age of twenty-one Pierre succeeded his father in his post at court, which he later sold to become secretary to the Duc de Vendôme. Meanwhile he had studied law and qualified as a barrister. His brush with the ageing Hardy in 1628 at about the date of his first play, the tragicomedy *Arétaphile*, has already been described.[1] Hardy's contemptuous references to 'affected court poets' and to 'excrements of the bar' both fit the younger Du Ryer. During the years 1628–34 he produced a total of eight plays, including six irregular romantic tragicomedies, one pastoral and a comedy of original conception, *Les Vendanges de Suresnes* (1633). This had a pastoral plot with bourgeois characters in a modern setting – the banks of the Seine near Paris.

In 1636, two years after Mairet's *Sophonisbe*, Du Ryer's first attempt at regular tragedy was performed. This was *Lucrèce*, the story from Livy of the rape of Lucretia by Sextus Tarquin after her boastful husband's unwise bet on her chastity. The rape occurs offstage, Lucretia's ultimate suicide on stage. By this act she preserves her *gloire*, founded on her *honneur*, but apart from this the Cornelian values are hardly in evidence. The plot is too brutal and the victimized heroine's distress too prominent for there to be any question of a code of chivalrous behaviour.

That position was directly reversed in Du Ryer's second tragedy, *Alcionée*, probably produced in 1637, shortly after *Le Cid*. One of the

[1] See above p. 106.

two or three major tragedies of Du Ryer and a play which continued to be remembered and appreciated for a generation, *Alcionée* was concerned with an idealized form of love which (unlike that of *Le Cid*) had ultimately tragic consequences. The story, adapted from Ariosto's *Orlando furioso*, was a simple one and in that sense 'classic'. The hero Alcionée, having been refused the hand of the princess Lydie because he is not of royal blood, rebels against her father and, after devastating the kingdom and holding the King at his mercy, he generously restores him to the throne. Having proved the strength of his passion by this warlike feat, he has enforced no terms, but considers he has received the promise of Lydie's hand from her defeated father. He wishes there to be no confusion between ambition for the throne, which he disclaims, and his personal love for the princess. But he has voluntarily placed himself in a materially weak position and is reduced to pleading for her hand. The King is non-committal and leaves the decision to his daughter. She, having secretly come to love Alcionée, feels that honour forbids her consent:

> Ici mon amour est un crime
> Et ma haine est une vertu.

She continues in this frame of mind, with *amour* gradually gaining the upper hand, but not until it is too late. Alcionée, dismissed by the King and, he believes, by the princess, commits suicide. He is brought in dying and learns at last that Lydie's hatred of him was feigned, in obedience to her 'vaine grandeur'. So the play has a pathetically romantic ending.

VI

Alcionée was followed by an unremarkable romantic tragicomedy, *Clarigène* (1637–8). Regular in construction, in compliance with the fashion now extending to tragicomedy, it had a complicated plot dependent on the coincidence that two different characters possessed identical names. The ending was happy. Without transition, Du Ryer then wrote two biblical tragedies, *Saül* and *Esther*.

Saül (1639–40) may have owed something to Jean de La Taille's tragedy of the 1550s, *Saül le furieux*,[1] as well as to the biblical sources, which contain all the essentials of the story. Du Ryer's main divergence

---

[1] See above p. 11.

from La Taille was that he did not introduce David into his play but concentrated the interest on the guilt-haunted Saul and his children and ended the tragedy with the lamentations and death of the old King. With the exception of Billard, who had written a *Saül* in *c.* 1610, no other dramatists are known to have used this admirable tragic subject. Though basically similar, Du Ryer's treatment of it is superior to Jean de La Taille's. There is considerable power in his presentation of a ruler in his last days, condemned (he believes) by heaven, suspecting everyone, confused as to his right course, threatened by external enemies and by internal revolt. In despair Saul consults the Pythoness (the Witch of Endor), who at his command raises up the ghost of Samuel. Samuel prophesies immediate disaster and the death of the King's children. Though Saul, who knows he has sinned by invoking infernal help, doubts for a time whether the ghost was really Samuel's or a lying spirit, the prophecy proves completely accurate.

The English reader will find some features of *Macbeth* in this story and its treatment, with the difference that Shakespeare shows Macbeth's crime as well as his punishment. Du Ryer's witch-scene seems in comparison to be tame and lacking in horror, though in the absence of stage directions the method of performance remains uncertain. The ghost of Samuel, however, must appear on stage to deliver its lines. Other effects also offend against the spirit of regular tragedy. In the last act there is the suggestion of a battle in the background, fighting-men come and go, Jonathan is carried in wounded and dies on stage where the bodies of two of Saul's other children are lying. Saul finally kills himself before the audience.

The unity of place is at best that of the modified multiple décor. While the scene of most of the play is Saul's palace, there is also the scene outside the witch's cave and the last act takes place in a wood near the battlefield. It would also be unrealistic to suppose that the unity of time is observed. The unity of action certainly is, though the material is rather thin for five acts and demands padding in the form of long *tirades* reminiscent of the sixteenth-century drama. Saul's final lamentation over his downfall, already factually known and psychologically registered, runs to over 200 lines.

The play, however, won some contemporary esteem and is noteworthy as a reasonably successful treatment of a theme apparently better suited to a different period and conception of drama.

Du Ryer's next tragedy was also drawn from the Bible, but in spite of this it was much nearer to the secular drama of the time. *Esther* (1642) was treated as a drama of court intrigue revolving on frustrated love and jealousy. The first three acts are concerned with the replacement of the disgraced Queen of Persia, Vasthi, by the sweet-natured Esther, and the intrigues of the King's minister Aman to prevent this, since he is secretly in love with Esther himself. This is his motivation and the political question of the Jews in exile remains in the background. Only between Acts III and IV does Aman persuade the King to decree the massacre of the Jews,[1] partly because of his hatred of them, but more specifically to ruin Esther, whom he will represent to the King as favouring them. At the same time he sets afoot a plot to assassinate the King.

All this springs from amorous frustration and the Jewish question in its more political form serves only to bring about the happy dénouement. In an attempt to save her people Esther risks everything by revealing that she is a Jewess, a fact unknown before both to the King and to Aman, while at the same time the King learns that the captive Jews have rendered him a signal service by unmasking another plot against him. Aman is sent to execution, his place as minister is given to the Jews' champion Mardochée, Esther becomes Queen, and the Jewish people, almost as a secondary consequence, are saved.

Earlier plays on the story of Esther had been written by Rivaudeau (*Aman*, 1566), Matthieu (*Vasthi* and *Aman*, both 1589) and Montchrestien (*Aman*, 1601), but the subject had not appeared on the professional stage in Du Ryer's time. Nor was it dramatized again until Racine's *Esther* of 1689, written for school performance.

VII

Leaving biblical subjects, Du Ryer next wrote a tragedy in Corneille's Roman vein. *Scévole* (1644) was his only venture in this manner and resulted in his most successful dramatic work. The story of the play contains the dilemmas which confront the characters and the moral assumptions which influence their decisions.

Tarquin, the expelled King of Rome, has returned to besiege the

---

[1] Racine was to place this at the beginning of his *Esther*.

city with the help of his ally Porsenne, King of Etruria. Junie, the daughter of the Lucius Brutus who led the rebellion against Tarquin (and is now dead), is captured and brought before Porsenne. Porsenne's son Arons, who knew her before the war, is in love with her. She, however, is in love with Scévole, a young Roman who turns up in the besieger's camp disguised as an Etruscan with a mission to assassinate Porsenne. Junie and Scévole are both animated by the inflexible Roman *vertu* – the resolve to serve their country whatever the consequences – but there are complicating factors. Porsenne treats Junie magnanimously, leaving her free on parole and so putting her morally in his debt; then her love for Scévole inclines her to dissuade him from attempting the assassination, which will all too probably be punished by his own death; unexpectedly Porsenne also proves to be in love with her and offers to make her a queen by marriage with his son Arons, since he recognizes that he himself is too old for her. With more or less difficulty she resists all these temptations and, acting *en vraie romaine*, urges on Scévole to do the deed.

In the event he fails by mistaking another man for the King and killing him instead. He is seized, defies Porsenne and Tarquin, who is represented as wholly villainous, and is ordered to be tortured. Another dilemma now appears, that of Arons whose life was once saved by Scévole in Rome. Is he to desert the friend who saved him or come to the help of his father's would-be murderer? And there is the further consideration that, as Scévole's rival in love, he has a personal (and so dishonourable) interest in his death. Finally he chooses the noblest course and intercedes for Scévole, but only after the latter has won the admiration of Porsenne by putting his own hand in the fire and allowing it to be burnt.

Scévole is pardoned, in spite of the reproachful threats of Tarquin, who exits invoking vengeance. Porsenne unites Junie to her heroic lover and proposes to offer peace terms to the besieged Romans.

This play bears evident resemblances to Corneille's *Cinna*, produced some four years earlier. The data of both tragedies include a magnanimous ruler who finally pardons, so securing a happy ending, the project of assassination, the pair of lovers animated by an ideal higher than love, and the secondary lover – Maxime in *Cinna* and Arons in *Scévole* – though his situation and character are different in the two plays. The motivation also stems from the same scheme of values, exaggerated in *Scévole* to almost superhuman heights, but recognizably 'Roman'. It was the last tragedy by an important dramatist to exalt the stoic virtues in so pure and uncompromising a form, with the partial exception of Corneille's own *Nicomède* (1650–1) and was written at a date when Corneille himself was writing plays based on different moral assumptions. Its contemporary success nevertheless showed that the public had not grown tired of heroic sublimity.[1]

The five other plays which Du Ryer was still to write included one nominal tragedy, *Thémistocle* (1646–7), of which the plot, bearing mainly on court intrigues and rivalries in love, has a certain political interest, faintly reminiscent of *Scévole*, in that it contains a conspiracy against the King of Persia and a test of the hero's patriotism. He is asked to fight against his own country, which has exiled him, and refuses. Apart, however, from this one display of patriotic *vertu*, the story is a romanesque one and ends happily thanks to the King's magnanimity. The other four plays are all frankly romanesque tragicomedies, ranging from *Bérénice* (published in 1645 and possibly written before *Scévole*) to Du Ryer's last play, *Anaxandre* (1655). His return to this type of play at that date, in spite of the undoubted success of the Roman *Scévole*, brings further confirmation of the popular trend of drama.

His *Bérénice* is notable as one of the few tragicomedies to be written in prose, though remarkable in no other way. The subject has no connection with that chosen later by Racine and Pierre Corneille.

VIII

Du Ryer's work can be related even less than Rotrou's to a dramatic or ethical norm. Of his nineteen plays, eleven were melodramatic or romanesque tragicomedies, irregular before 1637, technically regular

[1] *Scévole* was published in 1647 (*privilège* dated 31 August 1646) and soon after was included in the repertory of the Hôtel de Bourgogne (*Mémoire de Mahelot*). But there is a mention of 'the author of *Scévole*' in a document signed by Molière and others in 1644. The probability is that Molière's company bought the play in that year and acted it in the provinces after their departure from Paris in 1645. They certainly acted it in 1659, not long after their return to the capital. Meanwhile Du Ryer, having lost sight of them, had published his play and so enabled another company to perform it.

afterwards. He wrote one comedy, one pastoral comedy and the six tragedies considered in the preceding pages, ending with *Thémistocle*. He was a successful dramatist whose output was typical of his time, showing a preference for the romantic intrigue and several times exploiting (in tragicomedy) the notion of disguised or confused identities. His dramatic technique – the development of plot and the maintenance of suspense or at least interest – was professional. His versestyle is professionally adequate also, rising to greater heights only occasionally. He employs the lengthy *tirade* and also the dialectical debate. Though dramatic in that they bear on the development of the action, these debates often appear artificial, smacking of school rhetoric – in which of course Du Ryer was no exception among his contemporaries. His characters indulge in either repetition or *retournement* of their adversaries' phrases, *sentences* or near-*sentences*, near-epigrams and stichomythia. Many of his monologues and some of his duologues have a 'sung' quality in the tradition of Garnier and Montchrestien, dependent on the lulling rhythm of the alexandrines and on repetitions suggestive of opera. An example of this is *Alcionée*, III. v, which quickly becomes a duet between the two lovers:

ALCIONÉE   N'êtes-vous pas encor cette princesse même
             Qui permit l'espérance à mon amour extrême?
             N'êtes-vous pas encor cette divinité
             Qui semblait me conduire à ma félicité?
LYDIE   N'êtes-vous pas encor ce même Alcionée
             Qui fit trembler un trône où je suis destinée?
             N'êtes-vous pas encor ce ravisseur d'états
             Qui ne s'est signalé que par des attentats?
             N'êtes-vous pas encor ce funeste adversaire
             Que j'ai vu travailler au tombeau de mon père?
             Moi, je vous aimerais! Non, non, n'attendez pas
             Que le tyran des miens ait pour moi des appas.
             Voulez-vous voir enfin votre amour couronnée?
             Cesse d'avoir été le traître Alcionée.
             Voulez-vous plaire enfin à mon œil offensé?
             Faites plus que les dieux, révoquez le passé.
ALCIONÉE   En quel gouffre de maux est mon âme plongée?
             O dieux, quel changement!

LYDIE   Je ne suis point changée.
        La haine est dans mon cœur un vieux ressentiment
        De qui vos attentats sont le commencement.
        Non, je n'ai point changé, je suis toujours la même,
        Toujours prête à venger l'honneur du diadème.
        Non, je n'ai point changé, mais ce cœur plus ouvert
        Vous montre seulement un feu qu'il a couvert.
        Il est vrai que j'ai feint, mais il est équitable
        De feindre quelquefois pour punir un coupable . . .

The melodious quality of the verse – even when the character is
expressing indignation – is typical of Du Ryer. His imagery is usually
conventional, rarely departing from the ordinary clichés of the contemporary dramatic idiom. Very occasionally his metaphors are bolder,
verging on a style which might be classed as baroque, as in this description of Horatio, who has successfully held the bridge against the enemies
of Rome, swimming back to safety across the Tiber:

        On eût dit, à le voir balancé dessus l'eau,
        Que même son bouclier lui servait de vaisseau,
        Et qu'en poussant nos traits, tout notre effort n'excite
        Qu'un favorable vent qui le pousse plus vite.
        On eût dit qu'en tombant, le dieu même des flots
        Comme un autre dauphin le reçût sur son dos,
        Et que l'eau, secondant une si belle audace,
        Fût un char de cristal où triomphait Horace.

                                    (*Scévole*, I. iii)

As a poet, however, whose verse might deserve appreciation independently of its dramatic function, Du Ryer has less interest than the
third writer with whom this chapter is concerned.

                                    IX

Tristan L'Hermite (*c*. 1601–55) wrote the first of his eight plays at the
age of about thirty-five after an apparently varied and adventurous
youth. Almost the only information on his early life is drawn from
his obviously romanced autobiographical novel, *Le Page disgracié*,
which he published in 1643. According to this, he began as a page and
companion to the young Marquis de Verneuil, an illegitimate son of
Henri IV. When in trouble with his tutor he took refuge with a

company of players which acted at court (unidentified but, if this occurred before 1612, the troupe could have been Valleran le Conte's). In more serious trouble later as the result of a duel or a brawl, he fled abroad and visited, he says, England, Scotland and Norway. Returning to France, he was attached to the King's household in 1620 and then, from 1621 to 1646, to that of the King's unruly brother, Gaston d'Orléans. In his mid-thirties he turned to the theatre, having previously written court poetry of high quality in praise of the great or on the theme of *galant* love. He published further collections of lyric verse at intervals during his career as a dramatist.[1]

This opened with two tragedies, *La Mariane* (1636) and *Panthée* (1637). Both these subjects had been treated by Hardy[2] and, though there are alternative sources (Caussin's *La Cour sainte* and Josephus for *Mariane* and Xenophon for *Panthée*), there can be little doubt that Tristan was consciously influenced by the older dramatist's work. There are no close verbal resemblances in the dialogue, which would indeed be unexpected at a date when Hardy's language appeared thoroughly old-fashioned, but in the development of the plots and the situations Tristan broadly follows Hardy, though his dramatic technique is more skilful.

La Mariane, produced two years after Mairet's *Sophonisbe* and in the year before *Le Cid*, is notable as one of the earliest examples of regular tragedy. It observed the three unities and concentrated the interest fairly closely on the fate of the persecuted heroine and the reactions of the lovesick tyrant Herod. The activities of the secondary characters who plot against Mariane are integral to the story. Only the brief appearance of Mariane's mother, Alexandra, in Act IV, Sc. iv, is irrelevant, but was no doubt included because Tristan found it in both Hardy and his other probable sources. The whole of the fifth act is taken up by the narration of Mariane's exemplary death and Herod's regrets and extravagant lamentations. These are strongly reminiscent of sixteenth-century tragedy, but probably the influence was through Hardy and there is no necessary link between Garnier or Montchrestien and Tristan. The kind of delirium which Herod undergoes, together

---

[1] His principal collections were: *Les Plaintes d'Acante et autres œuvres* (1633), *Les Amours* (1638), *La Lyre* (1641), *Les Vers héroïques* (1648).

[2] For summaries of the stories, which are the same in outline in both dramatists, see above under Hardy's plays, p. 92.

with his dream of foreboding in Act I, are both in Hardy's tragedy, though Tristan eliminates the actual appearance of a ghost on the stage. In short, this was a technically regular tragedy incorporating certain features of earlier drama.

Panthée (1637) also retains the prophetic dream and the fifth act filled by a long messenger speech and lamentations – this time by the heroine, who commits suicide. As in Hardy, this is a disjointed play. It really falls into two parts and is given unity only by the character of Panthée, who in the first three acts is a captive princess determined to defend her virtue, and in the last two a loving wife fearing for her husband's safety. The double theme is inherent in the story and it may well have been the lack of unified interest which dissuaded later dramatists from taking it up. Tristan's play respects the unity of place as then understood and can also be held to respect the unity of time, though with a gross loss of probability.

Produced in the year of *Le Cid*, which must have overshadowed it, *Panthée* was Tristan's last play for several years. He then returned to the stage with a tragicomedy and three tragedies, all written and produced in close succession. *La Folie du sage*, his only tragicomedy,[1] attempted to combine a plot based on love and honour with the portrait of a character whose peculiar features have little bearing on the story. Ariste, the 'wise man', is a learned person whose feats of military engineering have enabled his King (the 'King of Sardinia') to win a victory over the Moors. In the course of the play he goes mad, then recovers his reason. He is widely read in the ancient philosophers and scientists, of whom he cites thirty-seven by name before throwing away their books as misleading. They had taught him that virtue was the sovereign good, fortifying the wise man against all adversities; experience has shown him that this was a lie. He is also interested in medicine and the composition of the human body and soul, on which he harangues a visiting doctor at some length. The doctor, ignorant or uninterested, or both, merely replies:

> Seigneur, sans perdre temps en définitions,
> Je vous le ferai voir par démonstrations.

[1] The *privilège* is dated 17 October 1644, the *achevé d'imprimer* 8 January 1645. Conjectured to have been first performed in 1642 or 1643.

Notable though Tristan's experiment is, there was no place in French tragedy or tragicomedy for this kind of character. It could be developed only in comedy, of which Molière's was the prime example.

The argument of the play, a romantic one containing moral dilemmas, does not require any such character as Ariste. The wise man's daughter is coveted by the King, first as his mistress, then, after Ariste's refusal, as his queen. She is in love with another man whom the King uses in ignorance as his go-between. After an attempted suicide from which she recovers and in face of her father's renewed opposition to the royal match, the King magnanimously renounces her and unites her to her original lover. The themes of personal honour and resistance to a demanding ruler might seem to suggest a Spanish source, but the story appears to have been Tristan's own invention.

X

At the same time as *La Folie du sage* Tristan published his third tragedy, *La Mort de Sénèque*, which was probably the later work. This again was a badly integrated play, with a nominal protagonist who is not central to the plot. The action turns on a conspiracy against Néron, of which one of the leaders is the beautiful Épicaris. The conspirators are betrayed. Épicaris is ordered to be tortured and is brought before Néron broken by the rack. With sublime Roman courage she still defies him and refuses to name her accomplices. Her motivation, unlike Émilie's in Corneille's *Cinna*, is not personal, but a pure hatred of Néron's vices and those of his new wife Sabine Poppée. Nor is there a love interest of any importance. Though one of the conspirators declares his love for Épicaris, he is brushed aside until the political objective is achieved and there is no development. The nominal hero Sénèque, when approached by the conspirators, has refused to join them in the attempt to assassinate his pupil and benefactor. His ruin, leading to his edifying suicide, is contrived by the hatred of Sabine Poppée. The death of the admired philosopher who, it is suggested, died more than half a Christian, thus furnishes the climax in accordance with the play's title, but in no way affects the main story of the weaving of the political plot and its discovery.

Of Tristan's two remaining tragedies the first, *La Mort de Chrispe* (1645), has a story similar to that of Racine's *Phèdre*, which fortuitously heightens its interest. The source, however, is not in any of the earlier

Hippolytus–Phaedra tragedies but in Caussin's *Cour sainte*, on which Tristan had already drawn for *La Mariane* and *La Mort de Sénèque*. In Caussin Tristan almost certainly found the account of the Emperor Constantine and his second wife Fausta, who fell in love with her stepson Chrispus and was executed together with him by the outraged Emperor. Tristan's Chrispe does not respond to Fauste's passion since he is in love with his cousin Constance, to whom the Emperor is hostile for political reasons. These four characters are in the same situation relative to each other as Racine's Thésée, Phèdre, Hippolyte and Aricie, and the development, if it is to be tragic, cannot differ fundamentally. The characterization, however, does. In the first two acts Fauste is experiencing Phèdre's dilemma, torn between passion and *honneur* and trembling at the prospect of a meeting with Chrispe.[1] At

---

[1] In a long monologue which opens the play Fauste describes a situation similar to Phèdre's, but she uses terms which are Cornelian rather than Racinian, balancing *désir* against *vertu*, *gloire* against *infamie*, *raison* against *amour*. The whole of her internal debate (to which she returns in Act II) is in fact an antithetical and rhythmical piece of rhetoric in the Cornelian convention which is less moving than Phèdre's desperate heart-searching, e.g.:

> Sors, idole charmante [Chrispe], abandonne la place,
> Le désir te retient, mais la vertu te chasse,
> Et trouve avec raison mes sens bien effrontés
> De prendre tant de droits dessus mes volontés.
> Ma raison doit sur eux agir comme une reine
> Et ne consentir pas d'être mise à la chaîne . . .
>
> Que ne dois-je craindre et qu'est-ce que j'espère
> Si j'ose aimer le fils, étant femme du père?
> Quel crime à celui-ci se pourrait comparer?
> En quels gouffres de maux serait-ce s'égarer?
> Ce prodige de mal tous les autres enserre,
> C'est la haine du ciel et l'horreur de la terre,
> C'est le plus noir poison dont l'honneur soit taché,
> C'est un monstre effroyable et non pas un péché.
> Mon âme toutefois est encore flattée
> De ces mêmes horreurs qui l'ont épouvantée:
> Je m'en sens tour à tour et brûler et glacer
> Et je ne les saurais ni souffrir ni chasser.
> O passion trop forte, ô loi trop rigoureuse!
> J'ai trop de retenue et suis trop amoureuse;
> Le devoir et l'amour avec trop de rigueur
> S'appliquent à la fois à déchirer mon cœur.

an early stage, however (in Act II), she learns of Chrispe's love for Constance and from that point much of her energy is devoted to thwarting the union of the pair and working for the destruction of her rival. There is an angry clash between the two women in Act IV, in which their antagonism and its cause is made quite plain. Chrispe, however, never becomes aware of Fauste's passion for him, in spite of a near-avowal in Act III, in which the Queen reveals her feelings as plainly as possible without actually spelling them out. At first she is determined to include Chrispe in her plans of vengeance but she later relents, intending to kill only Constance. In a melodramatic ending she sends a pair of poisoned gloves to her rival, but Chrispe is present when they arrive and their deadly fumes are breathed by both lovers together. Fauste, having confessed her responsibility to Constantin, commits suicide by plunging into a bath of boiling water (the deaths are all narrated). Her husband concludes, rather flatly:

> Il faut qu'on la retire et que soudainement
> On la fasse sans bruit porter au monument.[1]
> Elle avait des défauts, mais elle avait des charmes
> Qui m'obligent encore à répandre des larmes.

Tristan's Constantin has neither the stature nor the function of Racine's Thésée. He is in no way responsible for his son's death. Chrispe and Constance do roughly correspond to Hippolyte and Aricie, although Chrispe has less of the continent fascination of Racine's character and Constance considerably more maturity and aggressiveness than his sweetly virginal princess. Fauste has the potentialities of Phèdre, but she develops as a character in the wicked stepmother tradition and comes to resemble the evil elder women of Corneille's middle-period plays, goaded on, it is true, by passion but obsessed ultimately by the desire for revenge. If Racine took anything material

---

> Je frémis tout ensemble et brûle pour ce crime,
> La raison me gourmande et mon amour m'opprime.
> Mais il faut noblement achever son destin,
> Il faut vivre et mourir femme de Constantin . . .

Although there are sentiments here which Phèdre could have shared, Fauste is able to conclude resolutely in favour of *honneur* and *innocence*. Later, her smothered passion is diverted to desire for revenge.

[1] Tomb, mausoleum.

from this play it would be the invention of a young princess for his hero to fall in love with, though he gives a convincing alternative explanation of this in his preface to *Phèdre*. In spite of a certain number of verbal resemblances in the two texts, the existence of his debt has not been conclusively shown.

Neither is there much substance in the suggestion that Tristan's last tragedy, *La Mort du Grand Osman* (*c.* 1647), influenced Racine's *Bajazet*. *Osman* was a Turkish palace drama with a violent plot which can be classed as political since it concerned a revolt against a Sultan which occurred historically in 1622. Tristan adds, however, a powerful love motivation by developing the part of his heroine. Rejected by the Sultan, she contributes to his downfall, then kills herself out of remorse.

Dramas with Turkish settings were rare but not unknown to French theatre audiences. There were others in the same period as Tristan's venture. Mairet's *Solyman* and Dalibray's *Le Soliman* (both *c.* 1637 and both derived from Bonarelli's tragedy *Il Solimano*, printed in Venice in 1619) had been the first in the new theatre of the thirties. The *Roxelane* of Desmares was printed in 1643. Magnon's *Le Grand Tamerlan et Bajazet*, with Turkish and Tartar characters, was probably produced in 1646, the year before Tristan's *Osman*. Lancaster also records an amateurish tragedy entitled *Le Grand Sélim*, published in 1645 and attributed to Le Vayer de Boutigny. Though all these helped to create a minor dramatic tradition, the original impulse came from the novel rather than from the theatre. From the 1630s to the 1650s, Turkish settings and characters appeared constantly in prose fiction. An outstanding example among several was Madeleine de Scudéry's *Ibrahim, ou l'illustre Bassa* (1641). When Racine's contemporaries came to criticize *Bajazet* for its lack of Turkish atmosphere their minds were no doubt conditioned by the reading of such novels rather than by any knowledge of the real Turkey.

After *Osman*, Tristan reworked Rotrou's comedy *Célimène* as a pastoral, *Amaryllis* (1652), and wrote his only comedy, *Le Parasite* (1653). He died two years after this.

XI

Tristan's tragic dramas were of mixed inspiration. The first two were developments of Hardy. *La Folie du sage* contained a Cornelian situation of the type found in *Le Cid*, there was 'Roman' virtue in *Sénèque* mingled with melodrama, and an approximation to the *Rodogune* type of tragedy in the rather more melodramatic *Mort de Chrispe*. The inspiration of *Osman* was romanesque.

Nearly all these plays were badly constructed in comparison with those of Tristan's principal contemporaries. Technically regular in so far as they observed the unities of time and place, they contained passages and scenes not strictly required by dramatic necessity. Characters were lost sight of or introduced too late, with a consequent loss of dramatic effect. The main interest was sometimes divided or obscured. As already remarked, an over-concern with characterization was largely responsible for these structural weaknesses. They can also be reasonably ascribed in part to some influence of Hardy persisting later than *La Mariane* and *Panthée*. Not only those two tragedies but the three others all contain the prophetic dream dear to the old dramatist. All five tragedies conclude with the lamentations of an earlier tradition and in two (*La Mariane* and *Sénèque*) the lamentations lead to a fit of delirium.

It seems possible that Tristan was lastingly influenced by his youthful impressions of tragedy, whether that of Hardy or others, as acted by the troupe which, he claimed, befriended him as a boy, and this may account for his somewhat old-fashioned technique.[1] It might account also for the Cornelian elements in his later plays, which could be explained as only partially successful attempts to catch up with contemporary taste.

His interest is nevertheless considerable. By temperament he was a lyric and descriptive poet writing in a dramatic medium. He elaborates details which must appeal to students of the seventeenth-century background and sometimes have a bearing on character, but are otherwise irrelevant. The outstanding example is the enumeration of Ariste's books in *La Folie du sage* and his tirades on the question 'What is man?' and on the art of medicine. Others are the descriptions of Seneca's house (*Mort de Sénèque*, V. iv) and of Turkish customs and costume in *Osman*. The effect of these is to give colour and flavour by stressing particular qualities and this runs counter to the 'classical'

---

[1] It is more noticeable and continues to a later date than in Rotrou, although the latter was Hardy's immediate successor as a provider of plays for the Hôtel de Bourgogne and was exposed to the influence of a professional tradition.

theory of both lyric and dramatic poetry as first put forward by Malherbe.

Tristan's lyric qualities are particularly evident in his monologues, several of which take the form of *stances*, a poetic form not unusual in the drama of the period, and in other metrical departures from the couplet-rhyming alexandrine. Such is Araspe's soliloquy, some eighty lines long, in *Panthée*, II. i. The opening stanzas are:

> Hôtes du silence et de l'ombre,
> Où l'air est si frais et si sombre,
> Arbres qui connaissez l'état de ma langueur:
> Soyez les confidents des peines que j'endure
> Et souffrez que je grave en votre écorce dure
> Le beau nom que l'Amour a gravé dans mon cœur.

> Amour, ce conseiller perfide,
> Ce jeune aveugle qui me guide,
> A causé tous les maux qui me font soupirer:
> Il a porté mon âme à suivre ses caprices
> Et l'a conduite enfin parmi des précipices
> D'où jamais ma raison ne put la retirer.

This is the aria type of monologue already noted in sixteenth-century tragedy and, at Tristan's date, intermediate between pastoral and opera. The *stances* of *La Mort de Sénèque* (V. i) are reminiscent on the other hand of religious poets such as Sponde:

> Mon âme, apprête-toi pour sortir tout entière
> De cette fragile matière,
> Dont le confus mélange est un voile à tes yeux:
> Tu dois te réjouir du coup qui te menace,
> Pensant te faire injure on te va faire grâce:
> Si l'on te bannit de ces lieux
> En t'envoyant là-haut, c'est chez toi qu'on te chasse,
> Ton origine vient des cieux . . .

Tristan wrote a good deal of conventionally *galant* dialogue, which he handled skilfully, but his poetic imagery in general was freer and bolder than the contemporary norm. Thus Fauste, speaking of her rival Constance:

> Ah, serpent dangereux qui t'oses prendre à moi,
> Tu t'émancipes trop, ta mort en fera foi.
> Tu te repentiras de l'air dont tu me traites
> Tu crèveras bientôt du venin que tu jettes.[1]
>
> (*Mort de Chrispe*, IV. vii)

Usually, in contradistinction to the general run of seventeenth-century dramatic verse, the metaphor is fully elaborated:

> CYRUS   [*undecided*] Comme un morceau de fer qu'attire également
> La secrète vertu de deux pierres d'aimant,
> Par un contraire effort parmi l'air se balance,
> Tiré de deux côtés de même violence,
> Ainsi sur ce sujet mon esprit agité
> Vague entre la douceur et la sévérité.
>
> (*Panthée*, III. vii)

In *La Mort de Sénèque*, Sabine reasoning with Néron compares the hated Sénèque to a leech:

> Pour moi, je n'aime point cette avide sangsue
> Qui ne peut contenir l'humeur qu'elle a reçue,
> Et qui par le moyen de ses secrets ressorts
> Te veut avec le sang ôter l'âme du corps . . .

And Néron replies:

> Sabine, c'est sans doute une éponge à presser.
>
> (*Mort de Sénèque*, I. i)

As a dramatic poet Tristan was capable both of vigour and of melodious lyricism, and such qualities go far to redeem his weaknesses as a playwright.

---

[1] The 'poison' image recurs, appropriately, throughout this play.

XII

In Tristan's dramatic work the political motivations are of small importance. They can be found in such different plays as *La Mariane* and *Osman*, but in both instances, as in *La Mort de Chrispe*, a political manœuvre is set afoot as a result of personal frustration or jealousy and has little interest in itself. Even *La Mort de Sénèque*, in which the action depends entirely on the conspiracy against Néron, is weak as a political drama. Its most prominent themes are the hatred of Sabine Poppée for Sénèque and the noble behaviour of the latter, with the heroic but ineffectual fortitude of Épicaris as a subsidiary theme. But, as has been seen, these are not fully integrated into the story of the conspiracy.

The love interest present in all the plays, with the exception of *Sénèque*, varies in its nature and function. The explosive combination of love and jealousy, which might be considered to point forward to Racine, occurs in *La Mariane* and *La Mort de Chrispe*. In the first it increases the fury of the male tyrant Hérode, though it does not cause it. In the second it becomes the mainspring of the action and the direct causation of the tragic catastrophe. In *Osman* it is love scorned, not jealousy of a rival, which leads to disaster. Elsewhere there is constant mutual love in *La Folie du sage* and in *Panthée* (the heroine and her husband), and these cases rest on the moral imperatives of *vertu* and *honneur*. But they spring naturally from the stories that Tristan was dramatizing and one cannot find any consistent idealization of these qualities in his work. Only for the Fauste of *Chrispe* and, less conspicuously, for the Rosélie of *La Folie du sage*, do they create a moral dilemma of potentially tragic proportions.

It appears that Tristan was prepared to invoke ethical values current in other drama of his time, but unsystematically and without stressing their importance. For this, as well as for the structure of his plays and, most particularly, for his verse-style, he can certainly be described as a baroque dramatist if one wishes to classify writers in those terms. In other terms he was a dramatist whose considerable originality may have been largely due to unfamiliarity with the professional theatre, the influence of older models and a natural preference for the idiosyncratic and the picturesque.

8

PIERRE CORNEILLE:
THE SECOND PERIOD, 1659–1674

Corneille's return to the theatre – *Œdipe* – his love of complication also
shown in other plays – social and theatrical changes since 1651 – *La Toison
d'Or* – *Sertorius* – *Sophonisbe* and the polemic with d'Aubignac – *La
Pratique du théâtre* – *Othon, Agésilas, Attila* – *Tite et Bérénice* and Racine's
Bérénice – *Psyché, Pulchérie, Suréna* – Corneille's retirement and death –
general features of the later plays – politics, love, anti-sentimentality, plot
and characterization – summaries of plays from *Œdipe* to *Suréna*

After a break of just over seven years Corneille returned to the theatre
with a new tragedy, *Œdipe*, first acted at the Hôtel de Bourgogne in
January 1659. The inducement, he says in the *Au lecteur* and the
Examen of the play, was a 'notable favour' (no doubt a gift of money)
bestowed on him by the *Surintendant des finances*, Nicolas Foucquet,
still at the height of his influence as an immensely wealthy patron of the
arts. Foucquet offered him a choice of three subjects,[1] and in opting for
one of the greatest subjects in all tragedy Corneille laid himself dan-
gerously open to invidious comparisons. It was the only occasion, with
the doubtful exception of *Médée*, on which he took up a subject
treated by the Greek dramatists (though in both cases Seneca's version
was the more immediate source) and on a long view the decision was
no doubt unwise. But if one can forget Sophocles' *Oedipus* and look
on Corneille's *Œdipe* as a skilful adaptation to seventeenth-century
taste of a somewhat bare and barbarous theme, it was certainly not
inferior to other contemporary modernizations.

To achieve this result, Corneille complicated and 'enriched' the
originally stark and slender story. There was no love interest in it,
he remarked. To introduce one he provided Oedipus with a sister,

[1] The other two are believed to have been Stilicon and Camma, dramatized by
Corneille's younger brother Thomas in 1660 and 1661 respectively.

the Princess Dircé, and brought Theseus to the court of Thebes to sue for her hand. This pair of lovers comes to occupy the foreground, overshadowing the disillusionment and agony of Oedipus, who ceases to be the dominant character. He is transformed also, meeting his doom with stoical heroism in place of the broken resignation of the Sophoclean original.[1]

The problem of identity, paramount in the Greek tragedy, is no longer centred on the single figure of Oedipus but is diluted by extension to Theseus and, in its effects, to Dircé. Corneille invents a political interest, dependent on Dircé's rights to the throne at a time when she believes herself to be the only surviving child of King Laius. This theme of the political implications of the marriage of royalty, which had already appeared in different forms in *Rodogune* and *Pertharite*, was to become a constant factor in Corneille's later plays. At the same time he passed over the political element which *is* in Sophocles – the rivalry of Oedipus and Creon – but which has no connection with match-making or love. Creon is dropped from his list of characters and at the end it is Theseus and Dircé who seem ready to take charge of the kingless state.

Corneille's seemingly gratuitous additions to the simple Oedipus story, his modifications of character, his exploitation of 'love', his respect of the physical *bienséances* (the blinded Oedipus did not appear on the stage), and his use of suspense and of the melodramatic surprise, resulted in a play typical of French drama of the mid-seventeenth century – typical also of Corneille's talent, which was basically anticlassical. Further illustrations of this are provided by two more of his later plays, both of which invite comparisons with simpler dramatic works. They can be considered briefly here outside the chronological order of composition.

In January 1663 Corneille took up the story of Sophonisbe, treated by Mairet in 1634.[2] He was fully aware of his predecessor's play which,

---

[1]   Prévenons, a-t-il dit, l'injustice des dieux;
             Commençons à mourir avant qu'ils nous l'ordonnent;
             Qu'ainsi que mes forfaits mes supplices étonnent.
             Ne voyons plus le ciel après sa cruauté:
             Pour nous venger de lui dédaignons sa clarté.
             Refusons-lui nos yeux et gardons quelque vie
             Qui montre encore à tous quelle est sa tyrannie. (V. ix)

[2] See above pp. 117 ff.

he remarked in the *Au lecteur*, still survived on the stage. In his version neither Syphax nor Massinissa dies. This makes Sophonisbe's hurried marriage with Massinissa bigamous, though in Corneille it remains unconsummated. It gives scope for a continued rivalry between the two kings and for a dramatic confrontation between Sophonisbe and her first husband (III. v). The survival of Massinissa as a Roman satellite provokes Sophonisbe's scorn and rejection of him. In place of the Othello-like ending of Mairet, there is the suicide of Sophonisbe alone. She drinks her own poison, having contemptuously refused that which Massinissa sent her. These variations, considerable though they are, are less radical than Corneille's introduction of a second queen, Éryxe, who is a rival for Massinissa's hand. The competition between the two queens, their fluctuating feelings towards Massinissa, their jealousy and their ironical exchanges, occupy much of the play. From an austere viewpoint they are unnecessary, but full of opportunities for a dramatist who enjoys handling a complicated plot and exploiting the psychological implications which it can be made to yield.

In *Tite et Bérénice* (1670) the comparison is with Racine's *Bérénice*, produced almost simultaneously. The question of a deliberate act of rivalry between the two dramatists is discussed later.[1] Of immediate interest is the fact that Racine constructed his five-act tragedy (admittedly an exercise in extreme simplicity) around the reactions of two characters towards their situation and each other. A third character serves as a foil and intermediary, but Racine requires no others apart from the confidants and a messenger. Corneille could never have been content with this sparse story of an impossible mutual passion. He introduces a second pair of lovers, involves them closely with Tite and Bérénice, and in fact makes their fate of almost equal importance to that of the nominal hero and heroine. Bérénice's heroic renunciation closes his tragedy, as it does Racine's, but it is only reached after numerous vicissitudes, and it leaves the other pair of lovers in sight of marriage and a happy ending for them.

II

Meanwhile *Œdipe* was a contemporary success which evidently justified in Corneille's mind his decision to return to the theatre and embark on the second stage of his dramatic career. Conditions had already

[1] See below pp. 202–5.

changed since the failure of *Pertharite* at the end of 1651, and were about to change more. The Fronde, the last open revolt of a self-assertive aristocracy, had ended in 1653 and the centralization of absolute power in the crown was already under way, to be marked more openly by Louis XIV's personal assumption of government on the death of Mazarin in 1661. The feudal ethos of the French nobility has been overstressed as an influence in Corneille's drama and even if related to 'Roman' virtue it had begun to disappear from his work after *Pompée* (1642–3). This was several years before the Fronde which, as a historical event, is not reflected in Corneille's work. One may assume a general interest in violent political intrigue combined with a romanticized conception of the chief participants as a background to his plays over two or three decades, but any more precise interpretations encounter serious factual objections. The changing environment to which Corneille returned in 1659 was less a matter of social climate than a more narrowly professional question. Royal patronage, administered by Colbert, assumed an increased importance, together with the prestige and rewards of performances at court. Corneille, it is true, had been persuaded to return by Foucquet, but the *Surinten-dant*'s arrest in 1661 marked the fall of the last really great independent patron of the arts, and no one after him could devote the same lavish resources to drama as were provided by the royal treasury and Versailles. After *Œdipe*, only *La Toison d'Or* was supported by a private patron.

As to the Parisian theatres, their number was increased to three by Molière's return to the capital in the winter of 1658–9.[1] His troupe had re-established itself with a successful court performance at the Louvre. For this all-important occasion Molière chose to perform Corneille's *Nicomède*, followed by a farce of his own, *Le Docteur amoureux*. Some two years later he was installed permanently at the theatre of the Palais-Royal, built originally by Richelieu. This new personality and force in the Parisian theatre did not order a new play from Corneille until *Attila* in 1667 but often performed his older works, so helping to keep his name before the public. Of the other two theatres, the Marais still specialized in machine-plays, with the occasional performance of a

[1] He reached Paris after a season of performances at Rouen, where Corneille was then living. The two men were certainly in contact and it seems quite possible that this was one of the factors which influenced Corneille's own return to the theatre.

new tragedy. The Hôtel de Bourgogne remained the principal home of tragedy. It produced *Œdipe* and four of the other nine plays which Corneille was yet to write. The great Floridor remained its director until his death in 1671.

More important than any of this was the arrival of a new generation of playwrights. Corneille's contemporaries of the 1630s were either dead or had ceased to write. In their place pre-eminently were his younger brother, Thomas, and Philippe Quinault. There were minor writers such as Gilbert and the persistent Boyer.[1] Racine had his first tragedy performed by Molière in 1664 and established himself as a leading dramatist during the last ten years of Corneille's writing career.[2]

III

After *Œdipe*, Corneille was commissioned by the Marquis de Sourdéac to write the words of a lavishly mounted machine-play, *La Toison d'Or*. This was first performed in November 1660 in the Normandy château of the Marquis in celebration of the Peace of the Pyrenees and the marriage of Louis XIV to the Spanish princess Maria Teresa. The performers were the actors of the Marais, who shortly afterwards (February 1661) mounted the same production in their own theatre in Paris. Like Corneille's *Andromède* of 1650, this new play contained allegorical and mythological characters in addition to the human characters. The story of these last was based on the legend of the Golden Fleece which Jason and his Argonauts captured with the help of Medea. Corneille typically added a sub-plot by introducing a new character, Hypsipyle, who, as a former mistress of Jason, provided a rival for Medea. The production was highly successful and helped to maintain the Marais abreast of its two competitors.[3]

It was no doubt this connection which persuaded Corneille to give his next tragedy, *Sertorius*, to the Marais also. This again was a popular success, so much so that both Molière and the Hôtel de Bourgogne were soon producing their own unauthorized versions of it. Superficially it was another Roman tragedy, dealing with Roman policy

---

[1] The Abbé Claude Boyer (1618–98) abandoned drama like Corneille for a time, writing nothing for the theatre between 1647 and 1659.
[2] See the table on p. 221.
[3] See D.-Holsboer, *Le Théâtre du Marais*, II, pp. 121–42.

in the provinces (Spain) and adapting a historical situation described by Plutarch. The ethics, however, are not those of *Cinna* and *Horace* and, seen in the perspective of Corneille's later tragedies, it becomes clear that *Sertorius* belongs to a line of plays in which the chief interest is political intrigue involving marriages of convenience and that the 'Roman' setting is secondary. As such, it is a finely constructed and exciting drama and the most interesting and durable of all that Corneille wrote in his second period.

It was followed a year later (January 1663) by *Sophonisbe*, first produced at the Hôtel de Bourgogne, to which Corneille once again returned in preference to the Marais.[1] As with *Sertorius*, the subject of *Sophonisbe* was drawn from Roman history (though not Plutarch) and it also concerned Roman activity in the provinces. Corneille may also have been attracted by the challenge of composing an alternative version of Mairet's thirty-year-old classic, which he professed to admire and took particular pains to avoid imitating.[2] As has been seen above, his deliberate avoidance of imitation gave a weaker tragedy (though he could plead historical justification for some of his divergences) and the play was a partial failure. Its appearance was marked by a polemic which, though minor compared to the Quarrel of *Le Cid*, had a certain significance at that date. Corneille's principal critic was the Abbé d'Aubignac, an uncompromising advocate of 'classical' purity in drama. In a first *Dissertation* published in February 1663, the month following the first production of *Sophonisbe*, he attacked that play on the grounds of both *vraisemblance* and *bienséance*, arguing that it was faulty in both respects. Over-obviously, he charged Corneille with attempting an unsuccessful imitation of Mairet and criticized him for observing the unities imperfectly.

In April 1663 Corneille published his play with an introduction which justified his treatment of the story and also contained his reply to d'Aubignac by implication. Meanwhile he had exerted pressure to delay the publication of a second *Dissertation* by d'Aubignac, on *Sertorius*, as a result of which d'Aubignac was obliged to look for

---

[1] While his reasons for preferring the Hôtel at this date are not precisely known, a determining factor may well have been the transfer to that theatre from the Marais of the actress Des Œillets, who had created the part of Viriate in *Sertorius*. See D.-Holsboer, *Le Théâtre du Marais*, II, p. 145.

[2] See the *Au lecteur* of Corneille's *Sophonisbe*.

another publisher. This *Dissertation*, a third on *Œdipe* and a fourth on *Le Poème dramatique*, were all published eventually.

Others joined in the polemic, notably Donneau de Visé, a young literary opportunist who was then editing *Les Nouvelles Nouvelles*, in which he was conducting an attack on Molière's *École des femmes*. He achieved the feat of first attacking Corneille, then defending him in opposition to d'Aubignac, a change of attitude which was more journalistic than critical. But the main conflict was between d'Aubignac and Corneille. While largely a clash between personalities and coteries, there was an underlying divergence of doctrine which had critical importance.

A few years earlier d'Aubignac had published his main critical work, *La Pratique du théâtre*, which became a central statement of the seventeenth-century 'classical' conception of tragedy. Begun apparently in 1640, then laid aside and elaborated before its eventual publication in 1657, this work had its roots in the purist school of the 1630s and the Quarrel of *Le Cid*. It insisted on observance of the unities in the strictest sense and on the subordination of all the dramatic action to a single unified theme. It extolled the qualities of clarity and harmony and compared a dramatic work to a painting – a comparison which was in itself a potential source of error, since a painting of the sort that d'Aubignac knew presents itself as a static and finished whole, while a play develops itself in continuous movement before the spectators. The difference in medium is all-important.

All d'Aubignac's arguments derived from his conception of *vraisemblance*, which stemmed in turn from the theories of Chapelain, as the latter had expressed them in 1630.[1] The *vraisemblance* was what the spectator could believe in and accept when he saw it on the stage. This purely contingent criterion, put forward nevertheless in the name of 'reason', precluded the horrific, the sensational and the unexpected (d'Aubignac loads his case by giving extreme examples), even though such happenings may have been factually true. In a drama so largely based, or claiming to be based, on history, this was a crippling limitation. Violent events must not come as a surprise, but must be presented as a logical outcome of previous actions. In characterization the eccentric and the peculiar must be avoided and the historical figure endowed with qualities either similar to those of the seventeenth-century image

[1] See above p. 115.

of the *honnête homme* or recognizable in some other way to contemporaries through the established conventions of their literature, which for d'Aubignac were predominantly those of the novel.

Corneille partially accepted this interpretation of *vraisemblance*, and indeed his plays, in their manipulation of history, bear plentiful signs of a desire to conform to it. But he could never go the whole way. As a successful practising dramatist he knew the value of the unexpected *coup de théâtre*, he enjoyed handling a complicated plot and he had a seemingly temperamental interest in the unusual character. He had set out his own theories, his reservations and his problems in the three important *Discours* which appeared in 1660 at the head of the collective edition of his plays to that date. In places he contradicted *La Pratique du théâtre* without naming that work. It was plausibly for that reason that d'Aubignac took offence and decided to attack Corneille on the issue of *Sophonisbe*.

The polemic cannot be said to have done any immediate harm to Corneille's reputation. It was, however, a sign that the man still generally recognized as France's greatest dramatist was open to unfavourable criticism. His plays could be scrutinized and found faulty in the same ways as those of lesser men. The comparison, whether open or implied, was always with the plays of his great Roman period and the opinion grew that, as he neared his sixties, his powers were beginning to fail. This opinion took no account of the true nature of his later plays, from *Rodogune* on, nor of his willingness to experiment, even if unsuccessfully.

IV

His next three plays after *Sophonisbe* showed a continuing decline in popularity. *Othon* was first acted before the court at Fontainebleau on 31 July 1664, then at the Hôtel de Bourgogne in November 1664. This drama of political intrigue under the Roman emperors was only a qualified success. *Agésilas* (Hôtel de Bourgogne, February 1666), judging by the near-silence of contemporaries, was a failure, possibly because of Corneille's bold experiment in writing it in irregular verse.[1]

[1] Octosyllabic lines mixed with alexandrines. There were various rhyme-schemes, constructed mainly on cross-rhymes and interior rhymes, providing freedom from the conventional alexandrine couplet.

This, in his skilful hands, gave greater fluidity to the dialogue, endowing it with musical qualities more appropriate to opera and pastoral but also, unexpectedly enough, permitting a naturalness akin to that of ordinary speech. Corneille had used a similar technique in his machine-plays *Andromède* and *La Toison d'Or*, and it was to be used again in *Psyché* and in Molière's *Amphitryon*, but for seventeenth-century tragedy at least he was right in claiming it as a complete innovation – and one which found no imitators.

His next play, *Attila*, produced by Molière at the Palais-Royal (March 1667), was about equally unsuccessful. Corneille took an obvious interest in the character of the great barbarian king, the 'Scourge of God', and his period (Act I, Sc. ii, for example, contains more historical fact than is necessary for the exposition of the drama and reveals Corneille in the act of writing rhymed history). But his cruel and crafty and, at times, brutal-tongued tyrant was still bound in part by seventeenth-century convention, as though he had stepped out of the fifth century to spend at least a few months at the court of Versailles. This play exemplified Corneille's unresolved problem. He was caught between the *vrai* of history as it came to him from his sources and the *vraisemblable* of what his audiences and his critics could accept on the stage.[1] He was unable to fulfil satisfactorily the requirements of either. His Attila, with his modern love dilemma, was an incompletely savage tyrant, no match for Marlowe's sixteenth-century Tamburlaine or Garnier's Nabuchodonosor, though he shared some of their features. *Attila* does remind one of Garnier, though there is no evidence that he influenced Corneille directly. Besides the parallel with the tyrant king of *Les Juives*, the praises given in *Attila* to Mérovée and the future greatness of France, with the implied reference to Louis XIV, recall the

---

[1] In the first preface to *Britannicus* (1670), Racine derided the character of Attila as 'un héros ivre, qui se voudrait faire haïr de sa maîtresse de gaieté de cœur'. This was doubly unjust. Attila was never drunk – at least on the stage – and his motives for apparently trying to set his mistress (Ildione) against him are deeper and more subtle than *gaieté de cœur*. In the scene in question (*Attila*, III. ii) he has decided, or is in the process of deciding, to conquer his inclinations and reject a love marriage with Ildione in favour of a political marriage with her rival Honorie. Characteristically he resents emotion and wishes to assert his mastery over it in Ildione's presence. There is also a possibility that he is probing to discover whether she is in love with another man, as in fact she is. Racine could certainly have seen these implications had he wished to.

similar treatment of Charlemagne and his Frankish kingdom in *Brada-mante*.[1] This may easily have been a coincidence, though at the date of *Attila*, *Bradamante* was still a live subject.[2]

V

After *Attila*, Corneille produced nothing for over three and a half years. His next play, *Tite et Bérénice*, styled a *comédie héroïque*, was first acted at Molière's Palais-Royal on 28 November 1670, a week after the appearance of Racine's *Bérénice* at the Hôtel. The question of deliberate competition has been thrashed out in the past, but the evidence is still inconclusive. The story that Henrietta of England, wife of the homosexual Duc d'Orléans, personally suggested the subject to Racine has an eighteenth-century origin.[3] Whether completely discarded, as a study written near the beginning of this century[4] maintained that it should be, or retained, it has only a secondary importance now. The diametrically opposite theory that the almost simultaneous production of the two plays was a pure coincidence is even harder to accept. Its most solid basis consists in the silence of contemporaries on the point, apart from two disclaimers to which it is easy to give an ironical interpretation.[5] But that two dramatists who, if their mutual hostility has been exaggerated, were certainly watching each other's productions closely, should blindly have composed plays on the same subject

[1] See above pp. 27–8.
[2] It furnished plays by La Calprenède (1637) and by Thomas Corneille (1695, written *c.* 1680). In January 1664, some three years before *Attila*, a lost play entitled *Bradamante ridicule* was acted before the King at the command of one of his courtiers, the Duc de Saint-Aignan, who provided the play and 100 louis to pay for the evidently lavish costumes. The title makes it very probable that this was a burlesque, but whether of Garnier, of La Calprenède, or of some more recent work, also lost, it is impossible to say. (See Lancaster, *History*, III, p. 663 n., and *Le Registre de La Grange*, entries for January 1664.)
[3] First explicitly mentioned by Fontenelle (Corneille's nephew) in *La Vie de Corneille* (1729).
[4] G. Michaut, *La Bérénice de Racine* (1907).
[5] (1) Michel Le Clerc, in the preface to his tragedy *Iphigénie*, which appeared a few months after Racine's *Iphigénie*: 'Le hasard seul a fait que nous nous sommes rencontrés, comme il arriva à M. de Corneille et à lui [Racine] dans les deux *Bérénices*.'
    (2) Donneau de Visé in *Le Mercure galant* (April 1677), apropos of Pradon's *Phèdre et Hippolyte*. The subject, he says, was not chosen 'par un effet du hasard, comme tout le monde sait qu'il arriva des deux *Bérénices*'.

produced within a week of each other by two theatres then in strong competition strains credibility.

It is not necessary to assume that either had access to the other's text – there is in fact no evidence of plagiarism in the narrow sense. All that was needed was a 'leak' giving the subject and perhaps the sources in which it was to be found, and one dramatist could set out after the other. In that case, which followed which? An argument against Racine is that Corneille had produced nothing for over three years and therefore must have been working on *Tite et Bérénice* for some considerable time before Racine caught him up. But it is at least equally possible that after *Attila* Corneille had grown discouraged and was moved or persuaded to break silence in order to compete with Racine, who was following his then normal rhythm of one play a year. The problem remains unresolved.[1]

Some evidence of a more general kind and certainly of wider interest is contained in Racine's Prefaces to *Britannicus* and *Bérénice* (Corneille's *Tite et Bérénice* carries no preface). In the first Racine, smarting under an initial failure, refers pointedly to a 'malevolent old poet' and compares his own conception of tragedy to that which he transparently assigns to Corneille:

Que faudrait-il faire pour contenter des juges si difficiles? La chose serait aisée, pour peu qu'on voulût trahir le bon sens. Il ne faudrait que s'écarter du naturel pour se jeter dans l'extraordinaire. Au lieu d'une action simple, chargée de peu de matière, telle que doit être une action qui se passe en un seul jour, et qui s'avançant par degrés vers sa fin, n'est soutenue que par les intérêts, les sentiments et les passions des personnages, il faudrait remplir cette même action de quantité d'incidents qui ne se pourraient passer qu'en un mois, d'un grand nombre de jeux de théâtre, d'autant plus surprenants qu'ils seraient moins vraisemblables, d'une infinité de déclamations où l'on ferait dire aux acteurs tout le contraire de ce qu'ils devraient dire . . .

He goes on to criticize certain characters identifiable as Corneille's, including Attila, for their implausible behaviour.[2] While two of his

---

[1] Recent discussions of it are to be found in A. Adam, *Histoire de la littérature française au 17e siècle*, IV, pp. 335–8, and R. Picard, *La Carrière de Jean Racine*, pp. 154–61. These two critics draw different conclusions.

[2] See p. 201, footnote 1.

four examples could be identified alternatively with characters in Thomas Corneille and Quinault, it seems that the brunt of his attack bore on Pierre Corneille himself.

The Preface to *Bérénice* is less bitter. It reveals a man who has not only enjoyed a theatrical triumph, but who has succeeded in vindicating his conception of tragedy against the conception that violates *vraisemblance* by resorting to a multiplicity of incidents:

> . . . Il y avait longtemps que je voulais essayer si je pourrais faire une tragédie avec cette simplicité d'action qui a été si fort du goût des anciens . . . Il n'y a que le vraisemblable qui touche dans la tragédie. Et quelle vraisemblance y a-t-il qu'il arrive en un jour une multitude de choses qui pourraient à peine arriver en plusieurs semaines? Il y en a qui pensent que cette simplicité est une marque de peu d'invention. Ils ne songent pas qu'au contraire toute l'invention consiste à faire quelque chose de rien et que tout ce grand nombre d'incidents a toujours été le refuge des poètes qui ne sentaient dans leur génie ni assez d'abondance ni assez de force pour attacher durant cinq actes leurs spectateurs par une action simple, soutenue de la violence des passions, de la beauté des sentiments et de l'élégance de l'expression . . .

This contains an implicit condemnation of Corneille's system of drama, if not quite necessarily of Corneille himself. It is entirely in line with the precepts of d'Aubignac, showing the same disapproval of what both he and Racine considered as the Cornelian irregularity. The first sentence in the above quotation also implies that in *Bérénice* Racine had deliberately set out to construct a tragedy founded on the principle of 'simplicity'. He may even have done so in response to what he felt as a challenge, though not necessarily with prior knowledge of Corneille's *Tite*. But when the two plays appeared there was a strikingly apposite example of the two conceptions.

Racine could be satisfied. His play, he says in its Preface, was followed with as much interest at the thirtieth performance as at the first. Though this can hardly be meant to apply to the monetary takings – there was always a fall-off in receipts of later performances – *Bérénice* was evidently a major success. Corneille's play was less successful in comparison but it was far from being a failure, as has sometimes been supposed. Its initial run at the Palais-Royal (Molière's theatre) showed that the relatively complicated plot and the unexpected development could still draw abundant audiences.[1]

VI

At about the date of the première of *Tite et Bérénice* Corneille was called in, apparently at very short notice, to help Molière out with *Psyché*, a *tragédie-ballet* with machines, singing and dancing, commanded by the court.[2] There was a highly successful collaboration between Molière, who planned the whole production but lacked time to write all the verse, Quinault who wrote the words of the songs, and Corneille who wrote most of the last four acts 'in about a fortnight'. He employed the same kind of lightly harmonious irregular verse that he had used in *Agésilas*. The music was by Lully. Incidentally this has some bearing on the question of the possible rivalry over *Bérénice*. It shows that, if pressed, Corneille could still compose at speed.

After this Corneille still had two plays to write. In November 1672 came *Pulchérie*, styled a *comédie héroïque* like *Tite et Bérénice*. This was another drama of politics and love, set in the Byzantine Empire of the fifth century. It contained a situation comparable to that of *Tite*, but in this case it was an empress who decided not to marry her lover for reasons of state. Corneille gave this play to the Marais rather than to Molière or the Hôtel. The reason is unknown, though it has been conjectured that he did so as a generous gesture towards his old friends, hard hit by Lully's recently obtained monopoly of spectacles with music.

His next and last play, the tragedy of *Suréna*, was performed by the Hôtel de Bourgogne (December (?) 1674). The story, ostensibly

[1] La Grange's *Registre* shows that the initial run of *Tite et Bérénice* grossed 15,738 livres for 21 performances over some fourteen weeks (28 November 1670 to 8 March 1671). The première yielded 1,913 livres. It alternated with the highly popular *Bourgeois Gentilhomme*, which over much the same period (23 November 1670 to 27 February 1671) grossed 22,260 livres, also for 21 performances (première: 1,397 livres).

In contrast, *Attila* in 1667 had grossed only 6,363 livres for 16 performances in fourteen weeks (première: 1,027 livres) after which it was virtually dead.

In the absence of records for the Hôtel de Bourgogne the only basis of comparison for *Bérénice* is Racine's mention of '(at least) thirty well-followed performances'.

[2] First produced at the Tuileries, 17 January 1671.

set in Syria at the time of the Roman wars of the first century A.D., is predominantly romanesque, with some political motivation. There is a tyrant-king and an impeccably gallant and virtuous hero in Suréna himself, whose historical prototype is radically modified to meet the requirements of *vraisemblance* as d'Aubignac would have defined them. In spite of this the play failed and Corneille ceased to write for the theatre.

He lived on for a further ten years, dying in Paris at the age of seventy-eight on 1 October 1684. His last years were not, as an older legend has it, spent in poverty, but the royal pension of 2,000 livres, granted him in 1662, was discontinued in 1674 and restored only in the year of his death. His reputation was also in decline, though later the lasting popularity of his greatest plays restored him to his leading position on a par with Racine, with whom his name has become permanently coupled.

VII

Nearly all the nine plays of Corneille's second period (disregarding *La Toison d'Or*) are dramas of political intrigue involving political marriages. *Sophonisbe* is an exception, though even there marriage is treated as a political factor. It is also introduced into *Œdipe* as a secondary theme. In that play King Oedipus favours the marriage of Dircé, whom he believes to be his step-daughter, to her cousin Haemon rather than to Theseus for the reason that the latter is too powerful and might support Dircé in enforcing her rights to the Theban throne. This invention of Corneille's shows his obsessive interest in a theme which assumed great importance in the succeeding plays and dominated *Othon*, *Pulchérie* and *Suréna*.

After *Œdipe* Corneille returned in the main to Roman history (Rome itself or the Roman provinces), finding his primary material in the Greek and Latin historians, Plutarch, Livy, Tacitus, Cassius Dio, but adapting it radically to suit his purposes. Little was left, however, of the old Roman ethos, even in distorted forms. *Vertu* of the old kind is seldom in evidence; *gloire* is attached to the attainment of supreme power, considered as a character's right through heredity or some other reason, or else it is a vindication of *amour propre* and may entail revenge. 'Love', in the sense of a strong personal attraction unaffected by ambition or self-interest, is present in some characters. Sometimes it is sacrificed in a painful effort to save the loved one or some other character; sometimes in favour of what are usually considered the higher claims of kingship.

The nature of 'love' in these plays thus lends itself to several shades of interpretation, ranging from pure affection at one end of the scale to expediency or self-interest at the other. But these simple extremes rarely occur in an absolute state, which makes analysis of the plays from the point of view of 'love' both more interesting and more difficult. Expediency may reinforce or diminish affection, a character's rank or potential rank may form part of their attraction as a personality. Corneille provides a number of intermediate or ambiguous cases and the question is further complicated by the fact that the feelings or motivation of some of his characters can change in the course of the play. Thus Sertorius falls in love at some point after Act I, as does the Mandane of *Agésilas*. Pulchérie in the play of that name grows less attached to Léon, while Léon's response to her is not entirely consistent.

There are still a few perfect lovers: Thésée in *Œdipe*, Cotys in *Agésilas*, Bérénice in *Tite et Bérénice*, the subject-kings Valamir and Ardaric in *Attila* (but both are weak characters); and, as like-minded pairs (reminiscent of the Rodrigue and Chimène of *Le Cid* or the Nicomède and Laodice of *Nicomède*), Othon and Plautine in *Othon*, Spitridate and Elpinice in *Agésilas*, Suréna and Eurydice in *Suréna*. These lovers are irreducible in their feelings. Their 'heart' will not change whatever expediency or prudence may dictate, but even so they are too reasonable or too controlled to be credited with *amour-passion*, a concept which it remained for Racine to develop in its fullest and most effective form. Love in Corneille thus rarely acquires a tragic stature in itself. In the examples quoted only Suréna and Eurydice are led to disaster, obstinately rather than blindly; Bérénice achieves a noble renunciation, consoled by the certainty that at least she possesses her lover's heart; all the others finally attain their desires and for them Corneille contrives a happy ending in the comic and tragicomic conventions.

This went at least part of the way towards meeting the contemporary demand for love of a particular kind (virtuous desire ultimately fulfilled) in tragedy, and when expressed in *galant* and even *précieux* dialogue might conceivably have been enough to satisfy the sentimental women who formed an influential part of Corneille's audiences.[1]

[1] See three pertinent pages on this point in A. Adam, op. cit. IV, pp. 226-9.

But it was not enough when these plays of his later period are considered as a whole, since there was so much else in them to shock the conventions of *galanterie*. By stressing other elements, Corneille could equally well be represented as an anti-sentimental, as an adversary of the *doucereux* and the tender-hearted. So indeed he was by the gazette-writer Robinet, who wrote of *Pulchérie* in December 1672:

> O que dans ce sien dramatique
> On voit une noble critique
> Des sottes tendresses de cœur
> Qu'étale tout stérile auteur.

Robinet, no critic in his own right, was certainly echoing some section of contemporary opinion which at that date at least condemned the 'sottes tendresses de cœur' and preferred something more virile and even more cynical.

But to consider these late plays primarily from this angle is to distort their significance. Corneille's main interest is not in love, however defined or represented; it is in the power-game, in the fascination of the moves and counter-moves of the statesman, the politician and the political adventurer. Into this game, played in deadly earnest, with a throne as the reward for success and assassination or execution as the probable penalty of failure, marriage may enter as an empirical factor: it can cement an alliance or secure a crown. Love, as a personal emotion, may either advance or ruin a political calculation. In either case it introduces a complication. For Corneille this was probably its principal attraction.

These plays have many of the features already remarked in the earlier tragedies of 1644–51.[1] They can be seen to throw back to *Rodogune*, or even before that to *La Mort de Pompée*. But they are less melodramatic. They still contain surprising vicissitudes (as in the last act of *Othon*), but the general atmosphere is more rational. None contains situations as bizarre as those of *Théodore* and *Héraclius*. The mystery of the concealed identity occurs only in *Œdipe*, and even there it is exploited in a different way. There are no more evil queen-mothers of the Médée-Cléopâtre line. Even the male villains develop scruples or hesitations (Aspar in *Pulchérie*, Perpenna in *Sertorius*); only

---

[1] See above, pp. 146 ff.

Attila is consistently ruthless and only Martian in *Othon* has no redeeming features.

Pairs of rival women contending for a throne or a man, continuing the pattern of Rodelinde and Edwige in *Pertharite*, are much more frequent and occur in every play except *Œdipe* and *Suréna*. Their relationships are not consistently hostile. Rivalry between them may breed jealousy or a desire for revenge, but also complicity or a shared contempt for a male character, and in several instances gives rise to excellent scenes of ironical cattiness. The characterization in these late plays is more subtle and varied than before, precisely because the moral absolutes of Corneille's 'great' tragedies have decreased in importance and the mixed or fluid motivations mentioned above have largely taken their place. The partly amoral background of the plays produces few characters in the sublime convention and it would seem that Corneille's older admirers felt disappointed for that reason. They missed, for example, the 'generous' character and gesture, which in nine plays is found only in Agésilas, Bérénice, the sub-heroic pair of Valamir and Ardaric in *Attila*, and Pompée ultimately in *Sertorius*. At the same time the younger generation were incompletely satisfied because they did not appreciate Corneille's treatment of love.

His constant preoccupation with the attainment of political power may look dry and repetitive, but in fact none of these plays duplicates any of the others. They combine common factors in different ways, skilfully varying the interactions of situation and character. The plots are still complicated, though somewhat less so than in the *Rodogune–Pertharite* period and, above all, they *appear* simpler. This appearance was a result of Corneille's greater mastery in the art of plotting, not of a closer approximation to the strict 'classical' ideal. The examples of *Sophonisbe* and of *Tite et Bérénice* are sufficient to show how wide the gap still remained. It is true that the complexity of Corneille's later work is relative when compared to the contemporary plays of his brother Thomas and Quinault. But these were extreme cases, and the imbroglios and situations that distinguish them were in fact developments, more or less successful, of features which can all be found in Pierre Corneille's own tragedies. They exaggerate the qualities of their model but do not invalidate what has been said about the basically complex nature of his conception of drama.

Less immediately popular than these younger dramatists, in 'old'

Corneille there is still no question of failing powers. If he had returned to the theatre to write only *Sertorius*, *Othon*, *Attila* and *Pulchérie*, his return would have been fully justified.

CORNEILLE'S PLAYS FROM *ŒDIPE* TO *SURÉNA*

Œdipe, tragedy, 1659
Based on the Oedipus tragedies of Sophocles and Seneca, with Corneille's addition of a love story.

Thésée, Prince of Athens, is at the court of Œdipe, King of Thebes and husband of Jocaste. He wishes to marry Dircé, the daughter of Jocaste by her first marriage with the late king Laïus, who responds to him. For political reasons Œdipe wishes her to marry her cousin Hémon. Dircé resents Œdipe, who has taken over a throne which she considers hers by right. At the same time Thebes is being ravaged by plague. The oracles are mute, but the ghost of Laïus, invoked by Tirésias (offstage), declares that only the blood of his own family will appease the gods, angered because some great crime has gone unpunished.

The crime is taken to be the murder of Laïus while on a journey, and the required victim to be Dircé, Laïus's only known surviving child. She proudly offers herself as a sacrifice, despite the pleadings of her mother Jocaste and her lover Thésée. The latter, having heard a report that a son of Laïus and Jocaste, exposed on the mountain as an infant, survived and is now present in Thebes, attempts to save Dircé by claiming that he may be this son and so acceptable as a sacrifice in her place. But in that case he would be her brother and his love for her would become incestuous (there was a similar situation in *Héraclius*). In a dialogue with her he wavers, admits that whoever he is he certainly did not kill Laïus, but decides to maintain that he is Laïus's son at least until the real son appears.

A confrontation with Phorbas, one of Laïus's attendants when he was attacked and killed, shows that the killer was not Thésée but Œdipe himself. It is decided that Thésée and Œdipe shall fight a duel in which either the murderer of Laïus or his supposed son, Thésée, will perish. Meanwhile, Jocaste is torn between love for her present husband Œdipe and the detestation which she ought to feel for him as her first husband's murderer.

In the final act a messenger enlightens Œdipe on his true parentage and his incestuous marriage with his mother. News of Jocaste's suicide is brought to Thésée and Dircé, who now dominate the stage. Shortly after comes the news of Œdipe's self-blinding, which has the effect of immediately halting the plague in Thebes, with the recovery of the dying.

La Toison d'Or, tragedy with machines, 1660–1

See above p. 197.

Sertorius, tragedy, 1662

Source: Plutarch, with additions by Corneille.

Sertorius, the Roman general commanding in Spain, is envied by his lieutenant Perpenna, who is plotting to assassinate him. Sertorius is a supporter of the Roman dictator Sulla. Pompée, a supporter of Sulla's enemy Marius, is also in Spain, but less powerful there than Sertorius. The latter has given refuge to Pompée's first wife, Aristie, divorced on Sulla's orders in favour of Émilie, whom Pompée has married in Rome for political reasons. Also at Sertorius's headquarters is Viriate, Queen of Lusitania. She desires to marry Sertorius, whom she admires for his power and Roman *vertu*, and set up an independent kingdom with him in Spain. Sertorius is not at first in love with Viriate, but Perpenna is. Sertorius offers Viriate (without her knowledge) to Perpenna, while himself inclining to a marriage with Aristie, which would strengthen his position in Rome. Perpenna is overwhelmed by Sertorius's generosity.

Aristie now hesitantly offers her hand to Sertorius, but not her heart, if he thinks it will advance his interests and give her vengeance for her divorce. She shows, however, that she still loves Pompée and Sertorius advises her to wait until she knows Pompée's mind.

Sertorius offers Perpenna to Viriate, who frankly says she prefers Sertorius. She receives Perpenna somewhat contemptuously but persuades him to detach Aristie from Sertorius, to which he readily agrees.

Pompée now arrives and remains non-committal on Sertorius's suggestion that they should combine together against Sulla. He declares that he still loves Aristie and thanks Sertorius for protecting her. In a confrontation with Aristie, she tries to persuade Pompée to remarry her and vindicate her *gloire*. He meets her with political arguments, asking her to wait until Sulla has laid down his power. She refuses this compromise indignantly.

In Act IV Sertorius realizes that he loves Viriate emotionally, but when she responds by proposing an immediate marriage, he urges prudence and delay, using the same kind of arguments that Pompée used with Aristie. Viriate demands a decision by the next day and leaves him. Sertorius then tells Perpenna of Viriate's preference for himself, but says he is still willing to support Perpenna's claim while showing the political disadvantages of offending Viriate. Perpenna's confidant tells him that he is simply being played with and reminds him that he must make an early decision about the plot to assassinate Sertorius at a banquet that evening.

In Act V Viriate and Aristie meet for the first time. They are basically in agreement. Aristie is ready to refuse Sertorius, saying that she is is still attached to Pompée. Viriate affirms that she is ready to marry Sertorius at once, in order to consolidate his and her power in Spain and wean him from his Roman ambitions. A messenger arrives unexpectedly from Rome with news that Sulla has laid down his power and that Pompée's second wife Émilie has died in childbirth, leaving the way open for Pompée's return to Rome and his remarriage to Aristie. Immediately after comes news that Sertorius has been assassinated and that Perpenna has taken over his command. While Perpenna is triumphing, Pompée enters, now supreme in Spain. Perpenna tries to ingratiate himself by handing him letters containing the names of Romans who have been intriguing against him with Aristie. In a generous gesture Pompée burns them unread, takes back Aristie, and sends out Perpenna to be massacred by the angry populace.

From Corneille's *Examen*: '. . . les raisonnements de la politique, qui fait l'âme de toute cette tragédie.'

Sophonisbe, tragedy, 1663
Based primarily on Livy, but with awareness of the *Sophonisbe* tragedies of Trissino, Montchrestien and Mairet, all mentioned in Corneille's *Au lecteur*.

Sophonisbe is besieged in Syrta by the Romans aided by their ally Massinisse, to whom she has been betrothed in the past. An army led by her elderly husband Syphax, with whom she had contracted a political marriage, arrives to halt the siege and there are prospects of peace, but Sophonisbe persuades him to continue fighting. In the ensuing battle he is defeated and taken prisoner. Sophonisbe is now at the mercy of Massinisse and the Romans. With her is Éryxe, a captive queen who, as Massinisse's present fiancée, can now expect to dominate Sophonisbe, but for Massinisse's doubtful attitude. He offers his hand to Éryxe, but only as a feint, then is immediately married to Sophonisbe, whom he still loves, as a means of protecting her against the Romans. Sophonisbe accepts in order to conserve her position as Queen of Carthage and perhaps detach Massinisse from Rome. She warns him that if he cannot save her from the humiliation of a Roman triumph she will break off the marriage. In a confrontation with her first husband Syphax, brought in in chains, she justifies her second marriage. A Queen of Carthage cannot be the wife of a defeated captive. He should have killed himself.

The Romans hint that they might still come to terms with Syphax and they receive Massinisse's plea on behalf of Sophonisbe coldly. Massinisse goes to plead with their commander Scipion while Sophonisbe waits. A messenger brings Scipion's refusal and his command forbidding Massinisse to see his wife again. He also brings a letter from Massinisse and a dose of poison which she returns to him contemptuously: 'He needs it more than I.' With equal contempt she 'gives back' Massinisse to her rival Éryxe, then takes her own poison, dying proudly as a Carthaginian and the daughter of Hasdrubal. It is foreshadowed that Éryxe, in spite of her reluctance, might be persuaded by the Romans to conclude a political marriage with Massinisse, their satellite.

Othon, tragedy, 1664
Source: Tacitus.

The plot concerns a struggle for power under the ageing Roman Emperor Galba. There are two main factions, one led by the Consul Vinius, the other by the Prefect Lacus and Martian, a freedman of Galba and his influential councillor. These two favour the nomination of Pison as the next Emperor, since he is a weak character who would become their tool (he does not appear on the stage). Vinius is ready to support the claim of Othon, a senator, who has become engaged to marry Vinius's daughter Plautine – at first for political reasons, but the two are now sincerely in love.

An alternative marriage for Othon is with Camille, Galba's niece, which Vinius himself now recommends as politically preferable. Urged by Plautine (who believes that their lives depend on it), Othon proposes formally to Camille who, though she loves him passionately, is non-committal. The freedman Martian then unexpectedly offers his love and his hand to Plautine, promising to support Othon on condition that she accepts him. She refuses sarcastically. News now comes that Galba is in favour of Othon's marrying not his niece Camille but Plautine. This would exclude him from the Empire. In an angry scene with Lacus and Martian Camille declares her readiness to marry whichever man becomes Emperor, since she would then be the power behind the throne.

She is having second thoughts when Galba announces his choice of Pison as successor and suggests marrying Camille to him. Sensing her hesitation, he offers her a marriage to Othon, but without the throne. It is now Othon's turn to hesitate (for love of Plautine). He protests deceitfully that he must not rob Camille of the Empire. She sees through him and sends him back to Plautine. Plautine, however, urges him to return to Camille as the only safe course – there is the risk of a political assassination. On his refusal she reveals Martian's offer to her and proposes accepting it to save her lover's life. Othon is horrified. It is now learnt that Pison has been received coldly by the army when presented to them as Galba's successor and that they seem to prefer Othon. The latter hurries off to seize his opportunity. Further news soon comes of a rising in his favour.

In Act V Galba is shown hesitating, uncertain whom to trust. Vinius and Lacus quarrel violently in his presence. To them and Plautine, who arrives in great distress after hearing a report of Othon's death, Martian enters with a soldier, Atticus, who declares that he has killed Othon with his own hand. Galba, Vinius and Lacus leave to deal with the situation and restore calm. But before going Galba orders Plautine to marry Martian, who tries to impose himself upon her. The tables are immediately turned. The soldier Atticus reveals that he is a partisan of Othon, who is alive and well after all. Atticus and his men are masters of the palace. Martian is arrested and led away. Hard on this comes news of the deaths of Galba, Vinius and Lacus. The first two have been stabbed by Lacus, who has then killed himself.

Othon enters, now uncontestably Emperor. He lays the Empire at

Plautine's feet. She says that her first duty is to mourn her father, but hints at the possibility of marriage in the future. Camille has disappeared from the action, but Othon undertakes to console her as an act of friendship though not of love.

Agésilas, tragedy, 1666

Source in Plutarch's *Lives* of Agesilaus and Lysander, considerably romanticized.

Lysandre, the great Spartan general under King Agésilas, has arranged marriages for his two daughters Elpinice and Aglatide to Cotys, King of Paphlagonia, and Spitridate, a Persian lord at the court of Sparta, respectively. Discontented with their prospective husbands, the sisters consider the possibility of an exchange. Elpinice is attracted by Spitridate while the realistic Aglatide would prefer Cotys, not for love but because he is a king. Her ambition for a throne was fired by Agésilas, who has secretly shown that she attracts him. Elpinice objects that Cotys appears to be in love with Mandane, the beautiful sister of Spitridate.

The permutations set up by the existence of three couples of potential lovers are finally resolved by the marriage of Spitridate to Elpinice, whose mutual love has remained constant, Cotys to Mandane, and Agésilas to Aglatide, who is satisfied to find herself a queen after all. Before offering her his hand the generous Agésilas has conquered his love for Mandane, whom he really prefers, in order to unite her to Cotys.

Among the numerous complications which arise in the course of the play, the chief are caused by (1) Aglatide's determination to marry a king – either Cotys or Agésilas, (2) Cotys's refusal to give up Elpinice, whom he does not love, to Spitridate, unless he is given Mandane, whom he does love, (3) the political calculations of Lysandre, who is jealous of Agésilas and plotting against him (the plot is discovered and pardoned), (4) the precarious position of the Persians Spitridate and Mandane who, as exiles, are dependent on Agésilas's goodwill. The main interest lies in the reactions of the characters to each other in the context of these considerations.

Attila, tragedy, 1667

Primary sources: Marcellinus, perhaps through Mézeray's *Histoire de France*, and probably other historians; Jordanes, *Getica*, and Paulus Diaconus, *History of the Langobards*.

Attila, King of the Huns, is hesitating between a political marriage with Honorie, sister of Valentinian, Emperor of declining Rome, or Ildione, sister of the Frankish King Mérovée, whose power is rising. Both women are at Attila's camp and in his power, as are two subject kings, Ardaric of the Gepids and Valamir of the Visigoths. Ardaric is in love with Ildione, Valamir with Honorie. The princesses love their suitors but both feel that their *gloire* requires them to marry Attila.

Attila, though finding that he is in love with Ildione, eventually offers marriage to Honorie as the better political match. Having meanwhile been 'given' Attila by the indignant Ildione, Honorie contemptuously refuses to accept her rival's leavings and reveals her own love for Valamir. Attila roughly changes front. He will reject her and marry Ildione after all. This inspires Honorie with a desire for vengeance on Ildione. She informs Attila that Ildione is in love with Ardaric and suggests that she should be punished by being married to a subject. Attila turns the tables on her by ordering her to choose within an hour between marriage with himself or the captain of his guard, Octar. He then offers Ildione to her lover Ardaric on condition that the latter kills Valamir and proposes to offer Honorie to Valamir on similar conditions – Valamir to kill Ardaric.

Bound by friendship, both kings refuse these conditions. Attila then proposes that they should fight a duel. When Ardaric refuses this also, Attila says that he can find other killers, choosing them from among the worst criminals. These shall be rewarded by receiving the princesses as wives. When Honorie protests he exults in his cruelty. At this point Ildione brings her agreement to marriage with Attila. He accepts her and consents to postpone the murder of her lover Ardaric until the next day. After they have left for the marriage ceremony Honorie tries to persuade Octar to kill Attila, but he is powerless, since the mistrustful Attila has changed the composition of his guard.

Unexpectedly, news is brought of Attila's sudden death from a haemorrhage. Power passes to Ardaric and Valamir, who are united to the princesses of their choice.

Unusual features in this play are the mentions of prophecy and hallucination. Ardaric has been told by his soothsayers that a future Roman Emperor will descend from him. The dying Attila sees the ghosts of his murdered brother and of the six kings he has also murdered (offstage: narrated).

Tite et Bérénice, comédie héroïque, 1670

Sources: Cassius Dio, abridged by Xiphilinus. The story is also in Tacitus and Suetonius (summarized in French by Coeffeteau), in Scudéry's *Femmes illustres* (1642) and, much romanticized, in *Tite*, a tragicomedy by Magnon, printed in 1660. In this obscure play Berenice comes to Titus's court in male disguise and wins his hand in a happy ending.

The Emperor Tite is within four days of celebrating his long-promised marriage with Domitie, the daughter of Corbulon, an eminent Roman (now dead) who had formerly refused the offer of the Empire. There is mutual love between Domitie and Tite's brother Domitian, but Domitie feels that a higher duty calls her to the throne through marriage with Tite. Domitian privately considers thwarting the marriage by bringing back to Rome a former love of his brother's, Bérénice, Queen of Judea, whom Tite had banished from Rome in obedience to the people's wish.

Bérénice's return, contrived by Domitian's confidant, is suddenly announced. Tite is torn between his passion for her, which is far from dead, and his duty to Rome and Domitie. The latter, now inspired by jealousy, is more determined than ever to become Empress.

The rivalry between the two women is exasperated by the hesitations of the two men and their doubts about their sincerity. Bérénice unselfishly refuses Tite's desperate offer to abdicate and follow her to her own country, but she and Domitian agree, both for selfish reasons, to prevent the marriage of Domitie to Tite.

At the beginning of Act V Tite is still wavering between love and his duty as a Roman Emperor not to marry a queen. Bérénice declares her readiness to leave him, but in her own time and independently of the Senate's decision about her future. The last scene brings the unexpected news of the agreement of the Senate, influenced by Domitian, to her marriage.[1] Bérénice still refuses, seeing too much danger in this for Tite. She makes her final renunciation and prepares to leave: 'Votre cœur est à moi, j'y règne, c'est assez.' Domitian is named as Tite's heir and Domitie is to be persuaded to marry him after all.

---

[1] It is typical of Corneille's concern with real history that in his play the Senate has assembled to discuss the disaster of the Vesuvius eruption, which occurred in the same year. The question of Bérénice is discussed as a second item.

Pulchérie, comédie héroïque, 1672

Source: in the *Au lecteur* Corneille merely refers to 'all the historians' and no precise names can be given. The background story and the chief characters belong to a well-known phase in Byzantine history.

The throne of the Roman Empire of the East is vacant after the death of Theodosius, whose sister Pulchérie was the virtual ruler in his lifetime. If she marries his successor she will continue in power. She is in love with Léon, a candidate for the throne, but makes it clear that she will not marry him unless he is made Emperor. A rival candidate is Aspar, betrothed to Léon's sister Irène, but actuated predominantly by ambition. Other characters are Martian, an old and trusted counsellor of the deceased Emperor, and Martian's daughter Justine, who is secretly in love with Léon.

Pulchérie is confirmed in power by the Senate and required to choose a husband to reign with her. To Léon's distress she does not immediately name him, doubting whether he is the best candidate, though she still loves him. Ironically, she requests Justine to try to win his heart and so remove temptation from herself. Meanwhile Aspar has tried to advance his own interests, first by suggesting joining forces with Léon – but with himself as the dominant partner – next by contemplating abandoning his fiancée Irène and marrying Justine, as a better political match, then by aspiring to the hand of Pulchérie herself. All the women see through him.

Pulchérie begins to feel detached from Léon and, having been finally ordered by the Senate to choose a husband without delay, she names the elderly Martian, to his joy and astonishment. Earlier he had revealed in private his secret and hopeless love for her. She insists, however, on a *mariage blanc,* arguing that in that way she will not break faith with Léon. Léon will be groomed for the Empire under Martian and is ordered to marry Justine. The marriage of Irène to Aspar, 'cet esprit flottant', is foreshadowed.

Suréna, général des Parthes, tragedy, 1674

Sources: Plutarch, *Life of Crassus,* much altered; Appian, *Syrian Wars.*

Orode, King of Parthia, has defeated the Armenians and brought the Armenian princess Eurydice to his court to be married to his son Pacorus as a guarantee of peace. Eurydice dreads the prospect of this marriage and is in love with Suréna, the great Parthian general who has defeated the Romans led by Crassus. Suréna fully reciprocates Eurydice's love, but the King plans to marry him to his daughter Mandane as a reward for his services (Mandane does not appear on the stage). Suréna has a sister, Palmis, with whom the prince Pacorus was formerly in love.

Pacorus, who is now deeply in love with Eurydice, is disturbed by her lack of response: she merely shows submission. Pressed to say if she loves another man she takes offence, postpones the marriage and urges Pacorus to go back to Palmis. Pacorus is still intent on discovering his rival's name.

Orode tests out Suréna's feelings towards his daughter Mandane. When Suréna cunningly protests that he is unworthy of such a match, Orode frankly tells him that he is growing too powerful and that he wishes to attach him to him as his son-in-law. He orders him either to marry Mandane or to name a wife of his own choice (Suréna cannot do this because his choice would be Eurydice). Ironically, Orode sends him to persuade Eurydice into marriage with Pacorus.

It is then suspected that Orode has deduced that Suréna and Eurydice are in love, since both refuse the marriages proposed to them in favour of an unknown lover. Though guards have now been posted at the doors, Eurydice is unconvinced and unwilling to believe that Suréna is in real danger. Palmis vainly entreats her to save him by marrying Pacorus: 'Acceptez mon amant pour conserver mon frère.'

Both Pacorus and Orode threaten the lovers, with a final ultimatum from the King. He demands at least one marriage: either Eurydice to Pacorus or Suréna to Mandane.

Eurydice and Suréna remain irreducible. Suréna is ordered to leave the court for a few days and goes out confidently. His sister, full of foreboding, persists in her attempt to persuade Eurydice to give him up and urge him to marry Mandane, but Eurydice is incapable of the sacrifice. At the last moment she consents, but too late. On leaving the palace Suréna has been killed by an unknown hand. Eurydice collapses, apparently dying. Palmis desires to live on for revenge.

9

ROMANESQUE TRAGEDY: THOMAS CORNEILLE AND QUINAULT

The vogue of romanesque tragedy – T. Corneille's career and dramatic work as a whole: borrowings and adaptations – *Timocrate* – other identity plays – *Camma*, a melodrama – variations on P. Corneille: *Laodice, La Mort d'Annibal* – 'Racinian' plays: *Ariane* – *Ariane* and *Bajazet* – *Le Comte d'Essex* – ethos of T. Corneille's drama – conventional verse-idiom – Quinault's career and dramatic production – his reputation for *tendresse* – *Amalasonte* – his identity plays – *Agrippa* – *Astrate* – the tragic dilemma in *Astrate* – tragedies of devoted love: *La Mort de Cyrus* and others – the interrupted *récit* – love and *vertu* in Quinault – his diffident lovers

The two authors considered in this chapter were writing plays styled tragedies or, more rarely, tragicomedies, in the later 1650s and throughout the 1660s. These plays were contemporary with most of the productions of Pierre Corneille described in the previous chapter. They also overlapped Racine's work.[1] In a sense they formed a bridge between the work of the two major dramatists, though that statement in itself does not fully represent the true position in a drama in which cross-influences were of such importance. But it can at least be said that they reflected the majority taste of theatre audiences in the fifteen years beginning towards 1655. This taste was for romanesque tragedy, whose principal features were that it derived from contemporary or near-contemporary novels or, when ostensibly based on other sources, as it frequently was, observed the ethos and attitudes found in the novels.[2] The treatment of love was similar. The plots, full of misunder-

[1] See the table on opposite page.
[2] After Honoré d'Urfé's *L'Astrée* (1607–27), the chief were de Gomberville's *Polexandre* (1637), Madeleine de Scudéry's *Ibrahim* (1641), *Le Grand Cyrus* (1649–53) and *Clélie* (1654–60) and La Calprenède's *Cassandre* (1642–5), *Cléopâtre* (1646–57) and *Faramond* (1661–70). La Calprenède also wrote plays.

	P. CORNEILLE	T. CORNEILLE	QUINAULT	RACINE
1656		Timocrate	Le Fantôme amoureux TC	
1657		Bérénice / Mort de l'Empereur Commode	Amalasonte TC or T	
1658			Le Feint Alcibiade TC / (?) Le Mariage de Cambyse TC / La Mort de Cyrus TC	
1659	Œdipe	Darius		
1660		Stilicon		
1661		Camma		
1662	Sertorius	Maximian / Persée et Démétrius	(?) Agrippa, ou le faux Tibérinus TC or T	
1663	Sophonisbe	(?) Pyrrhus		
1664	Othon		Astrate, roi de Tyr	La Thébaïde
1665				Alexandre
1666	Agésilas	Antiochus T or TC		
1667	Attila			Andromaque
1668		Laodice	Pausanias	
1669		La Mort d'Annibal		Britannicus
1670	Tite et Bérénice CH		(or 1671?) Bellérophon	Bérénice
1671	(Psyché)		(Psyché)	
1672	Pulchérie CH	Ariane / Théodat		Bajazet
1673		La Mort d'Achille		Mithridate
1674	Suréna		operas	Iphigénie
1675				
1676				
1677				Phèdre
1678		Le Comte d'Essex		
1689		operas, machine-plays and comedies		Esther
1691				Athalie

All these plays are tragedies except where otherwise indicated
TC ... tragicomedy
CH ... comédie héroïque
(?) ... exact date of first production uncertain

standings between characters and surprising vicissitudes, depended excessively on cases of disguised or mistaken identity.

By no means all the plays written by Thomas Corneille in the period under review exhibit these characteristics, and Quinault also produced some exceptions. Nor can either author – and this applies particularly to Thomas – be judged only on his work written during these particular fifteen years. It is obvious too that the romanesque was no new phenomenon in French drama. It dated back to the 1630s and characterized the great majority of the plays performed since then, as has been seen in previous chapters. But these were the more ephemeral plays, of relative unimportance beside other plays in which romanesque elements were either lacking or subsidiary. Almost invariably the first had been styled tragicomedies. From the 1650s on there was no serious competition, except dubiously from the now less fashionable Pierre Corneille, for the romanesque play to face. It assumed the name of 'tragedy', came at times to deserve it, and for a time dominated the stage under that description. In this period of its greatest success and most extreme development Thomas Corneille and Quinault provided the best examples of it.

II

Thomas Corneille, Pierre's younger brother by nineteen years, was born in 1625 and died in 1709 at the end of a crowded and highly successful literary career. He put his name, alone or in collaboration, to forty-six dramatic productions, including four operas and four machine-plays. He began, like his brother and Rotrou before him, with a series of comedies, the first of which, *Les Engagements du hasard*, appeared in 1649. In 1656 he made a triumphant breakthrough in tragedy with *Timocrate*, which has been hailed (probably rightly, though statistical proof is lacking) as the greatest theatrical success of its century. Over the next seventeen years there followed a succession of fourteen other tragedies, interspersed with three more comedies. Then came the operas and the machine-plays, composed mainly in collaboration with Donneau de Visé,[1] and a few further comedies written with the same collaborator. He composed one more notable tragedy, *Le Comte d' Essex* (1678), which proved the longest lived of his

[1] With whom he became co-editor of the *Mercure galant*, the literary and social (and often scurrilous) periodical, in 1681.

tragic plays, and ended his dramatic career in 1695 with a version of *Bradamante* which he had written some fifteen years earlier and was persuaded against his better judgement to allow the Comédie-Française to perform. By that date he had become a distinguished and active member of the Académie Française, for which he compiled several learned works. When he died, half blind, at the age of eighty-four, it was in his house at Les Andelys, a town in that part of Normandy where his family had been established for generations.

Thomas Corneille flourished in the shadow of his greater brother. Their father having died when he was fourteen, Pierre seems to have assumed the role of a benevolent father-figure. Like Pierre, Thomas studied for the bar, though he did not practise. Pierre taught him to read Spanish, an immensely useful accomplishment for a would-be playwright. At the age of twenty-one Thomas married the younger sister of Pierre's wife, Marie de Lampérière. The two brothers remained in close and harmonious contact through the rest of the elder's life, sometimes sharing the same houses in Rouen and Paris. On Pierre's death Thomas was elected to his chair in the Académie Française (and received in a speech of welcome by Racine, the Académie's then director). For long after the two remained associated in the public mind. Critics coupled them, treating Thomas as an appendage to Pierre. Eighteenth- and nineteenth-century publishers printed selections of his plays in the same editions as those of his brother.

But while the persistent impression of a younger-brother relationship hardly does Thomas Corneille an injustice, it should not be taken to mean that his plays as a whole were imitative of Pierre's plays. Only a small number of them can be so described. Constantly in search of the immediate theatrical success, he adapted the work of several other dramatists, using them quite openly and often improving upon them. Imitation or competition was common practice in his century and was encouraged by the theatre companies, but in him it was more obvious and more frequent than in any of his contemporaries. He was the foremost adaptor of his age and was no doubt recognized as such by Molière's widow when she asked him to write a new version in verse of her husband's *Don Juan*.[1]

[1] T. Corneille's version, entitled *Le Festin de pierre* (Molière's alternative title), was reasonably faithful to the original, but omitted or altered passages to which the censors objected. But for this the play could not have been performed at all at that

Of his first eight comedies, seven were direct adaptations of Spanish comedies, by Calderón, Rojas and others, with a few probable borrowings from Scarron, who worked on the same Spanish material. The eighth was a dramatization of Sorel's burlesque novel *Le Berger extravagant*, with the same title. Several of these were comedies of intrigue based on mistaken identities, with the confused relationships which resulted from them.

Similar complications were paramount in several of his tragedies, as will be seen below. Meanwhile his first two tragedies were based on episodes found not in plays but in novels (*Timocrate* drew on La Calprenède's *Cléopâtre* and *Bérénice* on Mlle de Scudéry's *Grand Cyrus*). For the next seven (*Commode* to *Pyrrhus*) parallel situations can be found in his brother's plays, though the primary sources were usually historians such as Plutarch. *Laodice* has resemblances, including two character-names, to *Nicomède*, while *La Mort d'Annibal* is a deliberate variation on that play. Two other tragedies are imitations or variations of plays by Thomas Corneille's younger competitor Quinault: *Antiochus* has the same story and the same main characters as Quinault's *Stratonice*, with one important difference; *Théodat* was clearly suggested by Quinault's *Amalasonte*, though written fifteen years later. In the later tragedies some Racinian influence becomes perceptible, most noticeably in *Ariane* (1672) and, more distantly, in *La Mort d'Achille* (1673) and *Le Comte d'Essex* (1678). With Racine, however, there is no question of an open or a competitive treatment of the same story. In *Le Comte d'Essex* Thomas renewed a forty-year-old play of La Calprenède's, to whom he also turned for his *Bradamante* which he composed at about the same date.

This catalogue of borrowings would not in itself stamp Thomas Corneille as unoriginal. The originality might lie in the treatment, as it had done, for better or worse, in his brother's *Œdipe* and *Sophonisbe* and in numerous other plays of the time. But the difficulty is to find any consistency of treatment or approach in Thomas's drama. Neither is it possible to trace any consistent development. His plays can be grouped, approximately at least, but the groupings correspond to no

---

date. Corneille's reworking, however, replaced the original for an unnecessarily long time. One hundred and seventy years passed (1677–1846) before Molière's text was restored to the French stage.

definable pattern. They reflect rather whatever influence the author was submitting to at the moment and are less the productions of an identifiable talent than reflections of popular taste.

This remains their primary interest and makes it unnecessary in a book of this scope to take more than a few of them as examples of Thomas's varied gifts.

III

Timocrate, first performed at the Marais in December 1656, was the first new 'tragedy' of any note at all, with the possible exception of Cyrano de Bergerac's *Mort d'Agrippine*, to be produced on the Parisian stage since Pierre Corneille's unsuccessful *Pertharite* of 1651. In the intermediate five years the theatres had been closed for about nine months in 1653 owing to the troubles of the Fronde,[1] which in themselves created a generally unfavourable climate for theatregoing. But comedy managed to flourish, tragicomedy held its own, only tragedy appeared to be dying. *Timocrate* revived it, at least in name, but only by assimilating it to tragicomedy and giving it features which came near to removing it from the domain of serious drama.

The play hinges on a case of double identity. It is an outstanding example of that familiar comic device which had also been used tragically in such plays as the elder Corneille's *Héraclius*. Timocrate, King of Crete, is at war with Argos. The Cretan fleet under his command is even now attacking the enemy country. The widowed Queen of Argos, whose husband has died in an earlier campaign against the Cretans, has several champions at her court – three friendly kings or princes who are all suitors for the hand of her daughter Ériphile and a valiant soldier of non-noble birth who has already rendered her outstanding services in war. This soldier, known as Cléomène, is none other than Timocrate himself, a fact revealed to the audience and the Queen only at the end of Act IV. The motive for his ambiguous support of Argos and his presence incognito at its court is love for the princess Ériphile, whose heart he wishes to win in the guise of a commoner, though in that capacity he could not marry her. He succeeds and then to her confusion and indignation urges her to marry his other self, Timocrate. All comes right in the end, with the abdication of the Queen and the marriage of the recognized Timocrate to Ériphile, who

[1] See D.-Holsboer, *Le Théâtre du Marais*, II, pp. 41–2.

succeeds to the throne. But it is reached through a maze of false trails and ambiguities, including a reported combat in which 'Cléomène' defeats Timocrate and apparently takes him prisoner.

The false trails, designed to keep the audience guessing until a late stage in the action, provide the main interest of the play. Throughout there is a well-sustained excitement about who will do what and what will happen next. Comparison with the twentieth-century whodunit is inescapable, though the latter has developed conventions which demand a passably logical explanation of the false clues. The modern author is not supposed to cheat in the way Thomas Corneille sometimes does in this play and others. Nevertheless he constructed in *Timocrate* a model of what it seems justified to describe as the seventeenth-century whowasit, built on a very ingenious exploitation of an artificial situation.

This would not necessarily downgrade his play from the level normally expected of tragedy. The premisses of the *Oedipus Rex* are contrived and improbable, but the human drama which results from them is utterly convincing. This cannot be said of *Timocrate*. Of the three principal characters, the Queen is a conventional figure bent on avenging her husband's death – caused, she believes, by the father of Timocrate, whom she has sworn to kill if he falls into her hands. The solution of her dilemma, after she has learnt that Timocrate and the cherished Cléomène are the same person, is a trick one. Abdication releases her from her oath of vengeance, which bound her in her queenly capacity but would no longer bind her as a subject.[1] Her daughter Ériphile suffers an inner conflict also, first for having fallen in love with 'Cléomène' to whom, because of her royal blood, she cannot give her hand; and later, like Chimène in *Le Cid*, when she believes that her lover and Timocrate are engaged in a fight to the death. Even if 'Cléomène' wins, she ought to refuse him. Both turn out to be false dilemmas when the truth is known. Looking back at them from the end of the play, they appear parodies of the situations seriously developed in earlier tragedies, particularly those of the elder Corneille. But the most damaging parody – if parody had been intended – is in the behaviour and words of 'Cléomène'. He is presented as the perfect type of chivalrous lover. But in obeying part of the code he is obliged to make nonsense of the rest of it.

[1] There is a similar solution in Rotrou's *Venceslas*, but there it is better prepared and psychologically more plausible. See above p. 172, n. 1.

When Ériphile reproaches him for advising her to marry the hated Timocrate he protests, first that he will die voluntarily if the marriage takes place – that is his 'cruel duty', though it simply means that his Cléomène persona will disappear – and secondly that it is excess of love which leads him to sacrifice himself in order to place her on the throne of Crete as another man's wife. He puts this in extravagant terms whose ambiguity is not apparent at this point to the audience, though clues are planted in the last two lines quoted here:

> . . . Mais il est inouï peut-être avant ce jour
> Qu'aucun ait immolé l'amour même à l'amour.
> Pour consacrer mon nom au temple de mémoire
> C'est à moi que le ciel en réservait la gloire.
> Il la devait sans doute à ma fidélité,
> Et j'ose jusque-là flatter ma vanité
> Que d'un effort si grand, si beau, si peu croyable,
> S'il vous fit seule digne, il m'a fait seul capable.
>
> (*Timocrate*, II. iv)

This heroic abnegation of course collapses with the knowledge that Timocrate and Cléomène are the same, and with it goes the whole image of virtuous love as a serious concept. Cléomène's knightly boast in the same scene that he will conquer Timocrate in battle, since that is Ériphile's wish, goes the same way, since the combat is impossible and the danger illusory. Similarly, after having, as he says, defeated Timocrate, he claims Ériphile as his reward, arguing that, though his blood *may* not be royal, his prowess in battle has made him worthy of her (III. vi). His virile language is comparable to that of the Cid and other heroes of Pierre Corneille, until one realizes the situation, when it becomes more reminiscent of Matamore in *L'Illusion comique*.

The ethical counters of older tragedy – *devoir, vertu, gloire* – are rung out before the audience, but their value is depreciated. Though one can be sure that this is not intentional parody, it is perhaps something even more humiliating. The old values, which once possessed a moral reality, are invoked quite mechanically as the background of an ingenious melodrama.[1] Once again it is the principle of the modern detective story, in which the grim realities of violence and murder are conventionalized and subordinated to the requirements of a

[1] For signs of a similar tendency in P. Corneille himself see our comment on *Pertharite* (1651), p. 155 above.

guessing-game. From this point of view, *Timocrate* was the *Mousetrap* of the seventeenth century.[1] It convinced in performance and, when the agreeably surprising dénouement came, the audiences were evidently too involved to feel that they had been let down.[2]

IV

Thomas Corneille made the problem of concealed identity the central motif of three further tragedies, *Bérénice*, *Darius* and *Pyrrhus*, exploiting it with a complexity which grew from play to play, but repeating the success of *Timocrate* in none of them. Concealed identity also plays an important part in *Laodice* (1668), though here only some of the characters are in the dark. The audience learns the truth at an early stage (I. iii) and is able to relish the ironical ambiguity of the situations and the dialogue. After this Thomas abandoned the device altogether, except in a single comedy, *Don César d'Avalos* (1674), based on a Spanish original by Moreto.

Much earlier than this Thomas had experimented in tragedies reminiscent of his brother's, with the Roman Empire at stake, a conspiracy to secure the succession, the question of a political marriage and the intrusion of personal love. The first of these was *La Mort de L'Empereur Commode*, a much simpler play than his *Bérénice*, though produced in the same year.[3] The second was *Stilicon* (1660). This was followed by *Camma*, a great contemporary success and one of the most interesting of Thomas's earlier tragedies.[4]

[1] At the time of writing, Agatha Christie's *The Mousetrap* has been running for twenty consecutive years at the Ambassadors Theatre, London. No one would claim that it is so very greatly superior to numerous other thrillers which have enjoyed vastly shorter runs. It simply seems to have captured popular taste.

[2] The question of identity, the self as conceived by the self and the self as seen by others, has of course a deep philosophical and psychological significance when explored seriously. It was one of the preoccupations of seventeenth-century thought and of some of the drama. But as treated by Thomas Corneille, exteriorized and vulgarized, it becomes no more than a device. In the same way the detective stories exploit superficially the deeply serious problems of crime and motive which preoccupied a Dostoevsky.

[3] The Bérénice of T. Corneille's play was the lost daughter of a king, brought up in error as another man's child. The story was derived from *Le Grand Cyrus*.

[4] De Visé recalled (*Mercure galant*, January 1710) that the stage was so crowded with spectators at this play that the actors were unable to perform freely. Accordingly they gave extra performances on Thursdays, in addition to the three usual weekly performances on Sundays, Tuesdays and Fridays.

Camma starts from the basic premiss of the *Hamlet* story and shows what a clever mid-seventeenth-century playwright might have made of it, given enough imagination and a really free rein. Sinorix, the usurping King of Galatia, has poisoned his predecessor Sinatus partly to gain his throne, but more particularly his wife Camma.[1] She, however, does not respond, knowing that Sinorix was her husband's murderer (though he believes she does not know) and obsessed with a desire for revenge. She parries Sinorix's offer of marriage, having a plausible pretext for her refusal. The murdered king had betrothed Hésione, his daughter by a first marriage (and so Camma's step-daughter) to Sinorix, who ought now to marry her and make her queen. The princess Hésione does not know that Sinorix murdered her father but she bitterly resents his neglect of her and she also longs for revenge. The fourth important character is the prince Sostrate, unrelated to the others and passionately in love with Camma. Camma promises to marry Sostrate on condition that he first kills Sinorix who, as an additional complication, likes and trusts him. Independently, Hésione offers a similar bargain to Sostrate, who she mistakenly believes to be in love with her.

Cross-purposes and mutual deceptions fill the action until the first melodramatic highpoint in Act III. It has been preceded by two scenes in which Sinorix has had forebodings of disaster. He has had a dream in which the ghost of Sinatus appeared and foretold his assassination. He begins to feel remorse for his crime, then has a fresh presentiment of danger. Scene iii, no doubt suggested by a similar scene in Quinault's *Amalasonte* (IV. vi), follows, and can be quoted in its entirety. When it opens Sinorix is alone on the stage after his soliloquy.

CAMMA (*paraissant à un des côtés du théâtre et tirant un poignard*)
   L'occasion est belle, il est seul, avançons.
SINORIX [*back turned, still feeling remorse*]
   O Sinatus!
SOSTRATE (*paraissant à l'autre côté du théâtre et voyant Camma qui s'avance vers Sinorix un poignard à la main*)
   Que vois-je? Ah!

  J'ai perdu le mari pour acquérir la femme.
  Des beautés de la reine éperdument épris,
  D'un parricide affreux je l'ai faite le prix.   (I. i)

CAMMA   Perdons cet infâme.

*Dans l'instant que la reine lève le bras pour frapper Sinorix, Sostrate
lui saisit la main. Sinorix se détourne et le poignard tombe sans qu'il
puisse connaître de quelle main.*

Que fais-tu, malheureux?
SOSTRATE   Que faites-vous, Madame?
SINORIX *(se retournant et se saisissant du poignard)*
Justes dieux, un poignard! On en veut à mes jours.
A moi, gardes, à moi, qu'on vienne à mes secours!

The guard hurries in. Sinorix does not know which of the two has
attempted to kill him and the physically equivocal scene is followed
by verbal equivocation. Camma prevaricates, but Sostrate nobly
takes the blame on himself and demands death as his punishment. The
King is sure that he was pushed to the crime by Hésione who, when sent
for, instantly and defiantly assumes responsibility for it. She also
demands death but Sinorix generously offers to pardon them both if
Sostrate marries Hésione, whom he supposes him to love. Both hesitate, Hésione accusing Sinorix of guile: he desires this marriage to be
free to marry Camma himself. The third act ends with Sinorix's
demand that Hésione should give her consent within an hour. If not,
Sostrate shall die.

In Act IV Camma returns to the centre of the action. Still without
inculpating herself, she pleads with Sinorix for Sostrate's life and is
met with another ultimatum from Sinorix. If she will marry him
Sostrate will be spared. But if not, he adds sadistically, Sostrate will be
put to death with the most horrible tortures. Left alone with Camma,
who insists on marrying Sinorix to save him, Sostrate protests that
that would be an even worse torture. He would then die of despair,
suffering a thousand deaths instead of one.[1]

Hésione, who is certainly no Ophelia, now joins them and brings
further misunderstandings. She bitterly accuses Camma of consenting

[1] This comparison of physical torment with emotional torment recalls the
analogy pointed out earlier in connection with Garnier's tragedies (see pp. 19 ff.).
Thomas Corneille's handling of it is clumsy and unconvincing, mainly because the
reality of Sostrate's passion is never established. In the Racinian character it will
be. One can merely say of Thomas Corneille that he saw the possibilities but was
unable to exploit them.

to marry Sinorix through simple ambition for the throne, then, alone with Sostrate, she turns to the desperate prince saying: 'I know that it was for my sake that you tried to kill Sinorix. I am going to act. If I become queen you can hope everything from me.' She leaves to stir up the people to revolt and the act ends.

In the interval between Acts IV and V Hésione has apparently failed and has been arrested. The marriage ceremony of Sinorix and Camma has taken place, each drinking of the nuptial cup. Sostrate, sunk in despair, utters the line

> Tout me nuit, tout me perd, tout me devient funeste

and waylays Sinorix to confess his own love for Camma. The dénouement has now begun. Camma reveals her knowledge of her first husband's murder by Sinorix and her own responsibility for the attempted stabbing of Sinorix. Sinorix offers to kill himself but still denies his original crime. At this point he is called away to deal with a popular rising which has occurred after all. News is soon brought of his unexpected death in agony and of Hésione's raising to the throne by acclamation. Camma reveals that she had poisoned the wedding-cup and dies herself. Sostrate is prevented from stabbing himself, but his final speech is again one of despair.[1]

This might be described as a play which has everything, in almost too great abundance. There is murder and suicide, the attempted assassination scene on the stage, ambition, revenge, jealousy, emotional blackmail, political intrigue, a popular rising, a tyrant ruthlessly in love, chivalrous self-sacrificial love in Sostrate, the apparent treachery of a trusted friend,[2] the nominal marriage, the poisoned cup. All these elements had been used before and would be used afterwards, but rarely so many in the same play.

V

Laodice is equally melodramatic, but in a different way and with different characters. In Laodice, Queen of Cappodocia, Thomas Corneille aimed to create one of those female monsters which his brother

---

[1] Lancaster's summary of this play (*History*, III, p. 441) ends: 'The throne is left to Hésione, *who will probably marry Sostrate.*' There is no indication of this relatively satisfactory ending in the text.

[2] Sinorix's: 'Ingrat, de mes bienfaits est-ce la récompense?' (III. iv) is the equivalent of Auguste's long indictment of Cinna (*Cinna*, V. i) or, much further back, of the 'Et tu, Brute' of Shakespeare's *Julius Caesar*.

had presented so effectively. Her record is certainly impressive. Before
the action begins she has killed five of her six sons in order to secure
herself on the throne and she believes that the sixth, whom she had
sent away in infancy, is dead also. But having survived and grown
to manhood, he is at her court under an assumed name and is the
military champion of her kingdom, in the same way as Cléomène in
Timocrate.

His mother develops a weak link in her armour. She falls in love
with him and offers marriage, a proposition which he receives with
surprising calm in spite of his own love for a young princess. He supposes that Laodice's motive is political and he merely desires her
maternal affection and her motherly acceptance of him as her son and
heir when his true identity is revealed. (There is much in this character
which points forward to the bourgeois drama of the next century.)
When finally Laodice is enlightened her reaction is not one of horror
at the prospective incest as such but fury that he has usurped her
affections as a supposed lover and so 'corrupted' the hatred she desired
to feel for her last remaining son. This curious twist is intended to
preserve the integrity of her wickedness and to make her consistently
monstrous, but she falls somewhat short of Medea and once again
Thomas Corneille had attempted a character and an effect above the
level of his somewhat ordinary talent.

He did the same in his immediately following tragedy, *La Mort
d'Annibal*, a quite open variation on his brother's twenty-year-old
Nicomède, which had already provided suggestions for *Laodice*.[1]

In *La Mort d'Annibal* Thomas includes among his characters Prusias,
King of Bithynia, a weak and crafty figure as in the earlier play,
Flaminius the Roman, similar but acting with more obvious guile,
Attale, no longer the son of Prusias, but the king of a neighbouring
country[2] and still a protégé of Rome, and Nicomède, hostile to Rome
but no longer prominent.[3] Instead of Pierre Corneille's arrogant and

---

[1] Particularly in the political situation: the succession to the throne of a kingdom
under Roman influence, the intervention of a Roman ambassador, the final
resolution through a popular revolt.

[2] He has succeeded his elder brother, presumed to be dead. Later this brother reappears, robbing Attale of his political importance. The equivocation and the
resulting vicissitude are typical of Thomas's drama.

[3] For the summary of *Nicomède* see above pp. 163–4.

ironical pupil of Hannibal, Hannibal himself (still alive in this play, though in exile) is at least the nominal hero. A stoic but colourless figure, passive in the action – though the question of his fate is central to the plot – he is no substitute for Pierre Corneille's creation. There is a kind of Laodice in Thomas's Élise, Hannibal's irreducibly proud and scornful daughter whose hatred of Rome overrides all other considerations, even her love for Nicomède. Finally, in this play there is no Arsinoé, no unscrupulous Queen, as though Thomas had decided not to repeat the character he had presented a year before in his own *Laodice*.

His tragedy therefore discards or weakens the two most forceful characters of *Nicomède* and does not compensate for them in the new character, Hannibal. It also eliminates the attractively stoical love relationship of Nicomède and Laodice. In place of this there is an additional love complication. Not only Nicomède and Attale but Thomas Corneille's Prusias also is in love with Élise. The prospect of marrying her gives the old king a strong motive to double-cross both Attale and Nicomède, ostensibly on political grounds, and this further refinement is again typical of the author.

None of this, however, seems to have made the play popular. While his brother's *Nicomède* continued to enjoy constant revivals, *La Mort d'Annibal* quickly disappeared. Its initial run was short. First produced at the Hôtel de Bourgogne on 25 November 1669, it gave place on 13 December to Racine's *Britannicus* and was heard of no more on the Parisian stage. One must assume that, as the 1660s drew to an end, public taste was once again changing. Thomas Corneille must have recognized this, for henceforth he forsook the complicated imbroglios and the political machinery adapted from his brother's tragedies to write plays of considerably simpler construction in which the passion of love and its concomitant, jealousy, were the openly dominant characteristics.

VI

The first and best of these simpler tragedies of passion was *Ariane*, the story of which follows the legend and can be summarized in a few lines.

After slaying the Minotaur, Thésée has fled to Naxos with the two daughters of the King of Crete, Phèdre and Ariane. Thésée has promised to marry Ariane but, falling in love with Phèdre, postpones the marriage. Through his friend Pirithoüs he tries to persuade Ariane to marry Œnarus, King of Naxos, who is in love with her. Ariane realizes that she has a rival and is animated by a passionate desire for revenge, but does not identify the rival as her beloved sister and confidante, Phèdre. The latter, though hesitating to betray her sister, finally flees by night with Thésée. The outraged Ariane attempts to commit suicide, but her ultimate fate is left open.

This was a plain tragedy of passion, jealousy and betrayal, strongly concentrated round the heroine, but with important and essential parts for the two other principal characters, Phèdre and Thésée. The love of King Œnarus for Ariane, if theoretically less essential, is well integrated in the action. Comparisons have been suggested with earlier plays by Racine, including *Bérénice*, but there is a more striking resemblance to *Bajazet* which has not been pointed out. In both plays the heroine comes to suspect, then to realize, that the man she loves and expects to marry is in love with another woman. This rival is the woman she has made her trusted confidante, to whom she has revealed all her feelings and plans. In *Ariane* this situation is more poignant in that the rival is Phèdre, who is obliged to listen to her unsuspecting sister's plans for revenge:

PHÈDRE   . . . Pour venger votre amour que prétendez-vous faire?
ARIANE   L'aller trouver, la voir et, de ma propre main
             Lui mettre, lui plonger un poignard dans le sein.
             Mais pour mieux adoucir les peines que j'endure
             Je veux porter le coup aux yeux de mon parjure,
             Et qu'en son cœur les miens pénètrent à loisir
             Ce qu'aura de mortel son affreux déplaisir.
             Alors ma passion trouvera de doux charmes
             A jouir de ses pleurs comme il fait de mes larmes;
             Alors il me dira si se voir lâchement
             Arracher ce qu'on aime est un léger tourment.
                                    (*Ariane*, IV. iii)

Her rival is to die before the eyes of her perfidious lover (Thésée), whose 'affreux déplaisir' at the sight will make Ariane's vengeance all the sweeter. Racine's heroine envisages a parallel revenge. The rival (Atalide) shall be shown the body of her strangled lover, who will have expired within earshot of her cries of grief:

ROXANE   Qu'il n'ait, en expirant, que ses cris pour adieux.
        Qu'elle soit cependant fidèlement servie.
        Prends soin d'elle, ma haine a besoin de sa vie.
        Ah! si pour son amant facile à s'attendrir,
        La peur de son trépas la fit presque mourir,
        Quel surcroît de vengeance et de douceur nouvelle
        De le montrer bientôt pâle et mort devant elle,
        De voir sur cet objet ses regards arrêtés
        Me payer les plaisirs que je leur ai prêtés!
                            (*Bajazet*, IV. v)

Later, Roxane contemplates a different act of revenge similar to
Ariane's. She invites Bajazet to come and see his mistress put to death:

        Ma rivale est ici. Suis-moi sans différer;
        De ton cœur par sa mort viens me voir m'assurer.[1]
                            (*Bajazet*, V. iv)

Both heroines gloat in the same sadistic way over the 'doux charmes'
or the 'douceur' of the refined cruelty they have imagined. Both are
comparably indignant when they first discover how they have been
deceived:

ROXANE   Ma rivale à mes yeux s'est enfin déclarée.
        Voilà sur quelle foi je m'étais assurée!
        Depuis six mois entiers j'ai cru que, nuit et jour,
        Ardente, elle veillait au soin de mon amour:
        Et c'est moi qui, du sien ministre trop fidèle,
        Semble depuis six mois ne veiller que pour elle . . .
                        (*Bajazet*, IV. iv)

ARIANE   La rivale sur qui tombe cette fureur
        C'est Phèdre, cette Phèdre à qui j'ouvrais mon cœur.
        Quand je lui faisais voir ma peine sans égale,
        Que j'en marquais l'horreur, c'était à ma rivale!
        La perfide, abusant de ma tendre amitié,
        Montrait de ma disgrâce une fausse pitié,
        Et jouissant des maux que j'aimais à lui peindre,
        Elle en était la cause et feignait de me plaindre . . .
                        (*Ariane*, V. v)

---

[1] *Sic* in the first edition of 1672 and so presumably in the earliest acting version.
The stronger line, 'Dans les mains des muets viens la voir expirer', occurs only in
the later editions.

The parallel between the two plays cannot be drawn more closely. None of the three characters in the triangles is in the same position of strength or weakness in relation to the others. Racine's Bajazet and Atalide are virtually helpless before Roxane, whereas Thésée and Phèdre are not so before Ariane.[1] It is in Ariane's reactions that the echoes of *Bajazet* are strongest and, although there are no close verbal analogies, it seems probable that Thomas had some acquaintance with Racine's tragedy before writing at least parts of his play. Materially this was quite possible.

Bajazet was first performed at the Hôtel de Bourgogne on 5 January 1672 at the latest. *Ariane*, the immediately following production at the same theatre, was first performed there on 25 February or, less probably, 5 March. De Visé, who was to become T. Corneille's close associate, wrote long after in the *Mercure galant* of January 1710: '. . . ce qui doit surprendre tout le monde est que M. de Corneille, étant retiré à la campagne, avait fait cette pièce en quarante jours.' Though that figure is no doubt an approximation, it would be consistent with a plausible hypothesis that Thomas attended the première of *Bajazet* on 5 January, left Paris immediately after to work intensively on his play for five or six weeks, and delivered it completed to the actors in mid-February in time for it to be put into rehearsal for the 26th.

It is not even necessary to accept these not impossibly crowded dates. Thomas could well have written much of his play before attending the first performance of *Bajazet*, and have modified it after. Since he was writing for the same theatre company, he could equally well have attended a rehearsal or been shown Racine's script. Both plays contained a star part for the Hôtel's outstanding actress, la Champmeslé, and this would have been another inducement to Thomas to write a tragedy which gave her a somewhat similar role.[2]

---

[1] The material position of Racine's lovers is more nearly paralleled in *Théodat*, T. Corneille's immediately successive tragedy to *Ariane*. But the development is different and the play in no sense Racinian. It was suggested by Quinault's *Amalasonte* and also contains features of T. Corneille's own *Laodice*.

[2] It should perhaps be added that the *Mercure galant* of 5 March 1672, reporting the première of *Ariane*, suggests a long period of composition rather than the 'forty days' which de Visé mentioned later: 'Enfin *l'Ariane* de M. de Corneille le jeune, *qu'on attendait depuis si longtemps*, parut vendredi dernier.' The words italicized, however, were a usual publicity cliché, equivalent to 'eagerly awaited'. If taken

It is of course highly probable that the subject in broad outline was suggested to Thomas Corneille (as Lancaster observes, *History*, III, pp. 531 and 599) by de Visé's *Mariage de Bacchus et d'Ariane*, a machine-play with music produced at the Marais in the winter of 1671–2. But in this entertainment the story is developed quite differently and ends in the marriage of a triumphant Ariadne to the god Bacchus. Phaedra does not appear as her rival. These differences within the same framework of legend make the resemblances with *Bajazet* appear even more significant.

VII

Whatever the case with *Ariane*, what have come to be known as Racinian characteristics were evident in two of Thomas Corneille's remaining tragedies, *Achille* (1673) and *Le Comte d'Essex* (1678). The second was one of his most lasting successes and also has some interest as one of the few dramatizations of English history produced on the French stage.

Thomas says in his *Au lecteur* that he consulted the English historian William Camden, but speaks first of the play of the same title by La Calprenède, performed *c.* 1637, which has much greater importance for him. While reproducing the same story in outline, he altered details of the plot, changed some of the characters and reinforced the love motivation. His Essex is in love throughout with one Henriette, who responds to him but has married the Duc d'Irton to place herself beyond temptation and to allay the suspicions of Queen Elizabeth, who loves Essex jealously. Not knowing the reason of the marriage, Essex has attacked the royal palace to prevent it and is accused of treason. He is also accused of having conspired against the throne in Ireland. While his political enemies are securing his condemnation, Elizabeth is more interested in the question of his love for her and the identification of her rival. If he will respond to her in any way she will pardon him. But Essex proudly and obstinately refuses to ask for pardon. He is finally led to a hurried execution without the Queen's

---

literally, they may simply mean that *some* play from Thomas's pen had long been expected. Since his last tragedy, *La Mort d'Annibal*, in November 1669, he had produced only one comedy in 1670 and nothing in 1671. Even if the reference is specifically to *Ariane*, it would not prove that the play was *completed* long before its performance.

knowledge. She has bitter regrets and foresees that she will soon die herself.

In spite of its success the play has a tired air. It is built round Essex's inflexibility – but this, like the character, becomes monotonous – and the changing reactions of Elizabeth, which lack variety. There are not enough peripeteias. Having entirely abandoned the melodramatic surprises of his earlier plays, Thomas Corneille has nothing of sufficient vitality to put in their place. 'Love' is his prime motivation, but it ceases to be the *galant* love of the 1660s while falling short of the impassioned love of the 1670s. No doubt it was time for the author to abandon tragedy.

VIII

Thomas Corneille's ingenuity in the conception and elaboration of plots is his most obvious quality. He outdid his brother in this field and was not to be matched in it before the nineteenth century. The kind of situations that he used were to be found in the contemporary novel, but to compress and adapt them to the limits of a five-act play on a stage which permitted of very little physical action was a technical feat which deserved its immediate rewards. The motivations of his characters are the same as those found in his brother's later plays and, like those, can be classed comprehensively as: love, political ambition, hatred usually coupled with desire for revenge, *gloire* associated with either of the last two and based on an assertion of honour and/or personal dignity, which can be equated with *amour propre*. Among these predominantly aristocratic motives and qualities, conventional love has pride of place. It is a personal love of the kind later called romantic and is not often – certainly more rarely than in the elder Corneille – secondary to *gloire* or the desire for revenge. When incompatible with these, it nevertheless triumphs in the end in several plays, so satisfying the romanesque mentality. It is virtuous love in the sense that it respects the loved one's supposed interests and feelings, but it lacks the moral authority attached to that concept in Pierre Corneille. Even Chimène would have seemed too severe a heroine for his brother's plays. If stage drama ultimately stands or falls by its characters, too many of Thomas's are pleasant but mediocre, again according to the ethos of the novels. The villains are obvious but uninteresting and even a would-be monster like Laodice or a 'black' heroine like Camma fail in the end to evoke either horror or admiration. One is led to the conclusion that, while there is certainly no true tragic element in Thomas Corneille, the heroic is lacking also. This cannot be ascribed to any conscious 'demolition of the hero', but simply to a desire to satisfy the broadest possible stratum of contemporary taste.

Some of the ordinariness of Thomas Corneille's drama must be ascribed to his style. He wrote – rapidly, it can be safely assumed – in a conventional idiom which was the ultimate tired development of the literary purism of the 1630s. Its characteristics, or vices as they could easily become, were circumlocution and abstraction. In Thomas's hands these make too often for slack or turgid dialogue, influenced perhaps by the contemporary language of *préciosité* but by no means wholly explicable in that light:

> Je ne le vois que trop. L'accord qu'on nous propose
> Du mépris qui nous brave est la secrète cause,
> Madame, et de ma sœur l'ambitieux projet
> Court après ce faux charme et n'a plus d'autre objet.
> D'un diadème offert l'espérance confuse
> La livre tout entière à l'ardeur qui l'abuse,
> Et laisse dédaigner à ses sens éblouis
> Le mérite du père et la vertu du fils.

Thus the Emperor Honorius in *Stilicon* (I. iv) remarking to the Empress that the reason for his sister's contemptuous refusal of a proposed marriage with the 'virtuous' Euchérius, son of the worthy (but non-royal) Stilicon, is clearly the vague hope of achieving a royal match elsewhere. And thus the heroine of *Camma* (II. v) telling her lover that the time has come to make himself worthy of her hand and of the throne by killing the hated Sinorix:

> . . . c'est en servant ma haine
> Que tu peux égaler le destin d'une reine,
> Et trouver dans l'éclat d'un illustre projet
> A réparer l'affront du titre de sujet.

There are many such passages in these plays. As for the dialectical clashes in which his brother excelled, they are blurred and ineffective when they occur in Thomas. His highest skill shows in the ambiguous dialogues which the equivocal situations of several of his tragedies demanded. He became the master of the art of writing speeches capable of two interpretations, but this did not compensate for more serious or more psychologically sophisticated qualities.

IX

Though born ten years later than Thomas Corneille, Philippe Quinault (1635–88) may be considered as a contemporary in his theatrical career. This can be outlined briefly. It opened in 1653 with a comedy, *Les Rivales*, and continued with several other comedies and two immature tragicomedies, both derived from Calderón, until *Amalasonte* (1657), his first play which could be styled a tragedy.[1] From 1658 to 1670 he wrote eight more tragedies or tragicomedies and one more comedy – his best – *La Mère coquette*. In 1671 he was called in with Pierre Corneille to help out Molière with the musical machine-play, *Psyché*, and from then on was engaged exclusively by Lully as a librettist for his entertainments. In that capacity he wrote eleven *tragédies lyriques* or operas, one pastoral, and the lyrics for two court ballets. He received munificent rewards from the royal purse, but after an illness in 1686 religious scruples caused him to beg the King to release him from further work for the theatre. He died some two and a half years later.

His youthful years have some bearing on his dramatic work. He was the protégé and pupil of Tristan L'Hermite, whose household he entered as a boy. His first play, *Les Rivales*, was an adaptation of *Les Deux Pucelles*, a seventeen-year-old comedy by Rotrou, whose *Célimène* had been similarly brought up to date by Tristan for the Hôtel de Bourgogne in the previous year. It appears that Tristan passed on the second adaptation to his pupil, so launching him on his dramatic career. After Tristan's death in 1655, Quinault procured the publication of his last tragedy, *Osman*, so in some way repaying a debt to his master.

The link was thus close, and both personal and professional. Of particular interest is the fact that the lyric qualities which distinguish Tristan's dramatic verse are noticeable also in Quinault, though on a lower level and directed to more popular effects. The poetry of Tristan's moving soliloquies evolved too easily into sugary verses to be sung to Lully's music.

[1] It is so described in eighteenth-century editions, though earlier it was more usually called a tragicomedy. The distinction was becoming nebulous.

Before turning to opera Quinault had already acquired through his tragedies and tragicomedies a reputation for *tendresse* which was considered as his distinguishing mark. The critics and commentators of the sixties were almost sheepishly unanimous in singling out this particular quality, generally with approval.[1] An important exception was Boileau, of whose acid comment more must be said later. In the seventies the mood changed and more reservations were expressed.[2] But in the fifteen years that saw Thomas Corneille's greatest successes, Quinault was recognized as a master in the depiction of sentimental love. No doubt he deserved it, though there are other things in his plays.

X

In *Amalasonte* Quinault wrote his first nominally non-comic play with some claim to originality, since the story is not modelled on any identified source. Though a tragedy or a tragicomedy, it is constructed according to a familiar comic formula. A couple shown to be in love with each other at an early stage in the action are kept apart by various obstacles until their ultimately happy union in the last scene of Act V. The obstacles are melodramatic but seriously meant. They include a rival suitor for the heroine's hand, a second woman in love with the hero who intrigues against him through jealousy, an ambiguous letter sowing doubt in the heroine's mind, a political conspiracy, a false accusation of the hero, two attempts at murder which are both planted on the hero, and finally a poisoned letter intended for him but opened by the villain instead with fatal results. Three characters die and the hero and heroine are also in danger of their lives. But in spite of these dire perils the general formula remains comic and some of the situations also belong to comedy.[3]

[1] For a conspectus of quotations see Mélèse, *Répertoire*, pp. 59 ff. They range from Chapelain: 'Est un poète sans fond et sans art, mais d'un beau naturel, qui touche bien les tendresses amoureuses' (*Mémoire des gens de lettres*, 1662), to Chappuzeau: 'M. Quinault, qui sait parfaitement la Carte de Tendre et qui touche si bien les passions amoureuses' (*L'Europe vivante*, 1669).
[2] As by Saint-Évremond, conditioned no doubt at this date by Racinian tragedy: 'Dans les tragédies de Quinault vous désireriez souvent la douleur où vous ne voyez que de la tendresse.' (*Sur les tragédies*, III, 1677.)
[3] As when the hero's enemies are deceived into condemning him roundly in the presence of the heroine, who then announces she is about to marry the man they have been reviling (II. v).

This crudely written play already contains features soon to be recognized as characteristic of Quinault. It has an early example of the adoring lover in whom he specialized and of the 'tender' and not unsubtle exchanges between this lover and the heroine. The melodramatic machinery is similar to that found in Thomas Corneille, but it has a slightly different function. Whereas in Thomas the excitement and suspense which it sustains are in themselves the main attraction of the play and the love element is largely conventional, in Quinault the emphasis is reversed. Melodrama is used conventionally, though very conspicuously, to create impediments in the course of true love, whose eventual triumph or vindication is the real source of interest.

In *Amalasonte* only one important melodramatic device, the concealed identity, was lacking, but this was soon to be remedied. The plots of Quinault's next two tragicomedies, *Le Feint Alcibiade* and *Le Mariage de Cambyse*, depend upon it. Both were produced in the following year, 1658, less than two years after the model set up by T. Corneille's *Timocrate*. In the first the heroine Cléone impersonates her twin brother in order to approach her temporarily faithless lover and win him back. Numerous complications ensue; two other women fall in love with Cléone in her male persona; her lover challenges her to a duel; her murder is planned. But all turns out well in the end. *Le Mariage de Cambyse* rests on a case of infant substitution. Two princesses have been exchanged at birth and among the complications which result when they are old enough to have suitors not the least is the fear of incest, as in Pierre Corneille's *Héraclius*. After two plays which do not contain the concealed identity theme, Quinault returned to it in *Agrippa, ou le faux Tibérinus* (1662), which is probably the least credible specimen of its whole class.

The real Tibérinus, King of Alba, having been drowned, he is impersonated by Agrippa, who comes of a rival royal family and resembles him exactly. The impersonation has been arranged by Agrippa's father in order to place his son on the throne incognito. He accounts for his son's apparent disappearance by alleging that he was murdered on Tibérinus's orders. Agrippa's own sister Albine is taken in by the deception. She was in love with the real Tibérinus and now accuses the man she believes to be him of having murdered her brother and transferred his affection to another woman, the princess Lavinie, whom he loved when he was openly Agrippa and still does. Lavinie also believes that Agrippa is Tibérinus and so the murderer of her lover. She launches a plot to have him killed. She is prevented from seeing him by Agrippa's father until Act IV and when the meeting takes place her heart tells her that he is indeed her lover and she bursts into tears. Agrippa cannot resist revealing his true identity but by then the plot to assassinate him as Tibérinus is under way. He escapes thanks to his sister Albine, influenced as she believes by 'love' for Tibérinus, but in fact by 'nature' or family affection. She is left out in the cold, but the principal lovers are united and only a secondary lover of Lavinie's dies. For her sake he has taken part in the assassination plot and his last words are: 'Je meurs pour vous, princesse.'

Audiences who could accept the basic situation could be sure of an exciting afternoon at the theatre and come away with a warm feeling that love had triumphed in the end, and not least over politics. The questions of succession to the throne and of conspiracy, so important in Pierre Corneille, were now no more than machinery manufacturing the kind of obstacles we have already noted in *Amalasonte*.

XI

Quinault had one more identity play to write. *Astrate, Roi de Tyre* (1664) has claims to be considered his best tragedy and was among his greatest successes. The plot, though full of incident, is relatively simple. Élise, Queen of Tyr, has inherited the throne from her father, a usurper. To safeguard her position she has put to death the old king and two of his sons, held prisoners by her father for fifteen years. A third son is at liberty, hiding, as she learns from an oracle, in her own court, and she wishes to eliminate this potential danger to herself also. Meanwhile she has contracted to marry Agénor, a prince of her own blood, who is in love with both her throne and her person, but she keeps postponing the wedding. Her motive, unrevealed publicly, is love for Astrate, a great captain of apparently common origin who by his victories has become a pillar of the state. The fourth important character is Sichée, believed to be the father of Astrate. He is an elderly counsellor or minister similar to characters in *Amalasonte* (Theudion) and *Agrippa* (Tirrhène) and also in plays by both the Corneilles. Here he is a trusted servant taken over from the previous regime, but he proves to be plotting against both Élise and Agénor. When the Queen tells him of her love for Astrate he unaccountably tries to dissuade her from marrying him. The reason is made clear to all the principals in Act IV. Astrate, though brought up by Sichée as his son, is in fact the missing prince of the legitimate royal line. If he married Élise, Sichée's plans of vengeance would come to nothing.

This particular instance of concealed identity, certainly more plausible than the previous examples in Quinault, yields a situation of serious dramatic and even psychological interest. Astrate, who has seen himself as the Queen's defender and has been attempting to discover who is her hidden enemy at court, now finds that the man is himself. He is at first dismayed but quickly decides to put love above everything else and to continue defending her against the rebels whom Sichée has stirred up with the object of putting Astrate himself on the throne.

In the cause of love he also forgives the killing by Élise of his real father and his brothers:

> Je ne me connais plus et ne suis qu'un amant,
> Tout mon devoir s'oublie aux yeux de ce que j'aime.
>
> (IV. ii)

Élise's dilemma is more thorny. Fully aware of the 'crimes' which secured her on the throne, she realizes that her beloved Astrate ought to take vengeance on her. Remembering the oracle which predicted her downfall, she realizes also that she is in a trap baited by her own emotions, destroyed unsuspectingly by her only weakness:

> Je me vantais à tort d'un courage invincible,
> D'une âme à la terreur, au trouble inaccessible.
> L'ingénieux courroux du ciel plein de rigueur
> N'a que trop bien trouvé le faible de mon cœur.
> J'aurais bravé mon sort s'il ne m'eût point trompée;
> Je ne m'en gardais pas par où j'en suis frappée.
> De ce piège des dieux qui se fût défié?
> Mon cœur était sans doute assez fortifié
> Contre tous les dangers qui menaçaient ma vie,
> . . . Mais il ne l'était pas contre l'amour et vous.   (IV. iii)

Fate or the gods are occasionally called in question in a similar way in other tragedies of the period, but the mention in so many words of a deliberate trap seems to occur only in Quinault.[1] From this trap the only escape for Élise is suicide, which she commits by taking poison. In this way alone can she both prove her love for Astrate and fulfil the obligation of vengeance which love has prevented him from discharging himself:

> Je vous dois trop ma mort pour ne pas l'achever.
> Je ne puis moins, seigneur, pour vous rendre justice.
> Votre sang demandait de vous ce sacrifice,
> Et quand, par des transports mutuels entre nous,
> Vous l'oubliez pour moi, j'y dois songer pour vous.
>
> (V. v)

The contrived situation thus leads to a dilemma which deserves the name of tragic and can be resolved only by death. Such dilemmas are extremely rare in romanesque tragedy and it may well be that Quinault hit on this one by accident, drawn towards it by the given character of Élise and a conviction of the supremacy of love.

XII

Four remaining plays by Quinault glorify love without depending on concealed identities. *La Mort de Cyrus* (1659), a tragedy, and *Stratonice* (1660), a tragicomedy, date from before *Agrippa* and *Astrate*. *Pausanias* (1668) and *Bellérophon* (1670–1), both tragedies, were written several

---

[1] Racine's *Thébaïde*, which preceded *Astrate* by about six months, contains the same idea differently worded:

JOCASTE   Connaissez mieux du ciel la vengeance fatale:
               Toujours à ma douleur il met quelque intervalle,
               Mais hélas, quand sa main semble me secourir
               C'est alors qu'il s'apprête à me faire périr, etc.   (III. iii)

It is highly unlikely that Quinault borrowed anything from this unremarked first play by a novice in the theatre. The idea of a trap set by the gods was given full weight by Cocteau in his reworking of the Oedipus story, *La Machine infernale*. It did not occur to Sophocles nor, incidentally, to Pierre Corneille, whose Oedipus was merely defiant (see above p. 194).

years after and may owe something to Racine, since both were later than his highly successful *Andromaque*. In any case the plotting becomes progressively simpler, even though melodramatic inventions still persist. The plot structure in outline is the same in all these four plays, requiring three main characters with similar functions in each. They are the devoted lover, who 'languishes' in the two earlier plays but is more restrained in the last two, particularly in *Pausanias*; his beloved who responds, but for varying reasons (such as a betrothal elsewhere or a political peril) is prevented from doing so openly; and a jealous rival (a man in *Cyrus*, a woman in the other three plays) who tries to prevent the union of the principal lovers, successfully in *Cyrus* and *Pausanias*, unsuccessfully in *Stratonice* and *Bellérophon*. A fourth character and in *Cyrus* a fifth add variety to this basic scheme and save the stories of the plays from appearing repetitive. Their involvement with the other characters stems either from love or from political interests, sometimes from the two combined. But in every case Quinault works from his basic formula, which was already roughed out in *Amalasonte*, though obscured there by the melodramatic and comic elements, and applied in *Astrate*, though in that play it is overshadowed and in a curious way enriched by the theme of hidden identity. One advantage of the formula was that it could be used to yield either an unhappy or a happy ending without necessarily descending to the comic provided the handling of detail was sufficiently sensitive.

A noticeable if secondary feature in these plays of Quinault is his introduction of the supernatural. There are omens or oracles in *Cyrus* and *Bellérophon*, as there are in *Astrate*. Allied to this and belonging to a world of legend verging on the *merveilleux* and the operatic is the monster, apparently sent by the gods, which is ravaging the country in *Bellérophon*. In Act V it attacks the hero who finally succeeds in killing it. The description of its first appearance (V. iii) bears evident resemblances to Théramène's account of the death of Hippolyte in *Phèdre*, of course a later play. It is unnecessary to assume that Racine borrowed from Quinault, since he had all he needed in the Hippolytus story as dramatized by Euripides, Seneca and indeed Garnier. Of greater interest is the contrast in dramatic method. Théramène's *récit* stands as a piece of oratory in an older tradition, a shocking but beautiful finalization of the hero's life, after which it only remains for Phèdre to confess the truth and to kill herself. Quinault, on the other hand, divides his report of the monster's appearance into two parts. The first leads the audience and the characters of the play to believe that the hero has died. The jealous princess Sténobée, whose unjust accusation has brought him into disgrace with the King, proclaims his innocence and goes out to commit suicide. But then there is fresh news, a second *récit*. It was the monster that died and not the hero, and the latter comes in alive and well to be acclaimed and united to another princess of his own choosing.

It is as though in Racine's play Théramène had been mistaken, Hippolyte had survived and, Phèdre having disappeared, had concluded a happy marriage with Aricie. Purely on the score of dramatic excitement but on no other, Quinault's ending is superior to Racine's. It can be considered typical of many of the endings in romanesque drama.[1]

XIII

For all the sentimentalism implied in his reputation for *tendresse*, Quinault was groping towards *amour-passion*, but he was inhibited by the conventions of *galanterie* from realizing its true potential. His adoring lovers are submissive as part of the code and they have been rendered incapable of taking any action that is not self-sacrifice. The malady of love is physical in the Antiochus of *Stratonice*, who collapses in certain scenes of the play and is only revived when his father generously yields the woman he desires to him.

> Mon mal est bien plus grand que tu ne peux penser.
> Je me sens tout de flamme et toujours sans relâche
> Une fièvre maligne à mes humeurs s'attache.   (I. vi)

Elsewhere the sickness is of the mind rather than of the body. The great conqueror Cyrus, on the point of winning a battle, gives up and

---

[1] Racine himself used the device of the incomplete (and so misleading) *récit* in his first two plays, *La Thébaïde* and *Alexandre*. He could easily have introduced it into *Iphigénie*, where it would have heightened the excitement of the ending, but in this mature play he refrained from doing so. P. Corneille uses the device in *Horace*. In *Othon* the hero's death is falsely reported, though there is no *récit*.

lets himself be captured at the sight of the enemy queen facing him in her white armour:

> Je cessai, l'observant, de me croire invincible,
> Je crus en sa faveur ma défaite possible,
> Et reconnus d'abord, en voyant ses appas,
> Mille ennemis secrets que je n'attendais pas.
>
> *(Mort de Cyrus,* II. i)

Nearly all these male captives of love are represented as great warriors, as was Timocrate in Thomas Corneille's play. They have won battles and their courage is beyond dispute, though nothing in their characterization suggests the real soldier. They personify an ideal of chivalry adapted to the boudoir, in which the martial qualities, though assumed to be present, are completely obscured by devotion to the lady. This devotion is an end in itself and is its own justification. In Quinault it abolishes distinctions of rank, supersedes hatred and the vengeance obligation, and is higher than ambition for the throne. Contrary sentiments are sometimes expressed, but by 'bad' or ultimately discredited characters, not by the principal lovers. In these love subsumes virtue and honour, which are rarely mentioned as either separate or opposing concepts. The moral stiffening, as essential to the full knightly ethos as physical endurance, is thus omitted and its absence is made to appear unimportant.

The knight's beloved, his 'lady' in the convention of chivalry, is not always without *vertu* in the sense of moral scruples as opposed to love. The position of Thomiris in *Cyrus* is peculiar: in order to save the hero she contracts a marriage with the villain and, having done this in the cause of love, she is determined to respect the arrangement:

> J'aurai de la vertu, si je n'ai de l'amour.   (IV. vi)

Stratonice, in the play of that name, feels no scruples. She is engaged to the hero's father but she regards this as a purely political match which does not bind her morally. The Queen in *Astrate* is hampered by her previous crimes but, as seen above, the real obstacle is her lover's duty to take revenge on herself. Love leads her to discharge this duty for him. In *Pausanias* the captive princess Cléonice knows she ought to hate the hero, since he defeated and killed her father, but here again love is irresistibly stronger and leads her to an attempt to persuade him to desert his country and acquire a new empire with her.[1] Philonoé in *Bellérophon* is practically helpless; she has no motive to invoke *vertu* and her only torment is doubt about her lover's response.

Quinault's heroines are therefore sometimes aware of obligations which run counter to their amorous inclinations, but no deep conflicts are set up and it becomes pointless to look for them. Their jealous rivals, it is true, are motivated by a kind of passion rarely distinguishable from injured pride. It emerges as resentment or *dépit*, and is depreciated by the meanness as well as the melodramatic nature of the acts which it persuades them to perform. They do not constitute a tragic or even a dramatic centre for the plays and at the end are either discarded or discredited, even in those cases where they have been driven to suicide. Frequent in Quinault, they preserved in drama a familiar type of character without exploring its deeper implications.

Very much more conspicuous, especially in the text, is the 'tenderness' which so impressed contemporaries and which is conveyed with delicacy and skill in many scenes. Quinault is particularly good in his portrayals of the dawning of love, the first shy and uncertain indications that the heart has been touched. Thus Stratonice in a dialogue with her confidante Zénone:

ZÉNONE	Enfin vous confessez que l'amour vous surmonte?
STRATONICE	D'où me pourrait d'ailleurs provenir tant de honte?
	Je sens ce qu'en effet je ne puis exprimer,
	Mais je ne sais pas bien encor si c'est aimer.
ZÉNONE	Dieux! que me dites-vous?
STRATONICE	Que veux-tu que je die?
	L'amour m'est inconnu, je n'aimai de ma vie.
	Mais pourtant dans le trouble où mes sens sont réduits,
	Je crois que quand on aime on est comme je suis . . .

(*Stratonice*, II. v)

---

[1] She sums up the ethos of love-dominated heroism in four lines furnished with all the appropriate epithets:

> Ce crime au moins, s'il faut ainsi que l'on le nomme,
> Est un illustre crime et digne d'un grand homme;
> Est digne d'un héros intrépide, fameux;
> Et, pour tout dire enfin, d'un héros amoureux.

(*Pausanias*, IV. ii)

In the immediately following scene the lovers meet. Each knows
that he or she ought to hate the other and avoid the meeting, but they
feel drawn together and exchange what in fact are affectionate reproaches. The scene, which is written in a tone of comedy, ends in
a partial misunderstanding.

The modest avowal, in which the woman shows that she is not
indifferent to the man, is common in these plays. At its simplest, which
became almost a stage convention, it is expressed by a sigh: 'Hélas!'
The man then eagerly presses for a clearer declaration, whereupon the
woman replies, 'I have said more than enough already', and exits
hurriedly.

This coyness is elaborated in some of the plays to a point at which it
has much charm and even some psychological truth, if not at great
depth. The 'I hate you' ridiculed by Boileau[1] has an obvious place in
these lovers' exchanges, belonging both to the situation and to the tone
of the dialogue. Uttered half-seriously in *Stratonice*, the hatred motif
is developed into something genuinely pathetic in *Astrate*. In this scene
Astrate has just revealed his true identity to Élise and with it the knowledge that she was his father's murderer:

ÉLISE   Vous vous justifierez en immolant ma vie,
               Et serez innocent quand vous m'aurez punie.
               Vous devez vous venger et même me haïr.
               Votre sort vous l'ordonne . . .
ASTRATE   Hé! lui puis-je obéir?
               Vous, un objet pour moi de haine et de vengeance!
               Et vous me condamnez à cette obéissance!
ÉLISE   J'avouerai ma faiblesse, Astrate, et qu'en effet
               J'ai peine à vous presser d'obéir tout à fait.
               Ne suivez qu'à demi ce devoir trop funeste;
               Sauvez-m'en la moitié, je suis d'accord du reste.
               J'y consens sans regret. Vengez-vous, mais hélas!
               Astrate, s'il se peut, ne me haïssez pas.

                                      (*Astrate*, IV. iii)

---

[1] Les héros chez Quinault parlent bien autrement,
    Et jusqu'à *Je vous hais*, tout s'y dit tendrement.
                      Satire III (1665)

In most of his plays, however, Quinault keeps his lovers' conversations on a lighter level. As in *Stratonice*, they would seem more appropriate in comedy. It remained for Marivaux in the following century to write actual comedies in the same vein. It would be tempting if it were not anachronistic to speak of Quinault's *marivaudage*, but at least it can be said that he had established a precedent by achieving similar effects in tragicomedy.

10

JEAN RACINE

Education and apprenticeship – *La Thébaïde* – *Alexandre* – mature plays: *Andromaque* to *Mithridate* – Racine's position in 1673 – *Iphigénie* – *Phèdre* and the Quarrel of *Phèdre* – Pradon's *Phèdre et Hippolyte* – retirement and re-emergence – *Esther* and *Athalie* – romanesque features in Racine – conventional stagecraft – Racine's originality – characterization – *amour-passion* – amorality and predestination – Racine's verse-idiom – summaries of his tragedies

Jean Racine was born, in December 1639, of a family of local officials and lawyers established at La Ferté-Milon, a small town fifty miles north-east of Paris. Orphaned in infancy, he was brought up by pious relatives who took him to be educated in the Jansenist community of Port-Royal. Here he was taught some Greek and may well have been unconsciously conditioned by the Jansenist doctrine of predestination, but it is more hazardous than has sometimes been supposed to read any clear indication of either of these influences into his dramatic work. Thanks, however, to his connections with Port-Royal, he obtained an entry to Parisian society and the court and particularly to the theatre, on which his youthful ambitions became fixed. This thoroughly worldly streak in him eventually led to a break with his more puritanical relatives and masters.

From the age of twenty he was writing plays with the hope of production in the Parisian theatres. These were the same as when Pierre Corneille had returned to drama in 1659,[1] with Molière steadily strengthening his position at the theatre of the Palais-Royal and at court. The position was to remain unchanged until Molière's death in February 1673, when his company was merged with the troupe of the Marais to form the short-lived Théâtre Guénégaud. In 1680 the Guénégaud was merged with the Hôtel de Bourgogne and the combination was renamed the Comédie-Française, whose foundation as the sole officially sponsored Parisian theatre (apart from opera) dates from

[1] See above pp. 196–7.

then. None of these changes was to affect Racine who, after his early fumblings described below, was an Hôtel de Bourgogne author throughout his career.

Racine began by trying his hand at two or perhaps three plays which were not acted and have not survived.[1] His first play to reach the stage, the tragedy of *La Thébaïde, ou les frères ennemis*, was produced by Molière in June 1664 (a dead season in the theatre) and had a short and undistinguished run.

It was in any case an old-fashioned play for its date, in both the choice and treatment of the subject. It dealt with the bloody extinction of all the surviving members of the ill-starred family of Oedipus, brought about directly by the mutual hatred of Eteocles and Polyneices, the *frères ennemis* of the title. These kill each other in a combat in which their cousin Haemon also dies when trying to separate them. Their mother Jocasta and their sister Antigone commit suicide, while their uncle Creon falls unconscious, wishing for death. As with some of the characters of Thomas Corneille and Quinault, his fate remains inconclusive.

This tragedy, in which features of Cornelian drama, though badly assimilated, can be discerned, might be described as political. The two brothers and Creon all covet the throne of Thebes. 'Love,' said Racine in a Preface written twelve years later, 'which normally fills so large a place in tragedies, has hardly any in this one.' Nevertheless, besides including the traditional love of Haemon for Antigone, he supposes that Creon is in love with her also. This almost gratuitous addition of Creon's passion for his niece, absent as it is from all the possible sources, is a clumsy concession to romanesque tragedy having no necessary relationship to the main theme of the play, which is the

[1] Two of them, the first called *Amasie* and the second a play concerning Ovid, possibly entitled *Les Amours d'Ovide*, are referred to in his correspondence of 1660–1. In *c.* 1662, according to the not always reliable *Mémoires* of his son Louis Racine, he began a tragedy of *Théagène et Chariclée*, but abandoned it because of his dislike of 'romanesque adventures'. Molière's biographer Grimarest also credits the young Racine with a play of this title, 'qui à la vérité ne valait rien'. The source would have been the Greek romance by Heliodorus, previously dramatized by Hardy in his long serialization of the story (see above pp. 62–3). As other commentators have pointed out, at about these dates the minor dramatist Gilbert also wrote plays entitled *Théagène* (1662) and *Les Amours d'Ovide* (1663), both of which were performed. A possible inference is that the youthful Racine was attempting unsuccessfully to compete with Gilbert.

bitter feud between the two brothers. Indeed, *any* love interest, as Racine came to recognize, fits uneasily into what he calls 'the most tragic subject of antiquity'.

The reason why he chose the subject is by no means clear. The play might perhaps be described as an early example of the influence of Greek tragedy on Racine the Hellenist, but with considerable reservations. In his Preface, published after *Iphigénie* and not long before *Phèdre*, Racine claimed that 'Je dressai à peu près mon plan sur les *Phéniciennes* d'Euripide.' The importance of that 'à peu près' was pointed out long ago by Paul Mesnard.[1] Though the two plays deal, broadly speaking, with the same events, their emphasis, orientation and dénouements are quite different. Two scenes only in *La Thébaïde* might seem to reveal a direct imitation of Euripides. The *Antigone* of Sophocles, also mentioned in Racine's Preface though not claimed as a model, could have yielded him nothing, since it begins at a point when the action of *La Thébaïde* is over. Much more important was Rotrou's twenty-seven-year-old tragedy *Antigone*, which Racine recognized as a precedent, while criticizing its lack of unity.[2]

The direct Greek influence on *La Thébaïde* was therefore small and at most an indication of a road to be taken later in Racine's career. Possibly he already had some acquaintance with the Greek dramatists[3] and was trying to adapt his student knowledge to the different climate of the contemporary theatre. This is on the assumption that the choice of subject was his own, a point which cannot be decided categorically. His correspondence shows that he was working on the play in November and December 1663 in conjunction with various friends or advisers

---

[1] *Œuvres de Racine*, Grands Écrivains ed., Vol. I (Hachette, 1865), pp. 375–7.

[2] Looking back to Garnier (though there is no question of his influence on Racine) there is an interesting progression towards unity of theme which helps to typify the development of French tragedy. Garnier's *Antigone* (1580) combines three themes, each of them the subject of a different Greek tragedy: (1) the wanderings in exile of the blinded Oedipus after his downfall, (2) the struggle for the kingdom between his sons, ending in their deaths, (3) Antigone's defiance of Creon in her endeavour to bury the body of her brother Polyneices. Rotrou's *Antigone* (1637) omits the first theme but contains themes (2) and (3). Racine's tragedy, however inexperienced the execution, succeeds in concentrating on theme (2) alone.

[3] The fact that he studied them is proved by his annotations in the margins of various editions of Aeschylus, Sophocles and Euripides, but the dating of these annotations remains uncertain. It seems likely to have been later than *La Thébaïde*. (See P. Mesnard, *Œuvres*, Vol. VI, and R. C. Knight, *Racine et la Grèce*.)

whom he does not name, but who, according to one theory, were connected with the Hôtel de Bourgogne. Having finished his play, he learnt that it would have to wait its turn until after the production of three others. With natural impatience, he took it to Molière instead.

The other theory is that he worked from the start with Molière, who wanted a play to compete with a *Thébaïde* by Claude Boyer which the Hôtel intended to perform and gave Racine the subject and the whole plan of his tragedy. Then Boyer's play was postponed by the Hôtel, which might explain why Molière no longer found it urgent to produce Racine's tragedy, and in fact waited some six months before doing so.[1]

[1] The debate hinges on a sentence in one of Racine's letters to his friend Le Vasseur (Mesnard, *Œuvres*, VI, p. 507). After announcing the completion of his fifth act, he writes: 'On promet depuis hier *La Thébaïde* à l'Hôtel, mais ils ne la promettent qu'après trois autres pièces.' Previously Racine had referred to his own play as *Les Frères* [*ennemis*], though on production this became only its alternative title. If his reference was to Boyer's *Thébaïde*, there is complete lack of evidence that such a play existed at that date and there is no definite record of its production at any time. M. Raymond Picard (*La Carrière de Jean Racine*, p. 104) is convinced that it did exist and quotes two references, dated 1685 and 1687, to what appears to be this play, which imply that it was a memorable flop. But assuming that it was produced in the 1660s, would it have been so memorable that it was recalled some twenty years later, particularly in an age when theatrical flops were common and Boyer himself had several to his credit?

The statement that Molière caused Racine to write his tragedy is first found in Brossette's *Mémoires* (1702) and, more fully embroidered, in Grimarest's colourful but often inaccurate *Vie de Molière* (1705). Both were written some forty years after the event, but they may have drawn on some traditional account which was turning into legend. Grimarest maintains that Molière drew up the plan of the play, presented it to Racine, and helped him to correct each act as it was brought to him. This goes rather further than the credible.

Interesting support for the Molière theory was produced by M. J. Pommier (*Aspects de Racine*, 1954), who noticed that in Molière's *Critique de l'École des femmes* and his *Impromptu de Versailles*, both highly popular plays in the last months of 1663, the actress Marquise Du Parc (who belonged to his company and was later Racine's mistress) is described as a person 'qui se déhanche'. In one of his letters to Le Vasseur Racine wrote, 'La déhanchée fait la jeune princesse', meaning the Antigone of his play. Though there may well have been other actresses notorious for swaying their hips in a mincing way (the Hôtel de Bourgogne theory favoured la Beauchâteau, who had encouraged Racine in the past), it is highly probable that at that particular date la Du Parc would spring first to mind and that therefore Racine was writing *La Thébaïde* for Molière's troupe.

All that can be said with certainty is that Molière launched Racine as a dramatist, but why and with what degree of influence remains conjectural.

II

Racine's second play, *Alexandre*, conformed much more nearly to the prevailing fashion and can fairly be described as romanesque. It romanced the historical accounts of Alexander the Great's conquest of India by focusing the interest on the conqueror's love for an Indian princess and introducing an Indian queen of Racine's invention for the sub-hero to be in love with. In spite, however, of the *galanterie* of some of the dialogue, love is not the sole motivation. A pre-occupation with *gloire* gives a stiffening to some of the characters and Alexander's generosity rises to a Cornelian level. The excessive *tendresse* for which Quinault was renowned is avoided and at the same time the melodramatic complications of both Quinault and Thomas Corneille are absent from Racine's comparatively simple plot. Nevertheless the play derived from the general tradition of the novels and cannot be considered as a radical departure from it.

Alexandre was a success.[1] It established Racine as a dramatist, thanks in part to a manœuvre which cannot be interpreted to his credit. Molière had amply compensated him for the obscure production of *La Thébaïde* in the summer of 1664 by producing *Alexandre* at the height of the theatrical season of 1665–6. The première was on 4 December 1665. A fortnight later Molière's company were astonished to learn that the same play was being acted at the rival Hôtel de Bourgogne, to which it could only have been taken behind the original sponsors' backs. The two productions continued in competition for a few days, after which Molière's company gave up. Henceforth all Racine's plays up to and including *Phèdre* were produced by the better tragedians of the Hôtel, whom Racine was to serve as their most successful author.

Here again, but with much more certainty than in the case of *La Thébaïde*, a play of Boyer's was in question. The Hôtel had begun by

---

[1] Over six years later Mme de Sévigné, a good representative of contemporary taste if no critic, wrote: 'Jamais Racine n'ira plus loin qu'*Alexandre* et *Andromaque*.' (16 March 1672.) By that date Racine had also written *Britannicus*, *Bérénice* and *Bajazet*.

reviving a nineteen-year-old tragedy by Boyer, *Porus, ou la générosité d'Alexandre*. This was probably a riposte, thought up hastily, to the forthcoming *Alexandre* at the Palais-Royal, though there is the alternative possibility that the Boyer revival had been planned some time before and that Molière had commissioned Racine's play to compete with it, so repeating what may have occurred with *La Thébaïde*. This is unlikely and in any case unimportant. All the two plays have in common is the theme of Alexander in India and his chivalrous dealing with Porus. The rest of the plot and the other characters are all different. As soon as the Hôtel had secured Racine's tragedy they dropped Boyer's which, besides being old, was rightly considered as inferior.

III

During the first run of *Alexandre* Racine broke with Port-Royal in a polemic in which he defended the theatre against the perpetually recurrent charge of immorality and then passed acrimoniously to a personal attack on some of his old masters.[1] Having purged himself for a long time of any lingering religious scruples he went on unencumbered to write in ten years the seven tragedies which made his reputation. Emerging later from retirement, he wrote his two biblical plays, *Esther* (1689) and *Athalie* (1691), the second of which ranks among his masterpieces.

The most immediately conspicuous feature of this handful of plays is their variety. In *Andromaque*, produced in November 1667, two years after *Alexandre*, Racine wrote his first unquestionably important play. The interval was a long one and the visible superiority of his third tragedy over his second seems to suggest some change in Racine's personal life. A deeply felt love-affair, with the insights into actual passion and jealousy which it might give him, is a possible explanation. The woman in question would be the actress Marquise Du Parc, who had played the part of the Indian Queen Axiane in Molière's production of *Alexandre* and who transferred later to the Hôtel under, it is supposed, Racine's persuasion. Boileau, reminiscing thirty-six years later, observed that 'Racine was in love with la Du Parc . . . He wrote *Andromaque* for her.'[2] Though this flatly categorical statement was hardly

[1] For his two *Lettres à l'auteur des hérésies imaginaires* and the replies to them, see Mesnard, *Œuvres de Racine*, Vol. IV.
[2] Mathieu Marais, *Mémoires*, ed. Lescure (1863).

the whole story, it may well have had a substratum of truth. All serious critics have noticed a new maturity in *Andromaque* which would be hard to explain solely on the grounds of increasing literary skill.

Considered purely in a theatrical context, *Andromaque* still retained features of romanesque tragedy, notably in some of the situations and dialogue. But it went far beyond it in the intensity of the passions portrayed and the consequent ruthlessness of the characters. Neither the story nor the ethos derives from any seventeenth-century novel. The ultimate sources are Greek, in that the names of the characters and the background of the Trojan War occur in Homer and the Greek tragic dramatists as well as in Seneca and Virgil, from whose *Aeneid*, Book III, Racine quotes a short passage in his preface. One can therefore describe *Andromaque* in general terms as a play of Greek inspiration without deriving it in a close sense from any particular work of Sophocles or Euripides. As such, it was unusual for its period and carried suggestions of more brutal manners than were to be found in most contemporary plays.[1] Only Corneille's *Attila*, produced earlier in the same year, contains a comparable brutality, but more openly and crudely expressed. *Attila* was a failure while *Andromaque* was a great success, which tends to the conclusion that the public of the late sixties preferred the rapier to the bludgeon.

IV

More precisely Greek in its derivation was Racine's sole comedy, *Les Plaideurs*, which followed *Andromaque* at a year's interval. It was an adaptation to French manners and the French theatre of *The Wasps* of Aristophanes and, in spite of considerable alterations, is a proof, if one is needed, that Racine was a good enough Greek scholar to read and relish his author in the original.[2]

---

[1] Racine recognized this in his first Preface of 1668 and showed that his rejection of the romanesque was a conscious one. After admitting that he had softened the 'ferocity' of Pyrrhus as portrayed by Seneca and Virgil, he turned on critics who had judged his character to be still too brutal: 'J'avoue qu'il n'est pas assez résigné à la volonté de sa maîtresse [Andromaque] et que Céladon a mieux connu que lui le parfait amour. Mais que faire? Pyrrhus n'avait pas lu nos romans. Il était violent de son naturel . . .'

[2] For an excellent summing-up of the debt of *Les Plaideurs* to *The Wasps*, see R. C. Knight, *Racine et la Grèce*, pp. 286–8.

After this came the tragedies of *Britannicus* (1669) and *Bérénice* (1670), each with a Roman setting and each combining politics with love. The first, with an exciting if uncomplicated plot, was the most Cornelian of Racine's plays and was probably designed as a challenge to the old dramatist on his favourite ground. After an initial setback, ascribed partly to the hostility of Corneille and his supporters, partly to the fact that the first performance coincided with a public execution which drew off a large section of the potential audience, *Britannicus* soon established itself as one of Racine's most popular plays. As for *Bérénice*, its Roman background was all it had in common with Cornelian drama. The contrast and the circumstances of its composition have been discussed in an earlier chapter.[1] All that need be added at this point is that in its pathos it comes curiously near to the romanesque ethos – as though, not content with providing the demonstration in simplicity mentioned in his preface, Racine was also giving Quinault a lesson in how to use sentimentality without being dominated by it. The result, whether through reaction against his competitors or thanks to a faithful concentration on his own natural talent, was the most Racinian of his tragedies in the sense that this was a play which only Racine could have written successfully. But it can hardly be called the most typical, since none of the others resembled it.

In partial proof of this, his next tragedy, *Bajazet* (January 1672), was a violent drama – almost a melodrama – of intrigue and passion in a Turkish harem. Various sources have been found, including a real-life account which Racine claimed to have heard from a friend of a former French ambassador in Constantinople. More important was a *nouvelle* by Segrais, containing the story very nearly as Racine drama-tized it.[2] There were also the earlier plays and novels mentioned above in connection with Tristan's *Osman*.[3] That tragedy, performed *c.* 1647 and published by Quinault in 1656, at about the same date as Segrais's

---

[1] See above pp. 195 and 202 ff.

[2] *Floridon*, in the *Nouvelles françaises* (1656–7). In Segrais's story the Bajazet with whom the Sultaness falls in love is her stepson, and so in the same relationship as Hippolyte to Phèdre.

[3] See above p. 188. In *Bajazet*, II. i, there are references to the Sultans Solyman and Osman, but they are too general to show whether Racine derived them from earlier plays or from elsewhere.

nouvelle, was the last tragic Turkish play, with one minor exception,[1] to appear on the Parisian stage until Racine's.

It was therefore twenty years or more since French theatre audiences had seen this type of play and Racine's choice of subject and background was a bold venture at that date. It seems even bolder when one recalls that the only other *turquerie* nearly contemporary with it was the mock ceremony and the mock Turkish characters in Molière's *Bourgeois Gentilhomme*, first produced some sixteen months before *Bajazet* (in October 1670) and still being performed fairly frequently on dates when Racine must already have been writing his play.[2] To risk a possible comparison between his deadly serious drama and the clowning of Molière's stage Turks showed a self-confidence which was amply justified by success.

One year after *Bajazet*, Racine wrote *Mithridate* (January 1673), his third play on a Roman theme, but concerned this time, like several tragedies by Pierre Corneille (and two by his brother Thomas), with the wars of Rome outside Italy. He took as his hero Mithridates, King of Pontus, an implacable opponent of Rome, gave him two mutually hostile sons, one in favour of Rome and the other against, and added a woman with whom all three were in love. The tragedy had a Cornelian vigour and its sentimentally satisfying conclusion was too muted to disturb its generally tragic tone.

[1] Lancaster (*History*, III, p. 178) records a *Soliman, ou l'esclave généreuse* attributed to one Jacquelin and printed in 1653. It contains characters named Roxane and Bajazet.

[2] And indeed much later. The première of *Bajazet* was probably on 5 January 1672. La Grange's *Régistre* records an exceptional performance of *Le Bourgeois Gentilhomme* at the Palais-Royal on 27 December 1671. It was the first since July of that year and brought in 1,192 *livres*, a large sum for a play no longer new. It was repeated three times, with smaller receipts, from 29 December to 3 January 1672, then dropped until 24 May 1672. It is not impossible that the forthcoming production of *Bajazet* had some influence on Molière's choice of a post-Christmas entertainment and even on the public response to it.

M. Raymond Picard in his *Carrière de Jean Racine*, pp. 168 ff., argues that Racine conceived *Bajazet* to exploit a contemporary mode for things Turkish. But the only concrete evidence he quotes for this mode are a French translation dated 1670 of Ricaut's *History of the Present State of the Ottoman Empire* and the *Bourgeois Gentilhomme* itself, which certainly was influenced by a Turkish mission to Versailles earlier in 1670. By the time *Bajazet* reached the stage the mode was no longer new and one must at least discard the idea of Racine riding on a popular wave. In any case, he was riding it alone.

V

In the seven short years which had passed since the production of *Alexandre*, Racine had risen to a leading position in the theatre. His reputation stood well above that of his contemporaries and, whether his work was praised or criticized, the comparison even then was constantly drawn with Corneille. If these two dramatists, with Molière, have survived almost alone from the seventeenth century in the popular mind, it must be admitted that the seeds were sown early. Little is known of Racine's personal life at this period. He seems to have been wholly absorbed in his profession, that is the theatre and the contacts at court and among the nobility who could support him in his career. These connections certainly promoted his election to the Académie Française at the early age of thirty-three at almost the exact date of *Mithridate* (January 1673). His known mistresses also belonged to the theatre. La Du Parc died a year after the production of *Andromaque*. Soon afterwards Racine's name became linked with la Champmeslé, a great actress who joined the Hôtel in 1670 and played leading parts in all his tragedies from *Bérénice* to *Phèdre*. While it is hardly true that he 'wrote his plays for her', as Mme de Sévigné alleged, her contribution to his contemporary success cannot be entirely ignored.

Two plays remained for Racine to write and for la Champmeslé to act in. Both, in their different ways, had a Greek derivation.

Iphigénie, which received the honour of an elaborate first performance at Versailles in August 1674, belonged to the Trojan War complex and had such characters as Agamemnon, Achilles, Ulysses, Clytemnestra and Iphigenia. Racine took it principally from the *Iphigenia at Aulis* of Euripides,[1] with the adjustments necessary for the stage of his day. The original story ended with the sacrifice of Iphigenia, who was saved at the last moment by the intervention of a goddess. This dénouement, though suitable to a machine-play, could not be copied in a regular tragedy, and Racine invented a more rational pretext for his heroine's escape. Nevertheless, though the supernatural is excluded, or nearly so, the play has a certain legendary aura which was new in Racine and represented an extension of his dramatic range.

[1] He made certain other borrowings, notably from Rotrou's *Iphigénie*, a thirty-four-year-old adaptation of the same Greek play.

His rate of production was now slowing down. Having regularly written one play a year (counting *Les Plaideurs*) from *Andromaque* to *Mithridate*, he had waited nineteen months for the Versailles production of *Iphigénie* and up to two years for its first performance at the Hôtel in the winter of 1674–5. A further two years at least passed before the première of *Phèdre* on 1 January 1677. Here again the principal model was Euripides, and by modifying his *Hippolytus*[1] Racine achieved a perfect if improbable marriage between the primitive Hellenic inspiration and the sophisticated climate of Louis-Quatorzien drama. His *Phèdre* is of course not 'Greek', but it reflected the scholarly reading of a Hellenist who was also a great poet in his own language. But for that it would not stand out so highly among the many other French derivations from Greek drama, including some of those listed in the first footnote below.

Though it quickly established itself as one of Racine's finest plays, *Phèdre* was at first the subject of a bitter quarrel which momentarily threatened its success. Competing playwrights and jealous critics were no new phenomena in Racine's career. The latest example had been *Iphigénie*, against which a rival play by Le Clerc and Coras had been promoted. But since this play was not performed until several months after Racine's – thanks, it appears, to counter-measures taken by the latter – the effect was nil. Against *Phèdre* the opposition was better organized. Encouraged by the Duchess of Bouillon and her family and circle – a powerful faction opposed to the court where most of Racine's support lay – the minor dramatist Pradon composed a *Phèdre et Hippolyte* which was produced at the Théâtre Guénégaud two days after the première of *Phèdre*[2] at the Hôtel.

The almost universal contempt which critics have shown for Pradon's tragedy, justified though it may be on comparative grounds, has obscured the fact that it is quite a skilful piece of playmaking on the romanesque model. Pradon evidently had some knowledge of Racine's text, which had been circulating for some time before it was

[1] He also drew on the *Hippolytus* of Seneca. Several other French dramatizations of the story, based ultimately on Seneca or Euripides, had preceded Racine's. Among them were Garnier's *Hippolyte*, La Pinelière's *Hippolyte* (1635), Gilbert's *Hippolyte, ou le garçon insensible* (1647), Bidar's *Hippolyte* (1675). Tristan L'Hermite (as seen above pp. 185–8) used a similar story in his *Mort de Chrispe* (1645).

[2] Racine's tragedy was also entitled *Phèdre et Hippolyte* until the collective edition of 1687.

acted. He took the four principal characters and the story in the rough and proceeded to weave an exciting plot in the manner of Thomas Corneille. Much of the action depends on equivocations. Phèdre, who has taken Aricie as her confidante (there is no Nurse), becomes uncertain whether Hippolyte's sighs of love are for Aricie or herself. Thésée, whose part in Pradon is more active than in Racine, is also puzzled by the same sighs, but suspects that his son is in love with Phèdre. His first reaction is to decide that Hippolyte must marry Aricie, both to remove him from temptation and for political considerations which are embodied in the plot. He has what he believes to be final proof when he surprises Hippolyte on his knees before Phèdre, interceding in fact for Aricie, whom Phèdre by now (IV. iv) has spirited away and intends to kill. Later she releases Aricie, who becomes convinced that Hippolyte has deserted her for Phèdre. Aricie complains to Thésée, who has already called down the vengeance of the gods on Hippolyte but begins, as in Racine, to experience his first doubts. His mind is changed by the news that Phèdre has followed Hippolyte as he goes to his doom. It changes once again when Hippolyte's *gouverneur* Idas (the same part as Théramène) relates Hippolyte's horrific death and the suicide of Phèdre over his body.

These and several other peripeteias (all of which have parallels in earlier romanesque and Racinian tragedy, particularly in *Bajazet*) are handled with an ingenuity that could have gripped audiences while actually in the theatre, though it may have struck them as somewhat old-fashioned. Pradon's *Phèdre* is little more than a vicious and dangerous woman, resembling the Fauste in Tristan's *Mort de Chrispe*. Though the play met with some success initially, it faded from the repertory after sixteen consecutive performances and was revived only occasionally after that. Its relative failure could be taken as a sign that by that date melodrama was definitely out (though it was to creep back later) and high tragedy was in, if anyone remained to write it.

VI

The Quarrel of *Phèdre* and its aftermath, which led to personal threats against Racine by his aristocratic opponents, was no doubt one of the reasons that caused him to review his position and retire from the theatre. He renounced its evil ways, as they were then considered, embraced a sober piety, sought a reconciliation with his Jansenist educators at some date which cannot be specified and contracted a sensible bourgeois marriage. Above all, in the year of *Phèdre* he was given, with Boileau, an appointment as historiographer royal, which brought him a substantial salary and an established position at court.

This, so far as the drama was concerned, might have been the end of the matter, were it not that in 1688 he was called upon by Mme de Maintenon to write an entertainment suitable for performance by the young ladies of the college she had founded at Saint-Cyr. He chose the story of Esther, after much thought and straight from the Bible, according to his correspondence, but conceivably with at least some knowledge of previous dramatizations of the same subject.[1] Going back to Greek practice, which was also that of sixteenth-century French tragedy, he introduced choruses into his three-act play. For the most part these were sung and there was also a musical overture.

This delicately devised entertainment was an artistic and social success when produced in January 1689 and led to a demand for another biblical play for Saint-Cyr. Racine's response was to write *Athalie*, an altogether more ambitious work, this time in five acts and again with choruses. The subject was taken direct from the Old Testament, with additions from Josephus but with no dramatic precedents, except in two obscure school productions.[2] The story is a grim one, centring on the efforts of a threatened Hebrew community to defend its religion and its infant king against the ferocity of the impious Queen Athalie. She is one of Racine's great characters, a development perhaps of the evil monsters inaugurated by Corneille. She is led to destruction by 'the hand of God', though also by a perverse liking she conceives for the child Joas, whose true identity is concealed from her, but who is really her own grandson.

This situation is similar in outline to that of several earlier secular tragedies, such as Thomas Corneille's *Laodice*, after a removal of the love interest. But the religious setting may fairly be said to transform it and give altogether deeper implications to a familiar dramatic formula.

---

[1] See above p. 178.
[2] A Latin *Athalia* (1658) at the Collège de Clermont (see R. Lebègue in *Revue d'histoire du théâtre*, IV, 1948–9), and a French *Athalie* (1683) at a provincial school (see V.-L. Saulnier in *Rev. d'hist. litt. de la France*, Jan.–March 1949).

Unlike *Esther*, *Athalie* was performed very simply and privately at Saint-Cyr, probably because of a feeling that lavish productions, even of sacred plays, were unsuitable for the school, and perhaps also because some personal intrigue was mounted against the author. It remained almost unknown to the general public until the next century. Its first Parisian performance was at the Comédie-Française in 1716, after which it had frequent productions. At the date when he wrote it Racine had renounced the professional theatre and it was only through his connection with Mme de Maintenon that he composed – almost fortuitously – this work and *Esther*, so adding a great biblical tragedy to his varied range.

He lived for eight years longer, preoccupied by his duties at court and the challenge of maintaining his official and financial position. He brought up a family of seven in an atmosphere which was predominantly pious and Jansenistic. His own Jansenism, though discreet, was unconcealed and earned him dangerous enemies. By the time he died, on 21 April 1699, he had long since returned to the religion of his childhood.

VII

Racinian tragedy cannot be fully appreciated in isolation. However exceptional his talent, Racine belonged to his generation and practised a type of drama already established by lesser writers, who in their turn took much from Pierre Corneille and his generation. Racine's plays grew out of romanesque tragedy and should be approached as a development or adaptation of this rather than a radical departure from it.

He even made use of the physical stage effects so noticeable in Quinault. A prominent example is the overhearing scene in *Britannicus* (II. vi) in which Junie is forced to dissemble with her lover because she (and the audience) know that the dreaded Néron is listening in the wings. At a later point in the play (III. vi–viii), Néron makes a surprise entrance when Britannicus is kneeling before Junie and so learns the whole truth about their relationship. In *Bajazet* and even in the 'elegaic' *Bérénice* (V. v) letters are discovered which reveal a lover's true sentiments. They descend from the 'tablets' employed comparably by Quinault, as in *Amalasonte* and *La Mort de Cyrus*, and earlier still by Tristan in his *Panthée*. The sword snatched from

Hippolyte in *Phèdre* (II. v) is traditionally Euripidean and Senecan, but nevertheless it is snatched on stage and results in a kind of struggle between Phèdre and the nurse Œnone. Perhaps the most immediately exciting scene in all Racine occurs in *Mithridate* (V. ii–iii). The heroine, after a short farewell speech, is just about to drink the poisoned cup when a messenger rushes in crying 'Arrêtez! arrêtez!' and snatches it from her lips.

These physical devices all have an influence on the plot and are integral to the tragedies. Less obviously physical are the many scenes introducing a sudden change in the situation (usually by the entry of a particular character) and so enlivening the action with a surprise or an ironic contrast. They are to be found throughout the tragedies and illustrate Racine's cultivation of dramatic effects not far removed from melodrama.

On a more general plane is his use of ambiguity and its related elements considered in previous chapters. There are cases of infant substitution in *Andromaque* (Astyanax) and *Athalie* (Joas), though about the first there is no mystery and with the second only the evil queen and her supporters are unaware of the child's identity. There are ambiguous oracles in *La Thébaïde* and *Iphigénie*. There is doubt about who loves whom in the minds of at least some characters in *Andromaque*, *Bajazet*, *Mithridate*, *Iphigénie* and *Phèdre*. The doubt is of varying importance, but in *Bajazet* and *Mithridate* at least the play as written depends upon it. There is one outstanding case of concealed identity, that of Ériphile in *Iphigénie*. Indeed this play, the most 'Greek' of Racine's to that date but certainly not the most 'classical' according to seventeenth-century standards, is compounded of misunderstandings or *équivoques*.

First, there is the misleading oracle which appears to designate Agamemnon's daughter as the victim required by the gods. The discovery of 'another Iphigénie' in Ériphile, together with the revelation of her parentage, is delayed until the end, though prepared by two clues planted earlier (II. i and IV. iv). Without the character of Ériphile, wrote Racine in his Preface, 'I should never have dared to undertake this tragedy.' The character is really his invention, though he finds dubious authority for it in Pausanias.

The second main ambiguity, this time not invented but copied from Euripides, consists in the pretence that Iphigénie has been summoned to Aulis not to be sacrificed but to be married to her lover Achille. As far as Iphigénie and her group are concerned, the pretence is kept up until halfway through the play (III. v) and occasions several passages of double-edged irony. A letter intended to forestall the arrival of Iphigénie at Aulis and so save her life is delivered too late (again as in Euripides), but serves to give the heroine the false impression that her lover has deserted her. This équivoque is cleared up comparatively quickly.

The machinery of the plot lends a cat-and-mouse quality to the attempts to save Iphigénie. Can she be prevented from reaching Aulis? Once she is there, can her father or her lover protect her? Will the last-minute escape, decided by Agamemnon in IV. x, succeed? It fails because it is betrayed by Ériphile, Racine's 'necessary' character. Iphigénie is recaptured and only then fully accepts the necessity of her sacrifice (V. i). She is led towards the altar, a fight breaks out, and while her lover is defending her the treacherous Ériphile, who has gone out to witness her rival's death, is identified as the victim and kills herself to the sound of thunder.

Though this last part is only narrated, the narration is calculated to generate excitement and finally a happy relief that innocence has been spared and love has triumphed.

VIII

The love ethic of romanesque tragedy is also to be found in Racine, usually with the *galant* language which expresses it. This is not surprising in the immature *Thébaïde* and *Alexandre*, but even after *Andromaque* and Racine's own condemnation of the novelettish type of hero[1] there are a few perfect lovers in his plays: Antiochus, hope-lessly faithful to Bérénice, 'd'un inutile amour trop constante victime'; Britannicus, innocently sighing to Junie, 'Ma chère princesse . . . ma belle princesse' (V. i); Bajazet, conventionally typed as a brave young warrior,[2] though this has little significance in the tragedy; Xipharès,

---

[1] See above p. 258, footnote 1.
[2] See I. i:

ACOMAT   Toi-même, tu l'as vu courir dans les combats
               Emportant avec lui les cœurs des soldats,
               Et goûter, tout sanglant, le plaisir et la gloire
               Que donne aux jeunes cœurs la première victoire.

the true lover of Monime in *Mithridate*. On the female side there are modest princesses capable of the coy avowal already noted in Quinault: Monime in *Mithridate* (I. ii) and Aricie in *Phèdre* (II. iii). Some are capable also of extreme self-sacrifice in the cause of love: Bérénice in her particular way, Atalide in *Bajazet* ('J'aime assez mon amant pour renoncer à lui', III. i).

But it is significant that none of these lovers, male or female, with the single exception of Xipharès and Monime, avoids defeat or frustration. All become victims to circumstance or to the more ruthless characters who surround them.

IX

It is clear that Racine used, though with discretion, all the conventional apparatus of romanesque tragedy, from the melodramatic stage effect to the concealed identity and the adoring lover. Parallels for most, if not all, of his dramatic situations can be found either in romanesque tragedy or in Pierre Corneille. In a general history of the drama he falls into a natural place among a number of other playwrights. Yet he cannot be adequately described in this way. In what does his originality consist?

Most obviously, in the restraint with which he applies the romanesque techniques. These form an essential part of his dramatic machinery, including his 'dramaturgy', but do not dominate his work and at first sight may escape attention. Their presence and indeed their necessity become apparent if one compares his plays to sixteenth-century tragedy, in which the long moralizing tirades and the psychological torture-scenes succeed each other in a series of verbal tableaux, but without the connection, the suspense and the overall movement which make Racinian tragedy so excellent a model of dramatic craftsmanship.

This craftsmanship did not preclude simplification of plot, as has been seen in earlier chapters. The contrast between Racine's tragedies and those of his predecessors, including Corneille, is sufficient proof of this. Neverthelesss, even his outstanding exercise in plot simplicity, *Bérénice*, is not sustained merely by 'the violence of the passions, the beauty of the sentiments and the elegance of the language'. It depends also on the elements of suspense and surprise, less prominent than in *Bajazet*, *Mithridate* or *Iphigénie*, but of the same dramatic order. These elements are subordinate to the total effect, to which they contribute. Since nothing appears to be superfluous and a 'multiplicity of incidents' is avoided, the impression is certainly one of simplicity. But in drawing a distinction between Racine and other seventeenth-century dramatists, it would be more appropriate to stress his selectivity.

His type-characters conformed externally to familiar patterns. This was inevitable since he was working, not for some avant-garde group, but for a long-established company which at the same time was performing plays by other dramatists. Besides the appealing pairs of young lovers already mentioned, his character-scheme usually includes a king, in several cases a queen, sometimes a jealous rival, male or female and occasionally a counsellor or counsellor-confidant. It is when one looks at the different interrelationships of these conventional roles from play to play and the psychological composition of the characters within the roles that Racine's inventiveness becomes apparent. In the sense that because of their political authority they wield material power over the other characters, Pyrrhus, Néron, Titus, the absent Amurat, Mithridate, Agamemnon and Thésée are all 'kings', but all are different. The queens may be listed as Andromaque, Agrippine, Bérénice, Roxane, Clytemnestre and Phèdre, but here function and characterization become even more varied. Andromaque is a 'queen' in that her ultimate decision settles the fate of all the others, but at the same time she is the persecuted princess on whom the pathetic interest is focused. Agrippine, the only approach in Racine's drama (with the later exception of Athalie) to the Medea type of character, is portrayed at a moment when her power is waning and her cherished son, for whom her past crimes were committed, is on the point of rejecting her. The decline of the 'old monster' and the rise of the *monstre naissant* acquire a deep human interest of which Racine himself seems at first not to have been fully aware. It was in his second Preface to *Britannicus*, published some six years after the play's first production, that he wrote: 'C'est elle [Agrippine] que je me suis surtout efforcé de bien exprimer, et ma tragédie n'est pas moins la disgrâce d'Agrippine que la mort de Britannicus.'

As for Bérénice, she, like Andromaque, is a nominal queen but in effect a princess with whose suffering the audience is encouraged to identify. But her decision, again, is necessary to undo the emotional knot and conclude the tragedy on a note of 'majestic sadness'.

Clytemnestre is little more than a 'distressed mother', helplessly raging against her husband. Roxane and Phèdre are closer to the traditional queen and, if one supposes that Thésée, instead of returning in person, merely sent threatening messages like Roxane's absent consort, they would occupy the same material position with regard to the other characters. But because they are different psychological entities, with the consequence that *amour-passion*, which affects them both, does so with entirely different results, the whole situation is altered.

Characterization, implying a psychological truth and depth which are absent in Thomas Corneille and Quinault, is of obvious importance in Racine. Its most typical activation, as we have said, is *amour-passion*, which is rightly considered to be a feature of Racinian tragedy. Yet only three of his major tragedies, *Andromaque*, *Bajazet* and *Phèdre*, fully embody it. Néron has sadistic features, Ériphile in *Iphigénie* is impelled by sexual jealousy, but apart from these marginal instances one cannot claim the other tragedies as studies in the unbridled passion of love. Is this because the characters in them – and indeed in the three tragedies of passion also – attempt, successfully or not, to conform to some moral code?

It is noticeable in Racine that when dilemmas are posed or openly debated, they are rarely moral dilemmas. Usually they bear on questions of emotion and expediency, taking that term in its widest sense. Thus Mithridate (IV. v) is torn between anger against Xipharès and Monime and the affection which he feels for both of them, added to the desire that his son should live on to avenge him against Rome. Agamemnon (*Iphigénie*, IV. viii) is divided between love for his daughter and resentment against the defiant attitude of her lover Achille. (At this point he does not even recall his duty as a military leader.) No moral values are invoked. Taking the old Cornelian term *vertu* as a touchstone, one finds that it occurs most frequently in the romanesque *Alexandre*, but only in the conventional sense of 'worth, valour, courage'. It is a pure cliché. After this play it is found very rarely. For Andromaque, as for her confidante, *vertu* means faithfulness to the memory of her dead husband.[1] It is not opposed to passion, but to an equally strong personal feeling for her son. She uses the word herself

---

[1]   CÉPHISE   Madame, à votre époux c'est être assez fidèle.
Trop de vertu pourrait vous rendre criminelle.
(*Andromaque*, III. viii)

when she has found what she believes to be the solution: she will go through a marriage ceremony with her captor, having received his promise to protect her son, and kill herself immediately after:

> Mais aussitôt ma main, à moi seule funeste,
> D'une infidèle vie abrégera le reste,
> Et sauvant ma vertu, rendra ce que je dois
> A Pyrrhus, à mon fils, à mon époux, à moi.[1]

Phèdre, who, if she saw herself in a Cornelian-type situation, would seem the most likely of all Racine's characters to invoke *vertu*, never does so. Œnone does it once for her:

> Il faut d'un vain amour étouffer la pensée,
> Madame. Rappelez votre vertu passée.
>
> (*Phèdre*, III. iii)

But the low-born Œnone does not understand the crisis through which her mistress is passing. She can only apply conventional values to a situation which has gone far beyond them, and it is quite possible that Racine intended to convey this when he put the word into her mouth. Phèdre herself speaks only of her *gloire* (and then rarely) and once or twice of her impotent *raison*.

Bérénice is the only play in which *vertu* is used to imply an external obligation in the old sense incompatible with *amour*. Having finally made up his mind to send Bérénice away, Titus describes the inner struggle which has led to this decision:

> Je croyais ma vertu moins prête à succomber,
> Et j'ai honte du trouble où je la vois tomber.
>
> (*Bérénice*, V. vi)

Here *vertu*, exceptionally, represents his patriotic duty, which leaves him with only the two alternatives of renouncing his love or of killing himself.[2]

---

[1] Cf. Quinault's heroine Thomiris in a comparable situation. For her, *vertu* demands that she should fulfil the marriage vow she has just made. See above p. 248.

[2] One can, of course, interpret his threat of suicide as a ruse to prevent Bérénice's intended suicide: 'If you kill yourself, I will do the same.' But the bluff, if it is one, is not called.

With this one partial exception the dilemmas as Racine's characters conceive them do not refer to any general system of values in which such terms as *vertu*, *devoir* and *honneur* would possess a moral authority. Their dilemmas are personal and contingent, bearing on the satisfaction of their desires or the preservation of themselves or the individuals they love from disaster. The weak remnants of the code of chivalry, already debased by previous dramatists, sustain some of them, but nearly always ineffectively. Even when extended to unselfish love, the code is dubious. Antiochus has no choice but to respect it. Bérénice's noble resignation, apparently prompted by pure love for Titus, can also be explained as the sacrifice of herself to an idea of herself in a final bid to retain her self-respect. At least she can save that much from the wreck. If even such an august concept as self-sacrifice can become suspect, it is because Racinian tragedy tempts one to attribute all motives to *amour-propre*. Characters who have no moral code will not experience moral dilemmas, but instead will face choices between greater and lesser evils, as Phèdre does. Making the wrong choice (inasmuch as she is capable of choosing at all) she meets a tragic doom.

A chaotic morality is found in Rotrou, Thomas Corneille and others. In such dramatists it can be attributed to inconsistency, superficiality, or opportunism, or characterized in general terms as baroque. Is not Racine open to similar charges, particularly in view of the varied nature of his plays?

The reply often put forward, and justifiably so, is that his characters are dominated by a superior force against which neither personal attempts at self-assertion nor man-made (i.e. social) codes of conduct are of any avail. Stoicism is useless and so is heroism, whether based on that or any other humanist philosophy. This accounts for the absence of the heroic in Racinian drama, detectable only in the character of Mithridate and dubiously, as we have seen, in *Bérénice*. The basic amorality of Racine's characters, which makes them so interesting on the plane of human psychology, is thus not arbitrary but an inevitable consequence of a belief in the force of destiny. This might have been derived either from Greek tragedy or from the Jansenist interpretation of Christianity, which came very near to the doctrine of predetermination. In both cases it is ultimately religious, implying the existence of forces outside man which he is powerless to influence or resist. For the

Greeks, he was helpless against fate or the gods; for the Jansenists, in Pascal's phrase, there was 'the misery of man without God'.

No one, after studying Racine's theatrical career or reading his own comments on his plays, would maintain that he was consciously applying these theories of human existence. It is nevertheless perfectly possible that unconsciously he was conditioned by one or both of them, and the fact that his plays can be seen to illustrate them gives them a coherence and a philosophical significance which place them high above those of his contemporaries.

Racine's dramatic verse does more than contribute to the excellence of his tragedies; it forms an inseparable part of them. The analysis of it cannot be compressed satisfactorily into a short space and only a few general points can be made here.

To outward appearances it conformed to the contemporary conventions of dramatic poetry. Racine's rhetoric and his verbal dramaturgy were not considered as innovatory or even different. He used, for example, the *tirade* for passages of exposition, narrative or self-questioning at even greater lengths than was then becoming usual.[1] He obtained lyrical effects in aria-type monologue or dialogue. Occasionally he resorted to stichomythia (*Britannicus*, III. vii). Above all, he used the abstract imagery originally prescribed by Malherbe and progressively refined by dramatic poets until it had become conventional. It is in his discreet but telling use of this imagery, giving it new powers of suggestion and evocation which might well appear to be beyond its scope, that part of his strength lies; in that and in his readiness to dispense with imagery altogether whenever it is desirable to write with greater directness or greater urgency. His language is always appropriate to the character in the given situation. It is perfectly suited to the speaking voice. But beyond that it contains, in passage after passage, some of the finest examples of true poetry written within the French classical tradition.

---

[1] The celebrated *récit de Théramène* (interrupted after 72 lines) is by no means the longest. In *Britannicus* (IV. ii), Agrippine addresses a silent Néron for 108 lines. In *Mithridate* (III. i), the King expounds the political situation to his sons in a speech of exactly the same length. Each gives a 40–50-line reply.

RACINE'S PLAYS
(All are tragedies except *Les Plaideurs*.)

La Thébaïde, June 1664
Sources: in Rotrou's *Antigone* and Euripides' *Phoenissae*.

Thebes, ruled over by Étéocle, son of Œdipe, is being attacked by his brother Polynice, who wishes to replace him as king. Inside the city are their mother Jocaste, their sister Antigone and their uncle Créon. Créon's son Hémon, a supporter of Polynice, is in love with Antigone and she with him. Créon also proves to be in love with his niece.

Jocaste, though weighed down by a foreboding of disaster, tries to reconcile her sons, but they prove irreducible in their mutual hatred and their desire for the throne. Jocaste commits suicide when the brothers go out to a battle in which they kill each other. In an attempt to separate them Hémon is also killed, a disaster which provokes Antigone's suicide. Créon, who has encouraged the brothers' enmity in the hope of securing the throne for himself and making Antigone his queen, falls senseless, wishing for death.

Alexandre, December 1665
Sources: historical outline (less the love interest) in Quintus Curtius, Justin, and Plutarch, *Life of Alexander*.

Alexandre (Alexander the Great) is engaged on the conquest of India. He threatens the states of two native kings, Porus and Taxile, and of a native queen, Axiane. These kings are rivals for the love of Axiane, who prefers Porus. The latter is determined to resist Alexandre, but Taxile, influenced partly by jealousy of Porus, partly by the arguments of his sister Cléofile, is ready to accept the peace which Alexandre offers. Cléofile is swayed by her own love for Alexandre, which is returned in full. A battle follows in which Porus is defeated but not, as at first reported, killed. Taxile keeps out, but he is so taunted by Axiane that he rushes to attack not Alexandre but Porus, and is killed himself.

Alexandre magnanimously forgives the captured Porus and allows him to marry Axiane. Cléofile asks for time to mourn her brother, but does not deny her constant love for Alexandre.

Andromaque, November 1667
Source: germ in Virgil, *Aeneid*, *III*. Otherwise, Racine's adaptation of Greek legend.

Pyrrhus, son of Achilles and one of the victorious Greeks at Troy, has brought back captive to Epirus Hector's widow Andromaque and her small son Astyanax, the last of the Trojan royal line. Other Greek leaders send Oreste as an emissary to Epirus to demand the head of Astyanax, whom Pyrrhus appears to be sheltering. In fact he uses him to practise emotional blackmail on Andromaque whom he wishes to marry. At the same time he is formally betrothed to the Greek princess Hermione, but keeps her waiting. Oreste has long been in love with Hermione and hopes to detach her from Pyrrhus.

Andromaque, torn between faithfulness to the memory of her dead husband and the urge to save her child, finally consents to marry Pyrrhus on condition that he protects Astyanax, but is determined to kill herself immediately after. Hermione, furious at her rejection by Pyrrhus, persuades her would-be lover Oreste to kill Pyrrhus at the marriage ceremony. This is done, but Hermione repudiates the deed and goes out to kill herself on Pyrrhus's body. Oreste appears to go mad and is carried off senseless by his friends. Andromaque is left in command.

Les Plaideurs, comedy, 1668
Source: Aristophanes, *The Wasps*.

Britannicus, December 1669
Main source: Tacitus, *Annals*.

Néron, at an early stage in his reign, is just throwing off the influence of his mother Agrippine, thanks to whose intrigues he was made Emperor to the exclusion of Britannicus, who had a prior claim. He has carried off the princess Junie, with whom Britannicus is in love, and offers to marry her after divorcing his present wife Octavie, Britannicus's sister (this character does not appear). Junie refuses indignantly, but Néron forces her to appear cold to Britannicus, whose life will otherwise be in danger.

Agrippine, who feels her power slipping, sides with Britannicus against Néron, but they are betrayed by Narcisse, Britannicus's tutor, who is treacherously serving the Emperor. Agrippine is placed under guard and Britannicus, whom Junie has managed to reassure about her love for him, is arrested. Néron is persuaded by his own tutor, the honest and well-meaning Burrhus, to be reconciled with Britannicus, but immediately after the evil counsels of Narcisse persuade him to change his mind. Britannicus is poisoned at a banquet intended to seal the reconciliation, to the horror of Burrhus and Agrippine, who now fear the worst for themselves and Rome. Junie takes refuge with the Vestal Virgins, while Narcisse is murdered by the outraged crowd when he attempts to intercept her.

Bérénice, November 1670
Main historical source: Suetonius, *De Vita Caesarum.*

Bérénice, Queen of Palestine, is in Rome. She and Titus, who has just succeeded his father as Emperor, have long been in love. The only other important character, Antiochus, King of Comagène, is also in love with Bérénice, but has concealed the fact under an appearance of mere friendship. Believing, as does Bérénice, that her marriage with Titus is imminent, he comes to say goodbye and reveals his hopeless passion for the first time. She rejects it with scorn, confident of Titus's feelings for her.

These are passionate but, realizing that Rome will never accept a Queen as its Empress, Titus has reluctantly decided to obey his duty and send her away. Unable to tell her so himself, he asks Antiochus to do so for him. Antiochus unwillingly tells her and is met with an outburst of disbelief and suspicion. Later Titus confirms his decision to Bérénice, while declaring his undying love for her. Bérénice eventually appears to accept this and to be prepared to leave, but Titus learns from a letter she has written that she intends to kill herself. He swears that if she does so he will commit suicide in his turn. Convinced at last of his sincerity, Bérénice bids him a sad farewell and leaves for her own kingdom. She has renounced her great love and she bids the unhappy Antiochus to give up all hope of winning her for himself.

Bajazet, January 1672
Sources: Segrais, *Floridon,* etc. (See above pp. 259–60.)

The Sultan Amurat, engaged in a foreign war, has left his Sultaness Roxane in charge of affairs at Constantinople. With her are his younger brother Bajazet and the Grand Vizier Acomat. Through Acomat's intrigues Roxane has fallen in love with Bajazet and is ready for a *coup d'état* which will place him on the throne. Meanwhile he is entirely in her power. The absent Sultan has already sent an order to kill him, as a potential rival for the throne, but this order has been ignored. Roxane insists that Bajazet should marry her before she will act.

Bajazet angers her by refusing. He is secretly in love with his cousin Atalide, who has been used as a go-between in his dealings with Roxane. Realizing his danger, Atalide urges him to stifle his love for her and placate Roxane. Believing that he has done so too thoroughly, she begins to doubt Bajazet's love for herself. He reassures her, but his attitude and hers arouse Roxane's suspicions. While she is hesitating an envoy arrives from Amurat with news that the Sultan is returning and an insistent demand for Bajazet's death.

When told of this Atalide faints. A letter from Bajazet which is found on her definitely reveals his love for her and his indifference to Roxane. Though furiously jealous the Sultaness is ready to give Bajazet a last chance. She offers him pardon and her hand on condition that he will come with her to see Atalide put to death. He refuses and she sends him out to execution.

Meanwhile the Grand Vizier has started the revolt as a bold if desperate measure. But it is too late. Bajazet is already dead. Roxane is killed by the Sultan's envoy, who is then killed himself by Acomat's men. Atalide, lamenting that she has caused her lover's death – by her doubts of him and her weakness in fainting – stabs herself on the stage.

Mithridate, January 1673
Source in Plutarch, Cassius Dio and other historians.

Mithridate, King of Pontus, is engaged in an implacable struggle with Rome. He has two sons by previous wives: Pharnace, who favours Rome, and Xipharès, opposed to it. All three men are in love with Monime, a young princess whom the father intends to make his Queen. A false report of Mithridate's death encourages both sons to declare their love for her, but immediately after they are thrown into confusion by the King's return. Monime also, loving Xipharès secretly, dreads the consequences.

Mithridate is enraged at first only against Pharnace, whom he puts under arrest. A word from Pharnace, however, leads him to suspect Xipharès also, and he tricks Monime into declaring her love for him. Outraged by his duplicity, Monime refuses Mithridate's demand for an

immediate marriage to himself. Mithridate is hesitating (shall he punish
her and his favourite son?) when news comes that Pharnace has escaped
from arrest and is leading a revolt against him, supported by Romans
who have arrived by sea.

Mithridate goes out to battle, sending back an order for Monime
to be given poison. At the last moment this order is changed and the
cup is dashed from her hands. Mithridate has found the faithful
Xipharès fighting on his side and the enemy are routed at least temporarily, but only after Mithridate has stabbed himself to avoid falling
into their hands. He is carried in dying to unite the lovers and advise
them to escape and resume the struggle against Rome at a favourable
time.

Iphigénie, Versailles, August 1674; Paris, winter 1674–5
Sources: Euripides' *Iphigenia at Aulis*, Rotrou's *Iphigénie*.

The Greek fleet on its way to attack Troy is becalmed at Aulis.
Its leader Agamemnon has received an oracle from the priest Calchas
apparently demanding the sacrifice of his daughter Iphigénie before
the gods will permit the winds to blow again. He has reluctantly sent
word to his wife Clytemnestre to bring their daughter to Aulis,
pretexting her marriage to Achille, whom he believed to be fighting
elsewhere. Achille, however, has reached Aulis (earlier than expected)
when the play opens. Clytemnestre and Iphigénie arrive, bringing
with them Ériphile, a war-captive of Achille who has been put in
Clytemnestre's charge and who has secretly fallen in love with her
capturer. The vacillating Agamemnon has meanwhile sent a message
to Clytemnestre to prevent her arrival, but it has gone astray and is not
delivered until she is already at Aulis. It contains the false news that
Achille wishes to postpone the wedding, for the probable reason that
he prefers Ériphile. Achille clears up this misunderstanding, but not
before Iphigénie has realized that she has an actual rival in Ériphile.

Agamemnon's second pretence, that his daughter has been summoned
to Aulis to be married, not sacrificed, is exposed soon after, provoking
the indignant fury of Clytemnestre and Achille.

A last-minute change of feeling leads Agamemnon to send away his
wife and daughter clandestinely, but their escape is betrayed by Ériphile.
Iphigénie, recaptured, goes nobly resigned to the sacrificial altar.
Achille and his men intervene to rescue her, but as the battle is about

to begin the priest Calchas is inspired to recognize the required victim in Ériphile, whose hitherto unknown parentage is revealed: she was a daughter born secretly to Helen of Troy. Ériphile stabs herself on the altar, the winds blow, and Iphigénie is saved to be united to Achille.

Phèdre, January 1667
Primary source: the *Hippolytus* of Euripides (see also p. 261, n. 1 above).

Phèdre, the wife of Thésée, who is absent on a mysterious journey and is presently reported to be dead, has fallen hopelessly in love with her stepson Hippolyte. Though sick with desire almost to the point of death, she is determined never to reveal her passion, but is driven to do so at a meeting with him. Hippolyte, who admires and respects his father, is revolted. Moreover, he himself has just declared his love for the young and virginal princess Aricie, who is a virtual prisoner at the court. She responds to him.

The outward situation is transformed by the return of Thésée, the report of his death having proved false. The political question raised earlier of a disputed claim to the throne between Phèdre, Hippolyte and Aricie disappears. Phèdre feels both guilty and fearful that Hippolyte will denounce her to Thésée. Hippolyte only hints at her advances to him and asks to be allowed to leave the court.

To protect Phèdre, her nurse Œnone comes to Thésée and accuses Hippolyte of having attempted to rape his wife. She convinces him by showing him Hippolyte's sword, which Phèdre herself had snatched from him earlier with some intention of killing herself. The furious Thésée overrides his son's protests, calls down the vengeance of the god Neptune upon him, and sends him to exile. Phèdre is about to confess everything when she is checked by the bitter news that Hippolyte loves Aricie. She has a rival.

The pleadings of Aricie on Hippolyte's behalf, then the news that Œnone has killed herself and that Phèdre appears desperate, cause Thésée to have doubts on his son's guilt. But it is too late. Hippolyte's tutor Théramène arrives to describe the young prince's gory death, dragged along the rocky shore by his horses who bolted at the appearance of a sea-monster. Phèdre testifies to Hippolyte's innocence and dies by poison. Thésée is left to mourn his son and attempt to console Aricie.

Esther, Saint-Cyr, January 1689

In its main lines the play follows the Old Testament account in the Book of Esther.

The Jewess Esther has been chosen to be the Queen of Assuérus, King of Persia, in place of his present consort, 'the arrogant Vasthi' (who is mentioned only in passing). Esther is in secret communication with her uncle Mardochée, the champion of the Jewish people in exile. Assuérus has signed an order for the extermination of these, persuaded by their enemy, 'the impious Aman', his powerful and ambitious counsellor. Only Mardochée refuses to show respect for Aman, who hates him for this, for being a Jew and particularly because he has been obliged to honour him in public on the King's order. (This was Mardochée's reward for having exposed a plot against the King's life at some time in the past.)

At a banquet at her house Esther reveals her Jewish origin, of which Assuérus was unaware, obtains a reprieve for her people, condemnation of Aman and the elevation of Mardochée, who is given Aman's wealth and position.

The spoken and sung choruses, while not advancing the action of the play, are substantial. They stress the glory of the Jews' true God and his concern for the innocent and the oppressed.

Each of the three acts of the play has a different décor.

Athalie, privately at Saint-Cyr, January 1691; Comédie-Française, 1716

The story-source in outline only is 2 Kings 11.

Athalie, the reigning Queen of Judah, is a worshipper of Baal and an enemy of the true God of the Hebrews. On assuming power after the early death of her son Okosias (Ahaziah), she had ordered all her grandchildren to be slaughtered, so extinguishing the royal line of David. Only one, Joas, was secretly saved and is being brought up incognito in the Temple at Jerusalem by the High Priest Joad and his wife Josabet, who is the young boy's aunt.

Troubled by a dream of disaster, Athalie visits the Temple where she catches sight of the same child (Joas) who had appeared to stab her in her dream. Urged on by Mathan, a priest of Baal, and ignoring the objections of Abner, one of her captains who nevertheless is faithful to Jehovah, she questions the young Joas. Though his identity is not disclosed, Athalie leaves the Temple in a state of suspicion and anxiety.

This leads her to send Mathan to demand the child as a hostage: otherwise she will have the Temple burnt down and all its inmates – priests and other believers – killed. Having refused contemptuously, the High Priest boldly decides to reveal the identity of Joas and anoint him as King. Ignorant of this, Athalie surrounds the Temple with her troops and is enticed to go inside herself with a small guard chosen by Abner. Joas is revealed sitting on his throne, her guard deserts her, and she is led out by armed Levites to be killed. When the news of Joas's accession is proclaimed outside the Temple, the besieging crowds rally to him. The temple of Baal is invaded and Mathan slaughtered.

AFTER RACINE AND
CONCLUSION

Racine's contemporaries and successors – the Quarrel of the Ancients and the Moderns – the stagnation of tragedy – general summing-up: sixteenth-century tragedy – its legacy to the seventeenth century – Hardy and transition – growth of the professional theatre – dramatic theorists and their influence – regular 'classical' tragedy – persistence of freer types of drama – 'classical' tragedy vindicated by Racine – the long search for renewal

After Racine until the end of Louis XIV's reign there were no significant developments in French tragedy. The most successful of the older dramatists, Thomas Corneille and Quinault, had already abandoned it in the 1670s. The Abbé Claude Boyer (1618–98), a good journeyman who had been writing tragedies since the forties in search of a success which never came conclusively, had nothing new to offer. Having followed fashion conscientiously, he came nearest to a theatrical triumph with the biblical play of *Judith* which, with his earlier *Jephté*, was written for Saint-Cyr in the wake of Racine's *Athalie*. Produced professionally at the Comédie-Française in 1695, *Judith* met with considerable applause – largely due, according to Boileau, to the performance of la Champmeslé in the title-part. Boyer's career ended in 1697 with the libretto of an unsuccessful opera.

Jacques Pradon (1644–98) wrote ten tragedies in all, seven of which followed his notorious *Phèdre et Hippolyte*. This near-contemporary of Racine had begun in 1673 with *Pirame et Thisbé*, an attempted renewal of Théophile's fifty-year-old play. After *Phèdre* he wrote two tragedies on Greek subjects which had been treated by Seneca and Euripides, then turned to Roman history. This gave him his only real success, the tragedy of *Regulus* (1688). These later plays showed the influence of both Pierre and Thomas Corneille, with the romanesque tendencies associated particularly with the latter. The acid remark attributed to Racine, that 'the difference between M. Pradon and myself is that I know how to write', provides an acceptable explanation of Pradon's mediocrity.

Of a younger generation born in the 1650s, easily the most prolific was Jean-Galbert Campistron (1656–1723). Between 1683 and 1693 he produced nine tragedies in addition to a comedy and three opera libretti. Only three of his tragedies enjoyed any considerable contemporary success.[1] The others were complete or relative failures and two of them were never printed. The seven that survive were competent exercises in drama, Racinian in their regularity of construction if in no other respect, and generally derivative in their situations and characters. In *Alcibiade*, Campistron went back as far as Du Ryer's *Thémistocle* for the plot and other suggestions.

None of Campistron's contemporaries came near to equalling his output. Antoine de La Fosse (1653–1708) and Longepierre (1659–1721) are both remembered for one play among the three or four tragedies each wrote. The *Manlius Capitolinus* (1698) of the first had a complicated political plot, with the usual love element, based on Roman history. This play, a contemporary success when first produced, acquired an additional interest for critics and scholars as a partial imitation of the *Venice Preserved* (1682) of Thomas Otway, and so as a first faint sign of French awareness of English drama, though certainly not significant of a trend.[2] Longepierre's *Médée* (1694) was a renewal of the theme treated by Euripides, Seneca and Pierre Corneille. Described by the author in his Preface as 'une pièce à peu près dans le goût des Anciens' and a return (echoing d'Aubignac and Racine) to 'simplicity', this *Médée* failed on first production but became popular throughout the eighteenth century, after which it virtually disappeared.[3]

Like these two, other writers composed occasional tragedies, but failed to establish themselves as regular tragic dramatists. The only men who might be said to have done so belonged to a still younger generation which appeared round the turn of the century. Joseph La Grange-Chancel (1676–1758) produced eight tragedies between 1694 and 1716 and after a long interruption, due to his political opinions which earned him imprisonment and exile, two further tragedies acted

---

[1] *Andronic* (1685), *Alcibiade* (1685) and *Tiridate* (1691).
[2] Both tragedies had a common source in a French work, Saint-Réal's *Conjuration des Espagnols contre la République de Venise*.
[3] There is a modern edition edited by T. Tobari (Nizet, 1967).

in the 1730s. Claiming, no doubt with some justification, to have been advised by Racine, he failed, more markedly than even Campistron had done, to take over the succession. His main group of tragedies were based for the most part on nominally Greek themes but were more influenced by the French novel and treated in a romanesque way. The original story of his *Méléagre* (1699) is in Ovid, but had been dramatized long before by Benserade, whom he may have read, and by Hardy, whom he is unlikely to have known.

In the seven tragedies of Prosper-Jolyot Crébillon (1674–1762), produced between 1705 and 1726,[1] there are some signs of innovation, consisting principally in his cultivation of horror, which has often been stressed as his characteristic feature. He owed this reputation to his third tragedy, *Atrée et Thyeste* (1707), of which the story is certainly horrible, requiring a father to be deceived by his vengeful brother into eating a meal composed of the flesh of his own murdered sons. Crébillon educred this grisly feast (described with ghoulish relish in the original *Thyestes* of Seneca) to a cup of blood, and even that was not actually drunk. In his last plays there are one or two severed heads, but the audience does not see them. Crébillon's horrors were rhetorical rather than visual. In their day they represented a mild challenge to the old *bienséances*, which were to be more flagrantly violated in the *drame* than in tragedy itself.

If Crébillon's work can be found to contain certain intimations of the eighteenth-century taste for the macabre (the 'Gothic' sensibility), none of the other dramatists so far mentioned can be described as anything but backward-looking. They pillaged earlier dramatists for themes, only rarely going beyond the Roman, Greek and romanesque sources already drawn on. In their treatment of these themes they occasionally attempted new approaches but were incapable of establishing a new drama, or even the basis of one. Their timid innovations were generally melodramatic, better suited to tragicomedy if that class of play had still been current. But it had long ceased to be so[2] and for the *fin de siècle* playwrights the only alternatives to tragedy were

---

[1] He returned to the theatre late in life with two more tragedies on Roman themes, *Catilina* (1748) and *Le Triumvirat* (1754).

[2] The term, if not the concept, began to disappear in the early sixties. (See Chapter 9 above, on romanesque tragedy.) The last example of any note was T. Corneille's *Antiochus* (1666), alternatively styled a tragedy.

comedy, which was still flourishing, and various kinds of spectacle, principally opera. It is apparent that after Racine tragedy lost its drive, together with any clear sense of future direction. The causes were perhaps less in the writers than in the moment, an unusual one in the history of French literature.

The last three decades of Louis XIV's reign were a period of pause in French culture. New ideas were beginning to germinate in the social and political fields, though very tentatively. In art, the Quarrel of the Ancients and the Moderns, which occupied literary minds in the 1680s and 1690s, typified the situation. Against the Ancients and their champions, who argued that the Greeks and Latins had set up well-proved standards of excellence and that imitation of them in a broad sense was the only sure foundation for modern literature, the opponents of this classical tradition pointed to the brilliant talents which their own age had produced. But they were still looking back, though not so far as to Greece and Rome. Charles Perrault's poem, *Le Siècle de Louis le Grand* (1687), which was the immediate cause of this polemic, mentioned not a single French writer who was still alive at that date[1] and the majority of the examples given had flourished before 1650. The Quarrel reflected a certain pride, not to say self-satisfaction, felt by elderly Academicians in the achievements of the *Grand Siècle*, but contained nothing at all, beyond a vague theory of progress, which concerned future prospects. Anything less revolutionary, or even dynamic, it would be hard to conceive.

The period of 1680–1715 was thus one of stocktaking in the arts, of a disinclination to innovate, of a certain lassitude such as is perceptible in La Bruyère's *Caractères*, but particularly of a tendency to cling to acquired values. This was the predominant temper both of the ageing court and of educated society as a whole.

In the circumstances it was natural that tragedy, a genre recognized as one of the outstanding achievements of the reign, should stagnate. The foundation of the Comédie-Française in 1680 had left only one theatre in which it could be performed. Though the number of new tragedies produced in Paris did not decrease perceptibly, the theatre in its monopolistic position was disinclined to experiment. It could also be contented with shorter runs. If these were unprofitable for the

---

[1] Apart from an oblique reference to La Fontaine (not named) as a describer of the wonders of Versailles.

authors, it made little difference to the actors who had plenty of other material in hand. Lancaster has calculated that during 1689–1700 about fifty per cent of the performances of tragedy at the Comédie-Française were of Corneille and Racine, twenty-five per cent of other plays previously produced (going back as far as Du Ryer and Tristan), and only twenty-five per cent of new tragedies.[1] For these last the authors were paid their share of the takings but the others, in modern terms, were out of copyright.[2] A company which could draw on this rich repertory costing it nothing, using scenery and costumes so largely stylized that they were often interchangeable from play to play, naturally became conservative. Corneille and Racine still drew the necessary audiences and long continued to do so. Tragedy as a serious entertainment was not dead, it simply ceased to develop. The principal new interest, such as it was, centred on the actors and actresses and their art, on interpretation rather than on creation.

II

From this point it is possible to look back over the 150 years of tragic drama covered in this book and draw some general conclusions.

The sixteenth-century academics and their pupils introduced to France an idea of tragedy derived ostensibly, and sometimes actually, from the ancient Greek dramatists, but in practice more frequently from Seneca. From the experiments of the Boncourt–Coqueret group, beginning with Jodelle's, a form of play emerged which was consciously intended to replace, at least for cultivated audiences, the chaotic and spectacular medieval drama. It had five acts with choruses, a comparatively small number of actors, a limited playing-time, and was normally concerned with a single major event and the effect of this event on the principal character or characters. To interest its audiences it relied almost exclusively on words in preference to scenic effects, and, after a few early hesitations, these words were cast in the form of alexandrine couplets with alternate masculine and feminine rhymes. Verbal elaboration was of the first importance for the dramatists and the spectators

---

[1] See H. C. Lancaster, *History*, IV, p. 349.

[2] Though they may very exceptionally have received special payments as an act of grace. 'Il n'est pas impossible que Racine ait reçu des cadeaux des comédiens, qui jouent ses pièces plus que jamais . . .' (R. Picard, *La Carrière de Jean Racine*, p. 335, n. 1.)

alike and can convincingly be shown to be based on the principles of rhetoric as then taught in the schools. The result, as seen in the work of Garnier and later of Montchrestien, was often a display of splendid or florid eloquence – according to the point of view – and an overall impression of static speech-making which minimized the elements of continuity and surprise.

The lack of what were later to be considered as essential dramatic qualities in sixteenth-century tragedy is easy to point out, and in comparing it with seventeenth-century drama the contrast is too visible not to be remarked. Modern scholars have objected, however, that to apply such criteria to Renaissance tragedy is to ignore its true nature. It should be approached as a different art-form, entirely deserving of study in its own right.[1] While the argument, put in those terms, is a strong one, and a necessary corrective to the tendency to consider Garnier and his contemporaries merely as inept forerunners of Corneille and Racine, some comparisons are nevertheless illuminating and inevitable. The *form* established by humanist learned drama persisted, minus the choruses, in seventeenth-century tragedy, as did the virtual elimination of physical action. The rhetorical principles on which the first was largely based recurred in the second in such features as the *tirade*, the *récit*, stichomythia and the *sentence*, though the effects obtained from them might often be different, precisely because of the development of a 'dramatic' sense. More general features, such as the final speech of lamentations and the dream of foreboding,[2] also persisted in the later drama.

It is true that the seventeenth century could have drawn all this from alternative sources, going back as the sixteenth century had done, but independently, to Seneca or the Greeks or to Italian models and theory and readapting them to a new conception of drama. If insisted on, this interpretation would mean drawing a line after Renaissance tragedy and so segregating it in its period and implying an entirely fresh start towards 1630. But even if such an extreme position were adopted, it would still not exclude humanist tragedy from any general account of the emergence of tragic drama in France. Humanist tragedy would

---

[1] See e.g. R. Griffiths, *The Dramatic Technique of A. de Montchrestien* (O.U.P., 1970). See also pp. 44–6 above.
[2] Notably in Tristan's *Mariane* (1636), P. Corneille's *Polyeucte* (1642), Racine's *Athalie* (1691).

still be of interest as a first if ultimately sterile attempt to find a substitute for the dying drama of the Middle Ages.

But it was certainly more than that. Although there is little concrete evidence of any precise textual imitation of Garnier or Montchrestien by the dramatists of the 1630s (and this is natural, since the latter were consciously innovating in some contempt of the past, and particularly of its poetic diction), there are abundant traces of what can fairly be called a transition.

This should be placed in the period 1590–1620, a time of confusion and mediocrity in French drama, though not of sterility. The fact that Montchrestien's plays were written around 1600 and at least some of them were certainly performed, indicates that as late as this pure humanist tragedy could coexist with the cruder and apparently more popular types. The nature of some of these was mixed, proving again the persistence of the humanist influence, however debased, upon other writers. There was potential development here, unrealized for lack of talent and opportunity, but fortunately the example of the only considerable dramatist of the period proves beyond doubt that a transition of some kind was possible.

Alexandre Hardy apparently intended to write in the tradition of Garnier, who, with Seneca and Ronsard, was the only model he mentioned.[1] He used the apparatus of Renaissance tragedy, the warning ghosts, the over-ornamented speeches, the long rhetorical discussions, but he used it dynamically. While one or two of his tragedies are as deficient in movement and point as the sixteenth-century precedents, without the compensation of a convincing pathos, in the great majority there is a preoccupation with movement, often in the form of violent action on stage. His plays seem primitive because the action is episodic and badly co-ordinated with the story-line. In short, he was weak in plotting, so that in place of a steadily gathering interest he offers a series of shocks and surprises. It is hardly necessary to repeat that a more skilful playwright would have organized the material better. What is relevant here is that he achieved a kind of union between the static humanist tragedy and the tragic drama of his own century. His work can profitably be analysed from either point of view: both for what it preserves from the earlier age and for what it foreshadows in his successors.[2] If his surviving plays could be dated with any accuracy, it

[1] See above p. 73.   [2] For this, see above pp. 88 ff.

might be possible to trace a development within Hardy himself, but as things are this can only be conjectural. Whether or not his tragicomedies were the more recent part of his work, they certainly pointed forward to a type of play that flourished for several decades after him. Often derived from recent prose fiction, they contained in their totality all the principal features of the melodramatic tragicomedies of the 1630s and 1640s and even – making full allowance for the triumph of the *bienséances* and greatly improved techniques of plot construction – some of the features of the romanesque drama of the fifties and sixties.

III

No history of drama is entirely separable from the history of the theatre. The actors and audiences from whom the plays were written must influence their nature. Reciprocally, the standing and function of the theatre in a society is reflected, even if unconsciously, in the plays.

The learned tragedies of the Renaissance were originally acted by students and continued to be for a long time: not only in schools and universities but occasionally at court or in aristocratic houses when a special performance was called for to entertain the guests. Local fraternities not necessarily composed of students also combined in various towns to mount plays which were at least nominally tragedies and which seem to represent a communal effort similar to that shown in the medieval drama but on a more modest scale. Finally there were the travelling companies whose sole profession was to entertain and whose repertories evidently included both learned tragedies and other less regular types. There was thus considerable theatrical activity, both amateur and professional, of various kinds. But it had no focal point, no geographical centre which could have given it some social and cultural cohesion. Paris might have provided this, but even after 1600, as has been seen in an earlier chapter, it failed for some time to do so. The Hôtel de Bourgogne was used only intermittently by French companies, and then with dubious success. If Hardy, working for a manager who enjoyed security of tenure, had been able to write long enough for a public with known and constant tastes, his production might well have been less disjointed. As it was, he was obliged, like his lesser contemporaries, to improvise for various audiences whose responses must often have been unpredictable.

It was nevertheless the professional companies that eventually established a serious theatre in the capital and in the 1620s prepared the way for a new drama which could definitely equal the medieval drama in social importance and had sufficient prestige to attract and form writers of the first rank. In the 1630s the theatre became respectable (except for those who condemned it on religious grounds), it was securing influential patrons, and it could offer substantial rewards in money and status. Above all, it could now reflect, more immediately than any other art-form, the tastes and aspirations of the community as a whole. This position was maintained, with only minor variations, throughout most of the century.

The growing importance of the theatre attracted not only new dramatists but critics. There was interaction between them, making it impossible to define the share of each in the development of French classical tragedy, as it has come to be called. What can be said is that the dramatic theorists, as nearly always, were rarely the same men who wrote the plays. By far the greatest of these, Corneille, discussed, though for the most part at a later date, the underlying principles of his work. But both then, in the *Examens* and *Discours* of 1660, as in his earlier prefaces, the general tone of his writing is justificatory. If not necessarily on the defensive, he is seeking to reinterpret critical theory in the light of the proved effectiveness of his own plays. For him, the successful practitioner, the two things are not identical, however genuine his desire to reconcile them may have been. Other prominent dramatists – Rotrou, Du Ryer, Tristan L'Hermite – published their plays with fulsome dedications to aristocratic patrons, but without a sentence that could be construed as critical comment. Only Mairet in his preface to *Silvanire* and Scudéry in his *Observations sur le Cid* attempted anything approximating to dramatic theory. With Mairet this led to the actual composition of regular plays, though he departed from regularity in his later work, Scudéry applied some general criteria, which he attempted to observe in some of his own tragicomedies, to his examination of Corneille's play. But his *Observations* was primarily an opportunist work, brought into being by the desire to join in a contemporary polemic rather than to expound his own artistic creed. A polemical impulse can, of course, be ascribed to most, if not all, significant criticism, and this does not invalidate it, but when it is as occasional as Scudéry's it loses something in weight.

The critics who were not practising dramatists were polemists also.

They attacked and defended plays and their authors for personal motives, including the building-up of their own literary reputations. Yet their writings had a foundation of doctrine, expressed in somewhat fragmentary form in the 1630s and given its most complete expression in the Abbé d'Aubignac's *Pratique du théâtre* of 1657. It must be remarked in passing that d'Aubignac had composed towards 1640 three tragedies in strict accordance with his theories, though written exceptionally in prose since he had no talent for verse. They enjoyed only slight or very temporary success.[1] It is also noteworthy that his *Pratique du théâtre*, though it originated in the Quarrel of *Le Cid* and expanded certain critical ideas which he had expressed at that period, was published much too late to have exerted any formative influence on classical tragedy. It was a statement resuming what the theorists had desired or intended and its principal interest lies in that. It did not spring from the heart of a new movement and any influence which it had was on the generation of Racine.

All this may appear to lead towards the conclusion that French classical regular tragedy was an idea in the minds of theorists which was realized rarely in practice and, when it was, mainly in secondary works. This would be too extreme a view. It could only be based on conceptions of purity and conformity which may well be put forward as critical absolutes but are unattainable in the actual theatre. One has only to compare French tragic drama of the mid-century with earlier French drama, or with English Jacobean drama, or with Spanish drama up to and including Calderón, the contemporary of Corneille and Rotrou, to see the concrete results of the movement towards regularity. Linguistic and scenic proprieties were generally observed, with relatively minor exceptions in the latter. There was an awareness of moral *bienséance*, at least on a superficial level, though on the deeper level of moral utility it posed impossible conditions for writers of tragedy. *Vraisemblance* was aimed at conscientiously, though sometimes at the expense of twisting it into some very curious shapes. Play-construction, embracing structure, was immensely improved. It digested the more mechanical unities of time and place until they could go virtually unnoticed. It achieved in a fair number of plays the much more important unity of interest which is the characteristic feature of French classical

[1] For descriptions of his *Zénobie*, *Pucelle d'Orléans* and *Cyminde*, see Lancaster, *History*, II.

tragedy and the ultimate justification of all its other conditions. Much of value had to be discarded in the process, but for a long time it was accepted as a desideratum and inspired works which were not only typical, but major by any standards.

Plays which fell short of the 'classical' requirements on one or more points were nevertheless numerous – in fact very much more numerous than those that can strictly be said to have satisfied them all. They begin with the plays of the thirties that can clearly be seen to be irregular because they were so in a technical sense. They continue with plays that may appear conventionally regular, but which in their conception and often their structure are considerably removed from the classical norm. For the most part these are the plays classed under tragicomedy, but the distinction between this and tragedy is not absolute and can only be used as a rough working-guide. Tragedy also retained a strong element of melodrama, theoretically incompatible with the classical ideal, but generally present in practice. The single decade of the forties produced Corneille's *Rodogune*, *Théodore* and *Héraclius*, the major tragedies of Rotrou, and Tristan's *Mort de Sénèque* and *Mort de Chrispe*, in all of which the melodramatic element is perceptible, particularly in the violent and sometimes arbitrary nature of the dénouements. This may be concealed but is not removed by the fact that the worst violence occurs offstage.

It has become usual to describe this drama as baroque, a classification depending on analysis from several different angles, including the approach through language and prosody. One of the generally agreed features of the baroque is ambiguity, whether traced down to the deeper levels of consciousness and personality or seen merely as a display of distorting mirror-images. On that more superficial level the identity plays of the fifties and sixties can also be included in the baroque, which is thus extended to the time of Racine. But Racine himself, though he made some use of ambiguity, cannot be fairly classed as baroque. In his case the term ceases to be significant and it is more profitable to trace in his work the discreet persistence of the romanesque and the melodramatic, using those terms as we have done in the previous chapter.

On that basis he constructed plays which remain as the finest examples of French classical tragedy, a genre which without him would lose enormously in interest and standing. By his reaffirmation in

practice of the principles first laid down in the thirties, he saved it
for some time from the sterility into which it afterwards fell and which,
to judge by the work of his own contemporaries, was already threatening it when he began to write. He provides a striking example of an
exceptional talent working within an accepted formula which,
whatever its merits, can have no virtue in itself to create outstanding
work. Ultimately, even in the theatre, the individual talent is everything, while the method or the 'school' is at best an aid, at worst a
hindrance. With Racine conformism paid. With others it was a handi-
cap, even if unrealized at first.

In the course of the eighteenth century this began to be seen more
clearly, and the history of that drama is characterized by attempts at
modification or escape. They were still, however, not radical enough
to inspire a genuinely new drama. It was left to the Romantics to
reject openly what they saw as an intolerably restrictive tradition,
narrowed by then by several generations of mediocre tragic dramatists,
and to return to a vein which Pierre Corneille, among others, had
already opened up. The romanced historical dramas of Hugo and
Dumas *père* bore resemblances to seventeenth-century tragicomedy,
and particularly to the *comédie héroïque* as Corneille conceived it in
writing *Don Sanche d'Aragon*. For this play Corneille invoked the
example of Hardy to justify his introduction of Plebeian characters
(Dedication). He acknowledged his debt to the Spanish *comedia* in his
Examen. Rotrou might much more often have done the same.

BIBLIOGRAPHY

GENERAL STUDIES

ADAM, A. *Histoire de la littérature française au 17e siècle.* 5 vols. Paris, 1949–56.

BÉNICHOU, P. *Morales du Grand Siècle.* Paris, 1948.

BRAY, R. *La Formation de la doctrine classique en France.* Paris, 1927.

CHAMBERS, E. K. *The Elizabethan Stage.* 4 vols. London, 1924.

COHEN, G. *Histoire de la mise en scène dans le théâtre religieux français du moyen âge.* Paris, 1951.

DABNEY, L. E. *French Dramatic Literature in the Reign of Henri IV . . . 1589–1610.* Photocopied typescript. Austin, Texas, 1952.

DEIERKAUF-HOLSBOER, S. W. *Histoire de la mise en scène dans le théâtre français à Paris de 1600 à 1673.* Paris, 1960.

—— *Le Théâtre de l'Hôtel de Bourgogne.* 2 vols. Paris, 1968–70.

—— *Le Théâtre du Marais.* 2 vols. Paris, 1954–8.

FAGUET, E. *La Tragédie française au XVIe siècle.* Paris, 1912.

FORSYTH, E. *La Tragédie française de Jodelle à Corneille (1553–1640): Le Thème de la vengeance.* Paris, 1962.

FRANK, G. *The Medieval French Drama.* Oxford, 1954.

LANCASTER, H. C. *A History of French Dramatic Literature in the 17th Century.* 9 vols. Baltimore, 1929–42.

—— *Sunset, a History of Parisian Drama, 1701–15.* Baltimore, 1945.

—— *The French Tragi-Comedy . . . 1552–1628.* Baltimore, 1907.

LANSON, G. *Esquisse d'une histoire de la tragédie française.* Paris, 1926.

LAWRENSON, T. E. *The French Stage in the Seventeenth Century.* Manchester, 1957.

LEBÈGUE, R. *La Tragédie française de la Renaissance.* Brussels, 1954.

—— *La Tragédie religieuse en France: Les débuts (1514–73).* Paris, 1929.

MARSAN, J. *La Pastorale dramatique en France à la fin du 16e et au commencement du 17e siècle.* Paris, 1905.

MARTINENCHE, E. *La comedia espagnole en France de Hardy à Racine.* Paris, 1900.

MÉLÈSE, P. *Le Théâtre et le public à Paris sous Louis XIV, 1659–1715.* Paris, 1934.

MÉLÈSE, P. *Répertoire analytique de documents contemporains . . . concernant le théâtre à Paris sous Louis XIV.* Paris, 1934.

SCHERER, J. *La Dramaturgie classique en France.* Paris, 1959.

SHERGOLD, N. D. *A History of the Spanish Stage.* Oxford, 1967.

VALBUENA PRAT, A. *Historia del teatro español.* Barcelona, 1956.

—— *Literatura dramática española.* Barcelona, 1930.

THE DRAMATISTS: TEXTS AND STUDIES

Wherever a modern edition of a text exists, it has generally been preferred to earlier editions, on the grounds of relative accessibility. The studies listed under certain dramatists, particularly P. Corneille and Racine, are a small selection only from very wide fields.

T. DE BÈZE

Abraham sacrifiant. Ed. K. Cameron, K. M. Hall and F. Higman. Geneva, 1967.

P. CORNEILLE

Œuvres complètes. Ed. C. Marty-Laveaux. 12 vols. and album. Paris, 1862–8.

—— Ed. A. Stegmann. Paris, 1963.

Théâtre complet. Ed. P. Lièvre and R. Caillois. 2 vols. Paris, 1950.

Writings on the Theatre. Ed. H. T. Barnwell. Oxford, 1965.

LANSON, G. *Corneille.* Paris, 1898.

BRASILLACH, R. *Corneille.* Paris, 1938.

NADAL, O. *Le Sentiment de l'amour dans l'œuvre de P. Corneille.* Paris, 1948.

MAY, G. *Tragédie cornélienne, tragédie racinienne.* Urbana, 1948.

DORT, B. *P. Corneille dramaturge.* Paris, 1957.

COUTON, G. *Corneille.* Paris, 1958.

YARROW, P. J. *Corneille.* London, 1963.

DOUBROVSKY, S. *Corneille et la dialectique du héros.* Paris, 1965.

MAURENS, J. *La Tragédie sans tragique: le néo-stoïcisme dans l'œuvre de P. Corneille.* Paris, 1966.

FOGEL, H. *The Criticism of Cornelian Tragedy.* New York, 1967.

STEGMANN, A. *L'Héroïsme cornélien.* 2 vols. Paris, 1968.

T. CORNEILLE

Œuvres de T. Corneille. 9 vols. Savoye, Paris, 1758.
Timocrate. Ed. Y. Giraud. Geneva, 1970.
REYNIER, G. *T. Corneille, sa vie et son théâtre.* Paris, 1892.
COLLINS, D. A. *T. Corneille, Protean Dramatist.* The Hague, 1966.

L. DES MASURES

Tragédies saintes. Ed. C. Comte. Paris, 1932.

P. DU RYER

Alcionée. Ed. H. C. Lancaster. Baltimore and Paris, 1930.
Saül. Ed. H. C. Lancaster. Baltimore and Paris, 1931.
Scévole. Ed. G. Fasano. Bologna, 1966.
Thémistocle. Ed. P. E. Chaplin. Exeter, 1972.
Alcionée, Saül, Esther, Thémistocle and *Scévole.* In *Théâtre françois, ou*
   Recueil des meilleures pièces de théâtre. 12 vols. Vol. III. Paris, 1737.
LANCASTER, H. C. *P. Du Ryer Dramatist.* Washington, 1912.

R. GARNIER

Théâtre. Ed. L. Pinvert. Paris, 1923. (Contains *Porcie, Cornélie, Marc-*
   Antoine, Hippolyte.)
Œuvres complètes (sic). Ed. R. Lebègue. 2 vols. Paris, 1949–52. (Contains
   Les Juives, Bradamante, Poésies diverses, La Troade, Antigone.)
MOUFLARD, M. M. *R. Garnier, 1545–1590.* 3 vols. Paris, 1961–4.
GRAS, M. *R. Garnier, son art et sa méthode.* Geneva, 1965.
WITHERSPOON, A. M. *The Influence of R. Garnier on Elizabethan*
   Drama. Yale and Oxford, 1924.

J. GRÉVIN

Théâtre complet et poésies choisies. Ed. L. Pinvert. Paris, 1922.
César. Ed. E. S. Ginsberg. Geneva and Paris, 1971.

A. HARDY

Le Théâtre d'Alexandre Hardy. Ed. E. Stengel. 5 vols. Marburg, 1883–4.
Les Chastes et Loyales Amours de Théagène et Cariclée. Paris, Jacques
   Quesnel, 1623.
RIGAL, E. *Alexandre Hardy et le théâtre français à la fin du 16e et au*
   commencement du 17e siècle. Paris, 1889.

DEIERKAUF-HOLSBOER, S. W. *Vie d'A. Hardy, poète du roi*. Proceedings of the American Philosophical Society, Vol. 91. Philadelphia and Paris, 1947.

E. JODELLE

Œuvres complètes. Ed. E. Balmas. 2 vols. Paris, 1965–8.
Cléopâtre captive and *Didon se sacrifiant*. In *Ancien Théâtre français*. Ed. Viollet-le-Duc. Vol. IV. Paris, 1854.
Didon. Ed. D. Stone, Jnr. In *Four Renaissance Tragedies*. Harvard, 1966.
BALMAS, E. *Un poeta del rinascimento francese, E. Jodelle*. Florence, 1962.

JEAN DE LA TAILLE

Saül le furieux and *La Famine, ou les Gabéonites*. Ed. E. Forsyth. Paris, 1968. (This edition contains *De l'art de la tragédie*.)

J. MAIRET

Chryséide et Arimand. Ed. H. C. Lancaster. Baltimore, 1925.
Sylvie. Ed. J. Marsan. Paris, 1932.
Silvanire. Ed. R. Otto. Bamberg, 1890.
Sophonisbe. Ed. C. Dédéyan. Paris, 1945.
Solyman. In *Théâtre françois*. Vol. II. Paris, 1737.

A. DE MONCHRESTIEN

Tragédies. Ed. L. Petit de Julleville. Bib. elzévirienne. Paris, 1891.
La Reine d'Écosse. Ed. G. Michaut *et al*. Paris, 1905.
Aman. Ed. G. O. Seiver. Philadelphia, 1939.
Les Lacènss. Ed. G. E. Calkins. Philadelphia, 1943.
David. Ed. L. E. Dabney. Austin, Texas, 1963.
Les Tragédies d'Ant. de Montchrestien sieur de Vasteville plus une Bergerie et un poème de Susane. Rouen, Jean Petit, 1601. (Besides the *Bergerie*, this contains all the tragedies (except *Hector*) and a long non-dramatic poem on Susanna and the Elders. BM 11735. bbb. 5.)
GRIFFITHS, R. *The Dramatic Technique of A. de Montchrestien*. Oxford, 1970.

J. PRADON

Les Œuvres de Mr Pradon. Paris, P. Ribou, 1700.

P. QUINAULT

Théâtre de Quinault. 5 vols. Paris, 1715, 1739, 1778.
Théâtre choisi. Ed. V. Fournel. Paris, 1882. (Contains *Astrate*, 3 comedies and 6 *tragédies lyriques*.)
GROS, E. *P. Quinault, sa vie et son œuvre.* Paris, 1926.
BUIJTENDORP, J. B. A. *P. Quinault.* Amsterdam, 1928.

J. RACINE

Œuvres. Ed. P. Mesnard. 8 vols and 2 albums. Paris, 1865–73.
Œuvres complètes. Ed. R. Picard. 2 vols. Paris, 1951.
KNIGHT, R. C. *Racine et la Grèce.* Paris, 1951.
MOREAU, P. *Racine, l'homme et l'œuvre.* Paris, 1952.
VINAVER, E. *Racine and Poetic Tragedy.* Manchester, 1955.
LAPP, J. C. *Aspects of Racinian Tragedy.* Toronto and Oxford, 1955.
PICARD, R. *La Carrière de Jean Racine.* Paris, 1956.
—— *Corpus Racinianum.* Paris, 1956. With Supplements, 1961 onwards. (Related texts and documents.)
BUTLER, P. *Classicisme et baroque dans l'œuvre de Racine.* Paris, 1959.
KNIGHT, R. C. (ed.) *Racine, Modern Judgements.* London, 1969.
BRERETON, G. *Racine, a critical biography.* Rev. ed. London, 1973.

H. DE B. DE RACAN

Les Bergeries. Ed. L. Arnould. Paris, 1937.

A. DE RIVAUDEAU

Aman. Ed. K. Cameron. Geneva, 1969.

J. ROTROU

Œuvres. Ed. Viollet-le-Duc. 5 vols. Paris, 1820.
Théâtre choisi. Ed. F. Hémon. Paris, 1883 and 1925.
Le Véritable Saint Genest. Ed. T. F. Crane. Boston, 1907.
—— Ed. R. W. Ladborough. Cambridge, 1954.
Cosroès. Ed. J. Scherer. Paris, 1950.
Venceslas. Ed. W. Leiner. Saarbrücken, 1956.
Hercule mourant. Ed. D. A. Watts. Exeter, 1971.
DEL VALLEABAD, F. *Influencia española en la literatura francesa . . . Juan Rotrou.* Avila, 1946.

BUFFUM, I. *Studies in the Baroque from Montaigne to Rotrou.* Yale, 1957.
ORLANDO, F. *Rotrou dalla tragicommedia alla tragedia.* Turin, 1963.
VAN BAELEN, J. *Rotrou, le héros tragique et la révolte.* Paris, 1965.
MOREL, J. *Jean Rotrou, dramaturge de l'ambiguïté.* Paris, 1968.

TRISTAN L'HERMITE

La Mariane. Ed. J. Madeleine. Paris, 1939.
—— Ed. P. A. Jannini. Milan and Paris, 1969.
La Folie du sage. Ed. J. Madeleine. Paris, 1936.
La Mort de Sénèque. Ed. J. Madeleine. Paris, 1919.
Osman. G. de Luynes, Paris, 1656.
Panthée and *La Mort de Chrispe.* In *Théâtre françois.* Vol. II. Paris, 1737.
BERNARDIN, N. M. *Un Précurseur de Racine, Tristan L'Hermite.* Paris, 1895.
DALLA VALLE, D. *Il Teatro di Tristan L'Hermite.* Turin, 1964.

THÉOPHILE DE VIAU

Les Amours tragiques de Pyrame et Thisbé. Ed. G. Saba. Naples, 1967.

OTHER TEXTS AND DOCUMENTS

LAWTON, H. W. *Handbook of French Renaissance Dramatic Theory.* Manchester, 1949.
CHAPELAIN, J. *Opuscules critiques.* Ed. A. C. Hunter. Paris 1936.
GASTÉ, A. *La Querelle du Cid.* Paris, 1898. (Contains most of the relevant texts.)
AUBIGNAC, F.-H. D'. *La Pratique du théâtre.* Ed. P. Martino. Paris, 1927.
—— *Dissertations.* In François Granet, *Recueil de dissertations sur plusieurs tragédies de Corneille et Racine.* 2 vols. Paris, 1740.
Le Mémoire de Mahelot, Laurent et autres décorateurs de l'Hôtel de Bourgogne. Ed. H. C. Lancaster. Paris, 1920.
Le Régistre de La Grange, 1659–85. Facsimile reproduction. Ed. B. E. and G. P. Young. 2 vols. Paris, 1947.

INDEX

(Page numbers printed in bold type indicate summaries and main criticisms of plays)